CHANGE IN OFFICIAL CATHOLIC MORAL TEACHINGS

Readings in Moral Theology No. 13

Previous volumes in this series

CHANGE IN OFFICIAL CATHOLIC MORAL TEACHINGS

Readings in Moral Theology No. 13

Edited by
Charles E. Curran

PAULIST PRESS
New York/Mahwah, N.J.

Cover design by Tim McKeen

Library of Congress Cataloging-in Publication Data

Change in official Catholic moral teachings / edited by Charles E. Curran.
     p. cm.—(Readings in moral theology ; no. 13)
     Includes bibliographical references.
     ISBN 0-8091-4134-5
     1. Catholic Church—Teaching office. 2. Christian ethics—Catholic authors. I. Curran, Charles E. II. Series
BX1746 .C443 2002
241'.042—dc21

                                     2002009476

Published by Paulist Press
997 Macarthur Boulevard
Mahwah, New Jersey 07430 USA

www.paulistpress.com

Printed and bound in the United States of America

Contents

PART FIVE:
MORE THEORETICAL EXPLANATIONS OF CHANGE
IN OFFICIAL CATHOLIC MORAL TEACHINGS

Acknowledgments

"The Declaration on Religious Freedom" by John Courtney Murray is reprinted by permission of Paulist Press from *War, Poverty, Freedom: The Christian Response* (Concilium Vol. 15). "Religious Liberty" by Émile-Joseph De Smedt is reprinted by permission of Paulist Press from *Council Speeches of Vatican II,* edited by Yves Congar, Hans Küng and Daniel O'Hanlon. "Catholicism and Democracy: Conflict, Change and Collaboration" by J. Bryan Hehir is taken from *Christianity and Democracy in Global Conflict,* edited by John Witte, and is reprinted by permission of John Witte. "Churches and Human Rights: From Hostility/Reluctance to Acceptability" by Charles E. Curran is reprinted by permission of *Milltown Studies.* "Reflections on Slavery" by Diana Hayes, from *Rome Has Spoken: A Guide to Forgotten Papal Pronouncements and How They Have Changed through the Centuries,* edited by Maureen Fiedler and Linda Rabben, is reprinted by permission of The Crossroad Publishing Co. "Usury: The Amendment of Papal Teaching by Theologians" by John T. Noonan, Jr., from *Contraception: Authority and Dissent,* edited by Charles E. Curran, is reprinted by permission of John T. Noonan, Jr. The articles "The Right to Silence: Magisterial Development" by Patrick Granfield, "Whatever Happened to *Octogesima Adveniens?*" by Mary Elsbernd, and "Development in Moral Doctrine" by John T. Noonan, Jr., are reprinted by permission of *Theological Studies.* "Catholicism and Capital Punishment" by Avery Dulles is reprinted by permission of *First Things.* "To Kill or Not to Kill: The Catholic Church and the Problem of the Death Penalty" by E. Christian Brugger is reprinted by permission of E. Christian Brugger. "The Changing Anthropological Basis of Catholic Social Ethics," from *Directions in Catholic Social Ethics* by Charles E. Curran, is reprinted by permission of the University of Notre Dame Press. "Marriage and Sexuality: Magisterial Teaching from 1918 to the Present" by John Gallagher, from *Human Sexuality and Personhood,* is reprinted by permission of the National Catholic Bioethics Center, Brighton, MA. "Magisterial Teaching on Marriage 1880-1986: Historical Constancy or Radical Development?" by Joseph A. Selling, from *Historia: Memoria Futuri,* edited by Réal Tremblay and Dennis J. Billy, is reprinted by permission of Edacalf (Editiones Academiae Alphonsianiae, Rome). "Family and Catholic Social Teaching" is reprinted by permission from *Family: A Christian Social Perspective* by Lisa Sowle Cahill, copyright © 2000, Augsburg Fortress Publishers. "Encountering the Other: The Modern Papacy on Women" by Christine E. Gudorf is reprinted by permission of *Social Compass* and Christine E. Gudorf. The articles "Catholic Medical Ethics: A Tradition which Progresses" by Raphael Gallagher and "Progress in the Moral Tradition" by Marciano Vidal are reprinted by permission of the Continuum International Publishing Group from *Catholic Ethicists on HIV/AIDS,* edited by James F. Keenan, copyright © 2000 by James F. Keenan.

Foreword

Change in Official Catholic Moral Teachings is the thirteenth volume in the series *Readings in Moral Theology*. In keeping with the ethos of this series, this volume brings together previously published studies presenting the spectrum of positions on this topic. Many of the studies collected here try to explain how change has occurred on a specific issue. All agree that change has taken place in official Catholic moral teachings but not all agree on the nature of this change as is evident in the different explanations of capital punishment and the teaching on marriage and sexuality found in this volume. Most of the discussions of particular issues in this volume together with the theoretical explanations in Part Five press the issue of how such change occurs.

Commentators have pointed out that Catholic theology has paid little attention to the issue of change in moral teachings in comparison with the very abundant literature on the issue of the development of doctrine. By bringing these studies together, this volume tries to address the issue of change in official moral teachings and stimulate further discussion.

The essays collected in this volume address two important questions that need further study and discussion. First, what is the nature of the change that has taken place in official Catholic moral teaching? Some refer to this change as development, but others claim that the discontinuity is so great that one cannot properly speak of development. All agree that both continuity and discontinuity are involved in such changes, but disagreement exists over the extent of how these two aspects come together. Second, how have such changes occurred? What are the factors involved? This volume suggests important roles played in these changes by the Holy Spirit, anthropological insights, prophetic witness, human experience, theological interpretation, historical circumstances, and limitations in the official moral teachings themselves. But how do all these various aspects fit together? A better understanding of how these changes have occurred in the past will also throw some light on the possibility of change in the future.

As editor, I want to thank the many people who have contributed to the research and preparation of this volume: Jack Blanton and the late

Laura Lee Blanton, who generously endowed the Elizabeth Scurlock University Professorship of Human Values at Southern Methodist University, which I am privileged to hold; the scholars whose articles appear in this volume; Don Brophy and the staff at Paulist Press for their personal encouragement and professional skills; the librarians at the Bridwell Library of Southern Methodist University for their dedicated service to researchers; and Carol Swartz, my associate, for carefully preparing this manuscript for publication.

The continuation of this series serves as a memorial and a tribute to the co-editor of the first eleven volumes, Richard A. McCormick, S.J., who died February 12, 2000.

Charles E. Curran

Part One

RELIGIOUS FREEDOM, DEMOCRACY, AND HUMAN RIGHTS

1. The Declaration on Religious Freedom

John Courtney Murray

This chapter first appeared in *War, Poverty, Freedom: the Christian Response,* Concilium, No. 15 (New York: Paulist, 1966).

Narrow though its scope may be, the *Declaration* is nonetheless a document of considerable theological significance. This will become apparent if the document is considered in the light of the two great historical movements of the nineteenth century, both of which were bitterly opposed by the church.

THE SECULARITY OF SOCIETY AND STATE

The first movement was from the sacral conception of society and state to the secular conception. The sacral conception had been the heritage of medieval Christendom and, in a far more ambiguous form, of the ancien régime. For our purposes here, two of its characteristics should be briefly noted. First, the Christian world—or at least the Catholic nation— was considered to be somehow enclosed within the church, which was herself the one Great Society. Second, the religious prerogative of the prince extended to a care of the religion of his subjects and a care of their religious unity as essential to their political unity. (This religious prerogative of political rule was interpreted in a variety of more or less arbitrary ways, but these details need not detain us here.)

The nineteenth century saw the break with this conception of the sacrality of society and state, and a movement toward their secularity. As everybody knows, the church—both in Rome and in the so-called Catholic nations—opposed this movement with all the forces at her command. The reason was obvious. After the revolution in continental Europe (the new Federal Republic of the United States presents an altogether different case), the term of the historical movement was not a proper secularity of society and state. What emerged was the laicized state of rationalist or atheist inspiration, whose function was the laicization of society. In effect, what emerged was the ancien régime turned upside down, as Alexis de Tocqueville noted at the time. One might properly regard the Law of Separation (December 9, 1905) of the Third French Republic as the legislative symbol of the new order.

The church could not in principle accept this new order in its premises, in its ethos, or even in its institutions, primary among which was the institution of the so-called liberty of cult. Furthermore, the church did not in fact do a work of discernment of the signs of the times in order to discover, beneath the transitory historical forms assumed by the new movement, the true and valid dynamisms that were at work.

The overt revolt was against the sacrality of society and state as symbolized by the union of throne and altar. Few historians today would deny that this conception and its institutional symbol, for all their venerable antiquity, had become archaistic in the world of modernity. However, the true underlying direction of the new movement was toward a proper and legitimate secularity of society and state. In the depths, in which the hidden factors of historical change were operative, what was really going on was a work of differentiation, which is always a work of growth and progress. Civil society was seeking differentiation from the religious community, the church. The political functions of secular rule were being differentiated from the religious functions of ecclesiastical authority. The trouble was that this work of orderly progress was disrupted and deflected, as so often happens in history.

Chiefly to blame was the disastrous law of contradiction—that desire to deny and destroy the past, which was the very essence of Enlightenment rationalism (whereby it aroused the bitter antipathy, for instance, of Edmund Burke). What appeared on the surface, therefore, was not progress but simply revolution. Society as civil was not simply being differentiated from society as religious; the two societies were being violently separated, and civil society was being stripped of all religious substance. The order of civil law and political jurisdiction was not simply being differentiated from the order of moral law and ecclesiastical jurisdiction; a complete rupture was made between the two orders of law and the two authorities, and they were set at hostile variance, each with the other. Society and state were not invested with their due secularity; they were roughly clothed in the alien garments of continental laicism. At this horrid specter, stalking across the Europe of the Middle Ages, the church in the person of Pius IX hurled her unmitigated anathema.

Leo XIII first began to discern whither the deep currents of history were setting. In response, he restored to its proper centrality, and also developed, the traditional truth that Gelasius I had sought to enforce upon the Emperor Anastasius in A.D. 494: "Two there are, august Emperor, whereby this world is ruled by sovereign right *(principaliter),* the sacred authority of the priesthood and the royal power." However, Leo XIII transcended the historically conditioned medieval conception of the two powers in the one society called Christendom—a conception that, in debased form, had persisted under the ancien régime, with its Gallicanism and its famous device: "One faith, one law, one king." In a series of eight splendid texts, stretching from *Arcanum* (1880) to *Pervenuti* (1902), Leo XIII made it clear finally that there are two distinct societies, two distinct orders of law, as well as two distinct powers. This was the ancient affirmation in a new mode of understanding—an authentic development of doctrine. On this basis, Leo XIII was able to accomplish a second development. In scores of texts—more than a hundred in all, of which about one-fourth had to do with the Roman Question—he reiterated that the essential claim that the church makes on civil societies and their governments is stated in the ancient formula, "the freedom of the church." It was not possible for him to complete these two developments with a third—the affirmation of the freedom of society and of the duty of governments toward the freedom of the people. In any event, his doctrinal work cleared the way for further progress in understanding the rightful secularity of society and state, as against the ancient sacral conceptions.

This progress reaches its inevitable term in the *Declaration on Religious Freedom.* The sacrality of society and state is now transcended as archaistic. Government is not *defensor fidei.* Its duty and rights do not extend to what had long been called *cura religionis,* a direct care of religion itself and of the unity of the church within Christendom or the nation-state. The function of government is secular: That is, it is confined to a care of the free exercise of religion within society—a care therefore of the freedom of the church and of the freedom of the human person in religious affairs. The function is secular because freedom in society, for all that it is most precious to religion and the church, remains a secular value—the sort of value that government can protect and foster by the instrument of law. Moreover, to this conception of the state as secular, there corresponds a conception of society itself as secular. It is not only distinct from the church in its origin and finality; it is also autonomous in its structures and processes. Its structural and dynamic principles are proper to itself and proper to the secular order—the truth about the human person, the justice due to the human person, the love that is the properly human bond among persons and, not least, the freedom that is the basic constituent and requirement of the dignity of the person.

This is the true Christian understanding of society and state in their genuine secularity which appears in *Pacem in terris*. The *Declaration on Religious Freedom* adds to it the final clarity in the essential detail, namely, that in the secular society, under the secular state, the highest value that both state and society are called upon to protect and foster is the personal and social value of the free exercise of religion. The values of religion itself for men and society are to be protected and fostered by the church and by other religious communities availing themselves of their freedom. Thus the *Declaration* assumes its primary theological significance. Formally, it settles only the minor issue of religious freedom. In effect, it defines the church's basic contemporary view of the world— of human society, of its order of human law, and of the functions of the all too human powers that govern it. Therefore, the *Declaration* not only completes the *Decree on Ecumenism,* it also lays down the premise, and sets the focus, of the church's concern with the secular world, which is the subject of Chapter XIII. Not nostalgic yearnings to restore ancient sacralizations, not futile efforts to find new forms of sacralizing the terrestrial and temporal order in its structures and processes, but the purification of these processes and structures and the sure direction of them to their inherently secular ends—this is the aim and object of the action of the church in the world today.

In its own way, the *Declaration* is an act in that lengthy process known today as *consecratio mundi*. The document makes clear that the statute of religious freedom as a civil right is, in reality, a self-denying ordinance on the part of government. Secular government denies to itself the right to interfere with the free exercise of religion, unless an issue of civil offense against public order arises (in which case the state is acting only in the secular order, not in the order of religion). On the other hand, the ratification of the *Declaration* by Vatican Council II is, with equal clarity, a self-denying ordinance on the part of the church. To put the matter simply and in historical perspective, the church finally renounces, in principle, its long-cherished historical right to *auxilium brachii saecularis* (the phrase in Canon 2198 remains for the moment an odd bit of archaism). The secular arm is simply secular, inept for the furtherance of the proper purposes of the people of God. More exactly, the church has no secular arm. In ratifying the principle of religious freedom, the church accepts the full burden of the freedom, which is the single claim she is entitled to make on the secular world. Thus a lengthy, twisting, often tortuous development of doctrine comes to a term.

Like all developments, this one will initiate a further progress in doctrine, that is, a new *impostazione* of the doctrine of the church on the problem of church and state, as it is called, in order to restore, and to perfect in its own sense, the authentic tradition. This, however, is a subject in itself, not to be dealt with here.

HISTORICAL CONSCIOUSNESS

The second great trend of the nineteenth century was the movement from classicism to historical consciousness. The meaning of these two terms would require lengthy explanation, both historical and philosophical. Suffice it to say here that classicism designates a view of truth that holds objective truth, precisely because it is objective, to exist "already out there now" (to use Bernard Lonergan's descriptive phrase). Therefore, it also exists apart from its possession by anyone. In addition, it exists apart from history, formulated in propositions that are verbally immutable. If there is to be talk of development of doctrine, it can only mean that the truth, remaining itself unchanged in its formulation, may find different applications in the contingent world of historical change. In contrast, historical consciousness, while holding fast to the nature of truth as objective, is concerned with the possession of truth, with man's affirmations of truth, with the understanding contained in these affirmations, with the conditions—

both circumstantial and subjective—of understanding and affirmation, and therefore, with the historicity of truth and with progress in the grasp and penetration of what is true.

The church in the nineteenth century, and even in the twentieth, opposed this movement toward historical consciousness. Here, too, the reason was obvious. The term of the historical movement was modernism, that "conglomeration of all heresies," as *Pascendi dominici gregis* called it. The insight into the historicity of truth and the insight into the role of the subject in the possession of truth were systematically exploited to produce almost every kind of pernicious "ism," unto the destruction of the notion of truth itself—its objective character, its universality, its absoluteness. These systematizations were false, but the insights from which they issued were valid. Here again a work of discernment needed to be done and was not done. To be quite summary about it, this work had to wait until Vatican Council II. (I am not here speaking of the work of scholars.)

The sessions of the Council have made it clear that, despite resistance in certain quarters, classicism is giving way to historical consciousness. Obviously, neither of these theories has been debated, and perhaps they are not even understood as theories. The significant thing is that the Council has chosen to call itself "pastoral." The term has been misunderstood, as if the Council were somehow not concerned with truth and doctrine but only with life and practical directives for living. To so contrast the pastoral and doctrinal would be disastrous. The pastoral concern of the Council is a doctrinal concern. However, it is illuminated by historical consciousness: that is, by concern for the truth not simply as a proposition to be repeated but more importantly as a possession to be lived; by concern, therefore, for the subject to whom the truth is addressed; hence, also, by concern for the historical moment in which the truth is proclaimed to the living subject; and, consequently, by concern to seek that progress in the understanding of the truth demanded both by the historical moment and by the subject who must live in it. In a word, the fundamental concern of the Council is with the development of doctrine. The scholarly concern of the twentieth century has become also the pastoral concern of the church in the twentieth century.

Viewed in this light, the second theological significance of the *Declaration on Religious Freedom* appears. The *Declaration* is a pastoral exercise in the development of doctrine. (This, it may be said in passing, is why it met some opposition; classicism—if not as a theory, at least as an operative mentality—is still with us, here and there.) Briefly, the *Declaration* bases itself on a progress in doctrine that has, in fact, occurred since Leo XIII. It also carries this progress one inevitable step farther by discarding an older theory of civil tolerance in favor of a new doctrine of religious freedom more in harmony with the authentic and more fully understood tradition of the church. Only a bare outline of this progress can be suggested here.

The remote theological premise of the *Declaration* is the traditional teaching of the church, clarified by Leo XIII, with regard to the two orders of human life, the sacred and the secular, the civil and the religious. The immediate premise is the philosophy of society and its juridical organization—in this sense, a philosophy of the state—developed by Pius XII and given a more systematic statement by John XXIII in *Pacem in terris*. This philosophy is deeply rooted in tradition; it is also, by comparison to Leo XIII, new.

The Leonine doctrine, more Aristotelian and medieval in inspiration, rested on the conception of the common good as an ensemble of social virtues and values, chiefly the value of obedience to the laws. The Pian and Joannine doctrine, more profoundly Christian in inspiration, rests on the conception of the common good as consisting chiefly in the effective exercise of the rights, and the faithful discharge of the duties, of the human person. Correlatively, in the Leonine conception the function of government was primarily ethical, namely, the direction of the citizen-subject—who was considered more subject than citizen—toward the life of virtue by the force of good laws reflecting the demands of the moral order. In the Pian and Joannine doctrine, on the other hand, the primary function of government is juridical, namely, the protection and promotion of the exercise of human and civil rights and the facilitation of the discharge of human and civil duties by the citizen who is fully citizen, that is, not merely subject to, but also participant in, the processes of government.

The insight of Pius XII, which lay at the root of the new development, was stated thus: "Man as such, so far from being regarded as the object of social life or a passive element thereof, is rather to be considered its subject, foundation and end." In contrast, the customary focus of

Leo XIII's doctrine was on the *principes* (his favorite word), the rulers who wielded in society the power they had received from God. In this latter conception, society is to be built and rendered virtuous from the top down, as it were; the role of government is dominant. In the former conception, however, society is to be built and rendered virtuous from the bottom up, as it were; the role of government is subordinate, a role of service to the human person. Moreover, in Leo XIII's conception (except in *Rerum novarum*), government was not only personal but paternal; the "prince" was, *pater patriae,* as society was the family writ large. In Pius XII's conception, on the other hand, government is simply political; the relation between ruler and ruled is a civil relation, not familial. This was a return to tradition (notably to Aquinas), after the aberrations of continental absolutism and the exaggerations of the Roman-law jurists.

Leo XIII's paternal conception owed much to historical fact and to the political culture of his day. The pivotal fact was the *imperita multitudo,* the illiterate formless masses, which reappear time and again in his text. In contrast, Pius XII's political conception was a return to tradition, to the noble idea of "the people," a structured concept at whose root stands, as he said, "the citizen [who] feels within himself the consciousness of his own personality, of his duties and rights, and of his due freedom as joined with a respect for the freedom and dignity of others." This return to the tradition of "the free man under a limited government" (as someone has summarized the basic political insight of Aquinas) was likewise a progress in the understanding of the tradition.

Finally, in Leo XIII the traditional distinction between society and state was largely lost from view; its disappearance from history had been, in fact, part of the *damnosa haereditas*—the fateful heritage—of the ancien régime. It is a noteworthy fact that nowhere in the immense body of Leo XIII's writings is there to be found a satisfactory philosophy of human law and jurisprudence. He was always the moralist, not the jurist. His concern was to insist that the juridical order of society must recognize the imperatives of the objective moral order. This emphasis was indeed necessary against the moral antinomianism and juridical positivism of continental laicism. However, in consequence of this polemic necessity, Leo XIII gave little if any attention to the internal structure of the juridical order itself—the structure, that is, of the state.

This became the preoccupation of Pius XII, as the menace of totalitarianism loomed large, threatening the basic dignity of the human person, which is his freedom. Pius XII revived the distinction between society and state, the essential barrier against totalitarianism. He also made it a pillar of his concept of the juridical state. (The phrase is alien in English; we speak of "constitutional government.") The powers of government are not only limited to the terrestrial and temporal order. Since Leo XIII this had been clear doctrine, however much it may have been disregarded in practice. But even within this limited order, the powers of government are limited by the higher order of human rights, defined in detail in *Pacem in terris,* whose doctrine is completed by the *Declaration on Religious Freedom.* The safekeeping and promotion of these rights is government's first duty to the common good.

Even this rapid comparison may help to make clear that, although Leo XIII's theory of civil tolerance was coherent with his conception of society and state, it is not coherent with the more fully developed philosophy of Pius XII and John XXIII. For Leo XIII, the power of the ruler was *patria potestas,* a paternal power. The ruler-father can, and is obliged to, know what is true and good—the true religion and the moral law. His primary duty, as father-ruler, is to guide his children-subjects—the illiterate masses—to what is true and good. His consequent function is to protect them against religious error and moral aberration—against the preachments of the "sects" (that favorite Leonine word). The masses are to be regarded as children, *ad instar puerorum,* who are helpless to protect themselves. They must look to the ruler-father, who knows what is true and good and also knows what is good for them. In these circumstances, and given this personal conception of rule, the attitude of government toward what is error and evil could only be one of tolerance. Government permits by law what it cannot prevent by law. Moreover, this civil tolerance is no more than a dictate of necessity; it is practiced for the sake of a greater good—the peace of the community. This theory of civil tolerance may indeed be regarded as a counsel of practical wisdom. It can hardly be regarded as permanent Catholic doctrine, any more than the theory of government, with which it is correlative, may be so regarded. The roots of both theories are in the contingencies of history, not in the exigencies of abiding truth.

Therefore, the *Declaration on Religious Freedom* puts aside the post-Reformation and nineteenth-century theory of civil tolerance. The fault is not error but archaism. A new philosophy of society and state has been elaborated, more transtemporal in its manner of conception and statement, less time-conditioned, more differentiated, a progress in the understanding of the tradition. Briefly, the structural elements of this philosophy are the four principles of social order stated, and developed in their exigencies, in *Pacem in terris*—the principles of truth, justice, love, and freedom. The declaration of the human and civil right to the free exercise of religion is not only in harmony with, but also required by, these four principles. The foundation of the right is the truth of human dignity. The object of the right—freedom from coercion, in religious matters—is the first debt due in justice to the human person. The final motive for respect of the right is a love of appreciation of the personal dignity of man. Religious freedom itself is the first of all freedoms in a well-organized society, without which no other human and civil freedoms can be safe.

2. Religious Liberty

Émile-Joseph De Smedt

This chapter, an address by Bishop De Smedt of Bruges, Belgium, to the Third Session of Vatican II, first appeared in *Council Speeches of Vatican II,* ed. Hans Küng, Yves Congar, and Daniel O'Hanlon (Glen Rock, N.J.: Paulist Press, 1964).

In order that we might clearly understand the doctrine of the church on the extent and limits of the civil power's duty relating to religious liberty, we must, in a few words, develop the history of this doctrine. Bear with me, Venerable Fathers, if I seem to make more than just demands on your patience. But the Secretariat for Promoting Christian Unity is convinced that many difficulties and confusions can be avoided in this study of the schema if, before the discussion begins, I show very briefly what the Supreme Pontiffs since the time of Pius IX have taught concerning the duties of public authority in religious matters.

On the question of religious liberty, the principal document is the encyclical *Pacem in terris* in which Pope John XXIII especially developed these two points of doctrine: (1) by the law of nature, the human person has the right to the free exercise of religion in society according to the dictates of a sincere conscience *(conscientia recta)* whether the conscience be true *(conscientia vera),* or the captive either of error or of inadequate knowledge of truth and of sacred things. (2) To this right corresponds the duty incumbent upon other men and the public authority to recognize and respect that right in such a way that the human person in society is kept immune from all coercion of any kind (cf. *A.A.S.* 55, 1963, p. 299, p. 264, and pp. 273–274).

Moreover, this doctrine must be understood as the contemporary terminus of a process of evolution both in the doctrine on the dignity of the human person and in the church's pastoral solicitude for man's freedom. This doctrinal evolution took place according to a twofold law:

13

(1) *Law of continuity:* The church's doctrine and solicitude are always self-consistent, always remain the same. This perennial doctrine can be expressed in the words of Pope John: "The dignity of the human person demands this, that in his actions man should enjoy his own counsel and freedom" (ibid., p. 265). This doctrine has its deepest roots in the sacred scriptures, which teach that man was made to the image of God. From this doctrine stems the continual pastoral solicitude of the church for man's true freedom.

(2) *Law of progress:* The ecclesiastical magisterium adapts, explains, and defends genuine doctrine according to the demands of errors that are spread and according to the needs that arise from the development of man and of society. By this progress, the mind of the church is led to search more deeply into doctrine and to understand it more clearly.

In this way, there has arisen in two areas a distinction that no one has explained more clearly than Pope John XXIII in his encyclical *Pacem in terris:* (1) A clearer distinction between false *philosophical teachings* and the *endeavors and institutions* that these ideologies give rise to or nourish: While on the one hand the ideologies are always to be condemned, on the other hand the economic, social, and civil institutions that have arisen therefrom can contain something that is good and worthy of approval. (2) A clearer distinction between *errors* and the *person* who errs in good faith: While on the one hand errors must always be rejected, on the other hand the man in error "does not cease to be endowed with human nature, nor does he ever lose his dignity as a person, due consideration of which must always be maintained" (ibid., pp. 299–300).

These two laws of continuity and progress must be always kept before our eyes when the documents of the Apostolic See are read and interpreted.

In this way the door is opened to a correct understanding of many pontifical documents, which in the nineteenth century treated of religious liberty in such words that this liberty appeared as something that had to be condemned. The clearest example is found in the encyclical *Quanta Cura* of Pius IX, in which we read: "From this completely false concept of social rule (naturalism), they do not hesitate to foster that erroneous opinion which is especially injurious to the Catholic Church and the salvation of souls, called by our predecessor Gregory XVI *'deliramentum,'* namely that freedom of conscience and of cults is the proper right of each man, and this should be proclaimed and asserted in every rightly constituted society" (*A.S.S.* 3, 1867, p. 162).

As is evident, this freedom of conscience is condemned because of the ideology of the rationalists who founded their conclusions upon the principle that the individual conscience is under no law, and therefore, is subject to no divinely given norms (cf. *Syllabus,* prop. 3, *A.S.S.* 3, p. 168). Freedom of worship is also condemned when it is based upon religious indifferentism (ibid., prop. 15, p. 170). Finally there is condemned that separation of the church from the state that is based upon the rationalistic principle of the juridical omnicompetence of the state, according to which the church is to be incorporated into the monistic organism of the state and is to be subjected to its supreme authority (ibid., prop. 39, p. 172).

To understand those condemnations correctly, we must see in them the constant doctrine and solicitude of the church concerning the true dignity of the human person and his true liberty (law of continuity). For the ultimate basis of human dignity lies in the fact that man is a creature of God. He is not God himself, but an image of God. From this absolute dependence of man upon God, there flows every right and duty of man to claim for himself and for others true religious liberty. For man is subjectively bound to worship God according to the sincere dictates of his own conscience *(juxta rectam suae conscientiae normam)* because objectively he is absolutely dependent upon God.

In order, therefore, that his absolute dependence upon God might not be infringed on in any way, man must not be impeded in any way by others or even by public authority from freely practicing his religion. Therefore, in opposing the philosophical and political tenets of laicism, the church was fighting for the dignity and true liberty of the human person. In accordance with the law of continuity, then, the church, in spite of changing conditions, has remained consistent both in the past and in the present.

Leo XIII had already started this doctrinal development when he distinguished clearly between the church, the people of God, and the civil society, a terrestrial and temporal people (cf. *Immortale Dei, A.S.S.* 18, 1885, pp. 166–167). By this means, he opened the way to a new affirmation of the due and lawful autonomy that belongs to the civil order and to its juridical dispositions. Because of this, it was possible to take a step forward (law of progress) toward a new judgment on "modern freedoms."

These freedoms can be tolerated (cf. ibid., p. 174: *Libertas Praestantissimum, A.S.S.* 20, 1887, pp. 609–610). And yet, they were to be *tolerated* only. The reason was evident. For at that time in Europe the regimes that proclaimed the modern freedoms, religious liberty among them, consciously drew their inspiration from the laicist ideology. There was danger, therefore—Leo XIII sensed this—that the civil and political institutions of this kind of republic, since they were of laicist orientation, would lead to such abuses that they would necessarily do violence to the dignity and true liberty of the human person. In accordance with the law of continuity, what was dear to Leo XIII is always dear to the church— the safeguarding of the human person.

With the rise of state totalitarianism in its various forms, Pope Pius XI brought pastoral and doctrinal development to a new height. There is no longer any danger, as there was in the nineteenth century, that the false concept of liberty might do violence to human dignity. There is a new danger that every kind of human and civil liberty, and above all religious liberty, will be destroyed. For this reason, the church is beginning in a new way to manifest her concern, which through the centuries has never wavered, for human liberty and dignity. With the increase of her pastoral concern, the church's doctrine continues to develop.

Faithfully observing the law of continuity, Pius XI maintained the unstinting opposition of the church to antireligious laicism: "Those things which Pius X condemned we also condemn: as often as there is in 'laicism' any meaning or purpose that is harmful or contrary to God or religion, we condemn laicism, and openly declare that it must be condemned, as alien to God and religion" (*Maximam Gravissimamque, A.A.S.* 16, 1924, p. 10).

But observing the rule of progress no less, Pius XI introduced a new distinction that was of great importance for a deeper understanding of Catholic doctrine. He made a distinction between the "freedom of conscience" and the "freedom of consciences." The former he rejected as "equivocal" as often used by the laicist to signify "an absolute independence of conscience, which is an absurdity in man who was created and redeemed by God"; the latter however, "freedom of consciences," he accepted, stating that he would joyfully fight the good fight for "freedom of consciences" (*Non abbiamo bisogno, A.A.S.* 23, 1931, pp. 301–302).

Moreover, Pius XI not only fought for the religious liberty of the faithful, but he was at the same time compelled to show pastoral concern on a wider basis. For not only the Christian, but also the human reality was at stake, if we can rightly distinguish between two things that are in reality one.

By way of new advances, Pius XI developed a truly liberal and Christian doctrine when he taught: "Man as a person possesses God-given rights which must remain immune from all denial, privation, or interference on the part of society" (*Mit brennender Sorge, A.A.S.* 29, 1937, p. 159). And he continues in no ambiguous words: "The believer possesses the inalienable right to profess his faith and to practice it in a proper way. Laws that interfere with or render difficult this profession and practice are in contradiction to the natural law" (ibid., p. 160). No one who understands the condition of the times and the purpose of this encyclical can fail to understand the universal intent of this statement.

Deeply sharing the pastoral solicitude of his predecessor, Pius XII developed further and expanded his doctrine (law of progress). One thing he kept before his mind, the human person, created by God, redeemed by Christ Jesus, yet placed in stringent circumstances and surrounded on all sides by dangers.

In this context of doctrine and pastoral solicitude (law of continuity), we must read the text that in this matter is supreme. Enumerating "the fundamental rights of the person," which must be recognized and respected in every well-ordered society, he repeats the doctrine of Pius XI and vests it with new authority, affirming "the right to the private and public worship of God, including *'actio caritativa'*" (*Nuntius radiophonicus,* 24 Dec. 1942, *A.A.S.* 35, 1943, p.19).

The Roman pontiff did not propose this doctrine as a tenuous opinion or as a theory belonging to the schools. On the contrary, he carries the doctrine to its juridical conclusions so that it becomes a principle according to which just limits are placed on public authority: "The chief duty of any public authority is to safeguard the inviolable rights that are proper to men and so to provide that each one might more easily fulfill his duties" (*Nuntius radiophonicus*, 1 June 1941, *A.A.S.* 33, 1941, p. 200).

Here we must recall especially the doctrine of Pius XII on the limitation of the state, because it deals with the suppression of errors within society: "Could it be that in certain circumstances he (God) would not give men any mandate, would not impose any duty, and would not even communicate the right to impede or to repress what is erroneous and false? A look at things as they are gives an affirmative answer." Then, having cited the example of divine providence, he proceeds:

> Hence the affirmation: religious and moral error must always be impeded, when it is possible, because toleration of them is in itself immoral, is not valid absolutely and unconditionally. Moreover, God has not given even to human authority such an absolute and universal command in matters of faith and morality. Such a command is unknown to the common convictions of mankind, to Christian conscience, to the sources of revelation, and to the practice of the church. (*Ci riesce*, *A.A.S.* 45, 1953, pp. 798–799)

This declaration (law of progress) is of the greatest importance for our question, especially if we keep in mind what was in the past held concerning the role of the state.

At the end of this historical development comes the encyclical *Pacem in terris*. This document comes forth as a ripe fruit of a slow process of growth that has taken place within the church, under the light of the Holy Spirit throughout the whole of the last century.

Our schema had already been prepared and had been studied by the Central Commission and by the Commission for Coordination when Pope John, on April 11 of this year, published his last encyclical *Pacem in terris*. We believe that our text is in complete conformity with his pellucid doctrine, which was received within the church and outside the church with unprecedented praise.

We now submit for your consideration this text. In the historical conspectus of this doctrine, we have shown that in the pontifical documents, along with continuity, we must look for a progressive spelling out of doctrine. It is evident that certain quotations from the popes, because of a difference in words, can be put in opposition to our schema. But I beseech you, Venerable Fathers, not to force the text to speak outside of its historical and doctrinal context, not in other words to make the fish swim out of water.

3. Catholicism and Democracy: Conflict, Change, and Collaboration

J. Bryan Hehir

This chapter first appeared in *Christianity and Democracy in Global Context,* ed. John Witte, Jr. (Boulder, Col.: Westview, 1993).

I will confine my essay to a specific perspective on the broader topic of Christianity and democracy, namely, the relationship of the Catholic Church and democracy. The narrower lens is chosen because the relationship of Roman Catholicism to democracy has been more conflicted than in many other Christian churches. Yet developments in Catholicism over the last three decades have substantially changed Catholic doctrine and practice regarding democracy. It is the sources and significance of that change that this essay will explore.

The argument will move in three steps. First, the background of the Catholicism-democracy question since the nineteenth century will be sketched. Second, an assessment of Catholic theory and policy since Vatican II will be offered. Third, an analysis of the impact of John Paul II on the future relationship of Catholicism and democracy will be proposed.

CATHOLICISM AND DEMOCRACY: THE HISTORY AND THE SECOND VATICAN COUNCIL

The Catholic Church's relationship with the political order begins with the Roman Empire and is still being worked out today. The *dramatis personae* are relatively well known. On the ecclesiastical side it is Ambrose and Augustine, Aquinas and Vitoria, Lammenais and Pius IX, John Courtney Murray and John Paul II. On the political side the names are of emperors, kings, presidents, and dictators: Charlemagne, Philip the Fair, Richelieu, Talleyrand, Cavour, Mussolini, Stalin. The personalities on both sides struggled over principles and interests, theoretical categories and concrete claims.

Early in the story, A.D. 496 to be exact, the leitmotif was struck by Pope Gelasius in his letter, *Duo Sunt,* to the emperor. The famous "two swords" argument, holding that all authority comes from God but has been delegated in two ways to the spiritual and temporal powers in society, has been the baseline for the theology of church and state for fifteen centuries.[1] The terms of the debate have changed, from church and empire, to the church and the *Republica Christiana,* to the church and the nation state.

The interpretation of the *Duo Sunt* has ranged from hierocratic attempts to determine the temporal power to secularist attempts to stifle the public life of the church. But the *two swords* distinction, which then became the *two powers* relationship of the Middle Ages, and the *two societies* position of Leo XIII and Pius XII, has provided the central structural element for Catholicism's relationship to the political order.

In the eighteenth century, the democratic revolutions in France and the United States set a new context and posed a new question to an old teaching. The response of Catholicism to democratic polity can broadly be divided into two periods, with the Second Vatican Council being the dividing line.

THE NINETEENTH CENTURY: PIUS IX–LEO XIII

The democratic revolutions of the eighteenth century were not analyzed in a systematic fashion in Rome. The distinction between the rationale and dynamic of the American Revolution and that of the French Revolution was never a significant aspect of the Holy See's response to democracy. It was the French Revolution, in its theoretical and its practical aspects, which Rome equated with the meaning of democracy. Since both the theory and the practice ran counter to the Holy See's understanding of the best interests of the church's ministry, the response to democracy for a century after the French Revolution was unremittingly negative. The specifics of the response are found in Gregory XVI's *Mirari Vos* (1834) and in Pius IX's *Quanta Cura* (1864) and the *Syllabus Errorum* (1869). At the practical diplomatic-political

level, of course, the democratic movement in eighteenth- and
nineteenth-century Europe overthrew various representatives of the
ancien régime with which the Vatican had been aligned. But the more
significant question was the philosophical critique that Rome sustained
against democracy—and its allied conception of human rights—
throughout the nineteenth century.

Essentially the Catholic critique of democracy began with the idea
of freedom, extended through the prevailing notion of rights (especially
the right of religious freedom) and ended with a judgment against the
separation of church and state. The idea of freedom, which was at the
heart of the democratic movements, appeared in Catholic eyes (at least
in Rome) to be devoid of any normative framework that would relate
freedom to justice and order. Catholic teaching of the nineteenth century
was deeply suspicious of both political freedom and economic freedom.
The first threatened intellectual values; the second threatened social justice. The eighteenth-century view of rights, while analogous to that
found in Aquinas, in fact presupposed a very different order of relationships in society from the natural law teaching of the church. The neural-
gic point of conflict between Catholic teaching and democracy was the
idea of religious freedom. The democratic conception of the right
seemed in papal eyes to embody a mistaken notion of both liberty and
rights. The affirmation of freedom seemed to be cut off from any conception of an objective order of truth. The affirmation of right seemed
separated from the prior logic of the duty to seek religious truth.
Throughout the nineteenth century, Catholic teaching resisted the idea
of religious freedom in the name of standing against philosophical rela-
tivism and for the interests of the church.

The implacable opposition of Catholic teaching to democracy and
human rights eased somewhat with the pontificate of Leo XIII. If
Vatican II marks the dividing line between two distinct Catholic
responses to democracy and rights, Leo XIII is the pivotal figure who
begins the movement away from the nineteenth-century teaching and
sets the direction for a different approach, which he could not formulate,
but which he made possible.

While maintaining the Catholic philosophical critique of liberalism
and continuing to oppose the idea of separation of church and state, Leo
XIII made three moves which initiated a process of development in

Catholic teaching. First, Leo XIII argued that the reason for the existence of both the church and state was the welfare of the citizen. The person's spiritual welfare was the responsibility of the church and the citizen's temporal welfare (the common good of society) was the responsibility of the state. Hence the two institutions shared a moral obligation to cooperate for the good of the person. Second, while resisting the idea of the right to religious liberty, Leo XIII did expand the church's support for other rights of the person, particularly the rights of workers in the face of the Industrial Revolution. Third, Leo XIII restated the basic principle that should govern the "two swords" relationship: the freedom of the church to fulfill its spiritual ministry in society. Each of these ideas, as John Courtney Murray has demonstrated,[2] contained implications that Leo XIII did not grasp and never pursued. But his successors did.

As both Cardinal Newman and Murray have shown, development of doctrine does occur in Catholicism—but not simply or quickly. The potential for development inherent in Leo XIII's move away from the style of analysis of the other nineteenth-century popes was not taken up until the pontificate of Pius XII (1939–1958). As Murray argued, both Pius XII's political interest and intelligence, as well as the experience of the church with authoritarian-totalitarian regimes, led the pope to a recasting of Catholic teaching on democracy. The changes were rooted in Leo XIII but in each case went substantially beyond anything he had said.

First, Leo XIII's natural law teaching on rights focused on socioeconomic issues; he was more at home with the relationship of rights and justice than with rights and liberty. Pius XII turned his attention to rights in the political order, joining Catholic support for the traditional civil liberties to the range of socioeconomic rights affirmed by Leo XIII and Pius XI (1922–1939). It was in the context of this teaching that Pius XII addressed the topic of democracy. Prior to the Christmas Addresses of Pius XII, Catholic teaching on democracy was ambivalent. The association of democratic polity with the philosophy of liberalism and the revolutions of the eighteenth century, yielded a church judgment that was reserved, cautious, and minimalist in its legitimization of democracy. In a series of texts from 1941–1945, Pius XII moved to a clear affirmation of the principles and polity of democratic governance.[3]

Second, Pius XII accepted in principle the distinction between society and state, a fundamental notion for any democratic polity. Both the organic vision of society implicit in Catholic natural law philosophy and the desire to maintain a role for the state in "the care of religion" had been obstacles to the acceptance of the constitutional or limited role for the state. Thoroughly familiar with totalitarian claims of the left and right, Pius XII saw the wisdom of restricting the range of state power in the name of protecting basic human rights.

Third, Pius XII prepared the way for the acceptance of the right of religious liberty without ever quite taking that step himself. His contribution was to relativize the role that the nineteenth-century distinction of "Thesis-Hypothesis" had played in Catholic theology on church and state. The distinction posited an "ideal case" in which the state recognized the role of the Catholic Church in civil law (the thesis); all other church-state arrangements were "hypotheses," which could be tolerated, if implementing the thesis would be socially disruptive. It was this mode of argument that rendered suspect Catholic affirmations of either support for democracy or for religious liberty. Pius XII distanced himself from the distinction in a famous address of 1953 without ever disowning the formula.

In summary, Leo XIII had maintained both the premises and conclusions of nineteenth-century Catholicism on democracy, but within this framework, he introduced ideas that were incompatible with the old construct. Pius XII changed the premises of Catholic teaching on democracy and human rights, but stopped just short of changing the conclusion on religious liberty. That step, with its consequences for Catholic teaching and practice vis-à-vis democracy, was left to the Second Vatican Council.

VATICAN II DEMOCRACY AND THE CHURCH

Before analyzing how the development from Leo XIII and Pius XII reached fulfillment in the teaching of Vatican II, recognition should be accorded to two crucial contributions between Pius XII and Vatican II: one is the work of a theologian, John Courtney Murray, S.J.; the other is the encyclical of John XXIII, *Pacem in terris* (1963). While they are two different accomplishments, they illustrate, in tandem, how development of doctrine is effected in the Catholic tradition. Murray's work, an individual achievement of scholarship, extended over twenty-five years;

it often was done in tension with ecclesiastical teaching authority, and it found acceptance only after the event of the Council provided a new context for theological work in the church. Murray once described the theologian's role as standing on the growing edge of the tradition. It was exactly where Murray placed himself, between the experience of American democracy and the preconciliar teaching on church and state. Murray mediated that dialogue and helped to revise the teaching of Catholicism on democracy.

Murray used the combined resources of history, ecclesiology, and political philosophy to revise the teaching of Leo XIII and Pius XII. Essentially Murray argued that the historical reality that shaped nineteenth-century Catholic teaching on democracy had been transformed; that Leo XIII's view of the state should yield to Pius XII's more limited understanding of the state. Finally, in light of the first two changes, the church could affirm the right of religious liberty without threatening either Catholic doctrine on the church or the social order of society. The basic responsibility of the state should not be "the care of religion," but the protection of the right of religious freedom for each citizen. The basic demand of the church is not favoritism from the state but the freedom to function.

Murray worked with the categories of the tradition like a master craftsman. He took each of the major terms of the teaching and either redefined them (e.g., the state) or placed them in a new context (the idea of religious liberty). The end product of his effort was to provide a historical and theological explanation of Catholic tradition that allowed Vatican II to affirm a relationship with the political order substantially different from the nineteenth-century teaching on democracy, the state, and human rights. Murray stressed, before and during the Vatican II debate on religious liberty, how the church could restructure its relationship with a democratic state without simply contradicting the teaching of the past. He wove a complex argument that stressed continuity of key themes, while calling for change in the conclusions of earlier teaching.

Murray's research and writing from 1945–1965 was foundational for a Catholic theology of the state, but it was not authoritative. It was the insight of a single member of the church, urging the wider community—especially the papacy—to review and revise Catholic policy and practice in the political order. The first authoritative indication that the

Murray thesis could succeed was the encyclical of John XXIII, *Pacem in terris*. Published before the Vatican Council took up the topic of religious liberty, this very authoritative letter established a new framework for Catholicism's relationship to democracy, human rights, and religious liberty.

The dominant theme in *Pacem in terris* was its teaching on human rights. It not only provided the clearest and most comprehensive enunciation of which rights the church supported, it also sought to build a bridge across the old natural law versus natural rights debate. Without entering the dense specificity of how these two philosophical positions conceive of rights, of the nature of society, and of relationships between the citizen and the state, *Pacem in terris* shaped a natural law argument with a central place for rights claims. In style the argument sounds very similar to natural rights language; the framework of the rights argument, however, joins rights to duties, stresses the social nature of the person, and defines a more positive and expansive role for the constitutional state than natural rights conceptions usually yield.

The encyclical built extensively on the teaching of Pius XII, but in both style and substance, it created a much deeper and stronger linkage between Catholicism and democratic theory and polity than Pius XII had ever forged. In style, *Pacem in terris* was characterized by a more open attitude toward modernity (politically and culturally) than Pius XII ever demonstrated; in substance John XXIII took his predecessor's support for a constitutional state to a new level of specificity. Murray comments:

> The concept of constitutional government is more sharply described than in Pius XII, even to the point of recommending, for the first time in papal documents, the written constitution. And this concept of the limited functions of the state is brought into explicit correlation with a fully developed description of the juridical order of human and civil rights and freedoms, whose protection and promotion is the primary function of the state. This is Pius XII, of course, but speaking with a new accent—more affirmative, more confident that the present moment in history is the term of a progress that has been real, even though not unambiguous.[4]

Finally, for the first time in an authoritative Catholic document, there is a clear statement of the right to religious liberty. The text is not developed, nor is the correlative conception of church-state relations worked out. The significance of *Pacem in terris* is that, by its authority, it helped to prepare the way for the fuller statement of Vatican II.

The Second Vatican Council did not address explicitly the relationship of the church and democracy. In two texts, however, *The Declaration on Religious Liberty (Dignitatis Humanae)* and *The Pastoral Constitution on the Church in the Modern World (Gaudium et Spes)*, it completed the process of development begun by Leo XIII, and it established a new framework for the teaching and practice of the church in the political order.

Under the leadership of John XXIII, the Council adopted a relational view of the church's life. The intent and the method of the Council was to enter into dialogue with and relate to the multiplicity of institutions and communities that constitute the modern world. The relational conception of its pastoral role was reflected religiously in its document on ecumenism, intellectually in *Gaudium et Spes,* and politically in *Dignitatis Humanae.* The design of each text was to express a sense of the church's identity and then to find themes for dialogue and cooperation with other churches, with intellectual disciplines needed to understand the world, and with political institutions at the local, national, and international level.

Within this perspective, the principle contribution of Vatican II was its definition of religious liberty. Here the conciliar teaching was primarily designed to bring the church abreast of other religious and political communities that had long ago adopted this concept. The Council based the right on the dignity of the person, defined its scope in terms of protecting the person from coercion in religious affairs and guaranteeing both individuals and communities the right of free exercise of religious conviction, and finally, argued that such religious expression could be limited only in extreme conditions when it would threaten "the public order" of society.

In terms of Catholicism's relationship to democracy, defining clearly a right to religious liberty was a precondition for everything else. But the structural understanding of the church's role in the political community was the more important long-term contribution to the

Catholicism-democracy relationship. Murray's summary of the main elements of the Council's posture cannot be improved upon.[5] He identifies three ideas in the conciliar teaching: the acceptance of religious pluralism as the context of the church's life and ministry; the endorsement of the constitutional state; and the principle of the freedom of the church in society. The last two have appeared previously in this paper: Pius XII and John XXIII understood the value of placing constitutional limits on state power; Leo XIII and all of his predecessors understood the principle of *libertas ecclesiae.* Repetition of these themes by an ecumenical council solidified their place in Catholic teaching. But Vatican II's contribution went beyond that role in my view. By joining the acceptance of religious pluralism to the other two ideas, the council enhanced the church's ability to engage and support democratic polity. The church has had as difficult a time with pluralism as it had with the concept of freedom. Prior to the council, pluralism was a reality to be tolerated at best and resisted if possible. Acceptance of the fact of religious pluralism also meant accepting the fact that a constitutional state will almost inevitably be a secular state. This, in turn, makes even more significant the principle of the freedom of the church. Leo XIII endorsed the principle, but tied it to other claims for the legitimacy of a "Catholic state." Vatican II dropped any claims to such treatment; the regulating principle of church-state relations is the freedom of the church not favoritism for the church.

CATHOLICISM AND DEMOCRACY: POSTCONCILIAR RELATIONSHIPS

Both the experience and the teaching of Vatican II provided the church with a new basis for relating to democracy. To understand how that relationship has developed in the last twenty-five years, it is necessary to make a more general point about the postconciliar church. The document *Gaudium et Spes,* focused on defining the church's relationship to the world, has had a profound and systematic impact on the life of the church. While local situations would have to be examined in detail, a general pattern is clearly evident since 1965. The conciliar document not only legitimized social ministry, it also moved the social dimension of ministry toward the center of Catholic life. If one surveys the experience of the church since 1965, in situations as diverse as Latin America, Eastern Europe, and South Africa, it is virtually impossible to explain on an ad hoc basis the public role played by the Catholic hierarchy and the wider community of the church. The intensity of public engagement has escalated, and the willingness to confront major centers of political and economic power in the name of human rights and social justice has noticeably expanded.

In the search for a systemic rather than an ad hoc explanation (which could depend on accidents of history or a single personality), the most persuasive evidence always points to the event of Vatican II, its teaching, and the energy it generated throughout the church. *Gaudium et Spes* provided a rationale and a structural framework for interpreting the social role of the church. The rationale is the protection of human dignity. The defense of the human person is the basic reason for the church's social ministry. The principle did not originate with Vatican II; the popes have pressed it for the last century.

But *Gaudium et Spes* ties the defense of the person to the essential work of the church: "For she is at once a sign and a safeguard of the transcendence of the human person."[6] The sentence mandates a style of ministry for the church, an imperative that must be included in any evaluation of the church's work and service. The structural conception of how the church should fulfill this role distinguishes between a directly political role and a socially significant presence in society. Direct political involvement (e.g., association with political parties, priests or nuns in political office) is ruled out; the church has no special political gifts and such involvement is deemed harmful to the broader ministry of the church. But a socially activist role for the church is legitimized and encouraged. This style of social ministry involves both the teaching-preaching role of the church and use of church institutions to come to the defense and aid of those under repression or those marginalized in the economy. This distinction, opposing direct political involvement but not social ministry, is confusing to many observers of Catholicism, but it is rooted in Vatican II, and it has been a basic guideline for John Paul II.

In such an activist ministry how has Catholicism engaged democracy? The answer of the last twenty-five years is that it has fostered democracy principally through the church's work for human rights. The struggle for human rights has been the matrix from which democracy has emerged.

In a recent article Professor Samuel Huntington examined the democratization process that has moved more than thirty countries from authoritarian to democratic regimes since 1974. A central theme in Huntington's analysis of the "third wave" of democratization is the catalytic role of religion, and specifically, the role of the Catholic Church in the democratization process:

> In its first fifteen years the third wave was overwhelmingly Catholic....Everywhere, Catholic societies were in the lead, and roughly three-quarters of the countries that transited to democracy between 1974 and 1989 were Catholic.[7]

Huntington's analysis notes the historic connection between Protestantism and democracy, and the equally well-known presumption that Catholic faith and polity were unlikely supporters for democratic governance, not only within the church but within traditionally Catholic societies. Thus he goes on to state the Catholic thesis of his analysis:

> In the 1960s the church changed....Before 1960 the Catholic Church usually accommodated itself to authoritarian regimes and frequently legitimized them; only rarely did it oppose such regimes. After 1970, the church almost invariably opposed authoritarian regimes; and in some countries, such as Brazil, Chile, the Philippines, Poland, and in Central America, it played a central role in the efforts to change such regimes.[8]

Huntington's essay ably surveys a pattern that has been well known in theological writing for the past two decades but that has not received systematic attention in standard assessments of international politics. The key cases are Brazil and Chile in the 1970s; Central America and Poland in the early 1980s; and the Philippines, South Korea, and South Africa in the late 1980s.

My concern is to focus on two aspects of Huntington's Catholic thesis: first to comment on how a church, which took a century to recognize the right to religious liberty, transformed its theory and practice so decisively in two decades; and second, to highlight that there was a North American connection to the process of human rights advocacy, which Huntington and others have documented in the Catholic communities of the Third World and Eastern Europe.

Three major elements in postconciliar Catholicism were the moving forces in sparking and sustaining human rights advocacy. The first was doctrinal: There are two components of the doctrinal basis that legitimated and guided the Catholic Church's recent involvement with human rights and social justice issues. One dimension is papal social teaching, a body of philosophical reflection reaching from Leo XIII's first social encyclical *Rerum Novarum* (1891) to John Paul II's *Centesimus Annus* (1991). The social teaching prior to the 1940s stressed social and economic justice more prominently than it did political rights and democracy, but the movement noted earlier in this paper from Pius XII to John Paul II joined a social justice theme to advocacy of human rights and democratization. The second dimension is the way in which *Gaudium et Spes* of Vatican II incorporated the social themes into a definition of the religious ministry of the church. Accompanying the doctrinal legitimization of "social Catholicism" was an organizational or bureaucratic shift in Catholic polity, begun by Vatican II and carried forward by Paul VI after the Council. Essentially it involved a decentralizing process in Catholicism, a conscious choice at Vatican II to reorder relationships in the universal church. The pontificate of Pius XII had been the most centralized papacy in the history of Catholicism; it brought to fulfillment a long process of centralization begun in the Gregorian Reform (1073–1085) and culminating in the post-World War II papacy. Vatican II used an ancient theological principle, collegiality, to argue that the whole church is governed by the college of bishops with the Bishop of Rome at its center. The collegial principle then provided the basis for giving local churches (i.e., the church at the national or regional level) greater autonomy and scope for initiative in the realm of pastoral care and social advocacy. Collegiality was never framed as a challenge to Roman primacy or even a counterweight to papal leadership. It was cast in terms of providing for more effective episcopal collaboration of the pope and the bishops. Institutionally the principle of collegiality found expression in the creation of national episcopal conferences. These bodies have played a central role in the human rights and democracy struggles in Brazil, Chile, the Philippines, and Poland.

Paul VI, in his letter *Octogesima Adveniens* (1971), acknowledged that the papacy, on social questions, should be understood as setting a direction for the universal church, providing "principles of reflection, norms of judgment and directives for action."[9] But the local Christian communities had to analyze these particular situations and address them. This text was an invitation to the "local church" (at the national, diocesan, and parish levels) to become active agents of Catholic social teaching. The task of the local church was not simply to receive direction from the center of the church; it also had a creative role of leadership. Social advocacy was encouraged from "the bottom up" in the postconciliar period.

This process of decentralization, in turn, produced the third factor in the human rights ministry of the church: the engagement at the national and local levels of church life. The local engagement was to some degree a response to the theology and bureaucratic reforms stimulated by Vatican II; but it was also, very concretely, a response to local conditions and circumstances. Absent Vatican II, it is very likely that bishops, priests, religious, and laity in Brazil, El Salvador, South Korea, and Poland would have responded to injustice in these countries. But the conciliar theology and the postconciliar dynamic in the church gave qualitatively new support and legitimation to local movements for social justice and human rights. The contribution from the local level can be illustrated (but not adequately represented) by three examples: theological reflection, pastoral strategies, and personal leadership.

Theologically, local churches have begun to articulate distinctive forms of reflection, often joined specifically to social conditions. The principal example—to some degree the methodological model—has been the Theology of Liberation in Latin America. While the scope, range, and depth of this theological movement sets it apart from other local initiatives, it is useful to note that "Contextual Theology" in South Africa, an ecumenical endeavor, has its local roots and relevance, and there are variants of such local theology in both the Philippines and South Korea. In each case, the theology in question arises from the experience and pastoral challenge of the local church, it draws upon the broader themes of the church's biblical and theological tradition, and it returns to the local setting as a resource for pastoral activity and advocacy.

The pastoral strategies, which have been developed in the struggles for human rights and social justice, vary with the local conditions. Examples illustrate the differences: The Basic Ecclesial Communities in Latin America have become sources of spiritual nurture and units of social organization; the church-labor relationship forged in Poland in the 1980s has counterparts in Brazil and South Africa, but each is a unique alliance. The ecumenical character of pastoral strategies is very intense in parts of Latin America, in South Africa, and in South Korea. It is much less evident in Poland, but more visible in Czechoslovakia.

Finally, the local contributions to human rights advocacy include charismatic leadership by key figures. The names of hierarchical representatives tend to be the best known: Cardinals Sin (Philippines), Kim (South Korea), and Arns (Brazil). But the leadership of religious women is woven throughout the church: the slain missionaries in El Salvador, the nuns in the Philippines. The hardest to identify, but often the most heroic in their persistence and courage, is the lay leadership that sustains the social ministry in almost all of the cases cited above.

The final point to be made about postconciliar Catholicism's involvement with human rights is that a North American component has been part of the wider strategy. Huntington's article understandably focuses on the changes brought about in countries in Asia, Latin America, and Eastern Europe. But an understanding of how the church in the United States related to movements for human rights in other countries illustrates the transnational character of Catholic polity and responds to the theme of this volume.

Briefly, the movement in other local churches on human rights began in the late 1960s and became centrally important in the 1970s and 1980s. At approximately the same time, U.S. legislation in the Congress and then U.S. policy in the Carter administration raised the human rights issues here. The Catholic Bishops Conference testified at the opening hearings of Rep. Don Frazer's House Subcommittee, which developed the human rights legislation. Thereafter, in conjunction with the Protestant and Jewish communities, the Bishops Conference testified regularly on human rights policy affecting a wide variety of countries. Often the testimony was in response to requests from another local church or from U.S. missionaries working in Asia, Africa, or Latin America.

As Huntington notes, following a much earlier article by Ivan Vallier,[10] the transnational character of Catholicism provides added defense against authoritarian regimes. The local church can call on a network of other local churches. The ability to address the U.S. government in situations affecting Latin America, East Asia, and Eastern Europe was a particularly useful linkage for local churches confronting regimes that often were recipients of U.S. economic and military assistance. The policy used by the U.S. bishops involved three criteria. They would publicly address human rights issues if (1) evidence of abuses could be documented; (2) the local hierarchy approved of a U.S. church voice on the matter; and (3) U.S. policy was involved in the situation. These criteria legitimated action on a range of problems, but they also meant that certain situations were not addressed. If the local hierarchy was divided, if the data on abuses were not decisive, or if public protest here would put the local church in another country in greater danger, the U.S. bishops would not go public on an issue.

The successful transition to democracy in many countries poses new challenges for the church's social ministry. Huntington refers to the declining possibilities for Catholic leadership, since the countries now facing human rights struggles are not Catholic cultures. This assessment overlooks two quite current issues. First, in countries where the Catholic church is a minority, it often has an institutional role that continues to have influence: South Korea and South Africa are two examples. Second, in those countries in which democratic transition has occurred, the deeper socioeconomic problems associated with debt and development remain. The Catholic advocacy on human rights and democracy cannot be separated from these issues of poverty and social justice. For the local churches who led the way to democratization, and for the local church here addressing U.S. policy, these other issues are the next step in human rights advocacy.

CATHOLICISM AND DEMOCRACY: JOHN PAUL II

In both word and action John Paul II has forged a solid bond between the church and democracy. Huntington writes, "With the accession of John Paul II, the pope and the Vatican moved to center stage in the church's struggle against authoritarianism."[11] John Paul assumed the papacy after the local churches in several countries had already entered the arena of human rights and social justice. But he gave the whole enterprise a new urgency and a dramatic edge. His personal experience of opposition to communism, his public style, and his willingness to address very specific situations during his trips raised the visibility and the vitality of Catholic opposition to authoritarian rule.

He matched his deeds with words, addressing regularly the major themes of this paper: religious liberty, human rights, and democracy. A church that long was suspicious of the idea of religious liberty has a pope who presses the thesis that this is the fundamental or foundational right upon which all other human rights rest. His position does not, however, diminish attention to a broad range of other rights. In his 1979 address to the UN General Assembly, he analyzed all international affairs through the lens of human rights, endorsing the broad range of political, social, and economic rights found in UN documents.

His recent encyclical, *Centesimus Annus* (1991) contains, in my view, the strongest endorsement of democratic polity found in Catholic teaching. The text combines a series of supporting statements that are an enormous shift from the pre-1940 posture of Catholicism:

> The Church values the democratic system....
> The Church respects the legitimate autonomy of the democratic order....[12]

The record of this papacy thus far provides a solid basis of expectation that the principle of democratic governance will receive unstinting support from Rome and that the pope will continue to oppose authoritarian rule by his teaching and his witness. At the same time, it is clear that John Paul wishes to engage democratic societies in a conversation about some key characteristics of contemporary democracy. In brief, he is firmly committed to the political institutions of democracy, but he is also clearly worried about cultural presuppositions that often accompany democratic rule. His doubts are expressed in the following way:

> Nowadays there is a tendency to claim that agnosticism and
> skeptical relativism are the philosophy and the basic attitude
> which correspond to democratic forms of political life.[13]

The statement is not surprising from the position of a church
whose moral theology is grounded in both the authority of revealed truth
and a philosophy of natural law, premised on the idea of an objective
moral order. These foundational positions led many of John Paul's predecessors to doubt whether Catholicism and democracy were compatible.
They dissolved the tension by dismissing democracy. He is committed
to democracy but seeks to ground it in a definite vision of moral order.
The two realities—democracy and moral order—are not only compatible but, it would seem, complementary.

Yet the confidence of John Paul II in the church's ability to know
the moral order (not only in its premises, but in a wide range of conclusions) is not necessarily shared, particularly in the more secular soil of
postindustrial democracy. It would be a strange version of Catholicism
that did not pursue a critical conversation with the culture of democracy,
but it will not be a dialogue that produces quick or multiple conclusions.

The likelihood of an extended and complex dialogue raises two
final thoughts about John Paul II's style of engaging the conversation.
First, in the stark confrontation between advocacy for human rights and
authoritarian rule, the pope has proven himself an effective pastor,
diplomat, and moral leader. In the less stark, more subtle task of shaping
a moral consensus, under conditions of religious and cultural pluralism,
he may come across as too sure, too impatient, and immune to compromise on forging a civil consensus for a diverse populace. The very characteristics that enhance his role in stark confrontation may be less usable
after the battle for democracy has been won.

Second, there is the complex issue of governance within the
church itself. It is clear that democracy is not the polity of Catholicism,
and the pope's commitment to the role of democracy in civil society
should not be judged by the internal structure of the Catholic Church. It
is no secret that the premises of Catholicism as a faith are not of a democratic nature.

At the same time there is a spectrum of methods and modalities
about how authority is to be exercised even within Catholicism. This is
clearly a decisive papacy, prone to draw bright lines and to enforce the

limits vigorously. Without at all confusing the internal structure of the church with the structure of civil society, it is still possible to venture the idea that the pope's appreciation for freedom in the civil realm and his commitment to it will be enhanced or diminished in the public eye partly by his governance of his own institution.

That institution in the late twentieth century has moved dramatically in the direction of democratic governance. The future will offer it more possibilities to sustain a Catholic democratic commitment.

Notes

1. The interpretation of the Catholic tradition on democracy, which is now regarded as "classic," is that of John Courtney Murray, S.J. The first section of this paper depends heavily on his work, particularly on two essays: "The Problem of Religious Freedom," *Theological Studies* 25 (1964) 503–575 and "The Issue of Church and State at Vatican Council II," *Theological Studies* 27 (1966) 580–606.

2. Murray, "The Problem of Religious Freedom," 535–543.

3. The pertinent texts are the annual Christmas Address from 1942, 1943, 1944; see V. Yzermans, ed., *The Major Addresses of Pius XII: The Christmas Addresses* (St. Paul, Minn., 1961), 2:51–89; see also Murray, "The Problem of Religious Freedom," 543–548.

4. Murray, "The Problem of Religious Freedom," 553–554.

5. Murray, "The Issues of Church and State," 585–588.

6. Vatican II, *The Pastoral Constitution on the Church in the Modern World (Gaudium et Spes)* (Vatican, 1965), No. 76.

7. Samuel P. Huntington, "Religion and the Third Wave," *The National Interest* 24 (Summer, 1991) 30.

8. Ibid., 31.

9. Paul VI, *The Coming Eightieth (Octogesima Adveniens)* (Vatican, 1971), No. 3.

10. I. Vallier, "The Roman Catholic Church: A Transnational Actor," in *Transnational Relations and World Politics*, ed. R. Keohane and J. S. Nye Jr. (Cambridge, Mass., 1973) 129–152.

11. Huntington, "Religion and the Third Wave," 33.

12. John Paul II, *On the Hundredth Anniversary of Rerum Novarum (Centesimus Annus)* (Vatican, 1991), Nos. 46, 47.

13. Ibid., No. 46

4. Churches and Human Rights: From Hostility/Reluctance to Acceptability

Charles E. Curran

This chapter first appeared in *Milltown Studies*, No. 42 (Winter 1998).

The aim of this paper is twofold. First, to substantiate briefly the thesis enunciated in the title. The Christian churches, primarily Roman Catholic and Protestant in the Western world, have moved from hostility to, or reluctance about, human rights to an acceptance and even to a leadership role in the struggle for human rights in the world today.[1] Second, a much longer section will try to explain how this development occurred. A brief conclusion will reflect on what the churches can learn from this development.

From Hostility/Reluctance to Acceptance

Human rights in the Western tradition are primarily associated with the seventeenth-century philosophy of the Enlightenment, especially that of Thomas Hobbes and John Locke, and with the political systems that emerged from this approach and toppled the older political order. Some scholars have proposed that human rights as such arose only with the Enlightenment.[2] Both human rights and the Enlightenment are associated with opposition to religion in general and to Christianity in particular. Human rights have often been seen as coming from a growing secularism with its emphasis on human reason, the primacy of the individual, science, and a skepticism with regard to religious and Christian truth claims.[3]

Roman Catholicism disagreed with the Enlightenment precisely because of its emphasis on the individual and its secularism, which denied our relationship to God. Almost until the Second Vatican Council in the 1960s, Roman Catholicism strongly opposed the Enlightenment and its teaching on human rights. One of the primary rights proposed by the Enlightenment was the right to religious liberty, but it was only at Vatican II that Roman Catholicism accepted such a right.[4] A defensive and ultramontanist Roman Catholicism saw the Enlightenment as its primary opposition. Nineteenth-century papal documents, including the famous Syllabus of Errors, condemned and excoriated the theory and practice of the Enlightenment.[5] Gregory XVI's encyclical *Mirari vos* of 1832 well illustrates the Catholic Church's intransigent opposition to Enlightenment ideas. The pope strongly condemned liberalism, individualism, freedom of conscience (it is a *deliramentum*—a madness), freedom of opinion and of the press, democracy, and the separation of church and state. The remedies of these evils are found in the recognition that all authority comes from God, and the church has the role to teach the truth to all.[6] Hierarchical Catholic teaching only accepted democracy as the best form of government in the pontificate of Pius XII in the 1940s.[7]

In general, Protestantism was much more open to religious freedom and a role for freedom in human society, but it strongly opposed the rationalism and secularism associated with the Enlightenment and its emphasis on natural and human rights. Erich Weingärtner, who served as executive secretary of the Commission of the Churches on International Affairs (CCIA), now an important arm of the World Council of Churches (WCC), has recognized that for most of their history the Protestant churches opposed human rights "as the product of humanistic philosophy."[8] Calvinist theologians associated with the Free University of Amsterdam in the nineteenth century and the first part of the twentieth century fiercely criticized the idea of human rights even though they were often willing to accept the content of human rights. The idea of human rights basically repudiated the strong Calvinist belief in the sovereignty of God since it derives these rights from human reason and human beings.[9]

To make historical generalizations about Protestantism as a movement is quite difficult. Yes, there was opposition to the human rights movement, but this opposition in general was considerably less than the Catholic opposition and in many areas much quicker to change. As will be pointed out, many Protestants came to appreciate the content of the political and civil rights associated with the Enlightenment but had problems with the grounding and concept of human rights. I have chosen the word "reluctance" to refer to the general Protestant approach to human rights before the twentieth century.

Great change has occurred in the last fifty years. Obviously the churches were influenced by the 1948 Universal Declaration of Human Rights of the United Nations. As will be mentioned, other significant contemporary realities also influenced a decided change in the churches' attitude toward human rights. The churches have not only accepted human rights, but they have exercised significant leadership in the theoretical understanding of rights and the practical struggle for human rights across the globe. Max Stackhouse claims that the WCC "has done more for human rights among the peoples of the world than any other single international body."[10] Some might claim that Stackhouse as a Protestant theologian is somewhat prejudiced in the matter, but the subsequent pages will give some indication of the significant leadership role taken in this area by the WCC.

Human rights have also become central in the contemporary approach of Catholic social teaching. The first systematic development of human rights in hierarchical Catholic social teaching occurred only in 1963.[11] The Second Vatican Council and subsequent popes continued to insist on the importance of human rights for human existence on this globe. John Paul II in his social encyclicals and in his many trips throughout the world has made human rights the focus of his appeal to provide greater justice for human beings on our earth today. Pope John Paul's special relation to Eastern Europe and the dramatic changes that have taken place there have attracted great attention to his human rights approach.[12] The American political scientist, Samuel P. Huntington, has highlighted the important role of Catholicism in supporting democracy and human rights during the global struggles of the 1970s and 1980s.[13] Thus the Protestant and Catholic churches have moved from their opposition to human rights to a leadership role in promoting and defending human rights throughout the globe in the latter part of the twentieth century. Perhaps even more startling than the dramatic changes in the churches' acceptance of, and leadership in defending, human rights is the often mentioned argument that religion, and in this case Christianity, provides the best ground for the support and defense of human rights throughout the world.[14]

Catholic and Protestant thought today also share a general agreement about the content of human rights. Historically the Enlightenment identified human rights with civil and political rights to freedom from external coercion in matters of religion, speech, assembly, opinion, press, etc. Those who gave more importance to the social aspect of human existence stressed the social, economic, and cultural rights such as the right to food, clothing, shelter, and healthcare. These rights have been called the second stage of the human rights movement since they came to the fore after the civil and political rights associated with the Enlightenment and philosophical liberalism and were often associated with the socialist world. Some refer to a third stage in the human rights development associated with the rights of new nations especially in the South—nations that had been under the thumb of European colonizers. However, for our purposes this aspect can be included under social, economic, and cultural rights provided they are seen also in light of the two-thirds world.[15] The Protestant and Catholic churches have generally accepted the need for both kinds of rights.

Protestant and Catholic theorists, as perceptively pointed out by Joseph L. Allen, often recognize the same basis and grounding for human rights—the equal dignity and worth of the human person. This dignity itself is ultimately seen in terms of the person's relationship to God.[16] In explaining the relationship, some theological differences come to the fore in the different approaches of Catholics, Reformed Protestants, and Lutheran Protestants.[17] However, these different theological approaches to the grounding of human dignity do not detract from the acceptance of human dignity as the basis for human rights.

WHY THIS CHANGE?

As might be expected many factors have played a role in the changed understanding of Protestant and Catholic churches moving from reluctance or hostility to acceptance and leadership with regard to human rights. Looking back on the development it is obvious that the opposition to human rights was never absolute or total. There have been aspects of the Christian tradition that could be appealed to in defense of human rights. But the belated recognition of human rights and their acceptance came to life in the intellectual, historical, cultural, and economic developments regarding human existence and human rights. This section will try to answer the question of change by concentrating on three different but interrelated aspects of the question—human rights in general, civil and political rights, and finally social, cultural, and economic rights.

Human rights in general. Historically Roman Catholicism and Protestantism, to a lesser degree, have been seen in opposition to the human rights movement, which is usually associated with the Enlightenment and its aftermath. But history also shows some continuity with the churches' contemporary acceptance of human rights.

Scripture gives strong support to the dignity of human beings, which became the ecumenical basis for the contemporary acceptance of human rights. The Christian understanding of creation based on the Genesis narrative sees the human being as created in the image and likeness of God. The hierarchical notion of creation found in Genesis recognizes the human being as the crown and glory of all that God made—the one who was to have dominion over all other creatures. Some have even accused Christianity of being too anthropocentric.[18]

Thomas Aquinas insisted on the concept of the human being as the image of God and made this anthropology of image and participation the cornerstone of his ethical considerations. Aquinas begins the discussion of morality by recalling that the first part of the *Summa* has considered God, and now the second part will consider the human being who is an image of God precisely because, like God, the human being has intellect, free will, and the power of self-determination. Thus the greatest of the medieval theologians continued the Christian tradition of supporting the dignity of human beings and seeing the human being primarily in her rational and volitional aspects as an image of God.[19]

Aquinas also gave great importance to the concept of *ius*—the Latin word for *right*. Such an emphasis was in keeping with the Thomistic acceptance of natural law. However, *ius* in Aquinas did not mean a subjective right but rather a system of objectively right relationships. *Ius* in Aquinas often signifies "the just thing itself," or the object of justice.[20] Aquinas had not made the turn to the subject. The other cardinal virtues include a relationship to the agent, but the relationship involved in justice is not to the agent but to the equality of one thing to another as, for example, in salary for the work done.[21]

Most scholars, including Catholics, have seen the early seventeenth-century Enlightenment as the most significant place for the development of subjective rights. The Enlightenment emphasized the freedom, and consequently, the rights of the individual. It then had enormous ramifications in cultural, political, and economic life. The American Revolution and the French Revolution of the eighteenth century are clearly associated with Enlightenment ideas. As time went on Roman Catholicism became the implacable foe of the Enlightenment and the liberalism associated with it. By the nineteenth century, as illustrated in the pontificates of Pope Gregory XVI and Pius IX, Roman Catholicism saw itself as strongly opposing liberalism in all its forms. Theoretically liberalism stressed the freedom and rights of the individual person, whereas Catholics emphasized the law of God as mediated through the natural law and the duty to obey God's law. Individualistic liberalism strongly opposed the Catholic understanding of the individual as belonging to many different communities. Practically and politically the Catholic Church vehemently resisted political changes from the old order and castigated the concept of democracy. The Catholic Church insisted on the union of church and state.[22] In the first part of the nineteenth century, some Catholic liberals tried to be more supportive of democratic regimes and the autonomy of the political and social orders, thus recognizing rights even for religious freedom. However, by the middle of the century this incipient liberal movement was squelched. As a result the Catholic Church was seen by others and by itself as strongly opposed to liberalism. In a defensive and polemical posture, Catholicism failed to recognize the different shades of liberalism and some of its significant human aspirations.[23] In the Catholic approach associated with this nineteenth-century understanding, religious liberalism began when Luther insisted on the freedom of conscience and broke the bond between conscience and the teaching of the church. Philosophical liberalism by insisting on autonomous human reason cut people off from the law of God. Political liberalism rejected God's law by making the will of the majority determinative. However, this approach also condemned the economic liberalism of capitalism.[24] Without doubt the Catholic Church constituted a strong opposition to individualistic liberalism in the nineteenth century.

How did this staunch opposition change? As the twentieth century developed, the Catholic enemy (or to employ more ecumenical terms, the dialogue partner) changed. In the twentieth century totalitarianism came to the fore with its attempt to subordinate the individual to the good of society. In the light of Catholicism's defense of monarchies and denial of religious freedom, Catholicism was often somewhat tolerant of right wing authoritarianism but strongly disagreed with Marxism and Communism on the left. As the twentieth century progressed, Roman Catholicism little by little came to give much greater emphasis to the freedom, dignity, and rights of the human person. In this context the first cautious acceptance of democracy by the hierarchical magisterium came in the 1944 Christmas message of Pope Pius XII with his recognition that many people see a democratic form of government as a postulate of human reason.[25] One of those supporters of democracy was the Catholic neo-Thomist philosopher Jacques Maritain, who advocated democracy and human rights on the basis of his approach to Thomism and who later played a significant role in the 1948 United Nations' Universal Declaration of Human Rights.[26] As time went by the Catholic commitment to democracy became stronger.

The first full-blown development of human rights in hierarchical social teaching appeared in Pope John XXIII's 1963 encyclical *Pacem in terris*. Here John developed both political and civil rights as well as economic and social rights. These approaches to human rights are accompanied by a recognition of duties and found within a communitarian framework that still opposes the individualism often associated with Enlightenment liberalism.[27] From this time on human rights have been developed in theory and in practice to become the primary way in which the contemporary papacy has addressed the social issues of our world today.

Yes, there has been a dramatic change in the position of the Catholic Church with regard to human rights. However, this change does not mean that the Catholic Church has totally accepted the classical liberal approach associated with Enlightenment thought. Contemporary hierarchical Catholic teaching still insists on a communitarian basis for human rights and recognizes both political and civil rights as well as social and economic rights.[28]

The Catholic understanding of the historical development of human rights has also changed dramatically in the last two centuries. Evidence indicates that the understanding of this historical development was heavily influenced by the attitude taken to human rights. Catholic scholars in the nineteenth century who were strongly opposed to political and civil rights generally identified the origin of human rights with the Enlightenment tradition and the individualistic liberalism associated with it.

In the twentieth century Michel Villey wrote extensively on the history of human rights and its development. Villey sees a Catholic move toward the acceptance of subjective human rights in the work of the fourteenth-century philosopher and theologian William of Ockham. Thus the concept of human rights was not something unknown to Catholicism before the Enlightenment.[29]

Villey, who wrote about the historical development of human rights for almost forty years, strongly opposed the concept of subjective human rights, for he insisted on the Thomistic understanding of an objectively just order in which everyone possesses her or his just share. There was no need for egoistic clamoring for one's rights in the Thomistic approach. But the move to subjective human rights first appeared in the voluntarism and nominalism of William of Ockham. As a voluntarist, Ockham gave great importance to God's power and our power, not to rational ordering. As a nominalist, he insisted that only individuals have real existence so law must begin with the individual's claims. Thus it was the fourteenth-century Catholic nominalist who gave birth to the monstrous infant of understanding *ius* as a subjective power of the individual—a concept that paved the way for the excesses of the Enlightenment.[30]

Villey's approach well illustrates the neoscholasticism that Leo XIII authoritatively imposed on Catholic philosophy and theology in the last quarter of the nineteenth century and that remained the primary Catholic approach to philosophy and theology until Vatican II. Thomas Aquinas was the high point of philosophical and theological development. Periods of decline in Catholic intellectual life occurred when Aquinas was not acknowledged. In my judgment Leo XIII used Aquinas to prevent any dialogue with modern philosophies, especially those in any way associated with the Enlightenment. Neoscholasticism generally identified Ockham as one of the first villains whose nominalism and voluntarism destroyed the synthesis of Aquinas. However, Thomistic revivals in the sixteenth century and again in the nineteenth and twentieth centuries, thanks to Leo XIII's intervention, once again recognized the perennial philosophy of Thomas Aquinas that was so opposed to the concept of subjective human rights.[31]

In the last few years Brian Tierney and his student Charles Reid have convincingly challenged Villey's thesis.[32] Yes, Thomas Aquinas did not have an understanding of subjective rights, but the thirteenth-century canon lawyers known as the Decretalists possessed a well-developed, explicit understanding of subjective rights. In this view the Catholic legal system developed the theoretical and practical understanding of subjective rights before Ockham. Thus historically the concept of human rights did not begin with the Enlightenment or with Ockham, but these subjective rights are found in thirteenth-century canon lawyers. Yes, significant developments occurred with Ockham and later with Grotius and the Enlightenment, but the idea of subjective rights was not foreign to the earlier Catholic tradition.

The mainstream Protestant churches also had their problems with the concept of human rights. In general Protestantism was more open to the concept of freedom associated with the first generation of civil and political rights than was Roman Catholicism. Protestantism never saw itself in total opposition to the Enlightenment as did Roman Catholicism. However, Protestantism had problems with the concept of human rights and the anthropological foundation for these rights. According to Erich Weingärtner, for much of its history, mainstream Protestantism opposed human rights as the product of a humanistic philosophy.[33] Even after the United Nations' Declaration in 1948 many Protestants still had problems with the term and concept of human rights even though they agreed with the basic content involved.[34]

The problem with the term and concept of human rights comes from theological concerns. Human rights, natural rights, or the rights of man (to use the term often employed to describe the same reality) stress the rational and human perspective whereas many Protestants insisted on a distinctively theological foundation and basis for these realities in God's actions. However, since 1950 Protestant theologians and churches have come to propose such a theological foundation (God's gracious act of creation grounds human dignity and rights) and have become stalwart champions of human rights. Ironically, Roman Catholicism never had the same problem with the concept of human rights. The Catholic natural law theory was quite open to seeing human reason and human nature as the foundation for moral realities.

Political and civil rights. In discussing political and civil rights this section will concentrate on religious liberty, which from the viewpoint of the churches has been the most important and/or problematic of political rights. Here, too, the historical development shows the fascinating and tortuous path that led from reluctance or hostility to acceptance; but once again some elements in the Christian tradition from its very beginning were not necessarily hostile to religious liberty.[35]

The Gospels insist that Jesus freely calls disciples to follow him. Both the freedom of God in giving the gift and the freedom of the disciple in responding are emphasized. The free will of human beings is seen in the rejection of Jesus by many. The possibility of accepting or rejecting Jesus recognizes the fundamental importance of human freedom regarding religious belief.

A very significant development that profoundly influenced subsequent church teaching occurred with Augustine at the end of the fourth century. In the struggle with the Donatist dissidents, Augustine moved from his earlier position that the church should only use persuasion and justified the church's asking the state to use force to punish heretics and schismatics. Augustine argued from two New Testament passages: God used force to convert St. Paul; and, in the parable of the prepared banquet with no guests, the servants were sent out to compel people to come into the banquet (Luke 14:16–24). The famous Latin phrase *"compelle intrare"* set the tone for much of the subsequent Christian approach. Augustine maintained that if the state can prevent people from killing themselves physically it can prevent them from killing themselves spiritually. Thus began the long history of the Catholic Church's using force and violence against heretics in the name of the Gospel.[36]

Thomas Aquinas in the thirteenth century well summarizes the teaching and practice of the Catholic Church in the Middle Ages. Those who have never accepted the Catholic faith, such as gentiles and Jews, should not be forced to believe because to believe is an act of the free will. However, if these infidels impede or persecute the true Christian faith, then the faithful can make war against them. The treatment of

Native Americans by the Spanish conquistadors shows how this teaching could be abused in practice. However, heretics and schismatics should be physically forced to fulfill what they have promised and to hold on to what they have received. An important difference exists between those who once accepted the Catholic faith and those who never accepted it.[37]

However, since the beginning of the second millenium popes had insisted on the freedom of the church vis-à-vis the state. The church has to be free from the state in order to carry out its proper mission. The Catholic Church strongly insisted on the freedom of the church down through the years. However, this freedom of the church was not extended to the freedom of the believer until the second part of the twentieth century.[38]

The defensive posture of the Counter-Reformation only made Catholics insist all the more on the fact that the Catholic Church was the one true church and the need for the union of church and state. It seemed even more apparent, especially in the light of the Constantinian heritage of the union of church and state, that civil peace and unity could only exist in a country with religious unity.

The opposition to the Enlightenment only intensified the Catholic opposition to religious freedom. The excesses of the French Revolution and the attempt of European liberals to remove the church from public life and the public square heightened the Catholic opposition to the freedoms and rights of liberalism especially religious liberty. The Catholic Constantinian history and tradition, an authoritative or at least paternalistic notion of the state, and the subordination of freedom to truth, especially the religious truth of the Catholic religion, grounded the Catholic opposition to religious liberty until Vatican II.[39]

However, some changes were developing. The first change, as is often the case, was pragmatic. After Pope Pius IX's Syllabus of Errors, Bishop Felix Dupanloup of Orleans interpreted the strong condemnation of religious liberty in the light of the distinction between thesis and hypothesis. The thesis is the ideal, which should exist. The hypothesis is the historically necessary acceptance of something less than the ideal. Thus in religiously pluralistic countries one could tolerate the existence of religious freedom as a means of obtaining greater goods or avoiding greater evils.[40] Many Catholics, including popes, accepted this distinction, which in practice managed to moderate somewhat the strong opposition to religious liberty in Catholic hierarchical teaching. However, the implication of the distinction was still clear. If Catholics ever became the predominate religious group, the ideal of the union of church and state and the corresponding denial of religious liberty should come into play. The solution proposed by the distinction between thesis and hypothesis was a pragmatic way of living with the reality of a pluralistic society, but it fell far short of accepting a concept of religious liberty.

The second development concerned the Catholic opposition to collectivism and totalitarianism especially of the left as the twentieth century developed. Papal teaching began to recognize and even emphasize the dignity, freedom, and rights of the person over those of the state. In this movement toward accepting political and civil rights, religious liberty was the major obstacle and the last holdout. Finally Vatican II, in 1965, accepted religious liberty. However, the acceptance of religious liberty, especially in terms of its grounding, still differed in many ways from secular and Protestant justification. Yes, the freedom of the act of faith and the role of conscience are important, but the justification of religious liberty shows the influence of John Courtney Murray in seeing religious liberty primarily as an article of peace and not an article of faith. Religious liberty in society is not primarily a theological or moral issue but is a juridical or constitutional issue that has foundations in theology, ethics, and political philosophy. A limited constitutional government has no role to play in directing the religious lives of its citizens.[41] Thus only in 1965 did the Roman Catholic Church come to the acceptance of religious liberty after this long and somewhat tortuous development in which it obviously learned from many others the significance and importance of civil and political rights, especially the right to religious liberty. With religious liberty finally in place, the Catholic Church could then accept and propose the importance of these civil and political rights originally associated with liberalism. However, Catholicism sees these rights existing together with social and economic rights and both types of rights grounded in the community and not in an isolated individual.

Protestantism has been much more open to freedom in general than Catholicism. Mainstream Protestantism accepted religious liberty long before Catholicism, but again the first step in the direction of religious liberty was as pragmatic as it was much later for Catholicism.[42] Martin

Luther[43] and John Calvin[44] did not accept religious liberty. Roland Bainton, an influential American Protestant historian, uses Calvin to illustrate the peak of Protestant intolerance and persecution.[45]

The first movement toward religious liberty came from the left wing of the Protestant Reformation with such groups as the Mennonites, the Baptists, and the Quakers. These small minority groups had often been the object of persecution, and hence they strongly defended religious liberty against the majority religion. From 1500 into the 1700s religious wars wracked Europe. Some religions were again persecuted and called for religious liberty. As a result of these wars stronger national states arose that commanded the loyalty of people of different religions. Religious liberty in the United States resulted from the pragmatic fact that many different religions already existed in the territory of the colony. Pennsylvania, with its Quaker origins, had accepted religious liberty in a theoretical manner and not simply as a pragmatic adjustment to existing reality. As time went on, seventeenth-century Protestant thinkers gradually moved to seeing religious liberty as compatible with, and even based on, their faith and theology. By the end of the seventeenth century the theory of religious liberty was proposed as grounded in Protestant theology, but implementing religious liberty took some time.[46]

Protestantism thus accepted religious liberty much earlier than Catholicism and was also more open to the content of political and civil rights than was Catholicism. Protestantism put much more stress on conscience and its freedom. Protestant theology saw the church as a gathered community or voluntary association of individuals in contrast to the Catholic organic notion of the church as God's community of salvation, which was necessary for all those who were to be saved. Thus it was much easier for Protestants to see religious liberty for all as an implication of their own faith. Catholic understanding of the one true church as the only means of salvation made it much harder to accept religious liberty for other faiths. The greater Protestant emphasis on the individual and freedom of conscience together with the more democratic quality of Protestant churches resulted in a strong affinity between Protestantism and democracy as it developed in the Western world.[47] The famous thesis of Max Weber, which continues to be hotly debated, saw Protestantism as the ripe soil for capitalism.[48] However, Protestantism did not lose sight of the Christian concern for the poor and the needy. Despite problems with the concept or term of human rights or natural rights, mainstream Protestantism long before the twentieth century became sympathetic to and supportive of religious liberty and the concepts behind political and civil rights.

Religious liberty was a very significant topic in the modern Protestant ecumenical movement in the twentieth century. The International Missionary Council explicitly raised the religious liberty issue in the context of Protestant missionaries in colonial lands at its 1928 meeting in Jerusalem. Subsequent years saw the topic of religious liberty become quite significant in the international ecumenical movement. The Commission of the Churches on International Affairs (CCIA) played a very significant role in the final drafting of the article on religious liberty in the United Nations' Universal Declaration of Human Rights in 1948. The World Council of Churches from its first meeting in Amsterdam in 1948 gave great importance to religious liberty as the primary human right. The CCIA was also instrumental in bringing about the United Nations Commission on Human Rights and actively participated in the composition of the two 1966 International Covenants on Human Rights.[49] Thus the Protestant churches were comparatively very early and strong supporters of religious freedom, the freedom of conscience for all, and the content of civil and political rights despite some problems with the terminology of human or natural rights.

Social and economic rights. The Christian Church from its inception has insisted on the care and concern for the poor, the needy, the sick, the outcast, the marginalized. The church has tried to provide for people in need as illustrated in the origin of hospitals and places to care for the sick. Concern for the poor was very clear in the scriptures and exemplified in the work of deacons in the New Testament. Concern for orphans and widows has been rather constant in the Christian tradition.

As mentioned, eighteenth- and nineteenth-century Catholicism strongly opposed liberalism and the rights movement associated with the Enlightenment, but Catholics were more open to social and economic rights. Pope Leo XIII, in his 1891 encyclical *Rerum novarum,* marking the beginning of the modern papal social teaching, explicitly recognized such social and economic rights. The purpose of the encyclical in the light of the misery and wretchedness affecting the majority of the poor is to "define the relative rights and mutual duties of the wealthy and of the poor."[50] Leo XIII recognizes both duties and rights, bases these rights on the transcendent dignity of the human being, and recognizes the right to possess what is necessary for life, rights to food, clothing, and shelter, and the right to free association so that workers can protect themselves. The encyclical insists on the right to private property but wants that right extended in a wider way to the poor. The state should give special consideration to protecting the rights of the poor and the helpless. However, *Rerum novarum* does not recognize the civil and political rights associated with democracy; Leo generally held, at best, to a paternalistic and, at worst, an authoritarian view of the state. Leo strongly opposed the Enlightenment.

As mentioned the first full-blown discussion of human rights in the modern papal teaching occurred in *Pacem in terris,* with its insistence on duties and rights as well as political and economic rights. The primary difficulty for the Catholic tradition had been political and civil rights. There was no great controversy or dispute in accepting social and economic rights. However, social and economic rights occasioned serious tensions and divisions for Catholics in the subsequent years. After Vatican II greater emphasis shifted to national and local churches. In Latin America liberation theology came to the fore. In many countries the local Catholic Church was identified with the struggle on behalf of the poor and often opposed political oligarchies and dictators defending the status quo. Catholics could generally agree in theory about social and economic rights, but great disagreements centered about the concrete way of securing these rights. In Latin America, for example, some insisted on the need for a democratic socialist form of government while others emphasized the need to reform capitalism. The tensions and struggles were very serious.[51]

Mainstream Protestantism showed the same concerns with the poor and the needy, but they were much more open to the right to religious liberty and the contents of political and civil rights. The modern Protestant ecumenical movement in the twentieth century recognized many social problems in the first part of that century, some of which were associated with colonialism—economic justice, peace, racism, social change—but none of these were viewed from the concept or language of human rights. At the first meeting of the World Council of Churches at Amsterdam in 1948 and in subsequent years, the primary emphasis in human rights was given to religious liberty as the first and most important of political and civil rights.[52]

Developments on many fronts occurred in the 1960s and 1970s.[53] The Cold War, the invasion of the Dominican Republic by the United States in 1965 and that of Czechoslovakia by Russia in 1968, the Vietnam War, the rise of repressive regimes in many areas, the struggle of oppressed people for liberation, the Helsinki Accords, and many other significant events were the occasion for the discussion of human rights. The WCC itself knew the tensions existing among the churches of the First World, of the Second World, and of the Third World. Human rights and their vindication became a burning issue in both theory and in practice.

The WCC sponsored a meeting at St. Pölten in Austria in 1974 to deal with human rights. Some, especially from the First World, saw political and civil rights as primary and the only true human rights with singular importance given to religious liberty. The second approach stressed more the social nature of human beings and insisted on social and economic rights as well as what has been called the third generation of human rights—the rights of oppressed people and cultures to achieve their own identity and just desserts. Proponents of political and civil rights stressed denunciation and advocacy as the best strategy to promote human rights. But the second group logically called for political action to deal with the root causes of poverty, oppression, and exploitation. The St. Pölten consultation and the subsequent work of the Fifth Assembly of the WCC in Nairobi in 1975 achieved a remarkable consensus by recognizing the broad concept of human rights, embracing all human rights with no primacy given to religious liberty in particular or to political and civil rights in general. Likewise, the WCC from that time took a more active role in enabling oppressed people to secure their rights. Many practical tensions and divisions continued to erupt, but there was general agreement about the content of human rights and the strategies to implement these rights around the globe. The WCC's Program to Combat Racism, established in 1968, occasioned many tensions by contributing small amounts of money for humanitarian purposes to resistance groups in the Third World, some of whom advocated the use of violence.

This section has shown that the WCC experienced many more tensions in arriving at an acceptance of social and economic rights including rights in the Third World than had papal social teaching. This is explained by the nature of the WCC with member churches representing the different perspectives of First World countries, Second World countries, and

Third World countries and with their rightful insistence on practical ways of dealing with the root causes of social and economic rights. The Catholic papal tradition did not experience that many tensions in arriving at the theoretical insistence on social and political rights, but subsequently national and local Catholic Churches experienced similar divisions in trying to protect and promote social and economic rights for the poor and the oppressed.

Problems and tensions continue to exist with regard to understanding human rights and to implementing them. For example, on the theoretical level some now speak of the rights of future generations and of environmental rights as a fourth generation of rights. However, mainstream Protestantism and Roman Catholicism have come to a remarkable agreement on the theory, content, and practical promotion of human rights in our world.

CONCLUSION

What can the churches learn from the development of their approach to human rights? This concluding section will focus on the perspective of the Roman Catholic Church. The section will discuss four important points—methodology of theological social ethics, the learning church, dialogue, and development.

Moral methodology. The history shows the various elements that have entered into this change in the Catholic understanding of human rights. Scripture, tradition, theological concerns, historical and cultural realities, human experience, philosophical concepts, and pragmatic needs have all played a role in fashioning the development of the understanding of human rights in the Roman Catholic tradition. At its best the Catholic theological tradition has recognized in theory such a methodology, but it has not always applied it in practice.

This development shows the importance of two traditional methodological approaches in Catholic moral theology—the importance of tradition and a proper role for the human. The Catholic approach has recognized that the scripture alone is not sufficient for theology and the life of the church. The historical insistence on scripture and tradition often resulted in a poor understanding of both of these realities, but the recognition of the need for tradition is very significant. From a theological perspective tradition is based on the fact that the community of the church exists in time and space and continues to live under the inspiration of the Holy Spirit. The church must understand, live, and appropriate the word and work of Jesus in the light of the ongoing historical and cultural circumstances of time and place.

Catholic methodology has also recognized human reason and human nature as sources of moral wisdom and knowledge for the Christian. The Roman Catholic natural law theory has been criticized from many perspectives, but its insistence on the human as a source for moral wisdom is most important and helpful. The history of the development of the Catholic Church's understanding of human rights shows how much the church has learned from human sources of moral knowledge. The earlier Catholic tradition with its lack of historical consciousness did not give that much importance to human experience, but in the light of historical change and development, such as the one on human rights, we are very conscious of how important a role human experience plays in the church's understanding. Of course critical questions need to be raised to test human reason and human experience in order to determine if they are true and not erroneous. The development with regard to human rights thus illustrates the basic soundness of the Roman Catholic theological method with its acceptance of the human but also shows the importance of human experience as well as human reason as sources of wisdom and knowledge.

Dialogue as a way of learning. The development of the teaching on human rights together with the need for multiple sources of moral wisdom and knowledge underscores the importance of dialogue as necessary for learning about morality. Dialogue does not necessarily mean that one simply accepts the position expressed by others; these positions must also be tested. But dialogue recognizes the need to be open to learn from others. There is no doubt that the Catholic Church has learned from others the importance of religious liberty and of all the political and civil rights. However, here too the Catholic Church has not merely accepted in an uncritical way all that has been said by others. The Catholic position correctly insists on civil and political rights today, but it sees them as rooted in the reality of human society and community and not simply based on the rights of individuals seen as isolated monads. Likewise the acceptance of religious liberty is not based on a religious indifferentism, which has often characterized the approach of others. True dialogue will be always open to learn from others but is also prepared at times to criticize them when necessary.

Church as learner. The Roman Catholic tradition has often insisted on the role of the church as a moral teacher, but the developing understanding of human rights shows the importance of understanding the church as a learner. Without doubt the church has learned much from many sources to arrive at its contemporary understanding of human rights. The method of dialogue mentioned above and the learning process illustrated in the understanding of human rights point out that the church must learn even before it can teach. An older understanding of the deposit of faith thought that the church already had all that it needed in order to teach. However, even on questions of doctrine, the church itself has learned as illustrated in the very fundamental question of the understanding of God as Trinity. This doctrine was not found explicitly in the scripture but was only learned in the tradition through the community reflecting on its faith under the inspiration of the Holy Spirit. It is even more true in moral matters that the church has to learn before it can teach because the Catholic Church recognizes that its moral teaching depends heavily on human reason.

Development. No one can deny the tremendous development that has occurred in the Roman Catholic Church's teaching on human rights. Development properly understood includes both continuities and discontinuities as is well illustrated in this particular case.

The Roman Catholic tradition has had a tendency to overstress the continuities and downplay the discontinuities in its understanding of development with regard to its own teaching. Nowhere is this more clear than in its official understanding of the development that took place with regard to religious liberty. At the Second Vatican Council the question of religious liberty raised the even more basic question of change and development in official church teaching. Nineteenth-century papal teaching strongly condemned religious liberty. How could the Roman Catholic Church in the twentieth century teach what it denied in the nineteenth century? Proponents of the newer teaching maintained at that time that changing historical circumstances explained the development.

The nineteenth-century teaching was correct at that time, but in changed historical circumstances a different teaching is required. The proponents of religious liberty at Vatican II did not explicitly recognize that the earlier teaching in any time or place had been wrong.[54]

The Vatican II Declaration on Religious Liberty skips very quickly and loosely over the reality of past teachings on religious liberty. "Throughout the ages she has preserved and handed on the doctrine which she has received from her Master and the Apostles. Although in the life of the People of God in its pilgrimage through the vicissitudes of human history there has at times appeared a form of behavior which was hardly in keeping with the spirit of the Gospel and was even opposed to it, it has always remained the teaching of the church that no one is to be coerced into believing."[55] At best this statement is disingenuous. The document recognizes some error or problem with regard to occasional forms of behavior but not with regard to official church teaching. However, many papal documents justified the use of force in religious matters and denied religious liberty. While the Catholic tradition recognized even in the Middle Ages that no one was to be coerced into believing the first time as the Vatican document explicitly recognizes, the official teaching also accepted the use of force against heretics and schismatics—part of the teaching not mentioned in the Declaration on Religious Liberty. It is much too simplistic to explain the development by simply saying that the historical circumstances had changed and that the teaching was always right in the light of the circumstances. At the very minimum in a number of different areas, church teaching should have changed much earlier than it did.

The history of the church's attitude toward human rights shows that development involves both continuities and discontinuities. Too often hierarchical Catholic teaching has been unwilling to admit the discontinuities and has seen development almost solely in terms of evolution and continuities. Development is much messier and more complicated than a simple evolutionary theory is willing to recognize.

The shift in the Christian churches' understanding of human rights from reluctance or hostility to acceptance is a remarkable story that not only calls for an explanation of its development but also contributes to our understanding of the way in which the churches learn and teach morality.

Notes

1. The original title proposed by the committee organizing the Milltown Institute Conference on "Human Rights: Sacred or Secular?" was "Churches and Human Rights: From Hostility to Acceptability." A recent French article has accepted the same understanding of the approach to human rights—from hostility and a distrust of human rights to their defense. See J. F. Collange, "Le défi des droits de l'homme: L'avenir de l'humanité, les religions, et l'histoire. Rappels," *Revue d'éthique et de théologie morale: Le supplément* 203 (decembre 1997) 159–163. I have modified the suggested title because Protestant opposition to human rights was not as strong or perduring as Catholic opposition. Note the problem in speaking in general about Catholicism and Protestantism. The problem is less in dealing with Catholicism because of the role of the hierarchical teaching office. The discussion of Protestantism that follows generally refers to mainstream Protestant churches and in the twentieth century to the worldwide Protestant ecumenical movement.

2. C. B. MacPherson, *The Political Theory of Progressive Individualism: Hobbes to Locke* (Oxford: Clarendon, 1962).

3. R. Ashcroft, "Religion and Lockean Natural Rights," in *Religious Diversity and Human Rights,* ed. I. Bloom, J. P. Martin, and W. L. Proudfoot (New York: Columbia University Press, 1996) 195–197. Ashcroft here summarizes this generally accepted thesis, which he then refutes.

4. Declaration on Religious Liberty, in *Vatican Council II: The Conciliar and Post Conciliar Documents,* ed. A. Flannery, rev. ed. (Collegeville, Minn.: Liturgical, 1992) 799–812.

5. For an historical overview of this period see R. Aubert et al., *The Church in the Age of Liberalism* (New York: Crossroad, 1981).

6. Pope Gregory XVI, *Mirari vos,* nn. 14–21, in *The Papal Encyclicals 1740–1878,* ed. Claudia Carlen (Wilmington, N.C.: McGrath, 1981) 238–239.

7. P. E. Sigmund, "Catholicism and Liberal Democracy," in *Catholicism and Liberalism: Contributions to American Public Philosophy,* ed. R. B. Douglass and D. Hollenbach (New York: Cambridge University Press, 1994) 226.

8. E. Weingärtner, "Human Rights," in *Dictionary of the Ecumenical Movement,* ed. N. Lossky et al. (Grand Rapids, Mich.: Eerdmans, 1991) 486.

9. A. von Egmond, "Calvinist Thought and Human Rights," in *Human Rights and Religious Values: An Uneasy Relationship?* ed. A. An-Na'im, J. D. Gort, H. Jansen, and H. M. Vroom (Grand Rapids, Mich.: Eerdmans, 1995) 192.

10. M. L. Stackhouse, "Public Theology, Human Rights, and Mission," in *Human Rights and the Global Mission of the Church* (Cambridge, Mass.: Boston Theological Institute, 1985) 16.

11. Pope John XXIII, *Pacem in terris,* nn. 11–27, in *Catholic Social Thought: The Documentary Heritage,* ed. D. J. O'Brien and T. A. Shannon (Maryknoll, N.Y.: Orbis, 1992) 132–135.

12. J. B. Hehir, "Religious Activism for Human Rights: A Christian Case Study," in *Religious Human Rights in Global Perspective: Religious Perspectives,* ed. J. Witte and J. D. van der Vyver (The Hague: Martinus Nijhoff, 1996) 97–119.

13. S. P. Huntington, "Religion and the Third Wave," *The National Interest* 24 (Summer 1991) 30.

14. M. L. Stackhouse and S. E. Healey, "Religious and Human Rights: A Theological Apologetic," in *Religious Human Rights in Global Perspective,* ed. Witte and van der Vyver (The Hague: Martinus Nijhoff, 1996) 485–516.

15. Weingärtner, *Dictionary of the Ecumenical Movement,* ed. Lossky et al., 485. For some, the fourth generation of human rights refers to the rights of future generations and the environment.

16. J. L. Allen, "Catholic and Protestant Theories of Human Rights," *Religious Studies Review* 14 (1988) 347–348.

17. Ibid. See also J. Moltmann, "Christian Faith and Human Rights," in *Understanding Human Rights: An Interdisciplinary and Interfaith Study,* ed. A. D. Falconer (Dublin: Irish School of Ecumenics, 1980) 182–223.

18. J. M. Gustafson, *Ethics from a Theocentric Perspective,* 2 vols. (Chicago: University of Chicago Press, 1981, 1984).

19. Thomas Aquinas, *Summa theologiae,* 4 vols. (Rome: Marietti, 1952) I II, prologus.

20. B. Tierney, *The Idea of Natural Rights: Studies on Natural Rights, Natural Law, and Church Law* (Atlanta, Ga.: Scholars, 1997) 22–27, 256–265.

21. Aquinas, II II, q. 57 a. 1.

22. See footnotes 5–7.

23. P. Steinfels, "The Failed Encounter: Catholic Church and Liberalism in the Nineteenth Century," in *Catholicism and Liberalism,* ed. Douglass and Hollenbach, 19–44.

24. See, for example, W. J. Engelen, "Social Reflections VI: Deuteronomy versus Liberalism," *Central-Blatt and Social Justice* 15 (March 1923) 407–409; "Social Observations VII: The Saviour's Social Principles and Liberalism," *Central-Blatt and Social Justice* 16 (April 1923) 3–5.

25. Sigmund, in *Catholicism and Liberalism,* ed. Douglass and Hollenbach, 226.

26. J. W. Cooper, *The Legacy of Jacques Maritain and Reinhold Niebuhr* (Macon, Ga.: Mercer University Press, 1985) 108–109.

27. John XXIII, *Pacem in terris,* nn. 8–37, in *Catholic Social Thought,* ed. O'Brien and Shannon, 132–137.

28. D. Hollenbach, "A Communitarian Reconstruction of Human Rights: Contributions from Catholic Tradition," in *Catholicism and Liberalism,* ed. Douglass and Hollenbach, 127–150. See also his earlier study, D. Hollenbach, *Claims in Conflict: Retrieving and Renewing the Catholic Human Rights Tradition* (New York: Paulist, 1979).

29. For an overview of his position, see M. Villey, *Leçons d'histoire de la philosophie du droit,* rev. ed. (Paris: Dalloz, 1977).

30. M. Villey, "La genèse du droit subjectif chez Guillaume d'Occam," *Archives de philosophie du droit* 9 (1964) 97–127.

31. For a very significant study of nineteenth-century neoscholasticism see G. A. McCool, *Catholic Theology in the Nineteenth Century: The Quest for a Unitary Method* (New York: Seabury, 1977).

32. B. Tierney, *The Idea of Natural Rights,* 1–203; C. J. Reid Jr., "The Canonistic Contribution to the Western Rights Tradition: An Historical Inquiry," *Boston College Law Review* 33 (1991) 37–92.

33. Weingärtner, *Dictionary of the Ecumenical Movement,* ed. Lossky et al., 486.

34. Egmond, *Human Rights and Religious Values,* ed. An-Na'im et al., 193.

35. For an excellent essay on the historical development of religious liberty, see B. Tierney, "Religious Rights: An Historical Perspective," in *Religious Liberty in Western Thought,* ed. N. B. Reynolds and W. C. Durham Jr. (Atlanta, Ga.: Scholars, 1996) 29–57. This entire volume is most helpful on the topic of religious liberty.

36. R. Coste, *Théologie de la liberté religieuse: liberté de conscience— liberté de religion* (Gembloux, France: J. Duculot, 1969) 286–291.

37. Aquinas, II II, q. 10, a.8.

38. Tierney, *Religious Liberty in Western Thought,* ed. Reynolds and Durham, 34–36. Note that the Russian Orthodox Church today insists on the freedom of the church but has difficulty accepting the religious liberty of all citizens.

39. For the development from these arguments to the acceptance of religious liberty, see J. C. Murray, *The Problem of Religious Freedom* (Westminster, Md.: Newman, 1965).

40. R. Aubert, "Mgr. Dupanloup et le Syllabus," *Revue d'histoire ecclésiastique* 51 (1956) 79–142, 471–512, 837–915.

41. Murray, *The Problem of Religious Freedom,* 17–31. For an overview of Protestant approaches to human rights, see R. Traer, *Faith in Human Rights: Support in Religious Traditions for a Global Struggle* (Washington, D.C.: Georgetown University Press, 1991) 19–31; J. R. Nelson, "Human Rights in Creation and Redemption: A Protestant View," in *Human Rights in Religious Traditions,* ed. A. Swidler (New York: Pilgrim, 1982) 1–12.

42. S. Ozment, "Martin Luther on Religious Liberty," in *Religious Liberty in Western Thought,* ed. Reynolds and Durham, 75–82.

43. J. Witte Jr., "Moderate Religious Liberty in the Theology of John Calvin," in *Religious Liberty in Western Thought,* ed. Reynolds and Durham, 83–122. There are aspects in Calvin's theology that were later used to justify religious liberty.

44. R. H. Bainton, *The Travail of Religious Liberty: Nine Biographical Studies* (Philadelphia: Westminster, 1951) 54–71.

45. Tierney, in *Religious Liberty in Western Thought,* ed. Reynolds and Durham, 46–55.

46. G. Maddox, *Religion and the Rise of Democracy* (New York: Routledge, 1996).

47. M. Weber, *The Protestant Ethic and the Spirit of Capitalism* (New York: Charles Scribner's Sons, 1958).

48. Gort, in *Human Rights and Religious Values,* ed. An-Na'im et al., 206–207; N. Koshy, "Religious Liberty," in *Dictionary of the Ecumenical Movement,* ed. Lossky et al., 859–863.

49. Pope Leo XIII, *Rerum novarum,* nn. 1–2, in *Catholic Social Thought,* ed. O'Brien and Shannon, 14–15.

50. Ibid., nn. 30–38, in *Catholic Social Thought,* ed. O'Brien and Shannon, 28–34.

51. M. E. Crahan, "Catholicism and Human Rights in Latin America," in *Religious Diversity and Human Rights,* ed. Bloom, Martin, Proudfoot, 262–277; Hehir, in *Religious Rights in Global Perspective,* ed. Witte and van der Vyver, 111–117.

52. Gort, in *Human Rights and Religious Values,* ed. An-Na'im et al., 204–207.

53. The following overview of the work of the WCC is based on José Zalaquett, *The Human Rights Issues and the Human Rights Movement: Characterization, Evaluation, Propositions* (Geneva: WCC, 1981); Erich Weingärtner, *Human Rights on the Ecumenical Agenda: Report and Assessment* (Geneva: WCC, 1983).

54. E.-J. de Smet, "Religious Freedom," in *Council Speeches of Vatican II,* ed. Y. Congar, H. Küng, D. O'Hanlon (London: Sheed and Ward, 1964) 160–168; Murray, *The Problem of Religious Freedom,* 47–84.

55. Declaration on Religious Liberty, n. 12, in *Vatican Council II,* ed. Flannery, 809.

Part Two

OTHER SOCIAL ISSUES

5. Reflections on Slavery

Diana Hayes

This chapter first appeared in *Rome Has Spoken,* ed. Maureen Fiedler and Linda Rabben (New York: Crossroad, 1998). The editors compiled the documents.

From the beginning until the nineteenth century, church pronouncements often justified the practice of slavery. As late as 1866, the Holy Office said, "Slavery itself...is not at all contrary to the natural and divine law." But when Leo XIII condemned slavery in 1890, he ignored the long church justification, claiming that the church had worked strenuously for centuries to abolish slavery. Both *Rerum Novarum* (1891) and the Second Vatican Council (1965) unequivocally condemned slavery.

OFFICIAL DOCUMENTS

EARLY CHURCH

Council of Gangra, ca. 340:
"If anyone, on the pretext of religion, teaches another man's slave to despise his master, and to withdraw from his service, and not to serve his master with good will and all respect, let him be anathema" (see *Decretum,* below).

Context: This was a reaction to Manichean incitement of slaves to emancipate themselves. It was incorporated into canon law and cited for the next fourteen hundred years.

Gregory I, Deed of Manumission, 595:
"It is most fitting that by a grant of manumission, masters should restore those whom nature had set free into the world, but who had been condemned to the yoke of slavery by the *jus gentium,* to the freedom in which they were born."

Gregory, I, *Pastoral Rule,* **ca. 600:**
"Slaves should be told…not [to] despise their masters and recognize that they are only slaves."

Gregory I, *Expositio in Librum B. Job,* **ca. 600:**
"All men are equal by nature but…a hidden dispensation of providence has arranged a hierarchy of merit and rulership, in that the differences between classes of men have arisen as a result of sin and are ordained by divine justice."

Ninth Council of Toledo, 655:
Children of clerics were to be enslaved.
　　Context: This was an early attempt to enforce clerical celibacy. It was later incorporated into canon law.

MEDIEVAL CHURCH

Urban II, Council of Melfi, 1089:
"We remove from every sacred order those who from the subdiaconate wish to have leisure for wives, and we decree that they be without office and benefice of the church. But if, warned by the bishop, they fail to correct themselves, we give permission to rulers that they subject their women to servitude."
　　Context: This was part of the effort to enforce mandatory clerical celibacy. It was incorporated into canon law.

***Decretum,* 1140:**
"If anyone, on the pretext of religion, teaches another man's slave to despise his master, and to withdraw from his service and not to service his master with goodwill and all respect, let him be anathema."

Alexander III, 1174:
"Everyone has the same God in heaven who created all men to be equal and not slaves by nature."
　　Context: This was an appeal to a Moorish king to release Christian prisoners of war.

Third and Fourth Lateran Councils, Alexander III and Innocent III, twelfth and thirteenth centuries:
The Lateran Councils permitted enslavement of Christians who helped Saracens during the Crusades.

Nicholas V, *Dum Diversas*, 1452/54:
"We grant to you [Kings of Spain and Portugal] by these present documents, with our Apostolic Authority, full and free permission to invade, search out, capture, and subjugate the Saracens and pagans and any other unbelievers and enemies of Christ wherever they may be, as well as their kingdoms, duchies, counties, principalities, and other property...and to reduce their persons into perpetual slavery."
    Context: Pope Calixtus III confirmed this decree in 1456. Sixtus IV renewed it in 1481. Alexander VI extended it from Africa to America in 1493, and Leo X renewed it in 1514.

Pius II, Letter to a Bishop, 1462:
Pius II condemned "wicked Christians who were taking the recently baptized adult converts away into slavery."

COUNTER-REFORMATION

Paul III, *Sublimis Deus*, 1537:
Although Indians were non-Christians, they had not been deprived of their freedom or of ownership of possessions; they should not be reduced to slavery.
    Context: This decree was not considered to contradict earlier papal pronouncements because it did not apply to hostile non-Christians enslaved in just wars.

Paul III, *Motu Proprio*, 1548:
"Each and every person of either sex, whether Roman or non-Roman, whether secular or clerical...may freely and lawfully buy and sell publicly any slaves whatsoever of either sex...and publicly hold them as slaves and make use of their work, and compel them to do the work assigned to them....Slaves who flee to the Capitol and appeal for their liberty shall in no wise be freed from the bondage of their servitude,

but...shall be returned in slavery to their owners and if it seems proper...punished as runaways."
Context: Slaves in Rome were seeking sanctuary on church property.

Pius V, *Motu Proprio*, 1566:
Pius V restored local officials' right to emancipate slaves who sought sanctuary in the Capitol.

Gregory XIV, *Cum Sicuti*, 1591:
Cum Sicuti decreed the emancipation of all indigenous slaves in the Philippines, a Spanish possession.

Urban VIII, *Commissum Nobis*, 1639:
Commissum Nobis forbade enslavement and trade in Indians in Paraguay, Brazil, and the Rio de la Plata region.

Urban VIII, 1629, Innocent X, 1645, Alexander VIII, 1661:
All of these popes were personally involved in buying Muslim galley slaves.

Holy Office, 1686:
The Holy Office decreed that Africans enslaved in unjust wars should be freed.
Context: When the church learned how the cruelty of Portuguese and Spanish conquerors alienated Indians from Christianity, it tried to back away from Nicholas V's blanket authorization of 1452/54 (see above).

MODERN ERA

Benedict XIV, *Immensa Pastorum*, 1741:
Immensa Pastorum condemned the unjust enslavement of non-Christian and Christian Indians.

Sacred Congregation of the Index, eighteenth and nineteenth centuries:
Numerous antislavery tracts were placed on the Index of Forbidden Books.

Gregory XVI, *In Supremo Apostolatus,* **1839:**

"[We] do...admonish and adjure in the Lord all believers in Christ, of whatsoever condition, that no one hereafter may dare unjustly to molest Indians, Negroes, or other men of this sort; or to spoil them of their goods; or to reduce them to slavery; or to extend help or favor to others who perpetrate such things against them; or to exercise that inhuman trade by which Negroes, as if they were not men, but were animals, howsoever reduced into slavery, are, without any distinction, contrary to the laws of justice and humanity, bought and sold, and doomed sometimes to the most severe and exhausting labors."

Context: The British Parliament outlawed slavery and slave trade in all dominions in 1838. Gregory did not condemn "just" enslavement or slave trade; nor did he excommunicate slave traders. Bishops in the U.S. South decided his prohibition did not apply to U.S. slavery.

Holy Office, 1866:

"Slavery itself...is not at all contrary to the natural and divine law....For the sort of ownership which a slave owner has over a slave is understood as nothing other than the perpetual right of disposing of the work of a slave for one's own benefit—services which it is right for one human being to provide for another....The purchaser should carefully examine whether the slave who is put up for sale has been justly or unjustly deprived of his liberty, and that the vendor should do nothing which might endanger the life, virtue, or Catholic faith of the slave."

Context: The U.S. Emancipation Proclamation was issued in 1863, the U.S. Civil War ended in 1865, and the thirteenth amendment to the U.S. Constitution, adopted at that time, abolished slavery. "Rome had never unequivocally condemned slavery, mostly out of fear of offending Spanish and Portuguese royalty. Gregory XVI finally condemned the slave trade in 1839, but not slavery itself. If pressed, the Vatican fell back on the medieval argument that, while slavery was an evil, it was not an unmitigated evil, for it allowed slaves to be Christianized. Although the Vatican was officially neutral during the Civil War, Pius IX made no secret of his sympathies for the Confederacy. However deplorable its social system, the South at least was not infected with the virus of liberalism" (Morris, p. 78).

Pius IX, 1873:

"...attached an indulgence to a prayer for the 'wretched Ethiopians in Central Africa that Almighty God may at length remove the curse of Cham [Ham] from their hearts'" (Maxwell, p. 20).

Context: In Genesis 9:22–27, Noah cursed his son Ham for seeing his nakedness and declared Ham would be his brothers' slave. Theologians later used this passage to justify the enslavement of Africans.

Leo XIII, Letter to the Brazilian Bishops, 1888, Letter to All Bishops, 1890, and *Catholicae Ecclesiae,* 1890:

"From the beginning, almost nothing was more venerated in the Catholic Church...than the fact that she looked to see a slavery eased and abolished which was oppressing so many people....She...stood forth as a strenuous defender of liberty....Indeed the more slavery flourished from time to time, the more zealously she strove [to liberate slaves]....Many of our predecessors, including St. Gregory the Great, Hadrian I, Alexander III, Innocent III, Gregory IX, Pius VII, and Gregory XVI, made every effort to ensure that the institution of slavery should be abolished where it existed and that its roots should not revive where it had been destroyed."

Context: Brazil was the last country in the Western Hemisphere to abolish slavery, in May 1888. Maxwell (1975) comments, "With the greatest respect to Pope Leo XIII, [his statement] is historically inaccurate." Popes had condemned only "unjust" slavery (of captives taken in unjust wars), not all slavery.

Leo XIII, *Rerum Novarum,* 1891:

"The active force inherent in the person cannot be the property of anyone other than the person who exerts it, and it was given to him in the first place by nature for his own benefit."

Code of Canon Law, 1917:

"A lay person who has been legitimately declared guilty of the crime of selling a human being into slavery or for any other evil purpose...shall automatically be deprived of the right to legal ecclesiastical actions and of every position which he may have in the church....If a cleric has committed [the above crime]...he shall be punished by the ecclesiastical court...even with disposition, if the circumstances demand it."

Second Vatican Council, Pastoral Constitution on the Church in the Modern World, 1965:
"Whatever violates the integrity of the human person, such as mutilation, torture inflicted on body or mind, attempts to coerce the will itself, whatever insults human dignity, such as subhuman living conditions, arbitrary imprisonment, deportation, slavery, prostitution, and selling of women and children...all these things and others like them are infamous....Human institutions...should be bulwarks against any kind of political or social slavery and guardians of basic rights under any kind of government."

Context: "It should be noticed how very slender and scarce is the Catholic antislavery documentation since 1888 as compared with the very large volume of Catholic proslavery documentation right up to the time of the Second Vatican Council" (Maxwell, p. 125). John Paul II quoted this passage in Veritatis splendor *(1993).*

REFLECTIONS ON SLAVERY

Human slavery has existed as long as human beings have struggled for power and authority over one another. Historically the most usual forms of slavery resulted from wars, in which the defeated population became part of the spoils for the victors, or from poverty or indebtedness that forced the poor to sell themselves or their offspring. Although this state was seen as lasting the lifetime of the enslaved person, a slave had many ways to obtain his or her freedom, through marriage to a free person, as a result of exemplary work, through self-purchase, among others. More important, these forms of slavery did not carry with them, for the most part, the stigma of dehumanization or racial inferiority (as racial categories had not yet been invented). Once having obtained their freedom, former slaves were usually at liberty to live their lives as they chose in the same society in which they had been enslaved.

The most significant shift in the institution of slavery occurred with the opening of the Americas to European colonization. It brought with it a stigma that has lasted to this day, especially for people of African descent. As Fr. Cyprian Davis noted,

> Slavery was very much an accepted institution in the world of the sixteenth and seventeenth centuries. It was accepted as an institution by the church leaders of the time, despite the efforts of popes to regulate trafficking in slaves and of Catholic theologians to determine the legitimate basis for the enslavement of certain peoples. (Davis, 1990, p. 20)

The Roman Catholic Church's history regarding the institution of slavery in the New World is, clearly, not an unblemished one. Although, as the records show, efforts were made at various times to control slavery and its harshest impact upon the enslaved, "as is often the case, however, there was often a vast discrepancy between the theory and the practice. The fact that one individual had ownership of the person and the labor of another provided the framework for inevitable acts of oppression and brutality" (Davis, 1990, p. 20). Just like today, the Catholic faithful and the hierarchy interpreted not only scripture and tradition but papal and curial statements to fit their own situations and understandings.

It is often asserted that slavery in Catholic nations was more benign, since the enslaved were recognized as persons because of their baptism, with rights and privileges in accordance with their human dignity. The fact remains that they had little or no control over their lives and those of their husbands, wives, or children.

For centuries, the church saw slavery as a feature of the natural law: some people were meant to be slaves, while others were meant to be their masters. Theologians believed that sacred scripture, especially the writings of St. Paul, and tradition in a seemingly unbroken line from the early church fathers through the popes and councils supported slavery. This "unbroken" line did have breaks in it, when the Vatican exposed and condemned the sinful nature of slavery and of those who profited from the trade in human lives. But this perspective was rarely acknowledged until recent times, when we see a dramatic shift from the affirmation to the condemnation of slavery.

As the statements cited in this book show, from its very beginning, the church not only acknowledged but actively supported the "natural order" of slavery. As Pope Gregory I (ca. 600) noted: "A hidden dispensation of providence has arranged a hierarchy of merit and rulership, in that the difference between classes of men has arisen as a result of sin and is ordered by divine justice." The enslaved were slaves because of their own faults and failures, and the church did not see its role or responsibility to change this state of affairs.

Thus, when the Americas were first opened to exploration and colonization, it was assumed that the people found in those lands, so radically different from the claimants, were fit only to serve rather than be served or accepted as equals. Once again, slavery's defenders used sacred scripture to support the enslavement of the native peoples of both the Americas and Africa. They interpreted the curse of Ham and his son Canaan and the curse of Cain as especially significant prophecies of both the existence of people of color and the divine mandate for their capture and enslavement. Thus, slavery became an accepted part of the church's expansion in Africa and the Americas, as a result, it was believed, of God's providence. Less importance was given to the explorers' and colonizers' desire to exploit the riches of these lands, which required a massive application of cheap and abundant labor.

The spread of the faith was also a critical factor in this new understanding of slavery, transforming it into a huge global market that traded in human lives. The church itself used enslavement to punish those who questioned or contradicted church teachings. Proponents saw slavery as an instrument of God's salvific plan for a great harvest of souls, because it brought pagan Africans and indigenous people in contact with the teachings of Christ. The doctrine of just war was a further justification. Theologians upheld enslavement of those defeated in a just war, and condemned enslavement of those captured in an unjust war.

In his first sermon, Jesus proclaimed the realization of Isaiah's prophecy that one would come who would proclaim "good news to the poor...release to the captives [and that] the oppressed [would] go free" (Luke 4:18). It is ironic indeed that a church founded on such principles would become the legitimizer of a form of slavery that dehumanized native and African peoples and established a mindset that differentiated people on the basis of race. This consciousness fostered the rise of racism, an ideology that haunts humanity, especially in the United States, to the present day, both in and outside the church, as the U.S.

bishops acknowledged in their 1974 pastoral letter on racism, *Brothers and Sisters to Us.*

As Maxwell notes, Leo XIII's assertion that the church always opposed slavery is sadly inaccurate. Before the end of the slave trade in the nineteenth century, with few exceptions, the Roman Catholic Church did support and maintain with all its power, secular and spiritual, the enslavement not only of non-Catholics but of its own Catholic faithful. Although England and the United States abolished the slave trade in 1807 and 1808, slavery itself did not end in the United States until 1865, and the Catholic nations of Spain and Portugal continued engaging in the illegal slave trade. The denial of slaves' human dignity and baptism in Christ, which affirmed that dignity, meant that until this century, the church denied people of color, male and female, rights granted to all other faithful in the church, including access to parochial schools, the religious life, and the priesthood.

The impact has been global, but it is in the United States that we can see some of the most harmful effects. Fr. Cyprian Davis carefully sets out the extreme bias that many U.S. bishops in the nineteenth and early twentieth centuries showed toward people of African descent. This bias clearly affected their interpretation of mandates issued by Rome calling for the elimination of the slave trade and slavery itself, as well as an intensive evangelization effort among the newly freed slaves. In the South and throughout the United States, overt resistance to more recent church teachings opposing slavery and racism culminated in segregation, discrimination, and second-class citizenship for Black Catholics. This resistance was so widespread that discrimination is still being dismantled today, with great difficulty.

We must admit, however, that today the church is trying to erase the failures of the past. It is critical that these failures be acknowledged as the sins they were and continue to be (see the 1989 report, *The Church and Racism,* by the Pontifical Commission on Peace and Justice). Despite claims to the contrary, the church was instrumental in the spread of a new and vastly more horrific form of slavery to the New World and in the establishment of a racial caste system that haunts us to this day.

The interpretation of scripture and tradition by which the church supported such acts was a product of the times and the conditions of society during those times. Nonetheless, this interpretation was immoral then and still is today. Since all of humanity, in its great diversity, was created in the image and likeness of God, there can be no rationale for slavery. To differentiate among human beings based on the color of their skin or any other factor is a sin against God and must be condemned. "Whatever violates the integrity of the human person…whatever insults human dignity…all these things and others like them are infamous" *(Pastoral Constitution on the Church in the Modern World).*

Evidence of conversion in the hearts and minds of the leaders of our church, albeit late, is welcome. For slavery has not ended. It exists in Africa on both the west coast, where children are kidnapped, and the east coast, where Christians are enslaved by non-Christians. We continue to reap the horrors of what was sown so many years ago. When people are brutalized and dehumanized, whether by their own or others, in the name of God, there can be no peace. Their souls cry out to heaven, and we ignore them at our peril.

Thus the church's complicity in the enslavement of countless millions cannot be ignored. Nor can we rewrite history to place the church in a better light. Instead, our knowledge serves to help us recognize the humanity of those in the church who falter and stumble as the rest of us do. Recounting this history enables Catholics throughout the world to realize that what once may have seemed acceptable was not and never can be.

The church's understanding of itself and its role has changed continually throughout its history and continues to change today. Further change is still necessary and will occur, because no human institution, even one graced by the Holy Spirit, can remain static. The church is both the unchanging Christ and the fallible creation of fallible human beings. As such, we continue to seek perfection while recognizing that only God is perfect. We strive for perfection and approach it most closely when we acknowledge the sins of the past, learn from them, and strive to do better.

6. The Correction of the Common Catholic Teaching Concerning Slavery by Pope Leo XIII

John Francis Maxwell

This chapter first appeared in Maxwell, *Slavery and the Catholic Church* (Chichester and London: Barry Rose, 1975).

The preparations for the first Vatican Council (1869–70) and the revival of the study of scholastic philosophy had led to a critical reappraisal of medieval notions concerning human society and human relationships. Some moralists were more ready than hitherto to jettison ancient principles of Roman civil law, which did not measure up to nineteenth-century developments in secular jurisprudence. By 1888 the transatlantic Negro slave trade had long since been suppressed by the navies of the maritime powers. Motivated both by "liberal" revolutionary humanism as well as by Christianity, the governments of most of the European and American nations had passed municipal and international legal prohibitions directed against all slavery and slave trading, including the enslavement of prisoners of war and convicted criminals. Slavery had been abolished by law in Chile in 1823, in Spain in 1837, in the Dominican Republic in 1844, in Ecuador in 1851, and in Argentina in 1853, in Venezuela in 1854, in the United States of America in 1865, in Brazil in 1888.

Two letters of Pope Leo XIII on slavery—one in 1888 addressed to the bishops of Brazil, another in 1890 addressed to the bishops of the whole world—indicate that the pope was concerned about providing doctrinal and pastoral guidance even though slavery had ceased to be a serious political issue for most of the governments of Christian states. There was the question whether the common Catholic teaching rooted mainly in principles of Roman civil law could now be modified or altered.

The answer of Pope Leo XIII, or his advisers and "ghostwriters," was to try to interpret some of the ecclesiastical documents of the ordinary *magisterium* from the past in an "antislavery" sense. As mentioned above, a few Catholic historians had been rewriting the history of slavery "from the Catholic angle" (omitting references to the common Catholic teaching), from which it might be inferred that the Catholic Church had always and constantly been abolitionist. It would appear that the Catholic historians who helped to write these two letters for Pope Leo XIII had come to believe that this was the truth. As a consequence, both these two letters lack historical accuracy....

In both these two letters Pope Leo XIII singled out for special praise twelve popes who, he wrote, had made every effort to abolish slavery and prevent its recurrence. His later letter of 1890 addressed to the bishops of the whole world begins as follows:

> From the beginning, almost nothing was more venerated in the Catholic Church, which embraces all men with motherly love, than the fact that she looked to see a slavery eased and abolished, which was oppressing so many people...; she undertook the neglected cause of the slaves and stood forth as a strenuous defender of liberty, although she conducted her campaign gradually and prudently so far as times and circumstances permitted...; nor did this effort of the church to liberate slaves weaken in the course of time; indeed the more slavery flourished from time to time, the more zealously she strove. The clearest historical documents are evidence for this...and many of our predecessors, including St. Gregory the Great, Hadrian I, Alexander III, Innocent III, Gregory IX, Pius II, Leo X, Paul III, Urban VIII, Benedict XIV, Pius VII, and Gregory XVI, *made every effort to ensure that the institution of slavery should be abolished where it existed and that its roots should not revive where it had been destroyed.* (Emphasis added.)

With the greatest respect to Pope Leo XIII, this is historically inaccurate. In his earlier letter of 1888 he had made selective use of a number of documents written by these same twelve popes to suggest that there had been a constant "antislavery" tradition in the Catholic Church.[1] But a number of other conciliar and papal documents, as well as canons of general church law, are simply ignored; all these twelve popes, who are given special commendation, had only condemned what they and contemporary moral theology held to be *unjust* methods of enslavement or *unjust* titles of slave ownership. Five of the popes mentioned were the authors of other public documents that actually authorized enslavement as an institution, as a penalty for ecclesiastical crimes, or as a consequence of war. The historical inaccuracy of writing that these five popes "made every effort to ensure that the institution of slavery should be abolished where it existed and that its roots should not revive where it had been destroyed" is proved as follows:

Pope Alexander III with the Fathers of the Third General Council of the Lateran in 1179 authorized the penalty of enslavement for captured Christians who had assisted the Saracens; Pope Innocent III did the same with the Fathers of the Fourth General Council of the Lateran in 1215; and Pope Gregory IX repeated this enactment in a letter to the English in 1235. Pope Leo X in 1514 followed the example of three of his predecessors in authorizing the kings of Portugal to invade and conquer the newly discovered territories of the New World, to reduce the non-Christian inhabitants who lived there to perpetual slavery, and to expropriate their possessions. Finally Pope Paul III in 1535 sentenced King Henry VIII of England to the penalty of being exposed for capture and enslavement by the Catholic princes of Europe, and in 1548, gave full permission for all persons, clerical and lay, to own, buy, and sell slaves in the City of Rome, and abrogated the privilege of the *conservatori* of Rome to emancipate Christian slaves.

Finally there was no condemnation by any of the popes mentioned of the capture and enslavement of Moslem prisoners of war by the galleys of the pontifical squadron in the innumerable naval actions that are well documented from about 1500 to about 1800.

The significance of these two letters of Pope Leo XIII is that it was no longer individual Catholics, whether lay or clerical, who were expressing "antislavery" sentiments, it was the pope himself. For the popes who were held up for special praise were those who (whether historically accurately or not is here irrelevant) had "made every effort to ensure that the *institution* of slavery should be abolished where it existed and that its roots should not revive where it had been destroyed." No distinction was made between just and unjust enslavement; it was the institution as such that was equivalently condemned.

Pope Leo XIII offered no explanation for this change of theological attitude. He did not indicate in these two letters whether it was a correction of scriptural exegesis or the beginnings of the movement for revision of the canon law of the church or a correction of the philosophical analysis of the very nature of slavery or a growing awareness that economic and social circumstances and conditions in many countries had completely changed or a realization that rationalist humanists and Protestant Christians could have been assisted by the Holy Spirit. Clearly, this was already about 100 years too late to be of any effective value in the antislavery campaigns and civil wars and revolutions of the nineteenth century; the lay reformers and abolitionists had won their campaigns without much effective help or moral leadership from the teaching authority of the Catholic Church, which had hitherto consistently refused to condemn the institution of slavery or the practice of slave trading as such.

Note

1. Letter *In Plurimis* to the bishops of Brazil, May 5, 1888. Collectanea S. C. de Prop. Fide (1907), II, n. 1688, paragraphs 15–18.

7. Usury: The Amendment of Papal Teaching by Theologians

John T. Noonan, Jr.

This chapter first appeared in *Contraception: Authority and Dissent,* ed. Charles E. Curran (New York: Herder and Herder, 1969).

In the current controversy over the force of the encyclical *Humanae Vitae,* it has been sometimes stated or assumed that it is unheard arrogance for theologians to criticize or to correct a solemn authentic statement of Catholic moral teaching as to the requirements of divine and natural law issued after investigation, reflection, and prayer by a pope. *Humanae Vitae* is a document in which the pope "in virtue of the mandate given to us by Christ" replies to questions on conjugal life with a "teaching founded on the natural law illuminated and enriched by divine revelation," articulates a theory of God's will or plan for married life, and conclusively holds that certain acts preventing procreation must be "condemned." It may be helpful in understanding the nature of this document and the nature of teaching authority in the church if there is greater familiarity with other instances of similar papal documents criticized by the theologians in which the view advocated by the theologians prevailed as the teaching of the church.

I propose to explore the theologians' response to papal teaching on a single subject at a single point of time. I choose this instance because the papal teaching was set out to change the behavior of a mass of Catholics and to end a theological controversy, because the teaching was given after mature examination of the issues, because it was based on a foundation of natural law enriched by divine revelation, because it was given in solemn discharge of the pope's teaching office, and because it was substantially reshaped by the response of the theologians a few years after it was uttered.

A Commission Is Formed

In 1565 Charles Borromeo became archbishop of Milan. He found prevalent in his diocese the practice of deposit banking, exchange banking, and business investments in which the investor was guaranteed his capital and a return. He viewed these practices in the light of the church's teaching on usury, which had been the common teaching of theologians, bishops, and popes for more than 1,000 years. This teaching was succinctly stated in the Roman catechism of which Borromeo was the principal editor:

> Whatever is received beyond the principal and that capital which is given, whether it be money or whether it be any other thing which can be purchased or estimated in money, is usury; for it is written in Ezekiel, 'He has not lent at usury nor received an increase,' and in Luke the Lord says, 'Lend, hoping nothing thereby.' This was always a most grave crime, even among the gentiles, and especially odious. Hence the question, 'What is usury?' is answered, 'What is it to kill a man?' Those who commit usury sell the same thing twice or sell what is not.[1]

The rule on usury proclaimed by three general councils of the church and a dozen popes rested on the belief that by divine law (Luke 6, 35) profit on a loan was mortal sin,[2] and that by natural law it was intrinsically unjust to sell money in a loan at a price higher than its face value, for the law fixed its value, and the value of the use of money could not be separated from the value of the principal.[3] This view of divine law, this theory of money, and the existing rule forbidding usury were challenged by the financial practices of the people of Borromeo's diocese.

In the first provincial synod held under his presidency to reform the morals of the diocese, these customs were noted and characterized. They were "the more frequent" species of the genus usury in the province, and therefore, serious sin *(crimina)*. The plea "widows and orphans" as a defense for investment practices is an old slogan. The synod solemnly reminded the faithful that nothing beyond the principal might be taken on loans or on deposits, even if the depositors were widows or wards.[4]

To a reforming archbishop the question looked simple. But the practice of extending credit at a profit was inveterate, and much of the practice was justified by theories of some of the more recent theologians. In particular, three types of transaction had their defenders. One was the so-called triple contract. The classical medieval theologians had always accepted the principle that profit might be made by an investor in a partnership. Here the investor ran the risk of losing his capital, and his return depended on the success of the venture; he was not a lender with principal and profit owed to him whatever happened to the enterprise. The classical theologians also admitted the lawfulness of charging for insurance. The innovators proposed combining contracts of partnership and insurance. Suppose that the probable return from investment in a partnership was 12 percent; deduct 2 percent for insurance that the principal would be repaid; deduct 5 percent for insurance that a regular return of 5 percent would be made—by the threefold contract of partnership and guarantees, the effect is achieved of a loan at 5 percent; each step has been analytically defensible as lawful. The case had been first defended in 1485 by the Franciscan Angelo Carleto de Clavasio; it had been adopted by the liberal German theologians at the new University of Tübingen, Gabriel Biel and Conrad Summenhart; it had been popularized in Germany by John Eck; and it had been vigorously attacked as usurious by the Spanish Dominican professor at Salamanca, Domingo de Soto. By 1565 the triple contract was a way of justifying profit on a business loan—a way that subverted the postulates of the usury prohibition, for it implicitly treated money as fertile, a way contrary to the old prohibition, and a way debated by modern theologians.[5]

A second approach was in terms of annuities or contracts of *census.* The classical medieval theologians admitted the lawfulness of making of profit on a purchase. They also admitted that one could buy the right to an annual return from some fruitful property like a farm. The purchaser of an annuity was, of course, extending credit because he put up a lump sum of cash in exchange for the right to an annual payment; but an annuity was not identical with a loan if it had to be related to the expected returns from a fruitful base, if the annuity ceased should the base be destroyed, and if there was no obligation on the seller's part ever to refund the principal. A contract in the form of an annuity could, however, be virtually identical with a loan if it were personal—that is, based on the labor of the seller; if it were guaranteed—that is, the seller agreed to pay whatever happened to the base; and if it were redeemable at the buyer's option—that is, the buyer could call for the return of the principal. In the sixteenth century the Tübingen liberals began to champion the contracts by which an annuity was made indistinguishable from a loan, and Summenhart made a comprehensive defense of the personal, guaranteed, redeemable annuity. These German novelties were welcomed in Spain, with only slight reservations, by Soto. But they were warmly attacked by Soto's colleague at Salamanca, Navarrus. By 1565 there was here, too, a development of medieval theological principles, which contrary to their restrained use by the medieval theologians, subverted the usury theory, and in which a controversy between modern theologians needed decision.[6]

A third controverted approach to profit in credit transactions involved the purchase of foreign exchange. Where foreign currency was bought for cash across a counter, there was no problem at all—the exchange banker extended no credit and made a profit on his service; the foreign currency was properly treated not at its legal face value but as a commodity. The difficulty occurred when the banker paid for foreign currency to be delivered later. Then a purchase of money as a commodity was made, but credit was also extended. Was the profit on this transaction lawful or was it usury? The masters of medieval moral theology had judged the transaction usurious![7]

There was, however, a minority current of medieval moral opinions that defended the exchange bankers, and in the sixteenth century, this minority opinion had become dominant, so that by 1565, there was no substantial controversy over the lawfulness of the banker's profit when he bought a bill of foreign exchange.[8]

Controversy on exchange banking centered on two points. One was the theoretical ground on which the banker's profit rested. A theory of some theologians was that the profit depended on his "virtual transportation" of money from one city to another.[9] Taken literally this theory meant in practice that the price of foreign money ought to depend on the distance of the foreign places from the place of purchase of the exchange and on the difficulty of transporting species from there. The advantage of this theory was that it distinguished the purchase of foreign exchange from a loan by saying that money absent in space was different from money absent in time: There were "intrinsic" difficulties in transporting money in space, while there were no "intrinsic" difficulties to which money distant in time was subject. But it was generally recognized that "the foundation" of the exchange market was the supply and demand for money, and that profit depended on accurately gauging changes in this market. The transportation change was not the basis for moneymaking in the exchanges. A different theory therefore justified the banker's profit as lawful because it was made in the purchase of money as a commodity. Yet if money could be purchased at a profit in foreign exchange transactions, why could it not be purchased at a profit in loans? This question, posed by the alternative justification of exchange banking, wrecked the usury prohibition completely unless a distinction could be sustained.

A second controversy concerned the technical operations of the exchange bankers. In a typical transaction, the Medici bank in Florence bought from a customer a bill on Bruges. When the bill arrived for payment in Bruges, the Medici branch there acted for the customer and drew a new bill on him in Florence. When this bill reached Florence, the customer paid the Medici there. The customer had had credit for four months—the bills taking two months each way—and the bank determined its profit at the end of the *ricorsa* or exchange and reexchange.[10] This common form of credit had the effect of a short-term loan with an interest rate determined by fluctuations in the exchange market. Its moral lawfulness was in dispute. Clearly condemned by medieval moralists, its admission would remove a large area of commercial banking from the usury doctrine.

Finally, the exchange banks needed capital for their business, and they were often financed by deposits. These deposits were a *discrezione,* that is, the banker had discretion as to the return paid the depositor, and so, like income bonds, the deposits ran some of the risks of the enterprise.[11] But there was no uncertainty about the banker's obligation to repay the principal. The great moral judge of Florentine banking practice, St. Antoninus, had declared, "Although they call this a deposit, yet it is clearly usury."[12] Yet, clearly, too, the practice of deposit banking persisted, supported by the sense of the people that profit on a deposit was different from a profit on a loan. At a theological level these contracts received indirect support from the theory of the triple contract and by the argument of Catejan and Navarrus that the triple contract could be found "implicitly" even though the actual spelling out of three separate contracts had not been done.[13]

With the triple contract, annuities, and exchange banking all theologically defended and all presenting ways of avoiding the moral law on usury, Charles Borromeo pressed the pope to give direction. On November 18, 1567, he wrote Niccolo Ormaneto, the zealous reformer whom he had lent the pope, as follows:

> Today is the eighth day I have been in Varese, always with constant business. I have found this country full of usury and usurious contracts, made as much by priests as by laymen; and believing that this is caused in good part by the ignorance of many, I would be much satisfied if His Beatitude would put into effect that thought which he has already deigned to communicate to me of wanting to make a general statement on usury; and I recall also that I have named to His Holiness those persons who seem to me good for well chewing over this matter and drawing up the bull. You may now have an hour with a good opportunity to speak a word to His Holiness and to represent to him the need which I see particularly in these parts, which recalls to mind the need which there is everywhere.[14]

Within three weeks Ormaneto could report that there was now a papal commission in existence to study "all the disorders occurring in this matter and above all in annuities, deposits, and exchanges."[15]

Pressure on the pope to act had come not only from Borromeo, but also from the Jesuits. In 1522 the city of Augsburg had been brought back from Protestant control to a place within the Catholic Empire; and in 1560 the Jesuits, led by the great Dutch reformer Peter Canisius, had come to instill Catholic economic teaching in this financial capital, still bitterly divided between Catholics and Protestants.[16] The Jesuits had been pained to discover the general practice prevailed of investing in credit transactions with a 5-percent return; they were inclined to attribute the custom to pernicious Protestant example. Peter Canisius refused to absolve Catholics taking the 5 percent. "Real usury," he told the chapter of Augsburg cathedral, "is here openly committed and the divine commandment 'Lend freely hoping nothing thereby' is violated, whatever is objected by certain men skilled in the law who think according to the prudence of this world that many things of this kind are to be dissimulated, although contrary to the canons and the received opinion of old and new theologians and canonists."[17]

This zeal of the reforming leader of a still new religious order was not shared by all Catholics. The secular clergy of Augsburg continued to object to such rigor, and the Jesuit authorities in Rome counseled Canisius to proceed cautiously. But he would not connive in what he saw as open sin, and a quarrel about the lawfulness of the 5-percent contract or "the German contract" developed both inside and outside the Jesuit order.[18]

In 1565 Ursula Fugger entered the lists. A member by marriage of the great Fugger banking family, the richest bankers in Europe, she was also a convert of Canisius and a pious benefactress of the Jesuits. It was not easy to be the pious wife of a usurer, for all usury, as ill-gotten gain, was subject to a duty of restitution; and no one could lawfully receive gifts or inheritance made up of usuries. For a decent woman the thought that her husband was daily committing mortal sin in his business was itself anguish. Ursula Fugger wrote directly to the Jesuit General, Francis Borgia, asking his counsel "as to the usurious contracts in which our family is not a little entangled."[19] Borgia replied that these contracts "which are less candid than you wish" would be carefully considered with Canisius and others in Rome.[20] It was plain that the experience of the laity who used these contracts as proper for decent Christians was not to be neglected by the Jesuits at headquarters.

The controversy over the 5-percent contract continued. In July of 1567 Peter Canisius repeated triumphantly the report that the pope had decided the question.[21] The rumor was a false one. Only in the winter of 1567 did the combined requests of Charles Borromeo and the Jesuits lead to the constitution of a papal commission. By February 16, 1568, Borgia could assure the Jesuits in Lyons, "Of the deposits and other usurious contracts we expect some speedy resolution, because many theologians are looking at this matter by order of His Holiness, who wants to compose a *motu proprio,* or brief."[22] Again on March 15, 1568, Borgia reported the pope's plan to draft a *motu proprio* on deposits "together with exchanges and annuities."[23]

A commission had, then, come into existence on the main forms of European credit and the common practices of the financial world. The commission's task was to enable the pope to decide the theological controversies about the moral law that had divided theologians, confused the laity, and threatened to subvert the divine and natural law forbidding men to seek profit on a loan. The commission's head was Cardinal Gugliemo Sirleto, an excellent man whom Borromeo had supported for pope in the election of 1565.[24] The commission was directed to draw on theologians. It relied on Jesuits, but it also took the counsel of Navarrus, Soto's old foe at Salamanca, now chosen by Borromeo as canonist of the Sacred Penitentiary and a moralist of outstanding acuity.[25] The commission was thus composed of the choices of Borromeo, of Borgia, and of the pope; and its members were more than routinely distinguished for piety and learning.

The pope to whom the commission reported, Pius V, had been a Dominican and a high official in the Inquisition. He was not unfamiliar with the main lines of theological thought on usury, but as an especially vigorous administrator, he could not have been expected to master the complex distinctions pressed by casuists. Distinctions were the work of theologians; his task was to proclaim the law of God. Pius V was humble, pious, strict, unchangeable in his judgments once they were formed, and with little experience of worldly affairs. Above all, the pope was marked by his scrupulous care to discharge his office faithfully. He declared once that he would retire into privacy at the Lateran rather than allow anything he considered wrong. As Pastor has remarked, "Pius V was so imbued with the responsibilities of his office that he looked upon it as an obstacle in the way of salvation."[26] To preserve the integral Catholic doctrine on usury, Pius V acted upon the report of his commission.

A Burden Is Assumed

On January 19, 1569, Pius V issued the bull *Cum Onus*. It began as follows:

> Undertaking the burden of apostolic servitude, we have recognized that innumerable contracts of annuity were and are celebrated which are not only not within the limits set by our predecessors for such contracts, but what is worse, by agreements entirely contrary to these limits, due to the burning

prick of avarice, show manifest contempt for divine laws. Therefore we—bound as we are to care for the salvation of souls and satisfying the prayer of pious minds—cannot not medicate such a grave disease and deadly poison with a salutary antidote.[27]

The bull closed by saying that for no one was it lawful to infringe what the bull determined or "to contradict it with temerarious audacity." "But if anyone presumes to attempt this he will know that he has incurred the wrath of Almighty God and of His Blessed Apostles, Peter and Paul."

Pius V thus made it evident that he acted in discharge of his apostolic office; that he judged here and now that there were contracts of annuity in which certain additional agreements made the contracts offensive to the law of God; that he acted to save souls from mortal sin or "deadly poison"; that he invoked the authority of his office as successor to Peter; and that he called upon all who would dare to go against the teaching not merely ecclesiastical sanction but also the wrath of God.

In the body of the bull the pope decreed that an annuity "can in no way be created except of immovable property or property regarded as immovable, fruitful by nature, and designated for definite ends." He also taught that an agreement binding the seller of the annuity to pay although the property was destroyed was "in no way valid." He also declared that any agreement by the seller to pay interest determined in advance was null. An agreement to permit redemption of an annuity against the seller's will—that is, the forced repayment of the principal— was invalid. Resale of an annuity at a higher or lower figure than the original price, the pope proclaimed, "can never be done."

Cum Onus was a thorough-going determination that a personal, guaranteed, or redeemable annuity was morally impossible—for by the statement that such could never be done the pope clearly did not deny that such annuities could be sold, but that such annuities could be morally sold. By this determination Pius V specified the agreements that turned annuities into contracts in contempt of God's law, for it was precisely the agreements that were declared impossible or invalid that turned annuities into the equivalent of loans at a profit. The bull was a rejection of the Tübingen liberals and of the compromisers in the Jesuit order. It was a triumphant vindication of Charles Borromeo and Peter Canisius. It was a definitive theological victory for Navarrus over his old rival Soto at Salamanca. It was established on the basis of divine law that only annuities substantially distinct from loans could be purchased at a profit.

The problems occasioned by exchange banking were more complex than those of the annuity contracts, and Pius V was unable to fulfill his hope of dealing with all the species of usurious contracts in a single document. Only two years later was he ready to speak specifically on banking. On January 28, 1571, he issued the bull *In Eam.* Like *Cum Onus,* this bull began by setting out that the pope was discharging an apostolic duty: "We diligently exert ourselves on behalf of our pastoral office so that we do not delay in healthfully applying opportune remedies for the sheep of Our Lord." Like *Cum Onus,* the bull went on to make a judgment that here and now forms of the exchange contract violated divine law: under pretext of exchanges "usurious wickedness is exercised by some." Acting to prevent the practice of mortal sin as he had done in *Cum Onus,* the pope exercised the office of pastor, striving "in every way to snatch the flock committed to us from the danger of eternal damnation."[28]

As in *Cum Onus,* Pius V was conscious that he was giving moral teaching in his function of Chief Shepherd, that he was judging certain contracts to violate divine law, and that he was determining what contracts of credit could avoid the sin of usury. He then taught the moral truth that all "dry exchange" was usurious, defining such exchange to be contracts taking the form of a purchase in which bills of exchange were not sent to another place, or if sent, they were not paid there but returned to be paid by the seller of the bill in the same place, as it was agreed, or at least certainly intended by the parties. The pope also taught that the only basis on which foreign exchange prices might vary was distance in space; distance in time of payment could not be made a basis for a change.

In this document, following the example set by Charles Borromeo in the synod of Milan, Pius V made a formal identification of the *ricorsa* with usury, for the expectation of purchaser and seller to pay the bill of exchange after it had not been paid in the foreign city was the essence of the *ricorsa.* The pope not only taught that this common practice constituted the mortal sin of usury; he also embraced a theory of the true basis for the exchange banker's profit. He adopted the theory that the banker legitimately profited on "virtual transportation" of money, understanding this theory literally—not as a legal fiction, but as an accurate reflection of the way exchange banks worked.[29] He thereby rejected the theory that the banker's profit depended on the supply and demand for money, and he assumed seriously and literally that money distant in space could be the subject of a profit while money distant in time could not. By adopting this assumption and by rejecting the *ricorsa,* the pope made a sharp distinction between moral profit in exchange banking and sinful usury; and there could be no question of confusing a moral exchange transaction with a loan at a profit.

The triple contract itself was not dealt with. There is some evidence that Pius V personally hesitated more in regard to this practice than in regard to the others.[30] But *In Eam* did speak of deposits, and deposits were a form of commercial contract in which the liberals' theory of implicit contract provided the defense of "implicit triple contract." Without adverting to this defense, Pius V held simply "deposits," like dry exchange, to be usurious; and the defense of them fell before this proclamation of their true character.

The triple contract itself was given consideration only fifteen years later in a bull whose history belongs with *Cum Onus* and *In Eam.* In 1586 another friar, this time a Franciscan, another ex-inquisitor, another vigorous reformer, was pope—Sixtus V. With his burning zeal to sweep away corruptions of all sorts he issued a bull on usury devoted to the morally impermissible characteristics of contracts of partnership. "Detestable avarice," the bull ominously opened, has inflamed men's hearts, and the devil has led men "to immerse themselves in the whirlpool of usury, odious to God and men, condemned by the sacred canons, and contrary to Christian charity." These avaricious and misled men have used "the decent name of partnership as a pretext for their usurious contracts." In order to stem this "contagious disease" before it spread farther, the pope, "desiring to draw as fully as we can with the favor of God upon the plentitude of apostolic power granted to us," declared that all future agreements "must be condemned," by which "it is guaranteed to persons giving money, animals, or other property in the name of a partnership, that, even if in some fortuitous case some disaster, loss, or lack happens to occur, the principal will be always safe and restored entire by the partner receiving it."[31]

The mention of future agreements made the bull appear to be only prospective legislation. But it also dealt with existing agreements of the kind condemned. Any person now enforcing such agreements was to be treated as a manifest usurer and excommunicated and denied Christian burial according to the provisions of the general councils against manifest usurers.

In this bull as in the two documents of Pius V, an apostolic office was discharged—indeed explicitly here the maximum of apostolic power possible was used; certain contracts were here and now judged to be usurious; what these contracts were was determined by the specific provisions declaring the condemned contracts to be invalid; and sanctions were invoked that were founded on the determination made by the pope that those who used these contracts were in mortal sin, offenders of God and their neighbor. Concretely, by holding usurious any agreement to guarantee the return of partnership principal, *Detestabilis Avaritia* condemned the triple contract.

The three bulls stood together. In a period extending over seventeen years, these authentic acts of papal teaching authority had repulsed an attempt to subvert the usury prohibition. Faithful to the main lines of theological tradition approved and proclaimed by popes, bishops, and councils for more than a millennium, Pius V and Sixtus V had rejected theories and practices that removed the usury prohibition's rigor from the world of commercial credit. The popes and their advisers had correctly perceived that if the novel theories of the innovating theologians were accepted, the entire moral structure of Catholic thought on economic matter would crumble, that rethinking of the meaning of divine law on lending would be necessary, that the old absolute condemnations of profit on a loan would no longer hold. They saw that to admit a market in money in some forms would be to admit a market in other forms; that it was essential from the viewpoint of existing divine law to maintain a distinction between distance in space and distance in time; that no moral value could be given to the practice of those otherwise decent Christians who invested in credit believing that moderate profit in finance was not a sin; that it was a work of Christian charity to end the confusion and uncertainty caused by rival theological analyses of important issues of conduct.

By means of the bulls' determination of divine law, the ordinary forms of commercial credit and government finance in Western Europe were condemned; Christian businessmen, bankers, and investors were told that they were committing sin; their wives and children were informed by the usual rules on unjustly taken property that they were bound to restitution; their associates, lawyers, notaries, and agents were informed by the usual rules on cooperation that they would have to justify acts of every material cooperation with the condemned practices.[32] While the absolute number of persons affected was not enormous, almost every part of the bourgeois world was affected by the popes' forthright actions.

Challenging established procedures, the popes no doubt anticipated objection and the continuance of sin. But objection could be refuted, sin absolved, and reform effected. With zeal and with serenity, the popes assumed that there could be no compromise with evil custom, no abandonment of past theological tradition. The laity must be instructed, the theological innovators repressed.

How did the laity and the theologians respond?

A Process Is Continued

The first response came from the Jesuits. In April, 1569, three months after the issuance of *Cum Onus,* Peter Canisius treated this declaration of Pius V as ending the 5-percent controversy. With triumph and compassion, he wrote the General, "I know that for certain ones execution of this recent judgment will be displeasing and harsh...but with Christ as our leader we shall overcome these difficulties both on the part of those hearing confessions and on the part of those confessing."[33] But this assurance in the ultimate acceptance of the papal teaching was not shared by all his brethren. From Munich the Jesuit Georg Schorich wrote the secretary general of the Society of Jesus, "These Germans do not desire to understand how lending at 5 florins per hundred is not lawful for them, while in the states of the church it is 7, 8, 9, and even 10 *scudi* per hundred."[34] At the very moment of Canisius's triumph he was being succeeded by a new provincial, Paul Hoffaeus, who was inclined to take seriously the murmurs of the people that the 5-percent contract could not always be unjust.[35] To the dismay of Canisius, Hoffaeus began to work for a new decision.

In Rome Pius V himself revealed a strange weakness. Approached again by Francis Borgia, the pope said orally that "miserable persons," such as wards and widows who invested their funds in the 5-percent contracts, might be "excused."[36] But he vouchsafed no explanation of how intrinsically sinful acts like lending at usury became lawful because the persons engaging in them were poor. The Jesuit theologians must have read this report of papal mildness as a sign that Pius V was himself still unsure of whether lending at 5 percent could not be analyzed in terms of the other contracts that formally avoided the divine prohibition of profit on a loan.

The Jesuits set up their own commission of theologians to study the problems involved. At its head was one of the brightest of their young theologians, Francisco Toledo, a native of Córdoba, thirty-nine years old in 1571, and Navarrus's counterpart as the theological adviser of the Sacred Penitentiary.[37] To it Hoffaeus forwarded the arguments of the Fuggers' lawyer on behalf of the 5 percent.[38] The Jesuits also consulted Navarrus as one of the main authors responsible for *Cum Onus* as to whether the bull was "declaratory of natural and divine law, or only constitutive of human law."[39]

In answer to this inquiry Navarrus noted the opening passages of the bull that referred to contracts of annuity made in contempt of divine laws and the conclusion of the bull applying the sanctions against usury to violators of the bull, and judged accordingly that part of the bull must be declaratory of divine and natural law. At the same time he observed that there were a variety of conditions laid down by the bull for a morally lawful annuity, and that as these conditions were to be observed in the future, not all of them were natural and divine law. The necessarily prospective character of some of the requirements showed their merely human character; for what was natural law "began with the beginning of the rational creature." Navarrus's conclusion was that the law set out in *Cum Onus* was partly divine, partly natural, and partly pontifical.[40]

The question this response raised was, What part was only pontifical? Here it was Navarrus's cautious opinion that "it seemed to be of natural and divine law" that an annuity be constituted on fruitful, immobile property. Other requirements, such that annuities be bought in cash, were purely pontifical.[41]

The third and key question was, Did the bull then bind in conscience? Navarrus was clear that to the extent it declared the divine and natural law, it "bound all, even laymen, in kingdoms not subject to the temporal domain of the pope." As to the provisions that were only pontifical law, there was an obligation on all Christians to observe them in external and internal behavior. Yet since these provisions only provided presumptions as to what was usurious, "no one is to be judged usurious in the forum of the conscience because of presumptions induced by this document, if the contrary is true before God, because no law founded on presumption binds someone in the forum of the conscience or of God if the contrary of what is presumed is, before God, true."[42]

If these answers were taken as a good gloss on the intention of Pius V, a loophole was suggested by Navarrus's language on the limited force of presumptions created by purely papal law. Yet respect for the papal intention required finding some provisions of divine and natural law in the bull. Navarrus himself thought that his own opinion on the unlawfulness of personal annuities had been recognized as divine law by the pope; he furnished no guidance on how to classify the equally important prohibitions of guaranteed or redeemable annuities.

The Jesuit theologians acted on the silence of Navarrus, but not until Pius V was dead. Then on June 22, 1573, there was a meeting of Toledo's commission—himself, two other Spaniards, Pedro Paez and Diego Bernal, and one Portuguese, Leon Enriquez. They were joined by Jesuit provincials from France and Austria and by Canisius's foe Paul Hoffaeus. Canisius himself was excluded from the gathering, apparently by design.[43] The group issued a decision written to provide guidance for all Jesuit confessors, preachers, and moralists.

Ex genere, the 1573 Commission declared, a contract for 5 percent beyond the principal was morally unlawful. The cases excused by Pius V—wards and widows who could not otherwise support themselves—were specifically condemned. But the triple contract was lawful (this was before *Detestabilis Avaritia*), and so was an annuity redeemable by either seller or buyer. In other words, an annuity at 5 percent in which the purchaser could also demand the return of his principal was legitimate. At the same time the theologians added, "Where the Bull of Pius V obliges, the buyer cannot oblige the seller to repurchase."[44]

The decisions of 1573 were a careful step toward undermining the force of *Cum Onus*. The theologians still taught in accordance with the bull and with Navarrus that an annuity was to be founded on "fruitful property"; they did not accept the full-annuity theory of the liberals. But in treating redeemability by the buyer as objectively lawful, they supported the single feature of an annuity contract that made it closest to a loan. Moreover, in the general language "where the bull of Pius V obliges," the Jesuit theologians implied that there were areas in which it did not oblige; that it was purely positive law that might not oblige; and failed to specify what parts of the bull were divine law, what parts purely pontifical law.

This first cautious theological response to the determinations of *Cum Onus* was not decisive enough to end the controversy but was ambiguous enough to sharpen it. In Germany the confusion, uncertainty, and conflict among theologians and laity increased. The rigorist Jesuits, heartened by the bull, continued to refuse absolution to persons taking the 5 percent. They were backed by the bishop of Augsburg who threatened suspension to any priest absolving a man putting out money at 5 percent.[45] But the bishop died and a new bishop of Augsburg ordered Canisius not to permit teaching against the 5-percent contract and not to criticize secular priests who did absolve the 5-percent takers.[46] The papal nuncio, Feliciano Ninguarda, announced that the bull was binding in Germany.[47] A righteous Englishman and professor at the Jesuit University of Dillingen, Caspar Haywood, became convinced that many of his confreres were unbelievably lax on the subject, that "to save the Company from certain ruin" the 5-percent contract must be denounced, and that it was his personal mission to war upon the hydra of usury that appeared in these common commercial practices.[48] Pressed to quiet the mounting storm, the new pope, a learned lawyer, Gregory XIII, adopted a via media: The Jesuit General was told that the Jesuits should not absolve the takers of the 5 percent but that the Jesuits should keep from disputing publicly or preaching on the question.[49]

Until 1581 the conservative defenders of medieval theology had won every major controversy taken to the pope. Whatever weakness had been betrayed by Pius V's counsel on the 5-percent contracts of widows and orphans, whatever prudential circumspection had motivated Gregory XIII's order not to preach, there was an unbroken series of papal decisions rejecting on their merits every contract that substantially approximated a loan for a profit. But one decade after *Cum Onus,* two decades after the controversy had begun in Germany, neither the laity nor the theologians were convinced that the final answer had been given.

In 1581 Gregory XIII acted in response to a plaintive inquiry from Duke William of Bavaria, who was a pious ruler under serious moral pressure from the rigorists Canisius and Heywood.[50] In his perplexity, the duke first received conflicting advice from the theological faculty of Ingolstadt and then in 1580 received the opinion of a group of Roman theologians that left him still muddled. In desperation he wrote Charles Borromeo, describing his plight and how he was working in order that "the Supreme Pastor of the church with the consent and judgment of his brother cardinals pronounce authentically what must be judged about this kind of usury everywhere and put into practice without discrimination of souls or scruple of conscience."[51]

Again Charles Borromeo took an interest in obtaining a papal judgment. He sent his agent Spetiano at Rome a copy of the duke's letter; noted that in this business of usury and on the questions raised "by the English Jesuit father," the duke wanted a decision by the pope himself; observed that "it would be good that His Beatitude console this Prince in this matter"; and instructed Spetiano to speak to the pope in the duke's name.[52] Again the pope consulted with Jesuits and other "most learned theologians."[53] Heywood, apparently encouraged by the nuncio Ninguardo and Cardinal Como, intrepidly argued his case in Rome and was benignly heard by the pope.[54] But the pope also asked the advice of a select committee of theologians chosen by the new general of the Jesuits Claudio Aquaviva.[55] This committee had as its most brilliant member Gregorio de Valentia, a thirty-year-old Spaniard who had been scandalizing Heywood and others at Ingolstadt by his defense of the German contract.[56] In April, 1581, this committee gave its decision.

The Jesuit congregation reaffirmed three of the decisions of the Jesuits in 1571: a loan at 5 percent was "intrinsically evil," the triple contract was permissible, the redeemable annuity was permissible. It went on to teach that an annuity guaranteed to pay a return regardless of what happened to the base was also legitimate. Climactically, it taught that while annuities founded on personal labor were "most dangerous" and "not commonly to be tolerated," they were inherently moral. The cases in which the 5-percent contract was taken were approved "unless it had the character of a loan"; and the congregation added that the contract "has not necessarily such a character, unless it is made without respect of persons." The 5 percent was to be considered usury, if it was sought by force of a loan alone or if in a loan it was sought without pretext of title or with false title or with the deliberate exclusion of all titles or in a contract not called a loan in which no pretext existed. But if the person of the borrower was considered by the parties—that is, if the borrower were a merchant or the owner of fruitful lands or a working person, and the contract was made with him principally in consideration of his status, the 5-percent contract could be interpreted as either a triple contract or a real or personal *census*. It would then have "the character of a licit partnership or some tolerable *census*." The congregation stated specifically that the implicit intention of gaining in a licit way sufficed to justify the contract and that "although they [the parties] do not know of a type [of contract] expressed in such a way, yet if the circumstances are such on the part of the thing itself, so that they contract with a merchant or person not having fruitful goods, yet having the ability to work, there is no doubt that this 5 percent is licit."

In other words, whenever the ownership of money was temporarily transferred to a merchant or worker, if the parties intended to act licitly, the contract might be analyzed as a triple contract, or census, and the profit on the contract might be legitimized. The far-reaching implications of this decision are evident, and the influence of the decision was as widespread. In practice, it meant that only loans to aged or infirm persons without property or loans bearing a rate of interest beyond that obtainable in a triple contract, or census, needed to be considered as true loans falling within the usury prohibitions. The old usury prohibition was dead.[57]

How did the Jesuit theologians avoid the teaching of *Cum Onus*? Apparently by assuming that all of the specific provisions of the bull could be treated as purely pontifical law, which had failed to be accepted, the congregation found no need to mention the bull at all. The more difficult question of reconciling the new Jesuit decision with the earlier teaching of the papal magisterium on the divine law against usury was not faced but left to the ingenuity of theologians.

Gregory XIII had had the advice of the brightest Jesuits. He also knew the mind of Borromeo, for whom he felt "an almost incredible

esteem."[58] He knew, too, that the duke expected support for a strict position. On May 27, 1581, the pope answered Duke William, congratulated
him on his care for the salvation of his people, and gave his judgment.
All the duke had asked for was there in this solemn judgment of the
pope, except that Gregory XIII was cautious enough not to make a bull
out of his response. The pope declared that the contract for 5 percent
could "not be excused by any custom or human law, nor defended by
any good intention of the contracting parties, since it is prohibited by
divine and natural law....But if in Germany there is some other contract
in which 5 percent is received, which is celebrated in form and manner
different from the aforesaid, we do not by this intend to condemn or
approve it, unless it is particularly set out and considered that so what is
to be judged in its regard may be decreed, as is decreed in regard to what
has been proposed."[59] The response was a classic holding of the line.
Gregory XIII had ignored the advice of the Jesuits, invoked divine and
natural law, refused to reduce the 5-percent contract "implicitly" to
another licit contract, and had not even given approval to other contracts
that might be lawful. It is not surprising that the duke, receiving this
severe answer, believed it to be his duty to outlaw the 5-percent contract
of his country and ordered his courts not to enforce existing contracts.[60]

The duke's sweeping measure hit the commercial life of Bavaria
with force. Popular outcry was enormous; the legislature petitioned for
the revocation of his measure; and by 1583 in the face of general skepticism as to the soundness of his law following the decision of the pope,
the duke was compelled to reconsider. Now he knew who to turn to for
different theological advice, and he went to Gregorio de Valentia, who
was still teaching at Ingolstadt. Gregorio gave him the impression that
what was decisive were the Jesuit decisions of 1581, not the pope's
judgment.[61] He also provided contract forms which in his opinion met
the lenient requirements of the Jesuit theologians. The duke embraced
the advice and forms eagerly and told his subjects that while he could
never permit usury he would permit the redeemable annuity.[62] The legislature assured him that this was all that it had wanted, and with this wise
verbal compromise, there was no further confusion among the laity in
Germany. The 5-percent contract or "German contract" was now spoken
of as an annuity at 5 percent; it was everywhere adopted in Catholic
Germany; and even the German word for interest, *Zins*, was derived

from the Latin designation *census* for contracts of credit in the form of annuities.[63]

The conservatives among the Jesuits, however, were still uneasy and continued to raise troublesome doubts. But after a majority of the theologians of the German province had agreed with the Roman Jesuits' decisions of 1581, the General Claudio Aquaviva in 1589 ordered the licitness of "the German contract" to be held without dissent by the Jesuits in the province.[64] No papal action was undertaken to challenge this open undermining of Gregory XIII's judgment of 1581—not to mention the complete disregard now manifested of *Cum Onus* or *Detestabilis Avaritia*. A combination of theological and lay opposition had triumphed. Borromeo was not alive to see this end for the program of reform he had begun in 1565.

Later theologians followed the lead of the Jesuit congregation of 1581 and made explicit the reason it ignored *Cum Onus*. The most acute of Jesuit writers on economic morals, Leonard Lessius, said that the bull had set out positive law that had been neither promulgated nor received in northern Europe; in his country "the contrary practice has always continued."[65] He introduced a defense of the morality of personal annuities by referring to this constant practice in Belgium, Germany, and France and observing that "what so many learned and religious men do in so many provinces is not easily to be condemned."[66]

This approach to *Cum Onus* was not confined to the Jesuits. Martino Bonacina, a Milanese theologian who was a protégé of Cardinal Federico Borromeo and later titular bishop of Utica, taught that personal annuities were formally lawful: "Where the bull of Pius V was received," the contracts were to be "judged usurious."[67] But even in those regions this was a rule only for the external forum; in the internal forum, only a probable opinion held that the bull was binding.[68]

Bonacina adopted an additional technique for reducing the teaching of the bull. The pope had condemned discounting of annuities. But, Bonacina said, surely this determination could not apply when expense or effort was necessary to collect the return: "this case seems excepted by *epikeia*."[69] By this appeal to exceptions, which the legislator equitably must have intended, the way was open for the theologian's judgment as to what cases fell outside the absolute and universal condemnations of the pope.

Bonacina did not identify the countries in which *Cum Onus* was even binding as law in the external forum, but by the mid-eighteenth century, it was apparent that the bull was accepted as law nowhere. Alfonso Liguori, the most balanced and authoritative of eighteenth-century moralists, reported that the bull was not binding in Belgium, France, Germany, Spain, southern Italy, and even in Rome itself.[70] Liguori accepted as probably lawful all of the varieties of annuity that *Cum Onus* had condemned.

Cum Onus was discarded by being reinterpreted as positive pontifical law. *In Eam* was undermined by indirect contradiction and a distinction advanced by the leading Roman canonist, Navarrus. The indirect contradiction occurred in his teaching on the theory justifying exchange banking. The idea that the virtual transportation charge was literally the basis for the banker's profit was not only implied by the bull but also taught expressly by Pius V's Jesuit adviser, Toledo. But Navarrus had taught in 1556 that the price of money on the exchanges depended on the varying supply and demand and added that this was "recognized by the common sense of all good and bad men in Christendom and so, as it were, by the voice of God and nature."[71] When his work was turned into Latin from Spanish following the bull, Navarrus did not change his teaching; the contradiction of Pius V and Toledo was indirect in the sense that Navarrus did not bother to point out that the pope's notion of a profit founded on distance in space flew in the face of what was determined by God and nature. He tried instead to find a more plausible way of distinguishing between exchange banking and lending at a profit, and later theologians followed his example while ignoring the theory of the pope. In the words of Lessius, in contradiction to those of Pius V, variation in the price of exchange due to the time of payment "should probably not be disapproved when this variation occurs through the common judgment of merchants for reasons which commonly seem just to them."[72]

The distinction that Navarrus advanced was explicitly made to avoid the teaching of the bull. Whatever theory of exchanges one held, the bull had dealt a mortal blow to banking practice if its condemnation of the *ricorsa* was accepted. Asked about the *ricorsa* sometime after the death of Pius V, Navarrus responded that the bull condemned only bills of exchange that were unpaid in another city and returned for payment to the place in which the bill was drawn. But suppose, he said, that the bank purchasing the exchange has a branch in the other city that was willing to act as agent for the seller, pay the bill in his name, and draw a new bill for payment by him when the new bill is returned to the home bank. Surely in this case there was not a fictitious transaction that deserved the name of dry exchange because the seller actually transferred credit that he possessed in the foreign city in order to make a true payment there of the first bill of exchange. That the branch bank acted as both drawee and drawer was not an objection because one person could act in two different capacities.[73] By this mode of argument, Navarrus justified the usual form in which the *ricorsa* was practiced and at the same time deprived the bull of much practical significance for the bankers.

Bonacina thought such practice "very dangerous" and so advised Federico Borromeo.[74] But he did not dispute Navarrus's basic analysis, and to say "very dangerous" was not to follow Charles Borromeo's synod in declaring the *ricorsa* to be usury. In 1631 Navarrus's approach was formally adopted by a Roman commission of theologians.[75]

Detestabilis Avaritia met an even swifter rejection by the theologians than *Cum Onus* and *In Eam*. By the time it appeared in 1586 the Jesuits had gone on record twice, in the 1573 and 1581 decisions, as approving the triple contract; and both Toledo and Navarrus were solidly committed to it. The only prominent moralist who had directly challenged it was Soto, and when the bull first appeared, it was reported that here Soto's thought had vanquished Navarrus. But Sixtus V was quick to limit the significance of his teaching. He was reported to have said privately that he condemned only what "the classical doctors condemned"[76]—an ambiguous statement because the principles taught by classical doctors like Thomas Aquinas condemned the riskless loan but approved investment in a partnership, and the very question at issue was which principles were to be applied to a relatively new combination of contracts. More strikingly, Navarrus did not revise his teaching, and Toledo, now a cardinal, published an explicit defense of the triple contract in a work for confessors titled *A Summa of Cases of Conscience, or Instruction for Priests.*[77]

Another technique used by the theologians to correct the teaching of Sixtus V had been used in relation to the other bulls: to describe the document as positive pontifical law. *Detestabilis Avaritia* was found to be accepted nowhere. As lapsed positive law, then, it was found to be not binding.[78]

A second approach was taken by those who thought that the bull insisted too much on its basis in divine law to be merely a pontifical decree. These theologians taught that the bull merely prohibited contracts of partnership that were "naturally usurious"—those contracts in which the rate of return did not take into account the guarantee of the return of capital.[79] If the guarantee of capital was properly charged for, as by hypothesis it was charged for in the triple contract, then the bull's condemnation did not apply. This approach was implicit in Toledo's defense of contracts eliminating the risk of capital in partnerships. A footnote referred to the existence of *Detestabilis Avaritia* as though there was no conflict between its denunciation of agreements eliminating the risk of capital and Toledo's defense. By 1602 the Sacred Roman Rota had adopted this approach.[80] In doing so it reduced *Detestabilis Avaritia* as an act of pontifical authority to an aberrant nullity.

Conclusion

In the sixteenth century a transition in theological analysis and theological attitude toward lay experience in banking accompanied a change in economic conditions that made the old rule on profit-seeking on a loan obsolete. The theologians were unable to formulate a general theory that could explain how the old rule could change, for they identified this rule as unchanging divine and natural law. Instead of formulating a general theory, they advanced cases in which they proposed analyses justifying profit on credit. In these analyses they used principles familiar to their theological predecessors but hitherto restricted to prevent the undermining of the usury prohibition.

When the popes and bishops heard of the theological innovations, they correctly perceived that these devices were inconsistent with the maintenance of what they took to be the divine law on usury. In fulfillment of their duty they acted to repress the innovations. They acted with mature deliberation, after study and report by theologians. Three of the men most responsible for the decisions taken have been subsequently recognized by the church as saints—Charles Borromeo, Francis Borgia, and Pius V. But neither a sense of duty nor careful deliberation nor sanctity nor fidelity to the theology of the past assured that the papal teaching would determine in a final way the magisterium of the church. The papal teaching was an element in a complex process; its effect depended on the response of theologians and laity. Only in action and interaction was the teaching of the church established.

The theological task was not accomplished at once. It took twenty years of argument before the Jesuit decisions of 1581 were reached. The popes did not formally reconcile themselves to the theologians until the eighteenth century, although in practice by 1589 the theological analysis had replaced the papal one. But no automatic agency or influx of divine grace assumed that all would agree at once or that what the popes had given as authentic teaching would not be repealed.

In five ways—by reducing them to pontifical law (the Jesuit general congregations on annuities), by insisting on distinctions that the bulls had rejected (Navarrus on the *ricorsa*), by appeal to *epikeia* (Bonacina on the discount of annuities), by denying their theoretical assumptions (Navarrus and Lessius on exchange banking), and by restricting them to "naturally usurious" contracts as determined by the theologians' view of nature (Toledo on the triple contract), the theologians successfully resisted the papal attempts to teach what was morally permissible in credit taking. The theologians' efforts were successful, in part, because they were supported by the highest Jesuit authorities and by bishops like the bishop of Augsburg; they were also successful, in part, because Pius V and Sixtus V had short pontificates. But these administrative and personal contingencies should not obscure the fact that the accomplishment of the theologians was basically one of intellectual analysis stimulated by reflection on the common practice of Christians.

The theologians did not form their teaching on a close exegesis of the personal intention of the popes who promulgated the bulls or the personal intention of their advisers; plainly, the popes and the advisers who counseled them conceived of their task as the determination of divine and natural law. But the theologians controlled these personal papal intentions by appeal to a broader context of experience and principle. By this appeal they amended the teaching.

The theologians were weakest in not offering any explanation of the papal language that spoke of divine and natural law. This weakness related to their inability to explain how the whole divine and natural law on usury would not disappear if their approach to annuities, exchange banking, and commercial credit was adopted. A comprehensive theory of how these laws could be explained in terms of more basic values had to await the work of an eighteenth-century layman, Scipio Maffei, and it was not until the nineteenth century that Maffei's theory became a commonplace of the manuals. But if the question is asked, How and when did the usury prohibition change? the answer is, It changed in the sixteenth century, and it was changed by the theologians, over stubborn papal resistance, defending forms of behavior in which profit was sought in extending credit.

The theologians were strongest in recognizing that the experience and judgments of the laity had a value for moral teaching, in not abandoning principles or insights of their theological predecessors even when these principles led to results clearly undermining the usury rule, and in rejecting a facile but untrue explanation of the nature of banking. Thus, appealing to the experience of the faithful, Navarrus argued that an "infinite number of decent Christians" engaged in exchange banking, and he objected to any analysis that would "damn the whole world." Thus the principles permitting partnerships, insurance, the sale of rights, and the sale of exchange were not abandoned by any major theologian, although the implications of these principles undercut the usury rule. Thus, the pope's attempt to rest the distinction between exchange banking and lending upon an alleged distinction between distance in space and distance in time was ignored.

In this development of moral doctrine the three authentic acts of papal teaching, *Cum Onus, In Eam,* and *Detestabilis Avaritia* served the purpose of engaging theological attention in a close study of the conditions in which credit was extended. The weak, scrupulous, or badly informed were probably led by these bulls to abstain from contracts that those with access to more expert theological advice felt free to enter. In a short space of time—thirty years at the most—the bulls were deprived of force to influence anyone's behavior. Acts of papal authority, isolated from theological support and contrary to the conviction of Christians familiar with the practices condemned, could not prevail, however accurately they reflected the assumptions and traditions of an earlier age. The theologians were to have the last word, because acts of papal authority are inert unless taught by theologians, because those who cared consulted them, because they taught the next generation, and because the very categories in which the papal teaching was put were shaped by Christian experience and theological analysis.

Notes

1. *Catechismus Romanus* (Rome, 1871 ed.), "De septimo praecepto," 8, 11.

2. Urban III, *Consuluit, Decretales Gregorii IX,* ed. E. Friedberg (1879–1881), V, 19, 10.

3. St. Thomas Aquinas, *Summa theologica,* II–II, q. 78, a. 1.

4. Synod of Milan (1565), Part 2, "De usuris," *Constitutiones et decreta in provinciali synodo Mediolanensi, Actorum S. Mediolanensis Ecclesiae,* Vol. II, ed. Achille Ratti (1890).

Borromeo in his book for pastors also urged the necessity of preaching against the various contracts used to disguise usury. Under the heading "Sins which are more frequently committed against the commandments of the divine law and which are to be taken away by the zeal of the preacher," Borromeo enumerated "so many classes of contracts which have been devised in fraud of the law prohibiting all usury." *Pastorum instructiones* (Ghent, 1824 ed.), Part I, c. 12.

5. For a classic exposition of the triple contract, see Navarrus, *Enchiridion seu Manuale Confessariorum,* 17, n. 252, *Opera Omnia* (vol. 1; Lyons, 1589); for the history, see John T. Noonan, Jr., *The Scholastic Analysis of Usury* (1957), pp. 202–230.

6. For a full defense of personal annuities as known in Germany, see Conrad Summenhart, *Tractatus de contractibus licitis atque illicitis,* q. 79–84 (Venice, 1580); for the history, see Noonan, pp. 230–248.

7. The classic condemnation is St. Antoninus, *Summa sacrae theologiae,* 3, 8, 3 (Venice, 1581–1582).

8. For the sixteenth-century defense, see Cajetan, *De cambiis, Scripta philosophica: Opuscula oeconomica-socialia,* ed. P. Zammit (Rome, 1934); for the history, see Noonan, pp. 171–192, 310–335.

9. Cajetan, *In summam theologicam S. Thomae Aquinatis* (Leonine edition), II–II, 78, 1, ad 6.

10. Raymond De Roover, *The Rise and Decline of the Medici Bank* (1963), pp. 110–121.

11. Ibid., pp. 100–102.

12. *Summa sacrae theologiae* (Venice, 1581), 2, 1, 6 and 2.

13. Cajetan, *De societate negotiatoria,* nn. 422–423, in *Opuscula oeco-nomica-socialia,* ed. cited; Navarrus, *Manuale,* 17, 257; Navarrus, *Commentarius de usuris, Si foeneraveris,* 14, 33.

14. Borromeo to Ormaneto, November 18, 1587, reproduced in Pietro Ballerini, *Vindiciae iuris divini ac naturalis circa usuram* (Bologna, 1747), 4, 2. On Ormaneto's role with Pius V, see Ludwig Von Pastor, *History of the Popes,* trans. F. I. Antrobus, vol. V (St. Louis), pp. 138–139.

15. Ormaneto to Borromeo, December 6, 1587, in ibid.

16. James Broderick, *St. Peter Canisius* (1935), pp. 422–435.

17. Canisius to the Cathedral Chapter of Augsburg, June, 1564, in *Epistolae et acta,* ed. O. Braunsberger (1896–1923), vol. IV, p. 563.

18. Bernhard Duhr, "Die Deutschen Jesuiten im 5%-Streit des 16 Jahrhunderts," in *Zeitschrift für Katholische Theologie,* vol. 241 (1900), pp. 209–248; Ernest Joseph Van Roey, "Le Contractus Germanicus," in *Revue d'histoire ecclésiastique,* vol. III (1902), pp. 901–946 (1903).

19. Ursula of Liechtenstein, wife of George Fugger, to Borgia, April 25, 1565, in Canisius, *Epistolae,* vol. V, pp. 533–534. Ursula Fugger is described by Canisius in ibid., vol. III, pp. 653–654.

20. Borgia to Fugger, June 9, 1565, in ibid., vol. V, pp. 535–536.

21. Canisius to Borgia, July 26, 1587, in ibid., vol . V, p. 529.

22. Borgia to the Jesuit House at Lyons, February 16, 1568, in ibid., vol. V, p. 487.

23. Borgia, March 15, 1568, in ibid., vol. V, p. 487.

24. On Sirleto, see Pastor, op. cit., vol. 5, p. 37; on his role in the commission see Ballerini, op. cit. The man who was apparently first named as chairman, Cardinal Dolera, died in January, 1588.

25. On Navarrus, see Mariano Arigita y Lasa, *El Doctor Navarro Don Martin de Azplicueta y sus obras* (1905). On his choice for the Sacred Penitentiary by Borromeo, see ibid., p. 395.

26. Op. cit., vol. 5, pp. 53, 63–66.

27. *Bullarium Romanum* (Turin, 1863), vol. VII, p. 737.

28. Ibid., VII, p. 884.

29. The principal Jesuit adviser of the pope, Francisco Toledo, in his own later *Summa casuum conscientiae sive Instructio sacerdotum* (Cologne, 1610), stated, "It is not similar as to place and time": there was per se risk and labor in money absent in space, but not absent in time (Book 58, c. 53). The "excess or value ought to be proportionate to the distance" (58. 54).

30. On April 10, 1568, Borgia wrote Nicholas Lanoius, the Jesuit provincial in Austria, that Pius V, as a "private theologian," not as pope, approved the triple contract, in Canisius, *Epistolae,* vol. 5, p. 487.

31. *Bullarium Romanum* VIII, 783–785.

32. On restitution and cooperation, see St. Bernardine of Siena, *De contractibus*, 44, 3, 4, *De evangelio aeterno, Opera omnia.*

33. Canisius to Borgia, April 2, 1569, Canisius, *Epistolae*, VI, p. 287.

34. Schorich to Polanco, ibid., VI, p. 287.

35. Braunsberger in Canisius, *Epistolae*, VI, p. 287.

36. Borgia to Hoffaeus, June 17, 1510, ibid., VI, p. 410.

37. On Toledo, see *Bibliothèque de la Compagnie de Jésus*, ed. C. Sommervogel (1898), vol. 8, p. 64.

38. Hoffaeus to Borgia, June 17, 1571, ibid., VI, p. 416.

39. Navarrus reports only that he was consulted on behalf of the Jesuits by a "friend distinguished for learning and piety." Navarrus, *De usuris*, 22, n. 85, *Opera omnia*, vol. 1, p. 289.

40. Ibid., n. 105, vol. 1, p. 295.

41. Ibid., n. 105.

42. Ibid., nn. 106–107, vol. 1, p. 296.

43. On the commission and on the exclusion of Canisius, Braunsberger in Canisius, *Epistolae*, VII, pp. 671–672.

44. "Cases Disputed in a Congregation held in the name of the Reverend Father General, June 22, 1573," in ibid., VII, pp. 672–674.

45. Broderick, *St. Peter Canisius*, p. 737.

46. Theoderic Canisius, rector of Dillingen, to Edward Mercurian, General of the Society of Jesus, February 17, 1576, in Canisius, *Epistolae*, VII, pp. 341–343.

47. Ninguarda to Cardinal Como, December 2, 1580, in Duhr, op. cit., n. 18, p. 282.

48. Duhr, pp. 230, 237.

49. Mercurian to T. Canisius, March 16, 1576, ibid., VII, p. 321.

50. Hoffaeus to Oliverio Manareo, Vicar General of the Society of Jesus, October 2, 1580, ibid., VII, p. 575.

51. Duke William to Borromeo, February 8, 1581, Appendix to Pietro Ballerini, *De jure divino et naturali circa usuram libri sex* (Bologna, 1747) 1, p. 318.

52. Borromeo to Caesare Spetiano, procurator of Borromeo at Rome, February, 1581, in ibid., vol. 1, p. 318.

53. Spetiano to Borromeo, March 16, 1581, in ibid., vol. 1, p. 318.

54. Braunsberger in Canisius, *Epistolae*, VII, p. 389.

55. Ibid., p. 590; see Van Roey, op. cit., n. 18, pp. 939–940.

56. On Gregory de Valentia, 1551–1603, Duhr, op. cit., n. 18, p. 233; Sommervogel, vol. 8, cols. 388–389.

57. The decisions are summarized in Franz X. Zech, *Dissertationes tres, in quibus rigor moderatus doctrinae pontificae circa usuras a sanctissimo D. N.*

Benedicto XIV per epistolam encyclicam episcopis Italiae traditae exhibetur (Venice, 1762), reprinted in J. P. Migne, *Theologiae cursus completus,* vol. 16 (1841) Dissertation 2, nn. 259–264. See Braunsberger in Canisius, *Epistolae,* VI, p. 590. Evidence of the decisions of 1581 is provided not only by Zech but also by a manuscript described by Duhr, p. 240, *Tractatus circa contractum quinque pro centum, ex communi consensu patrum ad id in quarta congregatione generali Societatis Jesu deputatorum, confectus mense Aprili 1581.*

58. Pastor, vol. 19, p. 28.

59. Text of papal brief and accompanying papal judgment in Van Roey, p. 941, and in Ballerini op. cit., n. 50, 1, pp. 321–322.

60. Zech, Dissertation 2, n. 265–276

61. Valentia to Aquaviva, September 21, 1583, Duhr, p. 242; Van Roey, p. 943.

62. Duhr, p. 244; Zech, Dissertation 2, n. 270.

63. Franz X. Funk, *Zins und Wucher* (Tübingen, 1869), p. 115.

64. Aquaviva to Canisius, March 2, 1589, in Canisius, *Epistolae,* VIII, p. 282.

65. *De justitia et jure ceterisque virtutibus cardinalibus libri quatuor ad 2.2 D. Thomae quaestione 47 ad quaestionem* 171 (Lyons, 1630), 2, 22, 12, 98–99.

66. Ibid., 2, 22, 4, 10.

67. *De contractibus* 3, 4, 3, *Opera omnia* (Venice, 1754).

68. Ibid., 3, 4, 46.

69. Ibid., 3, 4, 43.

70. *Theologia moralis,* ed. Gaudé (Rome 1947), 3, 5, 3, 9, 849.

71. *Commentarium resolutorium de cambiis,* 20, 51 (Venice, 1602), *Opera,* vol. 1. On the dates see Arigita, pp. 276, 520.

72. *De justitia* 2, 23, 91.

73. Navarrus, *Consilia,* V, 19, 1, 6–10. This counsel was published posthumously in 1591 and in other later editions of Navarrus's works. Arigita, p. 527.

74. *De contractibus* 3, 5, 1, 10.

75. Juan de Lugo, *Disputationes scholasticae et morales* (Paris, 1893), vol. 8, Disputatio 28, 7, 84.

76. Liguori, Book 3, n. 908.

77. *Summa,* 58, 41.

78. Lessius, *De justitia* 25; 33; Book 3, n. 908.

79. Lugo, *Disputatio* 30, n. 37; Liguori, Book 3, n. 908.

80. "Coram Coccino, June 3, 1602," reported in Zech, op. cit., n. 54, Dissertatio 2, n. 175.

8. The Right to Silence: Magisterial Development

Patrick Granfield

This chapter first appeared in *Theological Studies* 26 (1965).

Modern legal systems, Continental and Anglo-American, agree that the criminally accused is not bound to confess his crime. Moralists today unanimously hold that this right to silence flows from the fundamental dignity of the human person and is adequately formulated by the ancient maxim *nemo tenetur prodere seipsum.*[1] History has shown that the law of obligatory self-incrimination was not observed in practice because it demanded too much of the individual.

Our present study concerns doctrinal development, one of the most pressing questions in contemporary theology. Taking the insights of Newman and Möhler, modern theologians such as Rahner and Lonergan have constructed theories of development. These attempts to refine the previously inadequate implicit-to-explicit explanation of development, besides possessing intrinsic value, also have far-reaching ecumenical import. Theologians, spurred on by Leo XIII's *vetera novis augere et perficere,* are more and more investigating the complex process of explicitation in a historical perspective. Traditional teachings of the church are being reconsidered in their various stages of emergence. In the controversial area of contraception, for example, we have a pioneer study by John T. Noonan, who earlier had written on the problem of usury.[2]

In this article we will analyze the development of the right to silence in the magisterial pronouncements of the church. That this is an intriguing problem can readily be seen from the fact that it was not until 1917, with the appearance of the Code of Canon Law, that the church officially guaranteed this right of the accused in ecclesiastical trials. In shocking contrast, the right to silence was a working part of English law by the early 1700's and was incorporated into the Federal Constitution by the Fifth Amendment in 1791. The restriction of the exercise of the privilege against self-incrimination in Communist Russia, Iron Curtain countries, and some Latin American dictatorships indicates that this problem is of considerable current interest.

What are the significant statements of the teaching authority of the church relevant to the right of the accused to remain silent when questioned about his crime? What is the historical background and value of these pronouncements? Can we derive from them evidence of a gradual, organic development of an enlightened view of man's rights? These are the questions that we hope to answer in this article. We will begin with a study of seven documents in chronological order.

DOCUMENTATION

"Such is the unity of all history that anyone who endeavors to tell a piece of it must feel that his first sentence tears a seamless web."[3] This is especially true to anyone who attempts to trace the development of a particular doctrine. Therefore, to understand correctly the documents to be given shortly, it is necessary to see them in their proper historical perspective. A few introductory remarks about the background of church law are in order.

It is understandable why the infant church used the existing legal system when it could, since many of the ordinary acts of its daily administration were of the same nature as civil actions. Roman law, then, became the supplementary source of ecclesiastical law, and thus the expression *ecclesia viget lege romana.*[4] Pope Gregory I (590–604), for example, ordered that Roman law be used when no ruling in ecclesiastical law was found to answer a disputed question.[5] Later codifications of church law, both the *Corpus iuris canonici* (the decretal collections) and the *Codex iuris canonici,* are basically Roman in spirit, as is the whole of European law.

In Roman law, under the empire, criminal procedure took on many inquisitorial features, since the state spared no effort to stamp out crime. The defendant, faced with the absolutist character of law enforcement, was put in a precarious position. No longer could he, as in the earlier accusatorial procedure, refuse to reveal his crime and go unpunished. The state by means of torture would force him to confess. Confession became the goal of every judge. Torture, although it was criticized by many jurists, became the usual means for eliciting confession, and it remained an essential part of Continental criminal procedure well into the eighteenth century. One author explains its success when he observes that "it is a mode of procedure so humanly obvious that it would be difficult for one to imagine an age in which it could not be found."[6] There is no provision in Roman law for allowing the accused to remain silent, since in serious crimes the law demanded a confession for conviction.

With this background in mind, we can now proceed to the documents.

The Response of Pope Nicholas I to the Bulgarians, 866

In the middle of the ninth century, Prince Boris of the Bulgarians desired to have his people become Christians. He turned first to Constantinople, but dissatisfied with his discussions with the church officials there, he sent a delegation to Rome in 866. They presented to Pope Nicholas I a list of 106 questions. On November 13 the responses were given. Response 86 deals with torture, which was used in the courts to get confessions from the accused. Pope Nicholas's reply is a formal condemnation of torture, which he says is against the divine and human law. His language is colorful:

> You say that in your land, when a thief or a brigand has been arrested and denies his guilt, the judge has him struck on the head and pricked in the sides with hot irons until he confesses. But neither divine nor human law can in any way admit this. For confession should be free; it should not be extorted by violence but voluntarily proffered. And then if after using these torments, you fail to discover anything, are you not ashamed and do you not see how impiously you judge? If, on the contrary, overcome by pain, the victim admits a crime he has not committed, on whom, I ask, falls the infamy of so great a wickedness if not on him who has forced the unfortunate man to lie? He who utters with his

mouth what is not in his heart, may speak indeed but does not acknowledge guilt. Drop these customs therefore and wholly condemn what hitherto you have done from ignorance.[7]

Pope Nicholas's statement is significant, because it is such an obvious condemnation of the Roman-law tradition advocating torture. While presuming the necessity of confession and making no allowance for silence, the pope insists that it should be voluntary. His words about the unreliability of confessions exacted by torture echo the sentiments of the jurist Ulpian three centuries earlier.[8] In condemning the barbaric institution of the *quaestio* (which in time became synonymous with torture), the pope clearly indicates his unwillingness to allow tribunals to use any and every means to procure confession. In view of his cultural milieu, his is a profound insight into human nature and only one step short of recognizing the moral impossibility of asking a man to condemn himself by his own words.

The Bull Ad extirpanda *of Innocent IV, 1252*

This "one step" unfortunately was not taken for many centuries, and torture, embedded deeply in the juridical structure of Europe, was not to be abolished by a single papal statement. While one may agree with Vacandard that torture "had left too many sorrowful memories in the minds of the Christians of the first centuries for them to dream of employing it in their own tribunals,"[9] nevertheless medieval justice, both civil and ecclesiastical, considered it an indispensable part of court procedure. The ordeal, with its hot iron, molten lead, and boiling water, became commonplace. From the eighth to the thirteenth century it was accepted by many local ecclesiastical courts with the approval of their bishops, who felt that it was a reliable way to discover the *judicium Dei.*[10] The popes, however, never approved of the ordeal and succeeded in finally condemning it in 1215 at the Fourth Lateran Council.[11]

The papacy in the thirteenth century, however, faced with the revival of Roman law and the practice of torture in the civil tribunals, and above all anxious at the presence of virulent heresy in the church, approved the use of torture by the secular arm against heretics. For a long time the church hesitated in advocating physical coercion in dealing with heretics.[12] In time, the threat of excommunication and other spiritual penalties failed to control the fanatical tendencies of the heretics, and more severe methods were deemed necessary.

The heresy of Catharism made this expedient. Catharism first appeared in the eleventh century and soon spread throughout Europe. Described as "an altogether alien and contradictory religion into which some Christian terms had been forced,"[13] Catharism denied the Incarnation, the Resurrection, the mass, and the sacraments, and was hostile to all ecclesiastical discipline. This heresy so endangered the state and the church that its suppression became a political necessity. Heresy, besides being a serious sin, was also considered a grave offense against civil authority.[14]

On May 15, 1252, the papal bull *Ad extirpanda* of Innocent IV decreed that civil power is bound to force heretics by torture to admit their error and denounce their accomplices. It was sent to civil and religious authorities of Romagna, Lombardy, and the March of Treviso. Law 25 of the bull states:

> Since heretics are really brigands and murderers of souls and thieves of God's sacraments and the Christian faith, the secular power or the ruler is bound to force, without loss of limb or danger of death, all heretics he apprehends to expressly confess their errors. He must also force them to reveal other heretics whom they know, their defenders, just as thieves and robbers of temporal things are bound to reveal their accomplices and to confess the evil deeds which they committed.[15]

Innocent IV states explicitly that it is the law for criminals to confess their evil deeds and to reveal their accomplices. He applies this to heretics ("thieves...of the Christian faith"). In both cases there is no thought of the accused appealing to his right of silence. Such a possibility was completely foreign to the legal conscience of the time. The solution proposed is quite simple: The accused must confess his crime; if he does not, then the court must use torture. It is obvious that if the court can torture the accused in order to elicit a confession, then a fortiori the accused must be obliged to confess his crime when legitimately questioned by the judge.[16] Otherwise you would have the paradoxical situation in which the court forces someone to do something which he is not bound to do.

Theologians felt that torture was necessary for the suppression of crime and that individual interests must be sacrificed to the common good. St. Alphonsus (1696–1787), for example, did not object to its use, but he added that it should be used only in serious crimes in which complete proof is impossible without a confession.[17] Torture was to be used when all other means failed. However, St. Alphonsus took a more lenient view in solving the practical problem of the confessor's absolving an accused person who is unwilling to confess his crime. He states: "All rightfully agree that if the accused is in good faith, and it may be thought difficult to persuade him to confess his crime when questioned by a judge, the confessor ought to leave him in good faith."[18]

A vexing problem is to reconcile the statement of Pope Nicholas I with the decree of Innocent IV. Vacandard remarks that Innocent IV in recommending the use of torture certainly did not know the existence of the text of Pope Nicholas I and that he was conforming to the customs of the times and following the practice of the civil courts.[19] Journet feels that there are two possible approaches to the problem.[20] First, he observes that historians might discover that torture was so much a part of the criminal procedure that it would have been most difficult for the church to forbid its use. If the church wanted the help of the secular power in suppressing heresy, it could hardly go against a practice of such long standing. In this supposition the church would not have approved of torture but in the light of the circumstances, merely tolerated its use with the hope that more just penal codes in the future would not require it. The other possibility is that historians may find that torture, far from being tolerated as a necessary evil, was positively approved and encouraged. In that supposition, the historian ought to condemn those who supported it and "to denounce a concession made to the powers of evil for which they alone should bear the responsibility before history, before the Church, and before God...."[21] Journet cautions against concluding from the use of torture in dealing with heretics that the sanctity of the church is affected. "The errors," he writes, "of the canonical power in purely particular decisions, due to the deficiencies of its ministers, do not touch her inner sanctity."[22]

The Catechism of the Council of Trent, 1566

More than three hundred years passed before there was another magisterial statement about the defendant's rights in court. When the Council of Trent met in 1545, there were already many catechisms in existence. However, the need was felt for a better manual of Christian doctrine that could be used by those beginning to study religion. The fathers of the Council ordered that such a catechism be drawn up and appointed St. Charles Borromeo to head a commission of theologians who were to undertake this task. This took place in the eighteenth session, Feb. 26, 1562. The theologians set to work on a catechism that could be used by children and uninstructed adults to prepare them for further religious education by giving them the rudiments of Catholic doctrine. On Sept. 11, 1563, the Council altered the original plan somewhat. They decided to make the catechism more thorough and complete, so that it could be used by parish priests in instructing the faithful. The work was completed and approved in 1566 under the title *Catechismus ex decreto Concilii Tridentini ad parochos, Pii V Pont. Max. jussu editus.* Since that time it has been known by many names: the Catechism of the Council of Trent, the Catechism for Parish Priests, the Roman Catechism, or the Catechism of Pius V.[23] Under the Eighth Commandment we find mention of the defendant's obligation:

> In regard to an accused person who is conscious of his own guilt, God commands him to confess the truth if he is interrogated judicially. By that confession he in some way bears witness to and proclaims the praise and glory of God; and of this we have a proof in these words of Josue, when exhorting Achan to confess the truth: "My son, give glory to the Lord the God of Israel."[24]

In this text the accused who is in fact guilty is said to be obliged by the divine law ("God commands him") to confess the truth when he is questioned in court. By his confession he gives glory to God by respecting the virtues of truth and obedience. The *Catechism* states this in the form of a principle without giving any explanation. What is the exact meaning of "judicial interrogation"? Are there any possible exceptions to the principle? Must the accused confess his crime even when he faces the death penalty?

The *Catechism* gives no answer. Inevitably, there were theological commentaries on the *Catechism* that did treat these difficulties. The most famous of these appeared over a hundred years after the publication of the *Catechism* and was written in 1694 by the Dominican theologian Natalis Alexander, who followed the teaching of St. Thomas and Cajetan. He explains that before the accused can be legitimately questioned by the judge, there must first be some evidence, infamy (public knowledge), or partial proof that the accused committed the crime. When one of these is present, then the accused must confess the truth "simply and without ambiguities, even though he knows certainly that by this confession he will condemn himself to death."[25]

Theologians of the sixteenth and seventeenth centuries, following the existing positive law demanding confession, agree with the Catechism of Trent. The majority of theologians support the opinion of St. Thomas, who taught that "the accused is in duty bound to tell the judge the truth, which the latter exacts from him according to the form of the law *(secundum formam iuris),*"[26] even if this admission would lead to condemnation. The virtue of obedience requires that the accused be bound *sub mortali* to obey the judge. "If he refuses to tell the truth which he is under obligation to tell, or if he mendaciously deny it, he sins mortally."[27] St. Thomas confronts the objection that no one is bound to condemn himself, or as St. John Chrysostom puts it, "I do not say that you should lay bare your guilt publicly, nor accuse yourself before others" *(Hom. 31 on Hebrews).* He says that the accused in court does not lay bare his guilt. Rather, the judge imposes an obligation and he must obey it. Instead of the accused revealing his own guilt, "his guilt is unmasked by another."[28] The operative phrase in St. Thomas's discussion is *"secundum formam iuris."* In other words, St. Thomas structures his teaching around the existing positive legislation, which was Roman in origin and required confession. If the law changes, then the corresponding obligation to reply would also change.

Not all theologians accepted St. Thomas's opinion. Yet we do find such men as Cajetan, Dominic Soto, Schmalzgrueber, and Salmanticenses following the Thomistic, or traditional, view. Others, including Abbas Panormitanus, Peter of Navarre, Emmanuel Rodriguez,

Lessius, Lugo,[29] Diana, and Reiffenstuel, opted for a less rigorous teaching.[30] They argued that it was inhuman for a man to condemn himself and that under certain conditions, when faced with severe penalties, the accused might deny his crime.

The Provincial Council of Rome, 1725

The next stage in the development of the church's recognition of the defendant's rights came in 1725, when the Provincial Council of Rome abolished all oaths in ecclesiastical criminal trials. The council observes that experience has shown that the oath *de veritate dicenda* is no guarantee that the defendant will tell the truth. It is useless, since even under oath defendants "usually deny the crimes of which they are charged." In suppressing this oath, the council decreed that it could be required of defendants only when they were "examined as witnesses in the trials of other individuals." The use of oaths in any other way renders the whole examination null and void. The text reads:

> It must not be judged reprehensible that, because of changing conditions of the times and for reasons of necessity and utility, human laws and customs sometimes vary.... Because of this, we consider the practice in some secular and ecclesiastical courts of judges, in the process of examining the defendant in criminal trials, to demand of them the oath *de veritate dicenda* to be well-established, even though the said practice was never established by law. On the other hand, as daily experience shows, no advantage accrues to the prosecution from this practice, and nothing is proven against the defendant by this custom (as the defendants usually deny the crimes of which they are charged)....Hence it is that we, having weighed both sides of the question carefully and following as closely as possible the practice of the well-organized tribunals, command that all oaths tendered to the defendants in criminal trials be completely abolished and suppressed....Nor do we wish an oath of this kind to be exacted of the defendants in the future (unless they are examined as witnesses in the trials of other individuals) by

> any judge or official under any pretext, cause, or artifice;
> otherwise an examination thus conducted and all the oaths
> of the process shall be null and void and shall lack all bind-
> ing force against the criminal.[31]

The use of oaths in ecclesiastical courts has a long history. The *Corpus iuris canonici* refers to the *iuramentum calumniae* and the *iuramentum de veritate dicenda.*[32] The former assured the judge of the good faith of the litigants and was given to protect the defendant from possible unjust prosecution of the plaintiff. Both parties took the oath *de veritate dicenda,* which apparently assured the truth of their statements. The judge had the right to question the parties.[33] If the question was legitimate and the accused refused to answer it without a sufficient reason, his refusal would be, depending on the type of question asked, the same as a confession of guilt.[34]

Although the Council of Rome was a provincial council that legislated only for the Italian dioceses, it is important because of the authority of the Roman See and practice. It was not long before diocesan tribunals throughout the world followed Rome's example and suppressed the oath *de veritate dicenda* in criminal trials. In time it became the universal law of the church.[35]

We cannot conclude from the Council of Rome that the accused was no longer bound to reply to the judge's questions.[36] The council's intention was to remove the proximate occasion of the sin of perjury, without releasing the defendant from his duty to confess his crime when questioned. The council's decree is noteworthy, since it indicates a realistic appreciation of the problem that is derived from everyday experience. It points the way to future legislation favoring the defendant.

The Jubilee Decrees of 1749, 1775, 1824

Nearly twenty-five years after the Council of Rome we find a series of papal constitutions that do little to encourage an amelioration of the harsh law of obligatory self-incrimination. In the jubilee decrees of 1749, 1775, and 1824, three popes reaffirmed the traditional teaching requiring the defendant's confession.

In the Constitution *Paterna caritas,* which was given at Rome on December 17, 1749, Pope Benedict XIV decreed that the jubilee indulgence could also be gained by certain classes of people who were unable to come to Rome and fulfill the necessary conditions. In the category are nuns, oblates, tertiaries, anchorites, hermits, the infirm, those over seventy years of age, those in prison, those awaiting trial or awaiting sentence, those in exile, and those in the galleys. Benedict XIV goes on to explain the powers that confessors have in dealing with these categories, and he points out the special duty the confessor has toward prisoners. The text is given here:

> Let the confessors thus chosen, having heard diligently the confessions of these people, absolve them from every sin, crime, and delict no matter how grave and serious it may be, even though it is reserved to the Holy See or contained in the Bull *Die coenae domini.* A salutary penance should be given them, and to others the sanctions provided for by the canons should be imposed as well as the rules of proper conduct. The confessors should warn especially those who are in prison and whose case is not yet finished that they are bound by a serious obligation to reveal the truth about their crimes to the judges when they are questioned by legitimate authority. If they do not intend to do this, they would not only receive sacramental absolution invalidly, but greater harm would come to their souls. If they have this intention and have the other dispositions, their sins may be rightly confessed. However, the absolution they will receive from the confessor, while it may be salutary and beneficial and useful in the internal forum, has no effect in taking away the temporal punishments they deserve in the external forum.[37]

According to this Constitution, confessors are directed to warn their penitents who are defendants in criminal cases that they have a serious obligation to make known the truth when they are legitimately questioned. This is an obligation, not a matter of counsel. Unless the penitent intends to do this, sacramental absolution must be denied him. The pope does not make any qualifications, nor does he mention any milder opinion permitting the accused to refuse to admit his crime.

Two other popes in instructions to jubilee confessors repeat the prescription of Benedict XIV. Pope Pius VI, in *Paterna caritas urget nos* (Feb. 26, 1775), gives the same instructions,[38] as does Leo XII in the Constitution *Studium paternae caritatis* (Oct. 18, 1824).[39] However, in the jubilees before and after these three popes, there is no mention of this particular restriction. The decrees of the jubilees of 1700, 1725, 1900, and 1925 are silent on this point.[40]

Theologians made very little use of the jubilee decrees. Those theologians who prefer the milder opinion do not feel that the decrees present any problem.[41] Pruner, for example, feels that the decree of Benedict XIV should not be taken as a decision in favor of the more rigorous view. The milder opinion, he points out, does not allow one to lie. At the same time, it does not require that one confess everything in court. Pruner interprets the words of the jubilee decree, "to reveal the truth about their crimes," to mean that the accused is bound to tell the truth in court, but not necessarily the whole truth.

Regatillo and Zalba refer to the Constitution *Paterna caritas* of Benedict XIV when they discuss the rights of the defendant.[42] They attempt to reconcile it with the present Code of Canon Law, which states in Canon 1743,1° that the defendant in criminal trials is not bound to answer direct questions about his crime. They argue that if Benedict XIV in *Paterna caritas* taught that absolution should be denied those defendants who conceal the truth, then it must be interpreted in the following manner: When the common good requires that the accomplices of the defendant be discovered in order to avoid serious harm to the community, which otherwise could not be averted, then the defendant must reveal the names of these accomplices. In other words, he is bound to testify concerning the crime of another, not about his own crime. Regatillo and Zalba seem to read into the papal Constitution a limitation that is not found in the text itself.

The Procedural Norms of the Roman Rota, 1910

In 1910 the Roman Rota published a detailed system of procedural norms to be used in ecclesiastical trials. These norms had a widespread influence, since the Roman Tribunal of the Sacred Rota stood as the model for diocesan curias all over the world. Many of these procedural regulations became the source for what is today the universal law of the church. Canons 1742–1746, dealing with the interrogation of the parties, follow these rules quite closely in some sections. In other respects, however, particularly concerning the obligation of the defendant to reply, we find some marked differences. Article 109, 1, for instance, decrees in harmony with the 1725 Council of Rome that in criminal trials no oath is to be given to the accused. Articles 137, 138, 139, and 141 concern us more, and they are here given in full:

> *Article 137.* 1. Both parties have the right to draw out of the judicial confession of the adverse party a proof of the facts pertinent to the cause.
>
> 2. It is permitted even in criminal causes, and generally in all other causes that have reference to the public good, that the promoter of justice propose interrogations and allegations upon which the defendant is to be examined.
>
> 3. In causes that are concerned with the matrimonial bond and the validity of sacred ordination, the defender of the bond enjoys the same privilege.
>
> *Article 138.* During the examination each party has the right to request that certain interrogations be made and allegations presented with a view to obtaining a confession from the adverse party. But the request must specify the individual counts regarding which an answer is sought from the adverse party.
>
> *Article 139.* When such a request is accepted by the court, it is the judge who orders the party to reply to the question or to affirm or deny the presented allegation. If the party flaunts the precept of the judge, then the alleged facts will be deemed as true, and as admitted and confessed by the party.
>
> *Article 141.* The decree by means of which the allegations and the interrogations are accepted by the court must contain along with the text of the proposed questions and assertions the warning and threat that, if the party refuses to answer or offers no reasonable excuse for his silence or his absence, the alleged facts will be regarded as true and substantiated by the party's confession.[43]

The Roman Rota, then, as late as 1910, demanded that the parties answer the questions the judge put to them. This applies even in criminal trials, in which the oath *de veritate dicenda* is not required. If the party refuses to answer the questions or offers no reasonable excuse, then the point in question is considered true. The regulations do not explain the nature of a "reasonable excuse," nor do they exempt the accused in criminal trials from confessing his own guilt.

The Code of Canon Law, 1917

The *terminus ad quem* of our study in the development of the right to silence is the Code of Canon Law, which went into effect on May 18, 1917.[44] A controversy that had lasted for six centuries was abruptly settled by the church when it explicitly recognized in its law the privilege against self-incrimination. Canon 1743, 1° reads: "The parties are bound to answer and manifest the truth to a judge who legitimately questions them, unless it is a question of a delict they themselves have committed."[45]

According to the Code, a person may volunteer such information if he wishes, but he cannot be forced in any way to do so. If the public good is involved, the judge has a duty and a right to question the party. Commentators, following canon 19, agree that it is not unlawful to question the accused about even his personal crimes.[46] However, although the judge may legitimately question the party, he cannot impose any obligation on him to answer. Furthermore, if the defendant refuses to answer, as is his right, his refusal or silence cannot be taken as a confession. The Code seeks to protect the accused. It makes no mention of *semi-plena probatio,* fear of severe punishment, or hope of escaping such punishments. The law clearly intends to relieve the accused from his dilemma of being either forced to condemn himself or to lie. To secure this right to silence, canon 1744 states that in criminal cases the judge is not permitted to give the oath *de veritate dicenda* to the accused.[47]

The Code makes other observations concerning interrogation. First of all, the judge must be competent to try the case before his court.[48] The questions asked must be pertinent, and no one, witness or defendant, can be obliged to testify if he fears that his answers will incriminate him or will harm the reputation of, or cause dangerous vexations to, himself or his relatives by either consanguinity or affinity.[49] Professional information is privileged, and information received from a sacramental confession cannot be used in any way.[50]

EVALUATION

1. On the magisterial level, no evidence of an organic development of the right to silence appears in the documents we have studied. Occasionally a progressive element may be noted (e.g., *Responsio* of Nicholas I and the Council of Rome), but subsequent history failed to develop it in any significant way.

Rather, we discover a sudden, abrupt change. The privilege against self-incrimination is officially recognized for the first time by the church in the Code of Canon Law. In all the pre-Code documents there is either an explicit or implicitly presumed affirmation of the necessity of self-incrimination. This was, as we have seen, supported by the positive law, which was Roman in origin. This practice was too strongly embedded in the cultural worldview of church law to be easily put aside. The balance, efficiency, and success of Roman-law methods were apparently too revered by the church to permit contrary customs to gain official approval. It is understandable that the status quo continued until powerful and popular forces necessitated a change.

The documents we have examined possess different magisterial value. There are a moral *responsio,* a papal bull, a catechism composed and approved by a general council, a statement from a provincial council, a series of papal constitutions, and some procedural norms of the Rota. In none of them is found a precise, unambiguous dogmatic statement on the right to silence proposed to the universal church as binding. The very absence of any definitive statement is a strong indication that the church's stand was conditioned by the existing culture. The church took for granted that the law of self-incrimination best served the cause of justice and saw no reason to change it.

2. On the theological level, on the other hand, there was a genuine development that was possible only because many theologians considered the magisterial statements as directive, not prescriptive. Since the time of St. Thomas there were two schools of thought on the rights of the defendant. Those advocating a more lenient view argued that the law

obliging the accused to confess his crime was unreasonable. Various degrees of probability were attached to this view, but the note *sententia communis* was reserved for the Thomistic position.

A remarkable change took place in the middle of the nineteenth century. Theologians began to teach that the defendant was not bound to confess his crime when questioned by the judge. They presented their position positively and not simply as an opinion that may be held. It was not proposed in opposition to the law but supported by it. The *ordo legis* had changed and with it theological thought.

Francis Patrick Kenrick, following American legal norms, affirms that the accused can plead "not guilty" without lying. He refers to the traditional theological opinion and concludes that "since our form of trial is different, we do not feel it is necessary to spend any more time discussing this opinion."[51] The Italian moralist Berardi is even more explicit. He holds that the natural law and the common good cannot force one to confess, and "regardless of any interrogation of a civil judge, he is not bound to do so."[52] Noldin and Génicot, both writing before the Code, agree that the accused is not bound to confess.[53] Génicot makes the accurate observation that the only controversy concerning this problem is found in canon law, in which the older opinion is still in force.

3. Ultimately it was a change in civil law that influenced theological and magisterial opinion. The privilege against self-incrimination evolved slowly in civil law. Although it was well established in English law by the beginning of the eighteenth century, it took another century and a half before Continental law adopted it. Before that time brutal and cruel mutilations were often given for petty crimes; the court was all-powerful, and the individual had little or no security against unjust persecution. The public, accustomed as they were to the situation, were apathetic to such abuses, and there was no general interest in reforming the law.

The first humanitarian reactions appeared on the Continent in the 1700's, and popular attention was drawn to the movement of legal reform by the writings of Montesquieu, Voltaire, and Beccaria.[54] Toleration, reason, and humanity was the rallying cry against the barbaric judicial system.

In France in 1788, the States General met and by means of *cahiers,* written recommendations of the constituents to their delegates, public opinion made itself felt. Some of the more important demands were: (1) equal rights before the law and mitigation of the cruel penal system; (2) suppression of discretionary powers of the judge; (3) abolition of oaths imposed on the accused; (4) abolition of torture.[55] Many of these suggestions are found in the law of October 8–9, 1789, which was enacted by the Constitutional Assembly. Oaths and torture were abolished, and Article 13 decreed that when the accused first appears before the judge, the complaint must be read to him and the name of the denunciator given. The judge must appoint a counsel for the accused if he does not have one. The Code of Criminal Examination of 1808 also provided for counsel for the accused.

In 1880 the French Code of Criminal Examination was reformed, and an explicit reference is made to the defendant's obligation to reply. Article 85 states that at the first interrogation, the following practice must be followed: "The examining magistrate establishes the identity of the prisoner, makes him cognizant of the facts charged against him, and receives his statements, after having warned him that he has the right to refuse to reply to the questions put to him."[56]

Legal reform in France and the writings of Voltaire and Beccaria had a wide influence throughout Europe. Frederick II of Prussia, in the years 1754–56, abolished torture and corrected many of the unjust severities of his criminal system. Empress Catherine II of Russia drew up an outline of a new criminal code that was based on Beccaria's principles, and although a war against the Turks prevented the full realization of her plan, the most obvious abuses were remedied. In Italy, the Grand Duke Leopold of Tuscany issued in 1786 a new criminal code favoring the defendant. At the time of the unification of Italy in 1859 many local legal codes had improved greatly, and the Italian Criminal Code of 1865 has a decided humanitarian orientation.[57]

4. The present position of the church on the right to silence as seen in the Code of Canon Law is not a spontaneous achievement but the result of a long theological history. Many factors have contributed to this movement, which may be called, in Lonergan's term, transcultural. It is a process from one way of thinking to another, from one highly particularized worldview to another. In other words, one experiential priority has been replaced by another.

The traditional teaching of medieval theology on the right to silence was possible only in a culture that did not recognize fully the rights of the individual. The overmastering role of the state and the common good were emphasized to such a degree that the correlative rights of man were often neglected. In defense of this position it must be admitted that any restriction was made in the cause of justice. Torture, moral coercion, and obligatory self-incrimination were advocated (some would say tolerated) because it was felt that in the long run they promoted the greater good of the community.

The development of the right to silence does not follow the classical example of Christological development. In the latter we have in a relatively short time, a movement from the concrete, graphic descriptions of Christ in the New Testament to the metaphysical, abstract analysis of the *mysterium Christi* by the fathers of Nicaea. The right to silence did develop but not, at least on the official magisterial level, by a gradual, organic process. The church's recognition of this right was sudden and long overdue.

It was the presence of a persistent contrary theological opinion and a dramatic change in the civil law that finally influenced the church. Germinally, the final solution goes back to the fifteenth century. The dissenting opinion, however, while openly taught, was always presented in deference to the long-standing traditional opinion. A sense of urgency was given by the change in the civil law. It was not long after that the church, moved by the Spirit "who breathes where He will," acknowledged the right of man to refuse to condemn himself by his own words.

Notes

1. Cf. P. Granfield, O.S.B., "The Right to Silence," *Theological Studies* 26 (1965) 280–98.

2. Cf. John T. Noonan, Jr., *Contraception: A History of Its Treatment by the Catholic Theologians and Canonists* (Cambridge, Mass., 1965); *The Scholastic Analysis of Usury* (Cambridge, Mass., 1957).

3. F. Pollock and F. W. Maitland, *History of English Law* 1 (2nd ed.; Cambridge, Mass., 1899) 1.

4. Cf. A. Esmein, *A History of Continental Criminal Procedure,* trans. J. Simpson (Boston, 1913) 24.

5. *Epist.* 13 (*MGH, Gregorii epistolae* 1, 47).

6. P. Morelli, "Tortura," *Enciclopedia cattolica* 12, 338.

7. *PL* 119, 1010. The English translation used here is from C. Journet, *The Church of the Word Incarnate* 1, trans. A. H. C. Downes (New York, 1955) 295.

8. Ulpian, one of the principal authors of the Digest of the *Corpus iuris civilis* of Justinian, warned in a classic passage that evidence obtained through torture is frequently useless; cf. *Digest* 48, 18, 1, 23. Augustine's remarks on torture are likewise of interest; cf. *De civitate Dei* 19, 6.

9. E. Vacandard, *L'Inquisition: Étude historique et critique sur le Pouvoir coercitif de l'église* (Paris, 1907) 175.

10. Cf. A. Michel, "Ordalies," *Dictionnaire de theologie catholique* 11, 1143 ff.

11. The following popes spoke out strongly against the use of ordeals in ecclesiastical trials: Nicholas I (+ 867), *PL* 119, 1144; Stephen V (+ 891), *PL* 129, 797; Alexander II (+ 1073), *PL* 146, 1406. Canon 18 of Lateran IV reads thus: "*Nullus quoque clericus rottariis aut balistariis aut huiusmodi viris sanguinum praeponatur, nec illam chirurgiae artem subdiaconus, diaconus vel sacerdos exerceant, quae ad ustionem vel incisionem inducit, nec quisquam purgationi aquae ferventis vel frigidae seu ferri candentis ritum cuiuslibet benedictionis aut consecrationis impendat, salvis nihilominus prohibitionibus de monomachiis sive duellis antea promulgatis.*"

12. Many felt that spiritual power alone should be used in punishing heretics; cf. the Council of Reims in 1049 and the Council of Toulouse in 1056 (Mansi 19, 737, 849).

13. M. L. Cozens, *A Handbook of Heresies* (New York, 1945) 60.

14. Cf. A. S. Tuberville, *The Spanish Inquisition* (London, 1932) 3.

15. *Bullarum, diplomatum et privilegiorum sanctorum Romanorum pontificum Taurinensis editio* 3 (Turin, 1858) 556.

16. What constitutes a "legitimate question"? According to Cajetan, commenting on St. Thomas's *Summa theologica* 2–2, q. 69, aa. 1–2, for a question to be legitimate one of three conditions must be fulfilled: The accused must be under infamy *(infamia seu clamorosa insinuatio)* for the crime; there must be clear evidence that he committed the crime; and there must exist partial proof *(semi-plena probatio)* against him. Cf. *Sancti Thomae Aquinatis opera omnia, cum commentariis Thomae de Vio Caietani* (Rome, 1897) tom. 9, q. 69, aa. 1–2. These restrictions helped preserve the efficiency of Continental law procedure by admitting to trial only those cases that had genuine value. Once the state agreed to bring a case to court, there was a good possibility that a conviction could be made. Other theologians argue that the accused is not obliged to answer questions that are not legitimate or are not legitimately proposed. Cf. L. Lessius,

De justitia et jure (Antwerp, 1612) lib. 2, c. 31, dub. 3, n. 8; J. de Lugo, *Disputationes scholasticae et morales* (Paris, 1869) tom. 7, disp. 40, section 1, n. 1.

17. St. Alphonsus Liguori, *Theologia moralis,* ed. L. Gaudé (Rome, 1907) tom. 2, lib. 4, c. 3, dub. 2, art. 3, n. 202.

18. Ibid., dub. 7, n. 274. Cf. Lugo, op. cit., n. 20.

19. E. Vacandard, "Inquisition," *Dictionnaire de théologie catholique* 7, 2061.

20. Journet, op. cit., 297–98.

21. Ibid., 297.

22. Ibid., 304.

23. Cf. E. Mangenot, "Catéchisme," *Dictionnaire de théologie catholique* 2, 1917 ff. Pius X, in his Encyclical *Acerbo nimis,* decreed that "catechetical instruction shall be based on the Catechism of the Council of Trent" (*ASS* 37, 621). Joseph Collins, S.S., could write in our own time: "The Catechism of the Council of Trent remains today the primary text upon which all our modern catechetical texts are based" (*Teaching Religion* [Milwaukee, 1953] 23).

24. The Latin text may be found in the edition of Paulus Mantius, *Catechismus Concilii Tridentini ad parochos* (Tournai, 1890) n. 364.

25. A. Natalis, *Theologia dogmatica et moralis secundum ordinem catechismi Concilii Tridentini* (Venice, 1705) tom. 2, lib. 4, c. 10, art. 3, reg. 3. Cf. also G. Antoine, *Theologia moralis universa,* 4 (Avignon, 1818) 335; D. Concina, *Theologia christiana dogmatico-moralis* (Naples, 1773) tom. 4, lib. 5, diss. 4, c. 5.

26. *Summa theologica* 2–2, q. 69, a. 1 c.

27. Ibid.

28. Ibid., ad 1m.

29. Lugo's teaching on this point presents us with a paradox. On the one hand, he defends the use of torture if there is *semi-plena probatio* against the accused (op. cit., tom. 6, disp. 37, sect. 13, n. 153). On the other hand, he argues that it is too much to require a voluntary confession from an accused man (ibid., tom. 7, disp. 40, sect. 1, n. 16). Lugo teaches that an accused may conceal his crime if he faces the death penalty or its equivalent, such as galleys or a great loss of property or reputation. A law demanding voluntary confession, he states, is not accommodated to human nature and can serve only "*ad illaqueandas conscientias*" (ibid., n. 15).

30. A few minor theologians referred to the laxists' moral propositions concerning mental reservation, which were condemned on March 2, 1679, during the pontificate of Innocent XI (cf. Denzinger-Schönmetzer 2126, 2127). De Cardenas favors the milder opinion, stating that some laws and precepts are

penal and do not bind in conscience. He concludes that one can understand "how a judge may juridically question and the accused may still not be bound to confess his crime under pain of sin" (J. de Cardenas, *Crisis theologica* [Venice, 1700] pars 4, diss. 19, c. 3, n. 30). J. M. Sbogar follows St. Thomas: *Theologia radicalis* (2nd ed.; Prague, 1708) c. unicum, n. 13. Finally, P. Sporer considers the opinion of Lugo probable and safe: *Theologia super decalogum* (3rd ed.; Salzburg, 1711) tom. 2, tract. 5, in 5 praecept. decalogi, c. 4, sect. 1, n. 14 ff.

31. Cf. E. J. Moriarty, *Oaths in Ecclesiastical Courts* (Washington, D.C., 1937) 2. Cf. R. Clune, *The Judicial Interrogation of the Parties* (Washington, D.C., 1949); J. Krol, *The Defendant in Contentious Trials* (Washington, D.C., 1937).

32. C. 1, X, *de postulatione praelatorum* 1, 5; glossa s.v. *Confessiones,* ad c. 11, X, *de probationibus* 2, 9.

33. Glossa s.v. *interrogandi,* ad c. 11, C. XXX, q. 5; glossa s.v. *de confessis,* ad c. 3, X, *de confessis* 2, 18; glossa s.v. *interrogationibus,* ad c. 6, X, *de iuramento calumniae* 2, 17.

34. Medieval canonists used the maxim *Qui tacet consentire videtur.* Cf. C. Magni, *Il silenzio nel diritto canonico* (Padua, 1934); G. Danuti, *Il silenzio come manifestazione di volontà: Studi di Pietro Bonfante* 4 (Milan, 1930) 461–84.

35. Canon 1744. There is, however, at least one instance after 1725 in which the oath *de veritate dicenda* was required in a criminal case. On Feb. 20, 1866, the Holy Office issued an Instruction concerning the Apostolic Constitution of Benedict XIV, *Sacramentum paenitentiae,* dealing with solicitation. The Instruction states: "When these things [previous examination of the witnesses] have been diligently performed, the defendant is brought into the courtroom before the judge…and bound by the oath *de veritate dicenda,* he must answer each and every point of the examination and the denunciation" (*Collectanea Sacrae Congregationis de Propaganda Fide* 1 [Rome, 1907] 709, n. 11). This exception applies to this case only, perhaps because of its seriousness. Some theologians say that the Instruction is directive rather than prescriptive and that it is not at all certain that a confessor would be guilty of mortal sin if he refused to admit his crime; cf. D. M. Prümmer, *Manuale theologiae moralis* 2 (12th ed.; Freiburg, 1955) 149; J. A. McHugh and C. J. Callan, *Moral Theology* 2 (New York, 1958) 194.

36. J. Loiseaux (Piato Montensi), *Praelectiones iuris regularis* 2 (Tournai, 1896) 406.

37. Benedict XIV, *Bullarii Romani continuatio* (Florence, 1846) tom. 3, pars prima, 197–98, n. 8.

38. Pius VI, *Bullarii Romani continuatio* (Florence, 1847) tom. 8, pars prima, 13–17, n. 6.

39. Leo XII, *Bullarii Romani continuatio* (Florence, 1854) tom. 18, 269–73, n. 12.

40. The jubilee of 1700: cf. Innocent XII, Constitution *Regi saeculorum,* May 18, 1699, in *Bullarum, diplomatum et privilegiorum sanctorum Romanorum pontificum Taurinensis editio* 20 (Naples, 1783) 876–81. Jubilee of 1725: cf. Benedict XIII, Constitution *Pontificia sollicitudo,* Jan. 20, 1725, in *Bullarum, diplomatum et privilegiorum sanctorum Romanorum pontificum Taurinensis editio* 22 (Turin, 1871) 122–24. Jubilee of 1900: cf. Leo XIII, Constitution *Aeterni pastoris,* Nov. 1, 1899, in *Leonis XIII pontificis maximi acta* 19 (Rome, 1900) 230–39. Jubilee of 1925: cf. Pius XI, Constitution *Apostolico muneri,* July 30, 1924, in *AAS* 16 (1924) 316–20.

41. For example, J. D'Annibale, *Summula theologiae moralis* 2, n. 602; Berardi, *Praxis confessariorum* 1, 671, 672; J.-Ev. Pruner, *Bibliothèque théologique du XIXe siècle* 2 (Paris, 1880) 501.

42. E. F. Regatillo and M. Zalba, *De statibus particularibus* (Santander, 1954) 41. Cf. M. Zalba, *Theologiae moralis compendium* 2, n. 313.

43. *Regulae servandae in iudiciis apud S. R. Rotae Tribunal,* Aug. 4, 1910 (*AAS* 2 [1910] 783–850; tr. in Clune, op. cit., 45–46).

44. In the *Motu proprio* of Mar. 19, 1904, *Arduum sane,* Pope Pius X announced that a new code of law was to be prepared in which there would be collected "with order and clearness all the laws of the church,…removing all that were abrogated or obsolete, adopting others as far as needed by the customs of the present time, and making new ones according to need and opportunity." The new code was promulgated May 27, 1917, by Benedict XV in the Constitution *Providentissima mater ecclesia.* It went into effect on May 18, 1918.

45. Canon 1743, 1°: *"Iudici legitime interroganti partes respondere tenentur et fateri veritatem, nisi agatur de delicto ab ipsis commisso."*

46. Canon 1742, 1. Cf. F. Roberti, *De processibus* 2 (Rome, 1926) n. 321; M. Coronata, *Institutiones iuris canonici* 3 (2nd ed.; Rome, 1941) n. 1270.

47. Wernz-Vidal feel that it is cruel and inhuman to force the accused to reveal the truth under oath, since he is torn between telling the truth or facing severe penalties; cf. F. X. Wernz and P. Vidal, *Ius canonicum* 6/1 (Rome, 1927) n. 422 a.

48. Canon 1559.

49. Canon 1755.

50. Cf. J. Noval, *Commentarium Codicis iuris canonici* 4, *De processibus*: 1, *De judiciis* (Turin, 1920) n. 432; G. Cocchi, *Commentarium in Codicem iuris canonici* 12 (Turin, 1940) n, 130; Coronata, loc. cit.

51. F. P. Kenrick, *Theologia moralis* 1 (Philadelphia, 1841) 387.

52. A. Berardi, *Praxis confessariorum* 1 (2nd ed.; Bologna, 1887) 672.

53. H. Noldin, *Summa theologiae moralis* 2 (5th ed.; Innsbruck, 1905) n. 721, 1; E. Génicot, *Theologiae moralis institutiones* 2 (6th ed.; Brussels, 1909) 13.

54. For a complete treatment of this problem, cf. M. T. Maestro, *Voltaire and Beccaria as Reformers of Criminal Law* (New York, 1942).

55. Cf. Esmein, op. cit., 379–402.

56. Ibid., 511.

57. Cf. C. L. Calisse, *A History of Italian Law* (Boston, 1928) 477 ff.

9. Catholicism and Capital Punishment

Avery Dulles

This chapter first appeared in *First Things* 112 (April 2001)

Among the major nations of the Western world, the United States is singular in still having the death penalty. After a five-year moratorium, from 1972 to 1977, capital punishment was reinstated in the U.S. courts. Objections to the practice have come from many quarters, including the American Catholic bishops, who have rather consistently opposed the death penalty. The National Conference of Catholic Bishops in 1980 published a predominantly negative statement on capital punishment, approved by a majority vote of those present though not by the required two-thirds majority of the entire conference.[1] Pope John Paul II has at various times expressed his opposition to the practice, as have other Catholic leaders in Europe.

Some Catholics, going beyond the bishops and the pope, maintain that the death penalty, like abortion and euthanasia, is a violation of the right to life and an unauthorized usurpation by human beings of God's sole lordship over life and death. Did not the Declaration of Independence, they ask, describe the right to life as "unalienable"?

While sociological and legal questions inevitably impinge upon any such reflection, I am here addressing the subject as a theologian. At this level the question has to be answered primarily in terms of revelation, as it comes to us through scripture and tradition, interpreted with the guidance of the ecclesiastical magisterium.

In the Old Testament the Mosaic Law specifies no less than thirty-six capital offenses calling for execution by stoning, burning, decapitation, or strangulation. Included in the list are idolatry, magic, blasphemy, violation of the Sabbath, murder, adultery, bestiality, pederasty, and incest. The death penalty was considered especially fitting as a punishment for murder for in his covenant with Noah God had laid down the principle, "Whoever sheds the blood of man, by man shall his blood be shed, for God made man in His own image" (Gen 9:6). In many cases God is portrayed as deservedly punishing culprits with death, as happened to Korah, Dathan, and Abiram (Num 16). In other cases individuals such as Daniel and Mordecai are God's agents in bringing a just death upon guilty persons.

In the New Testament the right of the state to put criminals to death seems to be taken for granted. Jesus himself refrains from using violence. He rebukes his disciples for wishing to call down fire from heaven to punish the Samaritans for their lack of hospitality (Luke 9:55). Later he admonishes Peter to put his sword in the scabbard rather than resist arrest (Matt 26:52). At no point, however, does Jesus deny that the state has authority to exact capital punishment. In his debates with the Pharisees, Jesus cites with approval the apparently harsh commandment, "He who speaks evil of father or mother, let him surely die" (Matt 15:4; Mark 7:10, referring to Exod 21:17; cf. Lev 20:9). When Pilate calls attention to his authority to crucify him, Jesus points out that Pilate's power comes to him from above—that is to say, from God (John 19:11). Jesus commends the good thief on the cross next to him, who has admitted that he and his fellow thief are receiving the due reward of their deeds (Luke 23:41).

The early Christians evidently had nothing against the death penalty. They approve of the divine punishment meted out to Ananias and Sapphira when they are rebuked by Peter for their fraudulent action (Acts 5:1–11). The Letter to the Hebrews makes an argument from the fact that "a man who has violated the law of Moses dies without mercy at the testimony of two or three witnesses" (10:28). Paul repeatedly refers to the connection between sin and death. He writes to the Romans, with an apparent reference to the death penalty, that the magistrate who holds authority "does not bear the sword in vain; for he is the servant of God to execute His wrath on the wrongdoer" (Rom 13:4). No passage in the New Testament disapproves of the death penalty.

Turning to Christian tradition, we may note that the Fathers and Doctors of the Church are virtually unanimous in their support for capital punishment, even though some of them, such as St. Ambrose, exhort members of the clergy not to pronounce capital sentences or serve as executioners. To answer the objection that the first commandment forbids killing, St. Augustine writes in *The City of God:*

> The same divine law which forbids the killing of a human
> being allows certain exceptions, as when God authorizes
> killing by a general law or when He gives an explicit com-
> mission to an individual for a limited time. Since the agent
> of authority is but a sword in the hand, and is not responsi-
> ble for the killing, it is in no way contrary to the command-
> ment, "Thou shalt not kill" to wage war at God's bidding, or
> for the representatives of the State's authority to put crimi-
> nals to death, according to law or the rule of rational justice.

In the Middle Ages a number of canonists teach that ecclesiastical courts should refrain from the death penalty and that civil courts should impose it only for major crimes. But leading canonists and theologians assert the right of civil courts to pronounce the death penalty for very grave offenses such as murder and treason. Thomas Aquinas and Duns Scotus invoke the authority of scripture and patristic tradition and give arguments from reason.

Giving magisterial authority to the death penalty, Pope Innocent III required disciples of Peter Waldo seeking reconciliation with the church to accept the proposition: "The secular power can, without mortal sin, exercise judgment of blood, provided that it punishes with justice, not out of hatred, with prudence, not precipitation." In the high Middle Ages and early modern times, the Holy See authorized the Inquisition to turn over heretics to the secular arm for execution. In the Papal States the death penalty was imposed for a variety of offenses. The Roman Catechism, issued in 1566, three years after the end of the Council of Trent, taught that the power of life and death had been entrusted by God to civil authorities and that the use of this power, far from involving the crime of murder, is an act of paramount obedience to the fifth commandment.

In modern times Doctors of the Church, such as Robert Bellarmine and Alphonsus Liguori, held that certain criminals should be punished by death. Venerable authorities, such as Francisco de Vitoria, Thomas More, and Francisco Suárez, agreed. John Henry Newman, in a letter to a friend, maintained that the magistrate had the right to bear the sword, and that the church should sanction its use, in the sense that Moses, Joshua, and Samuel used it against abominable crimes.

Throughout the first half of the twentieth century the consensus of Catholic theologians in favor of capital punishment in extreme cases remained solid, as may be seen from approved textbooks and encyclopedia articles of the day. The Vatican City State from 1929 until 1969 had a penal code that included the death penalty for anyone who might attempt to assassinate the pope. Pope Pius XII, in an important allocution to medical experts, declared that it was reserved to the public power to deprive the condemned of the benefit of life in expiation of their crimes.

Summarizing the verdict of scripture and tradition, we can glean some settled points of doctrine. It is agreed that crime deserves punishment in this life and not only in the next. In addition, it is agreed that the state has authority to administer appropriate punishment to those judged guilty of crimes and that this punishment may, in serious cases, include the sentence of death.

Yet, as we have seen, a rising chorus of voices in the Catholic community has raised objections to capital punishment. Some take the absolutist position that because the right to life is sacred and inviolable, the death penalty is always wrong. The respected Italian Franciscan Gino Concetti, writing in *L'Osservatore Romano* in 1977, made the following powerful statement:

> In light of the word of God, and thus of faith, life—all human life—is sacred and untouchable. No matter how heinous the crimes...[the criminal] does not lose his fundamental right to life, for it is primordial, inviolable, and inalienable, and thus comes under the power of no one whatsoever.
>
> If this right and its attributes are so absolute, it is because of the image which, at creation, God impressed on human nature itself. No force, no violence, no passion can erase or destroy it. By virtue of this divine image, man is a person endowed with dignity and rights.

To warrant this radical revision—one might almost say reversal—of the Catholic tradition, Father Concetti and others explain that the church from biblical times until our own day has failed to perceive the true significance of the image of God in man, which implies that even the terrestrial life of each individual person is sacred and inviolable. In past centuries, it is alleged, Jews and Christians failed to think through the consequences of this revealed doctrine. They were caught up in a barbaric culture of violence and in an absolutist theory of political power, both handed down from the ancient world. But in our day, a new recognition of the dignity and inalienable rights of the human person has dawned. Those who recognize the signs of the times will move beyond the outmoded doctrines that the state has a divinely delegated power to kill and that criminals forfeit their fundamental human rights. The teaching on capital punishment must today undergo a dramatic development corresponding to these new insights.

This abolitionist position has a tempting simplicity. But it is not really new. It has been held by sectarian Christians at least since the Middle Ages. Many pacifist groups, such as the Waldensians, the Quakers, the Hutterites, and the Mennonites, have shared this point of view. But, like pacifism itself, this absolutist interpretation of the right to life found no echo at the time among Catholic theologians, who accepted the death penalty as consonant with scripture, tradition, and the natural law.

The mounting opposition to the death penalty in Europe since the Enlightenment has gone hand in hand with a decline of faith in eternal life. In the nineteenth century the most consistent supporters of capital punishment were the Christian churches, and its most consistent opponents were groups hostile to the churches. When death came to be understood as the ultimate evil rather than as a stage on the way to eternal life, utilitarian philosophers such as Jeremy Bentham found it easy to dismiss capital punishment as "useless annihilation."

Many governments in Europe and elsewhere have eliminated the death penalty in the twentieth century, often against the protests of religious believers. While this change may be viewed as moral progress, it is probably due, in part, to the evaporation of the senses of sin, guilt, and retributive justice, all of which are essential to biblical religion and Catholic faith. The abolition of the death penalty in formerly Christian countries may owe more to secular humanism than to deeper penetration into the gospel.

Arguments from the progress of ethical consciousness have been used to promote a number of alleged human rights that the Catholic Church consistently rejects in the name of scripture and tradition. The magisterium appeals to these authorities as grounds for repudiating divorce, abortion, homosexual relations, and the ordination of women to the priesthood. If the church feels herself bound by scripture and tradition in these other areas, it seems inconsistent for Catholics to proclaim a "moral revolution" on the issue of capital punishment.

The Catholic magisterium does not, and never has, advocated unqualified abolition of the death penalty. I know of no official statement from popes or bishops, in the past or in the present, that denies the right of the state to execute offenders at least in certain extreme cases. The U.S. bishops, in their majority statement on capital punishment, conceded that "Catholic teaching has accepted the principle that the State has the right to take the life of a person guilty of an extremely serious crime." Joseph Cardinal Bernardin, in his famous speech on the "Consistent Ethic of Life" at Fordham in 1983, stated his concurrence with the "classical position" that the state has the right to inflict capital punishment.

Although Cardinal Bernardin advocated what he called a "consistent ethic of life," he made it clear that capital punishment should not be equated with the crimes of abortion, euthanasia, and suicide. Pope John Paul II spoke for the whole Catholic tradition when he proclaimed in *Evangelium Vitae* (1995) that "the direct and voluntary killing of an innocent human being is always gravely immoral." But he wisely included in that statement the word "innocent." He has never said that every criminal has a right to live nor has he denied that the state has the right in some cases to execute the guilty.

Catholic authorities justify the right of the state to inflict capital punishment on the ground that the state does not act on its own authority but as the agent of God, who is supreme lord of life and death. In so holding they can properly appeal to scripture. Paul holds that the ruler is God's minister in executing God's wrath against the evildoer (Rom 13:4). Peter admonishes Christians to be subject to emperors and governors, who have been sent by God to punish those who do wrong (1 Pet 2:13). Jesus, as already noted, apparently recognized that Pilate's authority over his life came from God (John 19:11).

Pius XII, in a further clarification of the standard argument, holds that when the state, acting by its ministerial power, uses the death penalty, it does not exercise dominion over human life but only recognizes that the criminal, by a kind of moral suicide, has deprived himself of the right to life. In the pope's words,

> Even when there is question of the execution of a condemned man, the state does not dispose of the individual's right to life. In this case it is reserved to the public power to deprive the condemned person of the enjoyment of life in expiation of his crime when, by his crime, he has already dispossessed himself of his right to life.

In light of all this it seems safe to conclude that the death penalty is not in itself a violation of the right to life. The real issue for Catholics is to determine the circumstances under which that penalty ought to be applied. It is appropriate, I contend, when it is necessary to achieve the purposes of punishment and when it does not have disproportionate evil effects. I say "necessary" because I am of the opinion that killing should be avoided if the purposes of punishment can be obtained by bloodless means.

The purposes of criminal punishment are rather unanimously delineated in the Catholic tradition. Punishment is held to have a variety of ends that may conveniently be reduced to the following four: rehabilitation, defense against the criminal, deterrence, and retribution.

Granted that punishment has these four aims, we may now inquire whether the death penalty is the apt or necessary means to attain them.

Rehabilitation. Capital punishment does not reintegrate the criminal into society; rather, it cuts off any possible rehabilitation. The sentence of death, however, can and sometimes does move the condemned person to repentance and conversion. There is a large body of Christian literature on the value of prayers and pastoral ministry for convicts on death row or on the scaffold. In cases where the criminal seems incapable of being reintegrated into human society, the death penalty may be a way of achieving the criminal's reconciliation with God.

Defense against the criminal. Capital punishment is obviously an effective way of preventing the wrongdoer from committing future crimes and protecting society from him. Whether execution is necessary is another question. One could no doubt imagine an extreme case in which the very fact that a criminal is alive constituted a threat that he might be released or escape and do further harm. But, as John Paul II remarks in *Evangelium Vitae,* modern improvements in the penal system have made it extremely rare for execution to be the only effective means of defending society against the criminal.

Deterrence. Executions, especially where they are painful, humiliating, and public, may create a sense of horror that would prevent others from being tempted to commit similar crimes. But the fathers of the church censured spectacles of violence such as those conducted at the Roman Colosseum. Vatican II's Pastoral Constitution on the Church in the Modern World explicitly disapproved of mutilation and torture as offensive to human dignity. In our day death is usually administered in private by relatively painless means, such as injections of drugs, and to that extent it may be less effective as a deterrent. Sociological evidence on the deterrent effect of the death penalty as currently practiced is ambiguous, conflicting, and far from probative.

Retribution. In principle, guilt calls for punishment. The graver the offense, the more severe the punishment ought to be. In holy scripture, as we have seen, death is regarded as the appropriate punishment for serious transgressions. Thomas Aquinas held that sin calls for the deprivation of some good, such as, in serious cases, the good of temporal or even eternal life. By consenting to the punishment of death, the wrongdoer is placed in a position to expiate his evil deeds and escape punishment in the next life. After noting this, St. Thomas adds that even if the malefactor is not repentant, he is benefited by being prevented from committing more sins. Retribution by the state has its limits because the state, unlike God, enjoys neither omniscience nor omnipotence. According to Christian faith, God "will render to every man according to his works" at the final judgment (Rom 2:6; cf. Matt 16:27). Retribution by the state can only be a symbolic anticipation of God's perfect justice.

For the symbolism to be authentic, the society must believe in the existence of a transcendent order of justice, which the state has an obligation to protect. This has been true in the past, but in our day the state is generally viewed simply as an instrument of the will of the governed. In this modern perspective, the death penalty expresses not the divine judgment on objective evil but rather the collective anger of the group. The retributive goal of punishment is misconstrued as a self-assertive act of vengeance.

The death penalty, we may conclude, has different values in relation to each of the four ends of punishment. It does not rehabilitate the criminal but may be an occasion for bringing about salutary repentance. It is an effective but rarely, if ever, a necessary means of defending society against the criminal. Whether it serves to deter others from similar crimes is a disputed question, difficult to settle. Its retributive value is impaired by lack of clarity about the role of the state. In general, then, capital punishment has some limited value, but its necessity is open to doubt.

There is more to be said. Thoughtful writers have contended that the death penalty, besides being unnecessary and often futile, can also be positively harmful. Four serious objections are commonly mentioned in the literature.

There is, first of all, a possibility that the convict may be innocent. John Stuart Mill, in his well-known defense of capital punishment, considers this to be the most serious objection. In responding, he cautions that the death penalty should not be imposed except in cases in which the accused is tried by a trustworthy court and found guilty beyond all shadow of doubt.

It is common knowledge that even when trials are conducted, biased or kangaroo courts can often render unjust convictions. Even in the United States, where serious efforts are made to achieve just verdicts, errors occur, although many of them are corrected by appellate courts. Poorly educated and penniless defendants often lack the means to procure competent legal counsel; witnesses can be suborned or can make honest mistakes about the facts of the case or the identities of persons; evidence can be fabricated or suppressed; and juries can be prejudiced or incompetent. Some "death row" convicts have been exonerated by newly available DNA evidence. Columbia Law School has recently published a powerful report on the percentage of reversible errors in capital sentences from 1973 to 1995. Since it is altogether likely that some innocent persons have been executed, this first objection is a serious one.

Another objection observes that the death penalty often has the effect of whetting an inordinate appetite for revenge rather than satisfying an authentic zeal for justice. By giving in to a perverse spirit of vindictiveness or a morbid attraction to the gruesome, the courts contribute to the degradation of the culture, replicating the worst features of the Roman Empire in its period of decline.

Furthermore, critics say, capital punishment cheapens the value of life. By giving the impression that human beings sometimes have the right to kill, it fosters a casual attitude toward evils such as abortion, suicide, and euthanasia. This was a major point in Cardinal Bernardin's speeches and articles on what he called a "consistent ethic of life." Although this argument may have some validity, its force should not be exaggerated. Many people who are strongly prolife on issues such as abortion support the death penalty, insisting that there is no inconsistency, since the innocent and the guilty do not have the same rights.

Finally, some hold that the death penalty is incompatible with the teaching of Jesus on forgiveness. This argument is complex at best, since the quoted sayings of Jesus have reference to forgiveness on the part of individual persons who have suffered injury. It is indeed praiseworthy for victims of crime to forgive their debtors, but such personal pardon does not absolve offenders from their obligations in justice. John Paul II points out that "reparation for evil and scandal, compensation for injury, and satisfaction for insult are conditions for forgiveness."

The relationship of the state to the criminal is not the same as that of a victim to an assailant. Governors and judges are responsible for maintaining a just public order. Their primary obligation is toward justice, but under certain conditions they may exercise clemency. In a careful discussion of this matter Pius XII concluded that the state ought not to issue pardons except when it is morally certain that the ends of punishment have been achieved. Under these conditions, requirements of public policy may warrant a partial or full remission of punishment. If clemency were granted to all convicts, the nation's prisons would be instantly emptied, but society would not be well served.

In practice, then, a delicate balance between justice and mercy must be maintained. The state's primary responsibility is for justice, although it may at times temper justice with mercy. The church rather represents the mercy of God. Showing forth the divine forgiveness that comes from Jesus Christ, the church is deliberately indulgent toward offenders, but it too must on occasion impose penalties. The Code of Canon Law contains an entire book devoted to crime and punishment. It would be clearly inappropriate for the church, as a spiritual society, to execute criminals, but the state is a different type of society. It cannot be expected to act as a church. In a predominantly Christian society, however, the state should be encouraged to lean toward mercy provided that it does not thereby violate the demands of justice.

It is sometimes asked whether a judge or executioner can impose or carry out the death penalty with love. It seems to me quite obvious that such officeholders can carry out their duty without hatred for the criminal, but rather with love, respect, and compassion. In enforcing the law, they may take comfort in believing that death is not the final evil; they may pray and hope that the convict will attain eternal life with God.

The four objections are therefore of different weight. The first of them, dealing with miscarriages of justice, is relatively strong; the second and third, dealing with vindictiveness and with the consistent ethic of life, have some probable force. The fourth objection, dealing with forgiveness, is relatively weak. But taken together, the four may suffice to tip the scale against the use of the death penalty.

The Catholic magisterium in recent years has become increasingly vocal in opposing the practice of capital punishment. Pope John Paul II in *Evangelium Vitae* declared that "as a result of steady improvements in the organization of the penal system," cases in which the execution of the offender would be absolutely necessary "are very rare, if not practically nonexistent." Again at St. Louis in January 1999 the pope appealed for a consensus to end the death penalty on the ground that it was "both cruel and unnecessary." The bishops of many countries have spoken to the same effect.

The U.S. bishops, for their part, had already declared in their majority statement of 1980 that "in the conditions of contemporary American society, the legitimate purposes of punishment do not justify the imposition of the death penalty." Since that time they have repeatedly intervened to ask for clemency in particular cases. Like the pope, the bishops do not rule out capital punishment altogether, but they say that it is not justifiable as practiced in the United States today.

In coming to this prudential conclusion, the magisterium is not changing the doctrine of the church. The doctrine remains what it has been: that the state, in principle, has the right to impose the death penalty on persons convicted of very serious crimes. But the classical tradition held that the state should not exercise this right when the evil effects outweigh the good effects. Thus the principle still leaves open the question whether and when the death penalty ought to be applied. The pope and the bishops, using their prudential judgment, have concluded that in contemporary society, at least in countries like our own, the death penalty ought not to be invoked, because, on balance, it does more harm than good. I personally support this position.

In a brief compass I have touched on numerous and complex problems. To indicate what I have tried to establish, I should like to propose, as a final summary, ten theses that encapsulate the church's doctrine, as I understand it.

1. The purpose of punishment in secular courts is fourfold: the rehabilitation of the criminal, the protection of society from the criminal, the deterrence of other potential criminals, and retributive justice.

2. Just retribution, which seeks to establish the right order of things, should not be confused with vindictiveness, which is reprehensible.

3. Punishment may and should be administered with respect and love for the person punished.

4. The person who does evil may deserve death. According to the biblical accounts, God sometimes administers the penalty himself and sometimes directs others to do so.

5. Individuals and private groups may not take it upon themselves to inflict death as a penalty.

6. The state has the right, in principle, to inflict capital punishment in cases in which there is no doubt about the gravity of the offense and the guilt of the accused.

7. The death penalty should not be imposed if the purposes of punishment can be equally well or better achieved by bloodless means, such as imprisonment.

8. The sentence of death may be improper if it has serious negative effects on society, such as miscarriages of justice, the increase of vindictiveness, or disrespect for the value of innocent human life.

9. Persons who specially represent the church, such as clergy and religious, in view of their specific vocation, should abstain from pronouncing or executing the sentence of death.

10. Catholics, in seeking to form their judgment as to whether the death penalty is to be supported as a general policy, or in a given situation, should be attentive to the guidance of the pope and the bishops. Current Catholic teaching should be understood, as I have sought to understand it, in continuity with scripture and tradition.

Note

1. The statement was adopted by a vote of 145 to 31, with 41 bishops abstaining, the highest number of abstentions ever recorded. In addition, a number of bishops were absent from the meeting or did not officially abstain. Thus the statement did not receive the two-thirds majority of the entire membership then required for approval of official statements. But no bishop rose to make the point of order.

10. To Kill or Not to Kill: The Catholic Church and the Problem of the Death Penalty

E. Christian Brugger

This chapter first appeared as the Yamauchi Lecture in Religion, March 18, 2001, published by the Department of Religious Studies of Loyola University, New Orleans.

INTRODUCTION: WHAT'S GOING ON?

On the evening of May 16, 2001, barring a presidential pardon, Timothy McVeigh, architect of the worst act of domestic terrorism in U.S. history,[1] having forgone all remaining appeals, will walk from his holding cell into the federal execution chamber at Terre Haute, Indiana, be strapped to a gurney, have catheters pressed into his veins, and upon the warden's signal, begin receiving an IV cocktail of deadly chemicals; first *sodium pentothal,* a barbiturate, will render him unconscious; then *pancuronium bromide,* a muscle relaxant, will paralyze his diaphragm and lungs; and finally, *potassium chloride* will cause cardiac arrest. A twitch or two, like the start of a man falling asleep, may be momentarily visible; but then all will be still. Timothy should be dead within ten minutes.

In the weeks preceding May 16, the Justice Department will receive last minute petitions for executive clemency from a variety of death-penalty opponents, among whom, no doubt, will be Catholic bishops, perhaps even the bishop of Rome.

Episcopal petitions for clemency for the condemned have a long history in the Catholic Church. Fathers like Gregory of Nazianzus, Ambrose, and Augustine[2] each urged Christian magistrates to use non-lethal means if at all possible in the exercise of their juridical duties. At the same time, each would have vigorously and publicly defended the basic right of civil authority to inflict the death penalty. In fact, from the earliest days of the Christian church up to the first half of the twentieth century, a confident, consistent, and coordinated defense of the right of the state to kill criminals was maintained by the Catholic Church. The first signs of a weakening in this regard were discernible as early as the 1950s. The weakening increases—albeit gradually—in the 60s. And in the 70s the floodgates burst. In the last thirty years literally hundreds of public statements opposing the death penalty—more perhaps than in the previous centuries combined—have been published by the Catholic hierarchy on a local, national, and international level.[3]

Leading the opposition is Pope John Paul II. Not only has he initiated a wide-scale rethinking on the thorny issue of capital punishment in the Catholic Church with the publication of his 1995 encyclical *Evangelium Vitae,* but he also has taken and continues to take every opportunity possible, pastoral and political, to protest the death penalty's infliction in the modern world and to admonish Catholic consciences to be committed to the cause of worldwide abolition as an expression of commitment to the dignity of the human person.

Now anyone with even modest historical knowledge of the church's past teachings on the subject and who looks at the writings of the last thirty years, particularly of the past decade, is bound to ask: What's going on? Has the church rejected the death penalty? If not, is she planning to? What in fact is the current position? Is it reasonable to refer to it as a doctrinal development over the traditional position? Can we anticipate the current teaching to progress further? These questions I intend to explore with you tonight.

What Is the Current Position?

To get a handle on the current teaching, we'd do well to look at its most complete articulation to date in the 1997 definitive edition of the *Catechism of the Catholic Church.*[4] Recall, now, that the text of this edition is the universal *Catechism*'s second attempt at the issue of capital punishment, its first being the 1992 French edition (from which all other translations at the time were prepared). The 1992 statement was subsequently revised to reflect the stronger opposition found in John Paul II's tenth and most widely read encyclical, *Evangelium Vitae.*

The 1997 statement, in Part III, article 5 of the *Catechism,* on the Fifth Precept of the Decalogue, reads as follows:

> Assuming that the guilty party's identity and responsibility have been fully determined, the traditional teaching of the church does not exclude recourse to the death penalty, if this is the only possible way of effectively defending human lives against the unjust aggressor.
>
> If, however, nonlethal means are sufficient to defend and protect people's safety from the aggressor, authority will limit itself to such means, as these are more in keeping with the concrete conditions of the common good and more in conformity with the dignity of the human person.
>
> Today, in fact, as a consequence of the possibilities that the state has for effectively preventing crime, by rendering one who has committed an offense incapable of doing harm—without definitively taking away from him the possibility of redeeming himself—the cases in which the execution of the offender is an absolute necessity 'are very rare, if not practically non-existent.' [Note to John Paul II, *Evangelium vitae* 561] (Paragraph number 2267)
>
> A popular interpretation of this section goes something like this:
>
> The church has always taught that the state has the right to inflict punishments on duly convicted criminals, including, if need be, the punishment of death. The exercise of that right, however, is only justified if it manifestly contributes to the building up of the common good. Given the rise of effective nonlethal alternatives in today's world, recourse to the death penalty is no longer necessary for preserving the common good. Therefore, its infliction in the modern world, while in principle legitimate, is effectively illegitimate.

The *Catechism's* account is understood here to be no more than the derivation of a new practical conclusion resulting from the application of an unchanging principle (viz., civil authority possesses the right to kill malefactors for the sake of the common good) to changing conditions.

If we look closer, however, I think we will see that something more is being said. A careful scrutiny of the *Catechism*'s text in context will show that it is not saying what the Catholic Church has always said about the morality of capital punishment, only in a new way. It is saying something new. It is saying, I will argue, that the act of capital punishment, conceived and executed for the purpose of killing a human being, is never legitimate. I will defend this interpretation by highlighting two principal elements of the *Catechism*'s analysis. First, its analysis strictly ties the death penalty to a model of self-defense. From this it follows that the act referred to in the text as *poena mortis* (capital punishment) is not, precisely speaking, an act of punishment, but an act of collective self-defense by the community against an internal threat. Second, capital punishment, as well as all acts of "legitimate" killing, are subsumed under a model of double effect. Implicit is an understanding of the death penalty that limits its lawful infliction to conditions traditionally circumscribing legitimate killing in private self-defense. It follows that the type of act traditionally referred to as capital punishment, such as an act whose precise specification entails an intent to kill, is morally wrong. Let us look at each assertion more closely.

First, its analysis strictly ties the death penalty to a model of self-defense. In order to appreciate this we must first be clear on the nature of punishment in general. Punishment properly understood is a retrospective action; its justification in the present is because something has been done in the past. Punishment, we might say, looks back at the already committed offense. We only punish people who commit crimes. This is because we believe certain acts deserve punishment. We say a criminal is "guilty" and therefore "is just getting what he deserves"; we say "a great evil has been done and must be punished"; we say the punishment should "match" or "fit" or "be proportionate to" the crime, and so on. These are all different ways of referring to punishment's retributive purpose. Whatever other purposes the punishing may serve (e.g., criminal reformation, deterrence of other would-be criminals, protection of the innocent from impending harm), punishment is punishment (as opposed to any other nonpenal coercive sanction, such as quarantines for the infected, asylums for the insane, enforced curfews for minors) to the extent that it is being carried out for a crime.

Having said this, we note at once that the *Catechism* ties its analysis of the death penalty, not to a model of punishment *qua* punishment but strictly to a model of self-defense. We see this in the first place in the title of the subsection in which capital punishment is treated. The section is titled "Legitimate Defense" *(defensio legitima),* a term uncommon in Catholic theology.[5] When Aquinas uses the related term, "blameless defense" *(inculpata tutela)*—he never to my knowledge uses the term *defensio legitima*—he is referring to a blameless act of self-defense; and this self-defending act, if it results in the harm or death of the aggressor, must neither include as its end nor means the death or injury of the assailant.[6] When the 1917 and 1983 Codes of Canon Law use the related term "legitimate defense" *(legitima tutela)* in treatments of justifiable homicide, they, like Aquinas, are referring to legitimate killing in private acts of self-defense.[7]

We see again the self-defense motif in the fact that the section insists that death is legitimate only when necessary for defending human lives against attack. But when the concept of "necessary defense" is found in theological literature prior to Vatican II, it rarely if ever is used in treatments on the morality of capital punishment. It is rather used to refer to the killing of aggressors by private persons in self-defense—in most cases specifying that the harm done must be unintended.[8] Finally, we see the section's intention to frame its discussion in terms of self-defense in the fact that it refers to the recipients of capital punishment (i.e., to those who are legitimately put to death) as "aggressors," not "criminals," "the condemned," "prisoners," and the like. An aggressor is one who attacks. To defend against an aggressor is to defend against one who is or soon will be attacking. And the kind of defense section 2267 refers to entails "rendering [the aggressor]…incapable of doing harm." This language is a red flag to anyone familiar with the church's tradition of justifiable homicide. "Rendering aggressors incapable of causing harm" is classical terminology used to refer to the lawful killing of aggressors by private persons in self-defense; and the tradition unambiguously asserts that that killing must be unintended (i.e., be no more than a side effect of an otherwise legitimate act of proportionate self-defense).[9]

Second, capital punishment, as well as all acts of "legitimate" killing, is subsumed under a model of double effect. Permit me a brief aside on the term *double effect.* The term is a name given to the insight, developed by Aquinas, that among the many true things that can be said about a particular instance of human behavior, what is "primary for the purposes of morally assessing that behavior is the intentional," or the ends and means chosen by the acting person for carrying out a plan of action.[10] But the same piece of behavior may also have effects that are unintended. Since the morality of an act is primarily (though not exclusively) determined by what is intended, and not according to what is unintended, it can be morally legitimate to proceed with an act one foresees (even clearly) will have bad side effects—perhaps even lethal side effects—provided one does not intend those effects.

But this is pure sophistry, you might say. If a person causes an effect, surely that effect was intended. Not necessarily. If a student with fragile health rides his bike to class in the rain, foreseeing he might catch cold, need it be he is intending (i.e., willing) himself to get sick? Or if a mother stays late at the office, foreseeing her lateness will cause her daughter loneliness, would it be correct to say she is intending her daughter to be lonely? Or more seriously, if a pregnant woman with life-threatening uterine cancer decides to have a hysterectomy, foreseeing that the nonviable child in her womb will die thereby; if she intends the good end of regaining her health by virtue of the good or at least neutral means of undergoing a surgical operation, and at no time intends but only foresees the bad effect to her baby, is she worthy of any blame? In each case traditional moral reflection answers no. Double effect, therefore, is a way of noting the morally significant distinction between intention and side effects.

This applies to the case at hand in this way. An act of self-defense may have two effects—one intended, the other not. One's intention can be one's own safety by an act of force proportionate to render the aggressor incapable of doing harm. Sometimes lethal force is necessary to stop an aggressor. In such a case the death of the aggressor is a legitimate unintended side effect of an otherwise legitimately intended act of self-defense.

Double-effect reasoning is used in the *Catechism* to situate its discussion of capital punishment—to situate, in fact, its discussion of every form of legitimate killing. The subsection titled "Legitimate Defense," in which capital punishment is treated, does not leave this context until we reach paragraph 2266, the section immediately preceding the section on capital punishment. The first paragraph in the subsection, number 2263, introduces double-effect reasoning to show that not all actions that result in killing are intentional killing and forbidden by the commandment[11]; the next paragraph, no. 2264, applies double-effect reasoning to lawful killing in self-defense[12]; and no. 2265 applies the same reasoning to the right and duty of anyone "responsible for the lives of others" to defend the relevant community—if need be with arms—against unjust aggressors (e.g., to defend the civil community against foreign aggressors).[13]

When we get to 2266, the context changes.[14] The text here considers the nature of punishment in general and the state's basic right to inflict it. The section specifies three aims or purposes of punishment, the primary purpose being to "redress" (correct, amend) the disorder introduced by a criminal's deliberate crime; we called this purpose above, punishment's retributive purpose. Two secondary aims are also mentioned, namely, criminal reformation and societal self-defense. In saying that retribution is primary, the *Catechism* tells us that punishment, while not excluding forward looking nonretributive purposes from its broader definition, is essentially defined by being an act of retribution—an act that responds to and corrects something that has happened in the past. While it would make sense to call an act punishment that had no other purpose than to respond to an already committed crime by striking back, so to speak, at the one who committed it, it would not be appropriate to refer, say, to an act of striking back at an aggressor in self-defense as punishment. Self-defense is a response to a crime in progress or being contemplated; punishment, a response to crime that has already been committed. To intend retribution without intending self-defense is still to intend punishment; the opposite is not the case. But as I have shown above, when we turn to 2267, the conditions for a morally legitimate exercise of "capital punishment" (so called in the section) do not conform to the *Catechism*'s own definition of punishment specified in 2266, but rather to self-defense as defined in sections 2263–2265. The text insists that recourse to killing is legitimate if, and only if, the need to defend people's lives and safety against the attacks of an unjust aggressor can be met by no other means, or execution is the absolutely necessary means of effectively rendering an aggressor incapable of doing harm. Let me be clear on what I am saying: According to the

Catechism's own definition of punishment, the act defined as *poena mortis* (capital punishment) in number 2267 is not in fact an act of punishment, but rather an act of collective self-defense on the community's behalf by the state.

Perhaps the clearest indication in support of my interpretation is seen when we compare the treatment of the death penalty outlined in the 1992 edition of the *Catechism* with the text of the 1997 *editio typica*. In 1992 the *Catechism* taught the following:

> The Church has acknowledged as well-founded the right and duty of legitimate public authority to punish malefactors by means of penalties commensurate with the gravity of the crime, *not excluding, in cases of extreme gravity, the death penalty.* (1992 *Catechism*, no. 2266, emphasis added)

This sentence can plausibly be understood as teaching that the gravity of a crime can be a legitimate basis for the infliction of the death penalty. In other words, some crimes, because of their extreme gravity (i.e., the magnitude of their wickedness and damage) can be deserving of the death penalty. This interpretation of no. 2266 as it stood in 1992 is made more plausible by the fact that the church had taught the same for centuries. What is remarkable is that in the 1997 definitive edition the clause I highlighted is suppressed. The revised section reads:

> The efforts of the state to curb the spread of behavior harmful to people's rights and to the basic rules of civil society correspond to the requirement of safeguarding the common good. Legitimate public authority has the right and the duty to inflict punishment proportionate to the gravity of the offense. Punishment has the primary aim.... (1997 *editio typica*, no. 2266)

Limiting the morally permissible exercise of capital punishment to norms normally invoked for the guidance of acts of private self-defense, section 2267 concludes that "the cases in which the execution of the offender is an absolute necessity *(absolute necessarium)* 'are very rare, if not practically nonexistent.'" The last statement is of course taken directly from the papal encyclical *Evangelium Vitae*.

The conclusions I find in the *Catechism*'s account are not stated explicitly in its text. The text rather lays the theoretical groundwork for a development of doctrine on the morality of capital punishment to be fully articulated at a later time. That doctrine would at minimum state that judicial killing, to the extent that it serves the purpose of retribution (i.e., to the extent that it aims to redress the disorder introduced by deliberate crime by intentionally killing the one responsible for the disorder— to the extent that it is punishment), is wrong.

How, we might ask, does this conclusion correspond to the church's traditional teaching on the subject?

THE CHURCH'S "TRADITIONAL" TEACHING

If one considers chronologically the most significant and influential statements on the morality of capital punishment in Catholic Christian history,[15] one arrives at a number of propositions that summarize what we might call the cumulative consensus of patristic, medieval, and modern ecclesiastical writers. These propositions include

A. lawful public authority alone is authorized by God to inflict the death penalty;
B. this truth is witnessed to in sacred scripture;
C. the death penalty serves
  1. to redress disorder caused by an offense by imposing on offenders proportionate and due punishment,
  2. to protect society by removing a harmful influence and to deter other members of the community from committing serious crimes;
D. clerics are forbidden from participating in the sentencing and inflicting of capital punishments; and
E. the death penalty's lawful infliction requires an upright intention.

I said these reflect the cumulative consensus, not universal consensus. The one premise, however, which is found throughout, representing the virtually unanimous agreement of authors from the time of the Apostles to the modem period, is this: Civil authority, as guardian of the public good, has been given by God the right to inflict punishments on evildoers, including the punishment of death. Avery Cardinal Dulles in his Fordham University *McGinley Lecture,* October, 2000, says: "I know of no official statement from popes or bishops, whether in the past or in the present, that denies the right of the state to execute offenders at least in certain extreme cases." If we could query Christian authors back to the Fathers on the origin of their judgment, the reply in the first place would be divine revelation. In the minds of everyone from Origen, Ambrose, and Augustine, to Gratian, Aquinas, and Innocent III, to Robert Bellarmine, Thomas More, and Alphonsus Liguori, to John Henry Newman and Pius XI, the state's right to exercise lethal authority is taught by God in sacred scripture (particularly in St. Paul, see Rom. 13:1–4), hence to deny it would be to deny revelation itself. Cardinal Dulles notes that even the U.S. bishops in their influential "Statement on Capital Punishment" in 1984, as well the late Cardinal Bernardin in his now famous speech at Fordham University on the "Consistent Ethic of Life," concur in their judgment that "the State has the right to inflict capital punishment."[16]

THE QUESTION OF DOCTRINAL DEVELOPMENT

Would it be legitimate then to refer to the current position as a development of doctrine relative to the traditional position? Not if we understand development of doctrine in its normative sense in the Tradition.[17] This sense can be summarized as follows:

Doctrinal development begins as a partial and imperfect understanding of revealed truth, living by faith in the mind of the church. Because of revelation's definitive and fully determined character—as Vatican II says, "no new public revelation is to be expected before" the return of Jesus Christ (*Dei Verbum,* 4), whatever is not at first explicit, or rather, understood explicitly, is nevertheless already indicated in the explicit; prompted by the contingencies of history and culture and the impulses of a living faith, new and up until now implicit aspects of the content of revelation, under the guidance of the Holy Spirit, emerge from the deposit of faith into the consciousness of the church, making way for a fuller and more perfect understanding (and hence verbal expression) of the divine mystery, while all the time maintaining continuity with antecedent principles and types.[18]

By now it should be clear that the continuity we would expect between the moral judgment anticipated in the *Catechism* and the church's traditional teaching is lacking. At the very least, the traditional teaching holds that lawful public authority is authorized by God to foresee, plan, and inflict capital punishments on duly convicted criminals. The conclusion I see anticipated in the *Catechism* says that no crime, no matter how grave, is sufficient warrant for killing a human person; the only justifiable reason for killing the guilty is that while incarcerated they still pose a grave threat to the body politic.

CAN WE GO THERE?

If it would not be legitimate to refer to the current position as an organic development of doctrine, could the church, nevertheless, limited by the requirements of sound biblical interpretation and dogmatic tradition, now or at some time in the future, justifiably teach in an authoritative way that capital punishment is always wrong? That is to say, can the church change its fundamental position? We can word this another way: Is the traditional Catholic teaching on the morality of capital punishment bound by an irreformable tradition, as is, say, the moral teaching on the intentional killing of the innocent?

This delicate question would no doubt be answered differently by different theologians based on the assumptions held about the nature of Catholic moral teaching. Some would conclude that the sheer magnitude of the Catholic consensus, stretching from the dawn of the Christian church up until yesterday, agreeing on one judgment on the morality of capital punishment, is a reliable indicator of the truthfulness of that judgment. Others would say that the church, having amended judgments in the past on difficult moral questions—say, for example, the question of the legitimacy of coercing heretics back to right belief, has set a precedent that justifies it in changing its judgment in the present on an issue like capital punishment. Both views it seems to me have weaknesses. The first threatens to deal simplistically with the complicated and necessary task of Catholic theology to consider the extent to which the Magisterium's authority is engaged in each legitimate exercise of church teaching.[19] The second threatens to be dismissive of the divine assistance that accompanies the Magisterium, even in its moral teaching and even in its noninfallible teaching capacity.

So back to the question, Could the church be justified in changing its teaching? The church's liberty to propose in the present a judgment that contradicts a judgment(s) from the past depends in part on the authoritative nature of the past judgment(s), in particular, whether any particular statement asserting this judgment, or the traditional teaching as a whole, has been proposed infallibly. In order, therefore, to wholly answer the question nothing less than a consideration of all extant authoritative statements from Catholic tradition on the subject would be required. This obviously is beyond our scope. But permit me to say a few things in this regard.

Vatican II teaches that doctrine can be infallibly taught in three ways, (1) by the pope when he speaks *ex cathedra,* or when acting in his capacity as supreme shepherd and teacher of the universal church, he proclaims in a definitive act a doctrine of faith or morals, (2) by the pope and bishops gathered together in a general council when they teach definitively on a matter of faith or morals, and (3) by the ordinary and universal Magisterium of the Catholic Church, such as when the bishops dispersed throughout the world, united in a bond of communion among themselves and with the successor of Peter, agree on a judgment as one to be definitively held.[20] Assertions proposed in any of these three ways are, according to Catholic teaching, protected from error by the Holy Spirit and hence are known to be true and irreformable.

Any moral judgment, therefore, not asserted in sacred scripture nor proposed in one of these three ways is not known with certitude to be true and, therefore, is in principle reformable. And if none of the five propositions mentioned above specifying the church's traditional teaching on the permissibility of capital punishment have been asserted in the Bible or otherwise proposed infallibly, then the church's traditional judgment on the morality of capital punishment can in principle be revised.

The danger, of course, with speaking about the reformability (changeability) of church teaching is it can lead to a sort of theological positivism in which noninfallible doctrines are treated as if they are without obligatory character.[21] This is not my intent. What is at stake is whether the traditional teaching on capital punishment is true. Identifying the conditions for a legitimate exercise of infallibility is one way to provide an answer. If it has not been proposed infallibly, the question *in principle* remains open. One might argue that even if it turns out to be noninfallible, its status in the tradition is such that a subsequent revision, even by an authoritative source, would be required to provide a satisfactory demonstration of insufficiency. Fair enough, but this is beyond my purpose. The evidence suggests a fundamental revision is on the horizon. My point here is to judge whether such a revision is possible. If and when the church were to take a next step, a more thorough authoritative apologia for the revision (i.e., more thorough than we find in the *Catechism of the Catholic Church* and *Evangelium Vitae*) may well be expected.

I would like now to consider with you a few important examples from the tradition in which the death penalty's legitimacy has been taught (or thought to have been taught) and illustrate for you the kind of work Catholic theology undertakes in considering the degree to which authority is engaged in the church's making of formal statements on matters of faith or morals.

Two papal statements in particular deserve attention. The first, by Pope Leo X, in his bull *Exsurge Domine* (1520), condemns a number of propositions ascribed to Martin Luther, among which is included the following: "That heretics *(haereticos)* be burned is against the will of the Spirit *(contra voluntatem Spiritus)*."[22] How do we determine the authority of this statement? First we consider the document in which it is made, viz., a papal bull. A Bull is an ecclesiastical document issued by a pope (sealed with a *bulla,* or a round seal), addressing points of doctrine; its scope is generally limited to specific ideas or trends, but its audience is generally the universal church. Bulls often contain solemn condemnations of points judged to be dangerous to the Christian faith. It is not uncommon for theologians to judge that the definitions contained in papal bulls have been promulgated with infallible authority.[23] Let's say for argument's sake that the censures contained in *Exsurge Domine* have been infallibly proposed. Does it follow that the falsity of Luther's proposition also has been infallibly proposed, implying that the burning of heretics is *not* against, or not always against, the will of the Holy Spirit? Before we can judge this we need to examine the nature of the papal censure. Following the list of Luther's 41 problematic propositions, the bull reads: "All and each of the above mentioned articles or errors, so to speak, as set before you, we condemn, disapprove, and entirely reject as respectively heretical, or scandalous, or false, or offensive to pious ears, seductive of simple minds, and in opposition to Catholic truth."[24] The precise language justifies us in concluding no more than that the proposition is among a set of articles whose members are either heretical or scandalous or false or offensive to pious ears or seductive of simple minds, and are obstructive to Catholic truth. So the answer to the question whether the falsity of Luther's statement has been infallibly proposed in *Exsurge Domine* is negative.

The second statement, made by Pope Innocent III in the early thirteenth century, is arguably the most influential ecclesiastical statement on the morality of capital punishment in church history. It falls in a profession of faith aimed at reconciling to the church several members of a heretical sect known as the Waldensians.[25] The oath was drafted originally in 1180 (or 1181),[26] and first used by the pope for reconciling Waldensians in 1208.[27] The 1180-1208 version makes no reference at all to the authority of the state to kill criminals. In 1210 Innocent amended the profession adding, for reasons that are uncertain, the following statement:

> We declare that the secular power can without mortal sin impose a judgment of blood provided the punishment is carried out not in hatred, but with good judgment, not inconsiderately, but after mature deliberation.[28]

With what authority was this statement proposed, or rather, was the profession of faith in which it appears proposed? Given that the profession is directed to a particular group (i.e., the breakaway group of Waldensians) and not to the universal church and that its promulgation is by means of personal disciplinary letter, not by means of a bull or otherwise universally authoritative document, not all the assertions in it should be taken as articles of faith, even though some of them already have been defined as articles of faith. If therefore one of the propositions is not already a defined doctrine, the presence of that proposition in the oath to the Waldensians does not alone suffice to constitute it as such. It is, therefore, my judgment that Innocent's statement does not constitute an infallible definition.

What about the traditional conclusion that the death penalty's legitimacy has been taught in sacred scripture and hence is part of divine revelation? (After all, death is prescribed nearly fifty times for more than twenty offenses throughout the various law codes of the Pentateuch.)

Examining this question relative to the moral teaching of the Old Testament, the patristic distinction, systematized by Aquinas, might help us with our answer. Aquinas distinguishes between the "moral" precepts of the Old Law (i.e., Old Testament) and its merely "ceremonial" and "judicial" precepts. The Old Law's moral precepts *(praecepta moralia),* Aquinas says given to the people by "God Himself *(per seipsum),"* relate by their very nature to good morals and hence are part of the natural law. They can be reduced, Aquinas tells us, to the Ten Commandments. The remaining precepts of the Old Law—given "through Moses *(per Moysen)"*—are "ceremonial and judicial *(caeremonialibus et iudicialibus)."*[29] With the coming of Christ, the ceremonial and judicial precepts passed away, leaving the Old Law's moral precepts alone to endure into the Christian dispensation. If this distinction is sound, then all the precepts taught in the legislative part of Deuteronomy, in the Covenant Code and in the Priestly and Holiness Codes, such as virtually all the places in the Pentateuch in which death is prescribed, are either ceremonial or judicial precepts. We are left, then, with the Fifth Commandment as the only Old Testament moral precept dealing with life and death. And though it has been traditionally interpreted to refer only to the innocent, the precept itself tells us no more than not to kill.

Coming to the New Testament, we find passages apparently supporting as well as opposing bloody punishment. On the one hand, we see the good thief in Luke's account of the crucifixion announcing that he and his partner are "justly…receiving the due reward" for their crimes (Luke 23:41), and Jesus leaving the statement unopposed. On the other hand, we see Christ in John 8 apparently rescinding the Mosaic punishment of death for adultery when he turns the accusations of the mob, thirsty for the adulteress' blood, back on themselves by confronting them with their own guilt. Passages like these can be multiplied.

But what are we to do with the well-known passage from Romans 13, which reads

> For (public) rulers are not a terror to good conduct, but to bad. Would you have no fear of him who is in authority? Then do what is good, and you will receive his approval, for he is God's servant for your good. But if you do wrong, be afraid, for he does not bear the sword in vain; he is the servant of God to execute his wrath on the wrongdoer. (v. 3–4)

Surely this is an example of divine revelation asserting the legitimacy, at least in principle, of the state's power to kill evildoers? As transparent as it seems, most contemporary biblical scholars do not interpret the term *the sword* in v. 4 as having reference to capital punishment but rather as a metaphor for the general coercive authority of the state.[30] And Pope Pius XII in 1954 explicitly denies that verse 4 refers to a specific rule of action. Addressing a congress of Italian Catholic jurists, he writes,

> the words of the sources [of revelation] and of the living teaching power do not refer to the specific content of individual juridical prescriptions or rules of action (cf. particularly Rom. 13:4), but rather to the essential foundation itself of penal power and of its immanent finality.[31]

The pope says in essence that to get to the heart of divine revelation's teaching on the nature of civil authority's penal power, the place to look is not in specific rules of action—he singles out Romans 13:4, but rather to the foundation of civil authority in general (i.e., in the authority of God) and its right to defend the common good through the infliction of punishment.

This brief and admittedly selective exercise in theological exegesis illustrates the kind of work necessary for resolving the larger question of the authority of the traditional Catholic teaching on capital punishment. Having considered with you tonight certain of the chief doctrinal examples in the tradition, and having done so elsewhere with many other significant statements,[32] it is my judgment that, despite the chronicity and uniformity of the traditional conclusion on the morality of capital punishment, the conditions necessary for an infallible exercise of the church's teaching authority have not been met. It follows that a rethinking of the traditional teaching along the lines I have described is possible, and that the conclusions I find implicit in the *Catechism*'s account could be made explicit without in any way compromising the integrity of Catholic doctrine.

WHY THE CHANGE?

The act of killing Timothy McVeigh, like his (and Terry Nichols's) act of blowing up the Murrah Federal Building in Oklahoma City, has been conceived and planned in advance, and will be carried out with full deliberation and intent. His killing will be participated in (morally speaking) by everyone from the federal prosecutor and his assistants, who petitioned for and secured his sentence, to the judge who mandated the sentence, to the U.S. president, who, it is to predict, will deny requests—should there be any—for clemency, to the federal prison warden at whose command the poison is administered. Each will be, as it were, accomplices in killing. And if what I have said is correct, each, according to Catholic moral teaching, will be accomplices to a morally bad act.

Why might the church consider an act of judicial killing bad, even when carried out with all necessary due process and assurance of distributive fairness? We might venture an answer by looking at the philosophical system of thought used by John Paul II, viz., personalism. Since his elevation to the Chair of Peter in 1978 he has not ceased to remind the church and the world of the godlike nature and priceless dignity of the human person—every human person, even one whose actions are most loathsome and wicked. In these admonitions, the pope has used unprecedentedly strong language, language, it seems to me, that relocates the boundary lines circumscribing legitimate killing. Throughout the encyclical *Evangelium Vitae,* for example, the good of human life and its derivative rights are referred to with terms like *inviolability, inviolable,* and *inalienable.* For example, the pope says he is providing "a precise and vigorous reaffirmation of the value of human life and its inviolability" (no. 5); the encyclical speaks elsewhere of "the original and inalienable right to life" (no. 20); and again of "the sacredness and inviolability of human life" (no. 53); examples like these can be multiplied.[33] In only three instances is the scope of application limited to innocent human life.[34] The rest are unqualified. One particularly noteworthy instance reads

> human life is sacred and inviolable at *every* stage and in *every* situation; it is an indivisible good. (No. 87, emphasis added)

A second states

> (The Hippocratic Oath) requires every doctor to commit himself to *absolute respect* for human life and its sacredness. (No. 89, emphasis added)

Still another says

> the overall message, which the New Testament will bring to perfection, is a forceful appeal for respect for the *inviolability of physical life* and the integrity of the person. (No. 40, emphasis added)

Language like this is not used in this way in Catholic tradition before the twentieth century and does not find prominence in papal writings before John XXIII's encyclical *Pacem in terris* (1963). Though the tradition has always affirmed the absolute immunity of innocent human life from intentional attacks and destruction, this "inviolability" has traditionally been understood to be forfeited by one who conscientiously chooses to carry out certain kinds of behavior. The tradition is quite clear that the lives of those who deliberately commit serious crimes are not inviolable. Aquinas says a grave sinner falls from human dignity and may be treated as a beast,[35] Pius XII says a dangerous criminal, "by his crime,...has been dispossessed of his right to live."[36] In both cases, the malefactor's life through his own deliberate act becomes violable. This is clearly not the teaching of the *Catechism,* nor *Evangelium Vitae.* In fact, John Paul II emphatically states in the latter that, "Not even a murderer loses his personal dignity" (No. 9). The intentional and unalterable destruction of human life which capital punishment entails is hard to reconcile with the language used in these instances to specify the moral claim that human dignity makes on our choices and the behaviors that carry them out.

CONCLUSION

I have touched upon a few important points of the church's capital punishment debate, none of which were treated exhaustively and several of which, I'm sure, only served to raise further questions. But if by this exercise I have led you to conclude that the issues at stake are more complicated and multifaceted than they once seemed, and that at least something new is going on in the church's relationship to the problem of capital punishment, then one purpose for my talk will have been fulfilled. And I'll have the satisfaction of knowing that fewer careless statements will be made about what's going on with the Catholic Church and the death penalty.

Notes

1. On April 19, 1995, around 9:03 a.m., a massive bomb inside a rental truck exploded, blowing to pieces half of the nine-story Alfred P. Murrah Federal Building in downtown Oklahoma City. 168 people, including 19 children, were killed, and 500 were injured in the worst terrorist attack on U.S. soil. In June 1997 a jury found Timothy McVeigh guilty of the act; he was subsequently sentenced to die by lethal injection.

2. Following their examples, Pius XII, in 1953, appealed to U.S. President Harry Truman on behalf of Julius and Ethel Rosenberg sentenced to death for espionage.

3. Since 1980 the U.S. bishops alone have issued—personally or collectively—more than 214; most are listed in the *Bibliography of Statements by U.S. Catholic Bishops on the Death Penalty: 1972–1999,* compiled by Catholics Against Capital Punishment (Arlington, Va., 1998); available at <http:www. igc.org/cacp/biblio.html>.

4. Sections 2263–67, *Catechismus Catholicae Ecclesiae (editio typica Latina) (Catechism of the Catholic Church* [hereafter *Catechism*]) (Rome: Libreria Editrice Vaticana, 1997). The original edition—in French—was released in 1992, and the English translation of the French in 1994. In September 1997, with the revisions of the first edition complete, the definitive Latin text was promulgated by Pope John Paul II. English references unless otherwise indicated are from the English translation of the *editio typica,* the 1994 Vatican approved English translation of the 1992 French edition with the inclusion of the additions and changes required by the 1997 *Corrigenda* (Amendments to the 1992 Edition, Vatican English translation).

5. The *Catechism*'s predecessor, the 1566 *Roman Catechism,* prepared pursuant to a decree of the Council of Trent, treats capital punishment under a subsection headed "exceptions" to the Fifth Commandment. (*Catechism of the Council of Trent for Parish Priests,* part III, cap. VI, par. 4, tr. John A. McHugh, O.P. and Charles J. Callan, O.P. [New York: Joseph F. Wagner, Inc., 1923] 421.) And most systematic treatises, at least since Trent, follow Aquinas and treat it under the heading, "whether it is lawful to kill malefactors," or something similar. (*"Utrum sit licitum occidere homines peccatores,"* Aquinas, *Summa Theologiae [ST],* II–II, q. 64, a. 2; other examples include Thomas Cardinal Cajetan, Commentary on q. 64, a. 2, from Commentaries of Thomas Cajetan, in Aquinas, *Opera Omnia,* tom. IX, Leonine ed. [1897] 69; Juan Cardinal De Lugo, *"De justitia et jure,"* *Disputationes Scholasticae et Morales* [Paris, 1893], disp. 10, sec. 2, par. 56, 69; Cardinal Bellarmine, *De Laicis sive Saecularibus [De Laicis],* trans. Kathleen E. Murphy [Connecticut: Hyperion Press, Inc., 1928], ch. 13, p. 54.)

6. Aquinas's term is repeated constantly throughout the tradition in treatments of legitimate acts of killing in self-defense; for example, Alphonsus Marie de Liguori, *Theologia Moralis,* tom, 1, lib. 3, tract. 4, cap. 1, dub. 3, par. 380 (Rome: Vaticana, 1905); M. Zalba, S.J., *Theologiae Moralis Compendium,* vol. I (Madrid: Biblioteca De Autores Cristianos, 1958), no. 1591, p. 871; I. Aertnys, C.SS.R. and C. Damen C.SS.R., *Theologia Moralis* (Rome: Marietti Editori Ltd., 1956), tom. I, lib. III, tract. V, cap. III, no. 571, p. 541.

7. *"Causa legitimae tutelae contra iniustum aggressorem, si debitum servetur moderamen, delictum omnino aufert: secus imputabilitatem tantummodo minuit, sicut etiam causa provocationis."* *Codex Iuris Canonici* (1917), can. 2205, § 4; *"legitimae tutelae causa contra iniustum sui vel alterius aggressorem egit, debitum servans moderamen"; "ab eo, qui legitimae tutelae causa contra iniustum sui vel alterius aggressorem egit, nec tamen debitum servavit moderamen";* John Paul II, *Codex Iuris Canonici* (Vatican City: Libreria Editrice Vaticana, 1983), can. 1323, 5°, 1324, 6°.

8. Aquinas, *ST,* II–II, q. 64, a. 7c, ad. 4; Alphonsus De Liguori, *Theologia Moralis,* tom. 1, lib. 3, tract. 4, cap. 1, dub. 3, par. 380, p. 631; Zalba, S.J., *Theologiae Moralis Compendium,* vol. 1, no. 1591, p. 869; McHugh and Callan, O.P., *Moral Theology: A Complete Course,* vol. 2 (New York: Joseph F. Wagner, Inc., 1930), no. 1828, p.105; Aertnys, Damen, *Theologia Moralis,* tom. 1, lib. III, tract. V, cap. III, no. 571, p. 541; A.J.J.F. Haine, *Theologiae Moralis* (Rome: Desclée, 1900), 4th ed., tom. 1, pars II, cap. III, I°, q. 130, p. 453; Dominic M. Prümmer, O.P., *Handbook of Moral Theology* (Cork: The Mercier Press, Ltd., 1956) 127; Genicot, S.J., *Institutiones Theologiae Moralis* (Brussels: Alb. Dewit, 1927), vol. 1, tract. VI, sect. V, cap. II, no. 366, p. 296; note the ambiguity in Scavini's use of the term *solam necessitatem,* Petro

Scavini, *Theologia Moralis Universa* (Paris: Jacobum Lecoffre, 1863), tom. III, tract. VII, disp. II, cap. 1, art. I, no. 75, q. 7, p. 74.

9. See Aquinas *ST*, II–II, q. 64, a. 7c.

10. John Finnis, *Aquinas* (Oxford University Press, 1998) 277.

11. "The legitimate defense of persons and societies is not an exception to the prohibition against the intentional killing of the innocent that constitutes murder. The act of self-defense can have a double effect: the preservation of one's own life; and the killing of the aggressor....The one is intended, the other not. (Aquinas *ST*, II–II, 64, 7c)"

12. "Love toward oneself remains a fundamental principle of morality. Therefore it is legitimate to insist on respect for one's own right to life. Someone who defends his life is not guilty of murder even if he is forced to deal his aggressor a lethal blow:

> If a man in self-defense uses more than necessary violence, it will be unlawful: whereas if he repels force with moderation, his defense will be lawful....Nor is it necessary for salvation that a man omit the act of moderate self-defense to avoid killing the other man, since one is bound to take more care of one's own life than of another's. (Aquinas, *ST,* 11–11, 64, 7c)"

13. "Legitimate defense can be not only a right but also a grave duty for one who is responsible for the lives of others. The defense of the common good requires that an unjust aggressor be rendered unable to cause harm. For this reason, those who legitimately hold authority also have the right to use arms to repel aggressors against the civil community entrusted to their responsibility."

Although the context has changed from addressing the needs of an individual to those of a community, and from the right of an individual to defend his own life to the rights and duties of public authority to defend the community for which it is responsible, the context is otherwise the same. We are still referring to the need (previously individual, and now corporate) to repel an aggressor and the requirement that in doing so, only force necessary to render him unable to cause harm is to be used. The act mentioned here is, like before, an act of self-defense. While 2265 does not explicitly state that any death following from this act of self-defense must be unintended, the reference to collective self-defense in 2263 requires that that be the meaning of 2265. The *Catechism* certainly supplies no basis for saying that the death of an aggressor following from an act of collective self-defense as described in this paragraph may be deliberately intended.

14. "The efforts of the state to curb the spread of behavior harmful to people's rights and to the basic rules of civil society correspond to the requirement of safeguarding the common good. Legitimate public authority has the right and the duty to inflict punishment proportionate to the gravity of the

offense. Punishment has the primary aim of redressing the disorder introduced by the offense. When it is willingly accepted by the guilty party, it assumes the value of expiation. Punishment then, in addition to defending public order and protecting people's safety, has a medicinal purpose: as far as possible, it must contribute to the correction of the guilty party."

15. By *authoritative* I refer not only to propositions asserted in formally authoritative ways (e.g., the statements of popes and ecumenical councils), but also to ones which are *de facto* authoritative by virtue of the influence and import of the works in which they are expressed, for example, the *Decretum Gratiani* and *Dictionnaire de Théologie Catholique,* or by virtue of the influence and import of the authors who asserted them, for example, the church fathers and Aquinas.

16. Avery Dulles, S.J., *The Death Penalty: A Right to Life Issue?,* Laurence J. McGinley Lecture, October 17, 2000, Fordham University, 10. Fr. Dulles says that John Paul II would likewise concur in this judgment, but unfortunately makes no reference to the pope's treatment of capital punishment in *Evangeiium Vitae* 56, nor ever even references the account found in the *Catechism of the Catholic Church.*

17. The primordial work on the notion of doctrinal development is by Vincent of Lerins (d. ca. A.D. 445), *A Commonitory: For the Antiquity and Universality of the Catholic Faith Against the Profane Novelties of All Heresies,* ch. 1, par. 3, ch. 2, par. 4 *(Nicene and Post-Nicene Fathers, Series II,* vol. 11, 132); the most extended and perhaps most famous work is John Henry Newman's, *An Essay on the Development of Christian Doctrine* (1st pub. 1848) (University of Notre Dame Press, 1989). The basic ideas of Vincent and Newman are repeated in the following ecclesiastical documents: Vatican I, *Dei Filius,* ch. 4 *(Documents of the Ecumenical Councils [DEC],* Vol. II, 809), Pius XI, *Mortalium animos, AAS* (1928), 14, Pius XII, *Humani Generis* (1950) (Denz., 2314), Vatican II, "Dogmatic Constitution on Divine Revelation" *(Dei Verbum),* no. 8 *(DEC-*II, 974), "Pastoral Constitution," *Gaudium et Spes* (no. 62) *(DEC-II,* 1112). A fine contemporary theological exploration of the idea of doctrinal development is Henri de Lubac's "Le problème du développement du dogme," *Recherches de science religieuse* 35 (1948), 130–160; tr. "The Problem of the Development of Dogma," in *Theology in History* (San Francisco: Ignatius Press, 1996) 248–80.

18. This definition is adapted from one found in my doctoral dissertation: *Capital Punishment, Abolition and Roman Catholic Moral Tradition,* University of Oxford, Trinity 2000, 256–57. This definition applies to doctrines of faith and doctrines of morality; John Paul II writes in *Veritatis Splendor,* par. 28, that doctrinal development in the church's moral teaching is "analogous to that which has taken place in the realm of the truths of faith." It can be applied

by extension also to what are sometimes referred to as secondary objects of infallibility, for example, nonrevealed truths necessarily connected to revealed truths; see *Ad Tuendam Fidem,* no. 3, as well as Cardinal Ratzinger's *Commentary on Profession of Faith's Concluding Paragraph* (June 1998), par. 6, *Origins* (July 1998), vol. 28, no. 8, p. 117.

19. "One must therefore take into account the proper character of every exercise of the Magisterium, considering the extent to which its authority is engaged." Congregation for the Doctrine of the Faith, *Instruction on the Ecclesial Vocation of the Theologian,* 24 May 1990, (Boston: St. Paul Books and Media), no 17.

20. *Lumen Gentium,* no. 25.

21. See Vatican II, *LG,* no. 25, Pius XII's statement on the teaching authority of encyclical letters, *Humani Generis,* 1950 (Denz. 2313), and the instruction of the CDF, *Ecclesial Vocation of the Theologian,* 23, 24, 33.

22. Denz. 773.

23. According to Francis A. Sullivan, S.J., theologians Louis Billot, in his work *Tractatus de Ecclesia Christi* (1898), and Edmond Dublanchy, in his article on infallibility in the *Dictionnaire de Théologie Catholique* (1927), judged there to be "dogmatic [i.e., irreformable] definitions" in *Exsurge Domine* (1520). Sullivan does not specify which articles singled out in the bull fall into this category. Sullivan's judgment on the matter is "that *Exsurge Domine* does not meet the requirements for a dogmatic definition." See Sullivan, *Creative Fidelity: Weighing and Interpreting Documents of the Magisterium* (Dublin: Gill & Macmillan, Ltd., 1996), 84–85.

24. Denz. 781.

25. The sect took its name from its twelfth century founder, an erstwhile Lyonnais merchant, Waldes, who having undergone a conversion not unlike Francis of Assisi, went about gathering followers and preaching a gospel of evangelical freedom. For an introduction to the rise of the Waldensian heresy in the twelfth century see Malcolm Lambert, *Medieval Heresy: Popular Movements from the Gregorian Reform to the Reformation,* 2d. ed. (Oxford: Blackwell, 1992) 62–87.

26. It was drafted by Waldes himself at a time when he was attempting to prove his orthodoxy before certain members of the Lyonnaise hierarchy.

27. The oath of December 1208 is preserved in a letter of Innocent III's dated the 18th of that month "to the archbishop and suffragans of the church of Tarragona" alerting them to the reconciliation of Durand, the leader of the breakaway group, and his followers (for the letter see *Innocenti III romani pontificis Regestorum sive epistolarum libri XV, XI.* 196 and translated in Walter L. Wakefield and Austin P. Evans, *Heresies of the High Middle Ages [HHM]* [New York: Columbia University Press, 1969], 222–226; the letter

168 / *E. Christian Brugger*

appears in Migne, *Patrologia Latina [PL]*, tom. CCXV, cols. 1510a–1513d, although it is dated 15 Jan. 1209); two copies of Innocent's 1208 letter were made, one sent to Durand himself and the other to certain laymen supervised by the Poor Catholics ([*Regesta XI.* 197, 198; in Migne, *PL*, tom. CCXV, col. 1514]; see also *HHM*, 716, n. 15).

28.   *"De potestate saeculari asserimus quod sine peccato mortali potest judicium sanguinis exercere, dummodo ad inferendam vindictam, non odio, sed judicio, non incaute sed consulte procedat"* (*PL*, tom. CCXV, col. 1512a), my translation; the entire revised 1210 profession is translated in Denzinger, *The Sources of Catholic Dogma*, trans. Roy J. Deferrari (London: B. Herder Book Co., 1954), nos. 420–427, esp. no. 425.

29.   Aquinas, *Summa Theologiae*, I–II, q. 99, q. 100, a. 2c, a. 3c.

30.   For examples, see T. W. Manson, *Peake's Commentary on the Bible* (1962) 950 [825 f.], J. Fitzmyer, *The New Jerome Biblical Commentary* (1989), 864:119, F. Davidson and R. Martin, *The New Bible Commentary Revised* (1970) 1041; for a more thorough treatment of the passage, see G. Cragg and J. Knox, *The Interpreter's Bible*, vol. IX (1954) 598–604; one exception is E. Best, "The Letter of Paul to the Romans," *The Cambridge Bible Commentary* (1967), 148; he interprets the authority spoken of in verse 4 as including "the right to enforce their punishments even to the extent of putting men to death."

31.   Pope Pius XII, *Address to the Italian Association of Catholic Jurists*, December 5, 1954; translation, *Catholic Mind*, vol. 53 (1955) 381.

32.   See Brugger, *Capital Punishment, Abolition and Roman Catholic Moral Tradition*, doctoral dissertation, University of Oxford, Trinity 2000, chs. 3–7.

33.   The encyclical uses the terms a dozen or so times, including in the cover page title of the encyclical itself. "On the value and inviolability of human life" *(De vitae humanae inviolabili bono)*. See nos. 5, 18, 20, 40, 53, 57, 60, 70, 71, 72, 81, 87, 96, 101; for the related word *sacred (sacredness)*, see nos. 22, 62, 102.

34.   Nos. 57, 60, 101.

35.   *ST,* II-II, q. 64, a. 2, ad. 3.

36.   "Il est réservé alors au pouvoir public de priver le condamné du *bien* de la vie, en expiation de sa faute, après que, par son crime, ilest déjà dépossédé de son *droit* à la vie." Pius XII, "Iis qui interfuerunt Conventui primo internationali de Histopathologia Systematis nervorum," *AAS* 44 (1952) 787.

Part Three

ANTHROPOLOGICAL AND METHODOLOGICAL CHANGES IN CATHOLIC SOCIAL TEACHING

11. The Changing Anthropological Bases of Catholic Social Teaching

Charles E. Curran

This chapter first appeared in Curran, *Directions in Catholic Social Ethics* (Notre Dame, Ind.: University of Notre Dame Press, 1985).

For one hundred years there has existed a body of official Catholic Church teaching on social ethics and the social mission of the church. There was a social teaching within the Catholic Church before that time, but from the pontificate of Leo XIII (1878–1903) one can speak of a body of authoritative social teaching worked out in a systematic way and often presented in the form of encyclicals or papal letters to the bishops and to the whole church. The purpose of this chapter is to point out some of the changing anthropological emphases in this body of social teaching, thereby proposing an approach that can and should be employed in Christian social ethics today. The limitation of our discussion primarily to the official body of papal teaching should not be construed as failing to recognize the other theological approaches within the Catholic community. However, the teaching of the hierarchical magisterium has a special degree of authority about it and historically has served as a basis for much of Catholic social teaching during the last hundred years. Also by limiting the discussion to this particular body of teaching it is possible to place some realistic perimeters on the study.

Until a few years ago Catholic commentators were generally reluctant to admit any development within the papal social teaching.[1] The popes themselves gave the impression of continuity and even went out of their way to smooth over any differences with their "predecessors of happy memory." Often Catholic commentaries on the papal teaching were uncritical—merely explaining and applying the papal teaching. John F. Cronin, one of the better known commentators on Catholic social teaching in the United States, while reminiscing in 1971, recognized his failure to appreciate the historical and cultural conditionings of this teaching and the importance of a proper hermeneutic in explaining it.[2] In the area of church and state relations and religious liberty, the historically and culturally conditioned aspect of the papal teaching was clearly recognized somewhat earlier.[3] In the last few years more scholars have realized the development and change that have occurred in Catholic social teaching.[4] Especially since the decade of 1960s, this development has become so pronounced that no one could deny its existence.

This study will concentrate on anthropology, but it will be impossible to treat all aspects of anthropology. The first section on the personal aspects of anthropology will trace the development culminating in an emphasis on the freedom, equality, and participation of the person. The second section will discuss some of the important methodological consequences of such an understanding. The third section will evaluate the social teaching of Pope John Paul II in the light of these changing anthropological bases.

Personal Aspects of Anthropology

Octogesima adveniens, the apostolic letter of Pope Paul VI written on the occasion of the eightieth anniversary of *Rerum novarum,* proposes an anthropology highlighting the freedom and dignity of the human person that are seen above all in two aspirations becoming evermore prevalent in our world—the aspiration to equality and the aspiration to participation.[5] Freedom, equality, and participation are the significant characteristics of the anthropology of *Octogesima adveniens.*

The differences with the writings of Leo XIII are striking. The church at the time of Leo was fearful of freedom and equality and looked on the majority of people as the untutored multitude who had to be guided or directed by their rulers.[6]

Pope Leo condemned the "modern liberties." Liberty of worship goes against the "chiefest and holiest human duty" demanding the worship of the one true God in the one true religion that can be easily recognized by its external signs. Liberty of speech and of the press means that nothing will remain sacred, for truth will be obscured by darkness, and error will prevail. There is only a right and duty to speak what is true and honorable and no right to speak what is false. A like judgment is passed on liberty of teaching. Finally liberty of conscience is considered. The only true meaning of the freedom of conscience is the freedom to follow the will of God and to do one's duty in obeying his commands. At best the public authority can tolerate what is at variance with truth and justice for the sake of avoiding greater evils or of preserving some greater good.[7] Leo XIII was certainly no supporter of civil liberties and the modern freedoms.

Leo XIII not only did not promote equality as a virtue or something to be striven for in society, but he stressed the importance of inequality. Inequality is a fact of nature. There are differences in health, beauty, intelligence, strength, and courage. These natural inequalities necessarily bring about social inequalities that are essential for the good functioning of society. In short, the inequality of rights and of power proceed from the very author of nature. Leo had a view of society as a hierarchical organism in which there are different roles and functions to fulfill but in which all will work for the common good of all.[8]

According to Leo:

> In like manner, no one doubts that all men are equal one to another, so far as regards their common origin and nature, or the last end that each one has to attain, or the rights and duties which are thence derived. But, as the abilities of all are not equal, as one differs from another in the powers of mind or body, and as there are many dissimilarities of manner, disposition and character, it is most repugnant to reason to endeavor to confine all within the same measure, and to extend complete equality to the institutions of civil life.[9]

Inequalities and some of the hardships connected with them will always be part of human existence in a world that is marked by the presence of original sin. To suffer and to endure is the lot of people. People should not be deluded by promises of undisturbed repose and constant enjoyment. We should look upon our world in a spirit of reality and at the same time seek elsewhere the solace to its troubles.[10]

Leo XIII likewise does not call for the active participation of all in social and political life, but rather he has a very hierarchical view of civil society that follows from the inequalities mentioned above. Leo's favorite word for the rulers of society is *principes*. The very word shows his hierarchical leanings. The citizen is primarily one who obeys the divine law, the natural law, and the human law that are handed down by the *principes*. Leo even quotes the maxim *qualis rex, talis grex* (as the king, so the herd—the people), which indicates the power of the ruler over all the citizens in practically every aspect of life.[11] The citizens are called by Leo the untutored multitude, who must be led and protected by the ruler.[12] At best, authority appears as paternalistic, and the subjects are children who are to obey and respect their rulers with a type of piety.[13] Leo was fearful of the liberalistic notion of the sovereignty of the people, which really meant that the people no longer owed obedience to God and God's law in all aspects of their public and private lives.[14]

In this authoritarian and paternalistic understanding, there is no distinction between society and the state, which had been present in classical thought but then lost during the period of absolutism. Leo's theory is that of the ethical society-state in which the total common good of the society is entrusted to the rulers. Society is constructed from the top down with the ruler guarding and protecting the untutored multitude from the many dangers of life just as the father has the function of protecting and guiding his children in the family.[15]

Leo's denial of liberty, equality, and participation can be somewhat understood in the light of the circumstances of the times in which he lived. The pope was an implacable foe of a liberalism that in his mind was the root cause of all the problems of the modern day. Liberalism substitutes foolish license for true liberty. The followers of liberalism deny the existence of any divine authority and proclaim that every human being is a law unto oneself. Liberalism proposes an independent morality in which the human being is freed from the divine law and authority and can do whatever one wants. Leo consequently attacks those forms of government that make the collective reason of the community the supreme guide of life in society. They substitute the decision of the majority for the rule of God. God and God's law are totally removed from society.[16]

Behind Leo's fear of equality lurks the same individualism present in liberalism. For Leo society is an organism. Human beings are by nature social and called to join together in political society for the common good. To live in society is not a restriction on individual human freedom, for by nature all of us are social. Each one has a different function to play in the hierarchically structured organism that resembles the organism of the human body with all its different parts, but each functioning for the good of the whole. Leo fears an understanding that sees society merely as a collection of equal individuals, for this would destroy any social fabric and true social ordering. Participation is also looked on as a threat, for this could readily be confused with the demands of liberalistic license and destroy the organic unity of a society in which each person has one's God-given function to perform. In the context of Leo's understanding of the untutored multitude, there could be little or no room for participation.

In general Leo rightly recognized some of the problems of liberalism and individualism. However, his only solution was to turn his back totally on all the developments that were then taking place in the modern world. At the very least Leo lacked the prophetic charisma to sort out the good from the bad in the newer developments that were taking place in the nineteenth century and to find a place for the legitimate demands of liberty, equality, and participation.[17] The picture emerges of a static and hierarchically structured authoritarian society governed by the law of God and the natural law under the protection and guidance of a paternalistic ruler who directs all to the common good and protects his subjects from physical and moral harm.

This explanation of Leo's approach shows the tremendous gulf that exists between his understanding of anthropology and that proposed by Pope Paul VI in *Octogesima adveniens.* However, one can trace some of the major lines of the development that occurred from Leo XIII to Paul VI.

Even in Leo XIII there are some aspects pointing in a different direction, but they are found mostly in his 1891 encyclical *Rerum novarum* on the rights of the worker. In his political writings Leo especially argues against a totalitarian democracy with its emphasis on majority rule and its lack of respect for divine and natural law, but he always upheld the basic rights of individual human beings, which might be abused because of the totalitarian democracy. In *Rerum novarum* he stresses even more the rights of the individual worker, and his approach is less authoritarian and paternalistic. In *Rerum novarum* Leo recalls, while pointing out the danger of socialism, that the human being is prior to the state and has natural rights that do not depend on the state.[18] The right to private property is based on our nature as rational and provident beings. Every individual has the right to marry. Marriage is older than the state and has its rights and duties independently of the state.[19] The state has an obligation to intervene to protect the rights of the workers, for public authority must step in when a particular class suffers or is threatened with harm that in no other way can be met or avoided.[20] Moreover, workers themselves have the right to organize into unions and associations to promote their own rights and interests.[21] Here appears the basis for participation in the shaping of one's own destiny.

In *Rerum novarum* Leo repeats his teaching on inequality. The condition of things inherent in human affairs must be borne with. These conditions include natural differences of the most important kinds—differences in capacities, skills, health, and strength. Unequal fortune is a necessary result of unequal conditions.[22] However, Leo appears to admit a basic equality of all to have their rights recognized and protected by the state. In fact the poor and badly off have a claim to special consideration.[23] As one would expect, Leo upholds the rights of the individual against socialism. In tension with his other emphases Leo's writings show differing degrees of recognition of some freedom, equality, and even of incipient participation as anthropological concerns.

Pope Pius XI (1922–1939) remains in continuity with his predecessor Leo XIII. Liberalism lies at the root of the problems of the modern world. The principal cause of the disturbed conditions in which we live is that the power of law and respect for authority have been considerably weakened ever since people came to deny that the origin of law and of authority was in God, the creator and ruler of the world. Liberalism has even fathered socialism and bolshevism. Pius XI insists on the importance of natural law and a hierarchical ordering of society based on it. In *Quadragesimo anno,* on the fortieth anniversary of Leo's encyclical *Rerum novarum,* Pius XI continues the discussion of justice and the economic order, insisting on the dignity and rights of the individual and also on the social nature of human beings. Here again the two extreme approaches of individualism and socialism are rejected on the basis of an anthropology that recognizes the dignity and rights of the individual as well as the social aspects of the human person.[24]

However, contact with different forms of totalitarianism brought to the fore an emphasis on the defense of the rights, dignity, and freedom of the individual. (There has been much discussion in the last few decades about the relationship of the Catholic Church to fascism, nazism, and communism. Without entering into the debate, it is safe to generalize that the Catholic Church was much more fearful of the left and showed itself more willing to compromise with the right.) Pius XI defends the transcendental character of the human person against materialistic and atheistic communism. Communism is condemned for stripping human beings of their liberty and for robbing the human person of dignity.[25] Now the church becomes the protector of human freedom and dignity. In *Non abbiamo bisogno* Pius XI even defends the freedom of conscience with the recognition that he is speaking about the true freedom of conscience and not the license that refuses to recognize the laws of God.[26]

The development continues in the pontificate of Pope Pius XII (1939–1958). The historical context of the struggle against totalitarianism remains, but the significant role of Christian Democratic parties in Europe adds an important new dimension. In his Christmas radio message in 1944 Pope Pius XII insisted on the dignity of human beings and on a system of government that will be more in accord with the dignity and freedom of the citizenry. This emphasis on the dignity and freedom of the human being also calls for greater participation and active involvement of all. The human being is not the object of social life or an inert element in it, but rather is the subject, foundation, and end of social life.[27]

In the light of these historical circumstances and of a theoretical insistence on the centrality of the dignity of the human person, Pius proposed an understanding of the state remarkably different from that of Leo XIII. As John Courtney Murray lucidly points out, Pius XII abandoned Leo XIII's ethical concept of the society-state and accepted a juridical or limited constitutional state. For Leo there is no distinction between society and the state, for the state is hierarchically ordered, with the rulers having the function of guarding and protecting the illiterate masses in every aspect of life. By emphasizing the dignity, freedom, and responsibility of the individual person Pius XII clearly accepts a limited view of the state which sees it as only a part of society with a function of defending the rights of human beings and of promoting the freedom of the people. The state has a limited juridical role and does not act as the parent who guides the entire lives of one's children. No longer is the state understood in terms of the relationship between *principes* and the untutored multitudes. The rulers are representatives of the people, and the people are responsible citizens.[28]

Despite these significant changes in the importance of the dignity of the person and the recognition of limited constitutional government, G. B. Guzzetti still detects an air of the aristocratic about Pius XII's approach.[29] Also on the matter of inequalities in society, Pius advances over Leo but still insists that natural inequalities of education, of earthly goods, and of social position are not obstacles to brotherhood and community provided they are not arbitrary and are in accord with justice and charity.[30]

The short pontificate of John XXIII (1958–1963) with its convocation of the Second Vatican Council had a great impact on Roman Catholicism. In the area of social ethics John in his two encyclicals *Mater et magistra* and *Pacem in terris* defends human dignity in the midst of the ever-increasing social relationships and interdependencies that characterize our modern world. *Pacem in terris* gives the most detailed statement, in the papal social tradition, of human rights based on the dignity of the person but also adds the corresponding duties, thereby avoiding the danger of individualism. The dignity of the human person requires that every individual enjoy the right to act freely and responsibly. The dignity, freedom, and equality of the human person are highlighted and defended, but many of the assumptions of an older liberalistic individualism are not accepted.[31]

There is one fascinating development even within John's own writings. The papal social tradition consistently emphasizes that life in society must be based on truth, justice, and love. John XXIII repeated the importance of this triad in *Mater et magistra* in 1961.[32] However, in 1963 in *Pacem in terris* a fourth element was added: A political society is well ordered, beneficial, and in keeping with human dignity if it is grounded on truth, justice, love, and freedom.[33] Even in John there was only a later recognition of the fundamental importance of freedom alongside truth, justice, and love.

From the first encyclical of Leo XIII on the question of economic ethics, there was some recognition for participation and responsibility, especially in terms of the workers' right to form organizations and unions to promote their own interests. John XXIII recognizes there is an innate need of human nature, calling for human beings engaged in productive activity to have an opportunity to assume responsibility and to perfect themselves by their efforts. Participation of workers in medium-size and larger enterprises calls for some type of partnership.[34]

Two documents of the Second Vatican Council are most significant for our purposes—the Declaration on Religious Freedom and the Pastoral Constitution on the Church in the Modern World. It was only at the Second Vatican Council that the Roman Catholic Church accepted the concept of religious liberty—a concept that was anathema to Leo XIII. However, the council is careful to show that its acceptance does not stem from the tenets of an older liberalism and indifferentism. Religious liberty is the right not to worship God as one pleases but rather the right to immunity from external coercion, forcing one to act in a way opposed to one's conscience or preventing one from acting in accord with one's conscience. The basis for religious liberty is stated very distinctly in the opening paragraph—the dignity of the human person, which has been impressing itself more and more deeply on the conscience of contemporary people, and a corresponding recognition of a constitutional government whose powers are limited. A limited government embraces only a small part of the life of people in society, and religion exists beyond the pale of the role of civil government.[35] The council brings out all the implications of a limited constitutional government that in principle had been accepted by Pius XII. The Roman Catholic Church thus became a defender of religious liberty even though in the nineteenth century the papacy stood as the most determined opponent of religious liberty.

The dignity of the human person serves as the cornerstone of the Pastoral Constitution on the Church in the Modern World—*Gaudium et spes*. The first chapter of the theoretical part of the document begins with the dignity of the human person and its meaning and importance. Authentic freedom as opposed to license is championed by the conciliar document. In earlier documents there was a great insistence on the moral law as the antidote to any tendency to license. Now the emphasis is on conscience—the most secret core and sanctuary of the human person in which one hears the call of God's voice. The shift from the role of law, which is traditionally called the objective norm of morality, to conscience, which is called the subjective norm of human action, is most significant in showing the move to the subject and to the person. Of course the document stresses the need for a correct conscience, but the impression is given that truth is found in the innermost depth of one's existence.[36]

Gaudium et spes gives much more importance to equality than some of the earlier documents. Inequalities are still recognized, but now the existence of inequalities appears in subordinate clauses with the main emphasis being on equality. For example: "True, all men are not alike from the point of view of varying physical power and the diversity of intellectual and moral resources. Nevertheless, with respect to the fundamental rights of the person, every type of discrimination, whether social or cultural, whether based on sex, race, color, social condition, language, or religion, is to be overcome and eradicated as contrary to God's intent."[37] "Moreover although rightful differences exist between men, the equal dignity of persons demands that a more humane and just condition of life be brought about. For excessive economic and social differences between the members of the one human family or population groups cause scandal, and militate against social justice, equity, the dignity of the human person as well as social and international peace."[38]

There is also a call for responsibility and participation. The will to play one's role in common endeavors should be encouraged. The largest possible number of citizens should participate in public affairs with genuine freedom.[39] A greater share in education and culture is required for all to exercise responsibility and participation. The active participation of all in running the economic enterprise should be promoted.[40] The juridical and political structure should afford all citizens the chance to participate freely and actively in establishing the constitutional basis of a political community, governing the state, determining the scope and purposes of different institutions, and choosing leaders.[41]

In the light of this line of development the teaching of Pope Paul VI in *Octogesima adveniens* on the eightieth anniversary of *Rerum novarum* does not come as a total surprise: "Two aspirations persistently make themselves felt in these new contexts, and they grow stronger to the extent that people become better informed and better educated: the aspiration to equality and the aspiration to participation, two forms of man's dignity and freedom."[42] Such an anthropology stressing freedom, equality, and participation should have significant methodological consequences for Christian social ethics.

Historical consciousness, which is very pronounced in *Octogesima adveniens* but clearly absent from the documents of Leo XIII, gives great significance to historical conditions, growth, change, and development, and has often been contrasted with a classicist approach. In the area of methodology the classicist approach emphasizes the eternal, the universal, and the unchanging and often employs a deductive methodology. The historically conscious approach emphasizes the particular, the individual, the contingent, and the historical, and often employs a more inductive methodology.[43]

The importance of historical consciousness becomes very evident in the deliberations of the Second Vatican Council on religious freedom. Pope Leo XIII had condemned religious liberty. Perhaps the most pressing question facing the fathers of Vatican II was how to reconcile Leo's condemnation with the acceptance of religious liberty less than a century later. John Courtney Murray, in his writings on religious liberty, provided a solution. One has to interpret Leo in the light of the circumstances of his own day. Leo was struggling against a Continental liberalism with its denial of any place for God in society and its acceptance of an omnicompetent state with no recognition whatsoever of divine law or of natural law. In reaction to this approach Leo called for the union of church and state as the way rightfully recognizing and protecting the role and function of the church. However, the constitutional understanding of separation of church and state was based not on a Continental liberalism but on a notion of a constitutional government, which claimed only a limited role for itself in the life of society. The constitutional understanding did not deny a role or a place for religion in society; the role and function of religion existed beyond the pale of the limited scope and function of the state. Murray's historically conscious hermeneutic distinguished the polemical-historical aspect of Leo's teaching from the doctrinal aspect. There has been no change in the doctrinal. The recognition of historical consciousness provided the key to the problem of development and change in the church's teaching.[44] Murray made a remarkable contribution by his historical hermeneutic. In retrospect it is both easy and necessary to criticize Murray's theory as too benevolent. One should admit some error in the church's teaching in the nineteenth century and even some doctrinal discontinuity and evolution in the teaching on religious liberty.

The acceptance of historical consciousness in our understanding of anthropology also has important methodological ramifications in the papal social teaching. The earlier teachings were deductive, stressing immutable eternal principles of natural law. However, a more inductive approach began to appear in the 1960s. The encyclical *Pacem in terris* is divided into four major parts: order among people, relations between individuals and public authority within a single state, relations between states, relations of people in political communities with the world community. Each part concludes with a section on the signs of the times—the distinctive characteristics of the contemporary age.[45] There was much debate about the term "signs of the times" at the Second Vatican Council. Early drafts and versions of the Constitution on the Church in the Modern World gave great importance to the term. In the final version "signs of the times" was used sparingly because some council fathers did not want to use a term whose biblical meaning was quite different—the eschatological signs of the last days.[46] However, in the second part of the Pastoral Constitution, which treats five problems of special urgency in the contemporary world, each consideration begins with an empirical description of the contemporary reality even though the terminology "signs of the times" is not employed. Such an approach gives greater emphasis to the contemporary historical situation and does not begin with a universal viewpoint and deduce an understanding applicable to all cultures and times.

The anthropology of the papal social teaching by the time of *Octogesima adveniens* in 1971 stresses freedom, equality, participation, and historical mindedness. The methodological consequences of such an anthropology are quite significant and show a remarkable change from the methodology employed in the earlier documents. The earlier approach highlighted the universal, all-embracing character of the teaching. In retrospect, however, the claimed universalism of the earlier encyclicals was really limited to European socioeconomic conditions. In the economic realm there appeared, especially with Pius XI in 1931, a plan for the reconstruction of the social order in accord with what was called a theory of moderate solidarism. Pope Pius XI was much more negative about the existing abuses and injustices of the social order than was Leo XIII. Undoubtedly the problem of the depression influenced Pius's negative judgment about the existing social order and the call for a more radical reconstruction of society according to a solidaristic model based in general on the guild system with its intermediary institutions bringing together both workers and owners. The pope continued to condemn laissez-faire capitalism and the opposite extreme of socialism. In place of these two systems Pius XI proposed a third way that would eliminate the bad features of extreme individualism and extreme socialism while giving due importance to the personal and social nature of the individual person. This third way, although somewhat vague in its development and detail, was thought to be a universally applicable plan.[47]

Pius XII continued in the same line as his predecessor with an emphasis on reconstruction and not merely on reform. Professional organizations and labor unions are provisional and transitory forms; the ultimate purpose is the bringing together and cooperation of employees and employers in order to provide together for the general welfare and the needs of the whole community. Pope Pius XII also distinguished his reconstruction plan from mere comanagement, or participation of workers in management. Pope Pius XII originally followed the footsteps of his predecessor in proposing a universally applicable plan of reconstruction deduced from the principles of the natural law and corresponding in significant ways to the guild system of the middle ages. However, after 1952 Pius rarely mentioned such a plan of reconstruction.[48] In *Mater et magistra* Pope John XXIII merely referred to Pius XI's orderly reorganization of society with smaller professional and economic groups existing in their own right and not prescribed by public authority.[49] In John's encyclicals, in the conciliar documents, and in Paul's teaching there was no further development of Pius XI's plan for social reconstruction.

Reasons for the abandonment of a plan of social reconstruction applicable throughout the world can be found in the later documents themselves. These documents recognize the complexity of the social problem and historical and cultural differences that make it difficult for a universal plan to be carried out in all different areas. *Mater et magistra* emphasized the complexity of the present scene, the multiplication of social relationships, and many new developments in the field of science, technology, and economics as well as developments in the social and political fields.[50] The social questions involve more than the rights and duties of labor and capital. In *Populorum progressio* Pope Paul VI early in his encyclical stated that today the principal fact that all must recognize is that the social question has become worldwide.[51] The complexity of the question increases enormously when one brings into consideration the entire world and the relationships between and among countries, especially poor nations and rich nations. The approach of the Pastoral Constitution on the Church in the Modern World by beginning with the signs of the times also called for doing away with a deductive methodology resulting in an eternal, immutable plan of God for the world.

At the same time as Pius XI and Pius XII were talking about a program of reconstruction according to solidaristic principles of organization, the term "social doctrine" was used by these popes to refer to the official body of church teaching consisting of the principles of the economic order derived from the natural law and the plan of reconstruction based on them. Pius XI distinguished this social doctrine from social and economic sciences. The social doctrine contains the immutable truths taught by the popes, whereas social science is the area for research and scholarly enterprise. Precisely the authoritative nature of the doctrine distinguishes it from the empirical social sciences of economics or sociology.[52] Such an approach was called for by some Catholic sociologists who claimed that the major of their argument was supplied by authoritative church teaching, the minor came from their scientific research, and from these one drew the conclusion.[53] Pope Pius XII frequently speaks about Catholic social doctrine. According to Pius XII the earlier papal teaching became the source of Catholic social doctrine by providing the children of the church with directives and means for a social reconstruction rich in fruit.[54] Social doctrine is the authoritative teaching proclaimed by the hierarchical magisterium, deduced from the eternal principles of the natural law, and distinguished from the contribution of the empirical sciences.

Both the term "social doctrine of the church" and the reality expressed by it—namely, a papal plan or ideology of social reconstruction—gradually disappear from official church documents after Pope Pius XII. Later references are to the social teaching of the gospel or the social teaching of the church. Gone is the vision of the universal plan deductively derived from natural law and proposed authoritatively by the church magisterium to be applied in all parts of the world. No longer will there be such a separation between ethically deduced moral principles and the economic and social analysis of the situation. Rather, one now begins with the signs of the times and with an analysis of the contemporary situation and not with some abstract principle divorced from historical reality.[55]

Octogesima adveniens, with an anthropology insisting on personal freedom, equality, participation, and historical consciousness, employs a methodology quite at variance with that employed in the early papal documents. Early in the document Pope Paul VI recognizes the wide diversity of situations in which Christians live throughout the world. In the face of such diversity it is difficult to utter a unified message or to put forward a solution that has universal validity. The Christian communities themselves must analyze with objectivity their own situation and shed on it the light of the gospel and the principles of the teaching of the church. It is up to the Christian communities, with the help of the Spirit in communion with the bishops and in dialogue with other Christians and people of good will, to discern the options and commitments necessary to bring about the urgently needed social and political changes.[56] Rather than a universal plan based on natural law, Pope Paul VI recalls the importance and significance of utopias. Utopias appeal to the imagination of responsible people to perceive in the present situation the disregarded possibilities within it and to provide direction toward a fresh future. Such an approach sustains social dynamism by the confidence that it gives to the inventive powers of the human mind and heart. "At the heart of the world there dwells the mystery of man discovering himself to be God's son in the course of a historical and psychological process in which constraint and freedom as well as the weight of sin and the breath of the Spirit alternate and struggle for the upper hand."[57]

The methodological changes are quite significant. There is no universal plan applicable to all situations, but rather Christians discern what to do in the midst of the situation in which they find themselves. What to do is not determined by a deductive reasoning process based on the eternal and immutable natural law. Rather, a careful and objective scrutiny of the present reality in the light of the gospel and of the teaching of the church is central to the discernment process. Commitments and options are discerned in the situation itself. The approach is dynamic rather than static. The appeal to utopias, imagination, and the mystery of the human person at the heart of the world all testify to a less rationalistic discernment process. There is also an admonition for the individual and the church to be self-critical, thereby recognizing the dangers that might come from one's own presuppositions.

Octogesima adveniens concludes with a call to action.[58] All along the church's social teaching has called for action, but the call is now more urgent and more central to the very notion of the social mission of the church. The condition of individual responsibility and the urgent need to change structures require the active involvement of all. Once again emphasis is on the need to take concrete action despite the fact that there can be a plurality of strategic options for Christians.

Both the anthropology and the methodology employed in *Octogesima adveniens* outline a different understanding of the role of persons in the church itself and in the social mission of the church. An older approach, especially associated with the concept of Catholic Action proposed by Pope Pius XI and Pope Pius XII, saw the function of the laity to carry out and put into practice the principles that were taught by the hierarchical magisterium. As is evident in this document, the whole church must discern what options are to be taken in the light of an analysis of the signs of the times and in the light of the gospel even though there remains a distinctive role for hierarchical magisterium. No longer are the laity the people who receive the principles and the instruction from the hierarchy and then put these plans into practice. All in the church have a role in discerning and in executing.[59]

Contemporary Catholic social ethics mirror and at times even go beyond the approach and methodology employed in *Octogesima adveniens*. David Hollenbach has recently employed a similar methodology in his attempt to revise and retrieve the Catholic human-rights tradition.[60] Political and liberation theologies show some of the same tendencies but even go beyond the methodological approach of *Octogesima adveniens*. Critical reason insists on the importance of action. Praxis becomes primary in many of these approaches, and theology becomes reflection on praxis. For many liberation theologians, true theology can only grow out of praxis.[61] At the very least the methodology of Catholic social ethics is thus greatly changed from the time of Leo XIII, especially in the light of changing anthropological understandings.

POPE JOHN PAUL II

Karol Wojtyla became Pope John Paul II in late 1978 and has continued the papal and Catholic tradition in social teaching. His major contribution in this area has been the encyclical *Laborem exercens,* which was originally scheduled to be issued on May 15, 1981, the ninetieth anniversary of *Rerum novarum,* but was delayed a few months because of the attempted assassination of the pope.[62] In addition to the encyclical Pope John Paul II has said much about Catholic social teaching in his many trips abroad, especially in Poland and Latin America.

The basic teaching of *Laborem exercens* is in keeping with the developing tradition. The encyclical is critical of both extremes of Marxism and capitalism, and perhaps the pope's criticism of capitalism is more profound than that given by his predecessors.[63] There have been, however, diverse interpretations of the social teaching of Pope John Paul II. In this context one should note the frequent tendency of Catholics to find support for their own particular approach in the official church teaching. Gregory Baum has argued that *Laborem exercens* embraces a moderate socialism.[64] Donal Dorr finds in the papal teaching a continuing of the recent "radical agenda" with its basis in an option for the poor and an openness to the liberation theology of South America.[65] James V. Schall interprets Pope John Paul II as defending a middle-class, free society as opposed to a radical, this-worldly, socialistic understanding of the social mission of the church.[66]

A complete evaluation of the social teaching of Pope John Paul II lies beyond the scope of this chapter. The question for the present study is how Pope John Paul II relates to the thesis about the changing anthropological bases of Catholic social ethics. Does he continue these developments or tend to block them?

The present pope certainly emphasized the importance of the person. The dignity, freedom, equality, and participation of the person are constantly emphasized in *Laborem exercens* and throughout his writings. The basic thesis and thrust of *Laborem exercens* rest primarily on the importance of the person over the work. The primary basis of the value of work is not what is done or made (the objective sense of work) but the person who is its subject. In this light the pope proposes the following as the basic principle for guiding the system of labor—"the principle of the substantial and real priority of labor, of the subjectivity of human labor and its effective participation in the whole production process, independent of the nature of the services provided by the worker."[67] In accord with this principle *Laborem exercens* condemns an economism that considers human labor solely according to its economic purpose.

There is one changed anthropological emphasis pointed out earlier that might not be as strong in Pope John Paul II as in his immediate predecessor. This possible difference concerns historical consciousness and its resulting substantive and methodological consequences. Historical consciousness looks to a more inductive methodology, which in *Octogesima adveniens* recognized that it was neither the pope's ambition nor mission to put forward a solution to social questions that has universal validity. The local Christian communities themselves must analyze their own situations and in the light of the gospel and the social teaching of the church discern what is to be done in their given situation.[68] It is impossible to make a definite judgment at this time, but it appears that the present pope has not given such a great support to historical consciousness and its consequences.

Part of the pope's hesitancy might come from his background as a philosopher and the very topic of his first encyclical on the social question. *Laborem exercens* discusses in a somewhat philosophical and deductive manner the meaning of work and its implications for a just society As a philosopher the pope is explaining a very important reality that is of great importance for all human beings and the whole world. No practical importance is given in the encyclical to the diverse situations existing in the various parts of the world. The encyclical proposes guidelines and directions that should be followed in any just social system that truly appreciates the priority of labor. The methodology is definitely not inductive, but in fairness it should be pointed out that the pontiff does on occasion become quite specific in addition to the more general guidelines that are laid down.

In his trips to Latin America it has become obvious that John Paul II has worried about what he might term extremes in liberation theology.[69] With this background one would not expect him to say what his predecessor had said about the importance of local communities discerning things for themselves. The present pontiff sees the need to criticize some of these local developments. Generally speaking, the Roman Catholic Church of the present time seems to be fearful of recognizing too much local diversity and pluralism—something that a more historically conscious approach would try to justify and approve. This fear of decentralization and the emphasis on central control go against the logical consequences of historical consciousness. In the present context there is little or no mention of historical consciousness and the consequences that logically follow from it.

Any discussion about Pope John Paul II and historical consciousness must mention a very fascinating discussion that has gone on about the term Catholic "social doctrine." In the late 1970s the French Dominican Marie-Dominique Chenu published a little book in French and Italian titled *The "Social Doctrine" of the Church as Ideology.*[70] As it is obvious from the title, Chenu understands the social doctrine of the church in a very pejorative sense. This term stands for an approach to the social question that is deductive and abstract and consequently insensitive to historical and geographical variations. Chenu sees such a methodology as especially harmful to the church in the third-world countries. The French Dominican traces the development in official church teaching in a way basically in accord with the analysis given above, indicating a shift to a more inductive methodology developing in the 1960s and reaching its culmination in *Octogesima adveniens.* The French Dominican titles his chapter on *Octogesima adveniens* "An Inductive Method."

Chenu supports his theory by an analysis of the use of the term *social doctrine.* The term regularly appears in the earlier papal documents and indicates a deductive and somewhat abstract approach used in elaborating the principles of Catholic social teaching. This term is frequently employed even in *Mater et magistra* in 1961, but according to Chenu it is absent in *Pacem in terris. Gaudium et spes* avoids the term except for one unauthorized later addition to the text. The French Dominican objects to the word *doctrine* here because of the abstractness and deductive methodology connoted by the term. *Gaudium et spes* tends to use the word *teaching* rather than *doctrine.* Pope Paul VI also studiously avoided the use of the term. This analysis of a gradual and purposeful disappearance of the term *social doctrine* supports the thesis that the official church documents have gradually adopted a more inductive methodology that is more open to change and the needs of local churches.

The Chenu thesis generated some controversy and debate especially in Italy. In this context there was some surprise when Pope John Paul II in his opening address to the Latin American Bishops' Conference at Puebla in January 1979 used "social doctrine of the church" four times within one comparatively short section near the end of his speech. Ironically, in the short paragraph that introduces the term, there is a reference to paragraph four of *Octogesima adveniens*,[71] the very paragraph used by Chenu to prove his own thesis.

The precise meaning of the pope's usage of *social doctrine* is open to different interpretations. The fact of its use and the citation from *Octogesima adveniens* to support its use argue for a direct contradiction of the Chenu thesis.[72] On the other hand, at Puebla Pope John Paul II used *social doctrine* synonymously with the more general term of *social teaching*. His use of the term according to Roger Heckel has been discrete and relatively rare.[73]

For all these reasons there is in my mind some question about the extent to which Pope John Paul II is committed to historical consciousness and the methodological and substantive consequences coming from it. However, in all the areas mentioned earlier there is no doubt that the present pope is continuing in the newer developments traced by his more immediate predecessors.

Notes

1. For the best commentary available in English, see Jean-Yves Calvez and Jacques Perrin, *The Church and Social Justice: The Social Teaching of the Popes from Leo XIII to Pius XII, 1878–1958* (Chicago: Henry Regnery Co., 1961); also Jean-Yves Calvez, *The Social Thought of John XXIII* (Chicago: Henry Regnery Co., 1964).

2. John F. Cronin, "Forty Years Later: Reflections and Reminiscences," *American Ecclesiastical Review* 164 (1971) 310–318. For Cronin's major contribution in the field, see John F. Cronin, *Social Principles and Economic Life*, rev. ed. (Milwaukee: Bruce Publishing Co., 1964).

3. The most significant contribution to an understanding of development in the papal teaching on religious liberty was made by John Courtney Murray. For a summary of his approach, see John Courtney Murray, *The Problem of Religious Freedom* (Westminster, Md.: Newman Press, 1965). This small volume originally appeared as a long article in *Theological Studies* 25 (1964) 503–575.

4. For the best study of development in the papal teaching on economic questions before the Second Vatican Council, see Richard L. Camp, *The Papal Ideology of Social Reform: A Study in Historical Development, 1878–1967* (Leiden: E. J. Brill, 1969). For other helpful studies showing development in Catholic social ethics, see Marie-Dominique Chenu, *La "dottrina sociale" della Chiesa: origine e sviluppo, 1891–1971* (Brescia: Editrice Queriniana, 1977); David Hollenbach, *Claims in Conflict: Retrieving and Renewing the Catholic Human Rights Tradition* (New York: Paulist Press, 1979).

5. To facilitate a further study of the papal and church documents, references will be given to readily available English translations. For the documents from the time of Pope John, see *The Gospel of Peace and Justice: Catholic Social Teaching Since Pope John,* ed. Joseph Gremillion (Maryknoll, New York: Orbis Books, 1976). References will include the page number in Gremillion as well as the paragraph numbers of the documents, which generally are the official paragraph numbers found in the original and in all authorized translations. Thus the present reference is: *Octogesima adveniens,* n. 22; Gremillion, 496. Another readily available compendium of Catholic Church teaching on social ethics is *Renewing the Face of the Earth: Catholic Documents on Peace, Justice, and Liberation,* ed. David J. O'Brien and Thomas A. Shannon (Garden City, New York: Doubleday Image Books, 1977).

6. References to the encyclicals of Pope Leo XIII will be to *The Church Speaks to the Modern World: The Social Teaching of Leo XIII,* ed. Etienne Gilson (Garden City, New York: Doubleday Image Books, 1954). Thus the present reference is *Libertas praestantissimum,* n. 23; Gilson, 72.

7. *Libertas praestantissimum,* nn. 19–37; Gilson, 70–79. See also *Immortale Dei,* nn. 31–42; Gilson, 174–180.

8. *Quod apostolici muneris,* especially nn. 5, 6; Gilson, 192, 193.

9. *Humanum genus,* n. 26; Gilson, 130.

10. *Rerum novarum,* nn. 18, 19; Gilson, 214, 215.

11. Murray, *The Problem of Religious Freedom,* 55, 56.

12. *Libertas praestantissimum,* n. 23; Gilson, 72.

13. *Immortale Dei,* n. 5; Gilson, 163.

14. *Immortale Dei,* n. 31; Gilson, 174, 175.

15. Murray, *The Problem of Religious Freedom,* 55–57.

16. *Libertas praestantissimum,* n. 15; Gilson, 66, 67.

17. For a similar judgment on Leo's approach to liberty, see Fr. Refoulé, "L'Église et les libertés de Léon XIII à Jean XXIII," in *Le Supplément* 125 (mai 1978) 243–259.

18. *Rerum novarum,* n. 7; Gilson, 208, 209.

19. *Rerum novarum,* nn. 6–12; Gilson, 208, 211.

20. *Rerum novarum,* n. 36; Gilson, 224, 225.

21. *Rerum novarum,* nn. 49–51; Gilson, 231–233.

22. *Rerum novarum,* n. 17; Gilson, 213, 214.

23. *Rerum novarum,* n. 37; Gilson, 225, 226. Here I disagree with Camp, who on page 32 of *The Papal Ideology of Social Reform* seems to deny in Leo a basic equality of all before the law.

24. Reference to the encyclicals of Pope Pius XI will be to *The Church and the Reconstruction of the Modern World: The Social Encyclicals of Pope Pius XI,* ed. Terence P. McLaughlin (Garden City, New York: Doubleday Image Books, 1957). McLaughlin, "Introduction," 6–15.

25. *Divini redemptoris,* n. 10; McLaughlin, 369–370.

26. For a further explanation of this change in the light of opposition to totalitarianism especially from the left, see G. B. Guzzetti, "L'impegno politico dei cattolici nel magistero pontificio dell'ultimo secolo con particolare riguardo all'ultimo ventennio," *La Scuola Cattolica* 194 (1976) 192–210.

27. Radio message, December 24, 1944; *Acta apostolicae sedis* 37 (1945) 11–12; 22.

28. Murray, *The Problem of Religious Freedom,* 65–67.

29. Guzzetti, "L'impegno politico dei cattolici," 202.

30. Radio message, December 24, 1944; *Acta apostolicae sedis* 37 (1945) 14.

31. *Pacem in terris,* nn. 8–34; Gremillion, 203–208. See David Hollenbach, *Claims in Conflict,* 62–69.

32. *Mater et magistra,* n. 212; Gremillion, 188.

33. *Pacem in terris,* n. 35; Gremillion, 208.

34. *Pacem in terris,* n. 35; Gremillion, 208.

35. *Dignitatis humanae,* nn. 1, 2; Gremillion, 337–339.

36. *Gaudium et spes,* nn. 12–22; Gremillion, 252–261.

37. *Gaudium et spes,* n. 29; Gremillion, 266.

38. Ibid.

39. *Gaudium et spes,* n. 31; Gremillion, 267.

40. *Gaudium et spes,* n. 68; Gremillion, 304–305.

41. *Gaudium et spes,* n. 75; Gremillion, 310–312.

42. *Octogesima adveniens,* n. 22; Gremillion, 496.

43. Bernard Lonergan, "A Transition from a Classicist World View to Historical Mindedness," in *Law for Liberty: The Role of Law in the Church Today,* ed. James E. Biechler (Baltimore: Helicon Press, 1967) 126–133.

44. John Courtney Murray, " Vers une intelligence du développement de la doctrine de l' Église sur la liberté religieuse," in *Vatican II: la liberté religieuse* (Paris: Les Éditions du Cerf, 1967) 11–147; Murray, "Religious Liberty and the Development of Doctrine," *The Catholic World* 204 (February 1967) 277–283.

45. *Pacem in terris,* nn. 39–45; 75–79; 126–129; 142–145; Gremillion, 209–210; 217–218; 227–228; 231–232.

46. Charles Moeller, "Preface and Introductory Statement," in *Commentary on the Documents of Vatican II, V: Pastoral Constitution on the Church in the Modern World,* ed. Herbert Vorgrimler (New York: Herder and Herder, 1969) 94.

47. *Quadragesimo anno,* nn. 76–149; McLaughlin, 246–274.

48. Camp, *The Papal Ideology of Social Reform,* 128–135.

49. *Mater et magistra,* n. 37; Gremillion, 150

50. *Mater et magistra,* nn. 46–60; Gremillion, 152–156.

51. *Populorum progressio,* n. 3; Gremillion, 388.

52. *Quadragesimo anno,* nn. 17–22; McLaughlin, 224, 225.

53. Paul Hanly Furfey, *Fire on the Earth* (New York: Macmillan, 1936) 8.

54. Calvez and Perrin, *The Church and Social Justice,* 3.

55. Bartolomeo Sorge, "E superato il concetto tradizionale di dottrina sociale della Chiesa?" *La civiltà cattolica* 119 (1968) 1, 423–436. However, I disagree with the assignment of roles that Sorge gives to the hierarchical magisterium and the laity. See also Sorge, "L'apporto dottrinale della lettera apostolica 'Octogesima Adveniens,'" *La civiltà cattolica* 122 (1971) 417–428.

56. *Octogesima adveniens,* n. 4 Gremillion, 487.

57. *Octogesima adveniens,* n. 37 Gremillion, 502.

58. *Octogesima adveniens,* nn. 48–52 Gremillion, 509–511.

59. The understanding of eschatology mentioned in endnote 5 that tends to overcome the dichotomy between the supernatural and the natural and the church and the world also influences the position taken here. For a refutation of a distinction of planes approach in the social mission of the church, see Gustavo Gutierrez, *A Theology of Liberation* (Maryknoll, New York: Orbis Press, 1973) 53–58. For an approach that still tends to distinguish too much between the teaching role of the hierarchy and the executing role of the laity, see the articles of Sorge mentioned in endnote 55.

60. David Hollenbach, *Claims in Conflict.*

61. Gutierrez, *A Theology of Liberation;* Juan Luis Segundo, *The Liberation of Theology* (Maryknoll, New York: Orbis Books, 1976).

62. There are a number of readily available translations of *Laborem exercens* in English. References will be given to the official paragraph numbers and to the page numbers of the text in the widely used commentary by Gregory Baum, *The Priority of Labor* (New York: Paulist Press, 1982).

63. *Laborem exercens,* nn. 7, 8, 11, 14; Baum, 106–110, 114–116, 122–125.

64. Baum, *The Priority of Labor.*

65. Donal Dorr, *Option for the Poor: A Hundred Years of Vatican Social Teaching* (Maryknoll, N.Y.: Orbis Books, 1983) 207–275.

66 .James V. Schall, *The Church, the State and Society in the Thought of John Paul II* (Chicago: Franciscan Herald Press, 1982).

67. *Laborem exercens,* n. 13; Baum, 119.

68. *Octogesima adveniens,* n. 4; Gremillion, 487.

69. For a one-sided interpretation of Pope John Paul's teaching as being almost totally opposed to liberation theology see Quentin L. Quade, ed., *The Pope and Revolution: John Paul II Confronts Liberation Theology* (Washington: Ethics and Public Policy Center, 1982). For an interpretation of John as more open to some of the positions of liberation theology, especially the option for the poor and the solidarity of the poor in trying to bring about social change, see Dorr, *Option for the Poor,* 207–251.

70. Marie-Dominique Chenu, *La "dottrina sociale" della Chiesa: origine e sviluppo* (Brescia: Editrice Queriniaria, 1977); *La "doctrine sociale" de l'église comme idéologie* (Paris: Cerf, 1979).

71. Pope John Paul II, "Opening Address at the Puebla Conference," in *Third General Conference of Latin American Bishops: Conclusions* (Washington: National Conference of Catholic Bishops, 1979) III, 7, 13.

72. For such an analysis see Peter Hebblethwaite, "The Popes and Politics: Shifting Patterns in 'Catholic Social Doctrine,'" in *Religion and America: Spirituality in a Secular Age,* ed. Mary Douglas and Steven M. Tipton (Boston: Beacon Press, 1983) 190–204.

73. Roger Heckel, *The Social Teaching of John Paul II*: booklet 1: *General Aspects of the Social Catechesis of John Paul II: The Use of the Expression "Social Doctrine" of the Church* (Vatican City: Pontifical Commission *Justitia et Pax,* 1980).

12. What Ever Happened to *Octogesima Adveniens*?

Mary Elsbernd

This chapter first appeared in *Theological Studies* 56 (1995).

Octogesima adveniens, Paul VI's letter in 1971 to Maurice Cardinal Roy,[1] marked the eightieth anniversary of *Rerum novarum.* The letter, in particular its paragraph 4, was heralded as a central expression of a historically conscious methodology in magisterial teaching. Paul VI there highlighted the historically constituted nature of the social teaching of the church, the role of the local community, and the difficulty as well as the undesirability of a single universal papal message or solution to problems. What has happened to this articulation of a historically conscious methodology in the last twenty years? One response to this question can be uncovered by tracing how and in which contexts this significant paragraph has been used in the encyclical teachings of John Paul II.

Although the historically constituted nature of the social teachings of the magisterium has already been documented,[2] one must remember first, that the works prior to Paul VI and Vatican Council II were not as devoid of historically conscious methodologies as some would like to believe,[3] and second, that *Gaudium et spes* and the writings of Paul VI were not as historically conscious as proponents would like to maintain.[4] Documentation has demonstrated, however, that the encyclical writings of John Paul II intentionally stray from the earlier emerging articulation of a historically conscious methodology[5] in preference for a transcendental[6] or Thomistic[7] personalism as the basis of universal and absolute norms transcending all historical contingency. This prior documentation provides a context for continuing theological reflection on the role of local Christian communities[8] as well as on the desirability of a single universal teaching.[9] There is a prevailing sense that the intentional straying from historically conscious methodology has left its impact in these areas as well.

In light of the above, this article proposes to examine John Paul II's use of *Octogesima adveniens,* in particular no. 4. We will begin with an examination of *Octogesima adveniens* in its historical and Catholic social-teaching context to determine its significance as an expression of a historically conscious methodology. Then we will examine how and in what contexts *Octogesima adveniens* no. 4 is quoted in the writings of John Paul II. Finally, we will draw some conclusions about John Paul II's use of the passage and spell out some implications for Catholic social thought.

It is our contention that John Paul II stresses the continuity of Catholic social doctrine back to the gospel itself in a kind of unbroken chain. This continuity is seen by the pope as resting in its fundamental inspiration; in its principles of reflection, criteria of judgment, and basic directives for action; and in its link with the gospel. This approach is a departure from *Octogesima adveniens,* which held that Catholic social teachings had been worked out in history, that is, that Catholic social teachings are historically constituted, that the local Christian community contributed to the development of Catholic social teachings, and that a single universal message is not the papal mission.

OCTOGESIMA ADVENIENS IN HISTORICAL CONTEXT

Octogesima adveniens was not written in a historical vacuum nor in discontinuity from Catholic social teachings of the previous decade. Rather the letter continued themes found in *Gaudium et spes* and *Mater et magistra* and responded to the historical context in which it was written.

To mark the eightieth anniversary of *Rerum novarum,* Paul VI did not write an encyclical letter, but rather an apostolic letter to Maurice Cardinal Roy, who was president of the Pontifical Commission *Justitia et Pax.* In fact, the last encyclical letter of his pontificate, *Humanae vitae,* was written three years prior to this letter and ten years before his death. The move away from the encyclical as a literary form already suggests Paul VI's awareness of the importance of human experience or a historically conscious methodology. A look at the structure of *Octogesima adveniens* confirms this awareness. After a seven paragraph introduction, *Octogesima adveniens* turns to a reading of the signs of the times (nos. 8–42), which highlight the challenges faced by particular groups of people (e.g., workers and women), worldwide issues (e.g., media influence and environment) and aspirations (e.g., participation and equality). The remainder of the letter provides some ecclesial reflections on these signs of the times and an exhortation to action. Thus, two-thirds of the letter (nos. 8–42) detail the historical context for any ecclesial reflection or action.

Paul VI himself had experienced firsthand the diverse situations in which Christians found themselves, especially in his journeys to Israel (1964), to the United States of America (1965), to India (1966), to Turkey and Portugal (1967), to Medellín, Colombia (1968), and to Uganda (1969). These encounters with the people of God, their poverty, and their misery profoundly moved Paul VI, as his Wednesday audience reflections attest.

In addition, the years since *Populorum progressio* and *Humanae vitae* had been years of student unrest, violence, war, and genocide; and their pain was not lost on Paul VI.[10] His concern over the Paris student uprisings came out in two letters to the Semaine Sociale in France and in Italy.[11] He lamented the assassinations of Robert F. Kennedy and Dr. Martin Luther King Jr.[12] He decried the Six Day War between Israel and the Arab nations, the war in Vietnam, the Czech-Soviet confrontation, and the Biafra civil war with its practices of genocide.

Octogesima Adveniens *No. 4*

Against the backdrop of this historical context, paragraph 4 appears as a papal reflection on Paul VI's experiences in this world, on its diversity, and on the widespread movements toward self-determination and participation:

> In the face of such widely varying situations it is difficult for us to utter a unified message and to put forward a solution which has universal validity. Such is not our ambition, nor is it our mission. It is up to the Christian communities to analyze with objectivity the situation which is proper to their own country, to shed on it the light of the Gospel's unalterable

words and to draw principles of reflection *(principia cogitandi),* norms of judgment *(iudicandi normas)* and directives
for action *(regulas operandi)* from the social teaching *(e
sociali doctrina)* of the church. This social teaching has been
worked out *(est confecta)* in the course of history....It is up to
these Christian communities, with the help of the Holy Spirit,
in communion with the bishops who hold responsibility and
in dialogue with other Christian brethren and all men (sic)[13] of
goodwill, to discern the options and commitments which are
called for in order to bring about the social, political and economic changes seen in many cases to be urgently needed. In
this search for the changes which must be promoted,
Christians must first of all renew their confidence in the
forcefulness and special character of the demands made by
the Gospel.

Paul VI here recognizes that worldwide diversity makes it difficult
to set forth a solution with universal validity, and he goes on to maintain
that one message and one solution is neither his ambition nor his mission. It is, rather, the task of local Christian communities to analyze the
local situation; to facilitate dialogue between the gospel, social teaching,
and the local situation; and from that to undertake action to bring about
change. This approach reflects the method developed in the 1920s by the
Belgian priest, Joseph Cardijn, as foundational principles for the emerging Lay Apostolate movement, namely, Observe, Judge, Act.[14] While
reminding the local Christian communities of the help of the Spirit, of
the special character of the gospel, of their communion with bishops, of
the necessity of dialogue with other Christians and concerned persons in
this task, Paul VI explicitly assigns all three steps of the Cardijn method
to the local Christian community.

John XXIII had earlier referred to the Cardijn method in *Mater et
magistra;* however, he saw it serving a different function. According to
Mater et magistra, the Cardijn method was a way that "should normally
be followed in the reduction of social principles into practice."[15] The surrounding paragraphs are concerned with how the social doctrine of the
church is known, taught, assimilated, and applied according to circumstances. *Mater et magistra* no. 220 specifically states that these social
principles are universal in application because they take into account

human nature, natural law, and the characteristics of contemporary society, although it also notes the contribution of a "very well-informed body of priests and laymen" in its construction. Thus John XXIII urged the use of the Observe, Judge, Act method as the way to apply social principles to specific situations. The principles were the starting point; the local situation was reviewed and then judged according to the principles in order to determine which principles the circumstances could tolerate in implementation.

In *Octogesima adveniens,* however, the local community was called, first, to analyze the local situations; second, to shed the light of the gospel's unalterable words as well as to draw principles of reflection, norms of judgment, directives for action from the social teaching of the church; third, to discern in light of the above the options and commitments needed to bring about social, political, and economic change. The starting point is reflection on the local situation by the local Christian community. The community then becomes the locus of dialogue between the situation and its traditions, namely scripture and social teaching, in order to bring about action. The process is not application of ahistorical principles to situations but dialogical discernment for action, emerging from concrete situations and the Christian traditions.

In light of future interpretations, the second of these steps, "judge," requires additional comment here. What is implied by *judge* relies on the resources both of the gospel and social teaching, unlike *Mater et magistra,* which relied only on social principles. Principles of reflection, norms of judgment, and directives for action are drawn from social teaching, which is constituted in history. Although this phrase will be interpreted otherwise, the interpretation, consistent with the whole of no. 4 (as well as no. 42), maintains that social teaching itself is historically constituted via a dialogical development in Christian communities between the resources of their traditions and their specific situation prior to discernment for action. This position is strengthened by the Latin text, in which the statement that "this social teaching has been worked out in the course of history" is part of the previous sentence. This approach recognizes the participation of local Christian communities in the development of social teaching.

In fact by 1971 the YCS/YCW movements had passed their zenith, at least in the United States. However, thousands of Catholics in the United States who grew up in the YCS/YCW movements took up the challenge of local initiative and participation in their Christian and human communities. These Catholics did not look to magisterial teaching for principles to apply to local social, political, and economic issues. Rather, trusting in the Spirit of Jesus, the community discerned a course of action through mutual dialogue with both the situation and the traditions expressed in the gospel and social teachings.[16]

Paul VI's quite remarkable statement of historical consciousness stands in contrast to the "Gospel's unalterable words," as well as the "forcefulness and special character" of its demands. Thus it seems that for Paul VI, the gospel stands as the universal and unchanging truth, while social teachings develop historically. However, throughout this paragraph *doctrina* is used in the singular, to which fact some students of the encyclicals point as evidence of a well-defined and unchanging body of thought, that is, doctrine.[17] The context does not support this understanding, although it may well be one of the instances in which Paul VI is not as inductive as proponents of a historically conscious approach would like him to be.[18]

Later, in *Octogesima adveniens* no. 42, Paul VI raises the question of the role of the universal church, perhaps as a counterbalance to the role given to the local church in no. 4. Here he states:

> If today the problems seem original in their breadth and their urgency, is man without the means of solving them? It is with all its dynamism that the social teaching of the Church *(socialis ecclesiae doctrina)* accompanies men in their search. If it does not intervene to authenticate a given structure or propose a ready-made model, it does not thereby limit itself to recalling general principles. It develops *(crescit)* through reflection applied to the changing situations of this world, under the driving force of the Gospel as the source of renewal when its message is accepted in its totality and with all its demands. It also develops with sensitivity proper to the Church which is characterized by a disinterested will to serve and by attention to the poorest. Finally it draws upon its rich experience of many centuries which enables it, while continuing its permanent preoccupations, to undertake the

daring and creative innovations which the present state of the world requires.

Paul VI's reflections here reveal an understanding of the church as a pilgrim people searching for solutions to the urgent problems of the world. The passage then attempts to delineate a middle ground for social teaching between "recalling general principles" and concrete intervention. In his effort to find this middle ground, Paul VI restates the position that social teaching develops through reflection on the changing situations of each era in the light of the gospel. The gospel is unchanging; contemporary situations are changing; and social teachings are the historically constituted responses emerging from the dialogue between gospel and contemporary situations. In this mediating role, social teaching lives under the gospel, serves the building up of the reign of God in the world, attends to the poorest, and draws on its centuries-long experience. This approach provides fertile soil for permanent preoccupations (not answers) and creative innovations within the social teaching of the church.

Octogesima Adveniens *and* Gaudium et Spes

Thus, while Paul VI's statements add to John XXIII's use of the Cardijn method (Observe, Judge, Act), *Octogesima adveniens* also reflects several significant themes from *Gaudium et spes*. The concept of the church as the people of God alive by the Spirit of Jesus in the world provides a conceptual framework, which *Octogesima adveniens* both draws on and takes a step farther. This can be seen particularly in the proposed methodologies and in the role of the whole people of God. Three points serve to illustrate this change:

First, *Gaudium et spes* no. 4 proposes a methodology of "scrutinizing the signs of the times and of interpreting them in the light of the Gospel" in order to discern appropriate social action. *Gaudium et spes* no. 4 presents this methodology as the church's duty in carrying out the mission of Christ to understand the world and respond to its perennial questions. No. 11 invites the people of God to take up the task:

> The people of God believes that it is led by the Lord's Spirit, who fills the earth. Motivated by this faith, it labors to decipher authentic signs of God's presence and purpose in the

happenings, needs and desires in which this people has a part along with other men of our age. For faith throws a new light on everything, manifests God's design for man's total vocation, and thus directs the mind to solutions which are fully human.

The Spirit present in the whole Earth enables the people of God to scrutinize the signs of the times, to interpret them in the light of faith so as to determine fully human solutions. This constellation of the whole people, the Spirit, and social action are essential aspects in *Octogesima adveniens* no. 4.

Second, with its articulation of the church in the world, *Gaudium et spes* recognizes that the church is a historical reality with visible social structures and that there is mutual exchange and assistance between the church and the world. No. 44, which most clearly acknowledges this mutual exchange, begins by noting that the church has profited from past experiences, the sciences, human culture, and philosophy. It continues

> For thus the ability to express Christ's message in its own way is developed in each nation, and at the same time there is fostered a living exchange between the Church and the diverse cultures of people. To promote such exchange, especially in our days, the Church requires the special help of those who live in the world, are versed in different institutions and specialties, and grasp their innermost significance in the eyes of both believers and unbelievers. With the help of the Holy Spirit, it is the task of the entire people of God, especially pastors and theologians, to hear, distinguish, and interpret the many voices of our age, and to judge them in the light of the divine Word. In this way, revealed truth can always be more deeply penetrated, better understood, and set forth to greater advantage.

Living as the church in the world requires the special help of those who live in the world as well as the whole people of God to discern the signs of the times and to interpret them, in the light of the gospel. In fact this living exchange ought to be promoted. In this context, then, the task of the whole people of God is delineated as hearing, distinguishing, and interpreting the contemporary situation and judging it in light of the gospel in order to understand and articulate the truth. No. 44 concludes that whoever helps the human community also contributes to the church. *Octogesima adveniens* no. 4 will build on this mutual exchange between church and world as well as on the task of the whole people of God and the place of the gospel.

Third, the conciliar understanding of the church in the world results in a synthesis of religious life and earthly affairs, as well as in defining a distinct role for the laity:

> Laymen should also know that it is generally the function of their well-formed Christian conscience to see that the divine law[19] is inscribed in the life of the earthly city; from priests they may look for spiritual light and nourishment. Let the layman not imagine that his pastors are always such experts, that to every problem which arises, however complicated, they can readily give him a concrete solution, or even that such is their mission. Rather enlightened by Christian wisdom and giving close attention to the teaching authority of the Church, let the layman take on his own distinctive role.[20]

Self-directed action by the laity is a consequence of a well-formed Christian conscience (compare *Gaudium et spes* no. 16) enlightened by Christian wisdom and attentive to the teaching authority of the church. Pastors provide light and nourishment but not concrete solutions, which stand outside the mission of the priest. Paragraph 43 goes on to say that the laity have an active role in the whole church, are called to penetrate the world with a Christian spirit, and are invited to witness to Christ in all things. *Octogesima adveniens* no. 4 is shaped by the same primacy of conscience and the same synthesis of church and world.

Thus, we see that many of the ideas put forth by Paul VI in *Octogesima adveniens* emerge from *Gaudium et spes*. Conciliar theology set forth a distinct role for the laity rooted in informed Christian conscience and wisdom that cannot expect pastors to give solutions. *Octogesima adveniens* took a further step, stating that unified messages and universally valid solutions are not the mission of papal teaching but belong to local Christian communities, that is, a collective informed Christian conscience.[21]

Conciliar theology described the church as the pilgrim people of God integrally connected with the whole of humankind and its history: "The joys and the hopes, the griefs and the anxieties of the men of this age, especially those who are poor or in any way afflicted, these are the joys and the hopes, the griefs and anxieties of the followers of Christ."[22] From this theological starting point, Paul VI could maintain that "social teaching has been worked out in history."

Finally, conciliar theology sets forth a methodology for reading the signs of the times and interpreting them in the light of the gospel. *Octogesima adveniens* elaborates this methodology by including the place of social teaching and highlighting the social-action or praxis orientation of the project.

USE OF *OCTOGESIMA ADVENIENS* BY JOHN PAUL II

As one would expect, it is John Paul II's fundamental understanding of the church and the role of the laity that provide the theological context within which he describes Catholic social doctrine. A study of John Paul II's use and reinterpretation of *Octogesima adveniens* no. 4 provides a tool with which to probe his understanding of social doctrine.

Although study of the theological context out of which John Paul II writes is outside of our scope and has been done by others,[23] mention of a few conclusions pertinent to our topic is in order. First, John Paul II's philosophical training in phenomenology leaves him more at home with philosophical concepts than with scriptural exegesis. Thus while he considers scripture the source of social doctrine, one looks in vain for a critical, exegetical incorporation of the scriptural tradition into social doctrine. His studied conviction that phenomenology could not provide objective moral norms led John Paul II to build a system on universal truths, permanent principles, absolute norms, and a material-spiritual dualism.[24] Since the spiritual world is superior to the material world, hierarchical order, suspicion of and domination over the material world become central concepts.[25] John Paul II's philosophical contact with personalism is apparent in his insistence on human dignity and rights, albeit with an individualistic slant that influences concepts like common good, structural change, and sin.[26]

From his Polish Catholic experience within political systems of the extreme right during World War II and of the left in the postwar eastern bloc, John Paul II knows the reality of a church in conflict with society, the need for a united front against the opposing forces, and the dichotomy between church and world. In such a lived reality there is little place for local autonomy or diversity but rather much insistence on a unity of doctrine as a corpus or an organic body of truths of which the church is the guardian and teacher.[27] It is within this general theophilosophical framework that John Paul II uses and reinterprets *Octogesima adveniens* no. 4.

Opening Address at Puebla

The first time John Paul II refers to *Octogesima adveniens* is during the opening address at the South American Bishops Conference meeting at Puebla in January, 1979.

> What we have already recalled constitutes a rich and complex heritage, which *Evangelii nuntiandi* (no. 38) calls the social doctrine or social teaching of the church.[28] This teaching comes into being, in the light of the word of God and the authentic magisterium, from the presence of Christians in the midst of the changing situations of the world, in contact with the challenges that result from those situations. This social doctrine involves, therefore, both principles for reflection and also norms for judgment and guidelines for action (compare *Octogesima adveniens* no. 4).
>
> Placing responsible confidence in this social doctrine, even though some people seek to sow doubts and lack of confidence in it, to give it serious study, to try to apply it, to be faithful to it—all this is the guarantee, in a member of the church, of his commitment in the delicate and demanding social tasks and of his efforts in favor of the liberation or advancement of his brothers and sisters.[29]

This initial use of *Octogesima adveniens* no. 4 by John Paul II appears to focus on three categories: principles for reflection, norms for judgment, and guidelines for action. They are already stripped from their context in the overall schema of Observe, Judge, Act. There is no reference to local Christian communities observing the local situation; there is no reference to judging these situations in light of the gospel and Catholic social teaching; and there is no reference to discernment of the options and commitments necessary to effect change.

In addition, the relationship between social doctrine and action of Christians, as presented in *Evangelii nuntiandi* no. 38, is blurred. Social doctrine was presented there as a foundation of wisdom and experience, which the Christian must "concretely translate into forms of action, participation, and commitment" for the liberation of many. This is not accurately reflected in John Paul II's statement.

Instead John Paul II tells the South American bishops, first, that the source of social doctrine is the presence of Christians in a challenging world enlightened by the gospel and the magisterium (not social teaching, unless social teaching is equated with the magisterium); second, that social doctrine is equated with principles for reflection, norms for judgment, and guidelines for action (not a method for utilizing social teaching); and third, that members of the church are to study, apply, be faithful to social doctrine, as a guarantee of commitment to social action and liberation. Thus, although the members of the church are present in the world, their role is to apply and be faithful to the social doctrine they have been given; their role is not active discernment of the situation using the gospel and social teaching to determine a course of action. There is no mention of the Spirit or consultation with the Christian and human communities.[30]

John Paul II's Early Encyclicals

John Paul II does not quote *Octogesima adveniens* no. 4 in his first three social encyclicals, namely *Redemptor hominis,*[31] *Dives in misericordia,* and *Laborem exercens,* although *Redemptor hominis* no. 16 does refer in a footnote to *Octogesima adveniens* no. 42, when it calls for "daring creative resolves in keeping with man's authentic dignity."[32] Its appearance in a section on the economic threats and challenges of the contemporary era does resemble the context of *Octogesima adveniens* no. 42 on the role of the church in accompanying the Christian in a world of new questions and problems.

When he wrote *Laborem exercens,* John Paul II did not refer in a footnote to *Octogesima adveniens* no. 4, nor for that matter *Rerum novarum,* whose ninetieth anniversary *Laborem exercens* celebrates. *Laborem exercens* nos. 2 and 3 do, however, shed some light on John Paul II's method as well as his understanding of who contributes to social teaching. First, John Paul views *Laborem exercens* "in organic connection with the whole tradition of this [the church's] teaching and activity." That is, while the social doctrine embraces both teaching and activity, there is one organic unity traced back to the scriptures. According to John Paul II, this "traditional patrimony was inherited and developed by the teaching of the popes." His use of footnotes underscores his efforts to link his teaching back to the gospel source.[33]

Laborem exercens nos. 2 and 3 make four references to development of church doctrine. While this could signal a historically conscious methodology, a closer look yields a different picture. First, the text makes clear that it is the magisterium itself that brings about the "development" by bringing up to date "ageless Christian truth." The people, the historical situation, and the activities of practitioners apply the teaching but do not shape its development. Second, the "trend of development of the church's teaching and commitment in the social question exactly corresponds to the objective recognition of the affairs." In other words, a parallel-track system is operative: on the one hand, the "objective recognition of the state of affairs," which apparently is one step removed from the actual state of affairs and filtered through those who do the recognizing, and on the other, "the development of the church's teaching." The context of this sentence in no. 2 does not suggest that social doctrine was shaped by its historical context but rather that the unfolding of world events corresponded to the wisdom of a developing social doctrine, albeit in two disparate spheres (i.e., of the parallel-track system we just mentioned).

The parallel-track approach in John Paul's methodology also manifests itself in other divisions and distinctions such as between teaching and activity, doctrine and commitment. Doctrine maintains ageless Christian teaching, which is more fully understood in the passage of time, while activity and commitment constitute its applications throughout the ages. Thus, John Paul II's neglect of *Octogesima adveniens* no. 4 appears to signal at least an unconscious shift from its historically conscious methodology.

This conclusion is supported by John Paul's comments, in these same two paragraphs of *Laborem exercens,* concerning the question of who contributes to social teaching. He notes that the social question has engaged the church's attention in three locations: first, "the documents of the magisterium issued by the popes and the Second Vatican Council";[34] second, "pronouncements by individual episcopates"; and third, "the activity of various centers of thought and of practical apostolic initiatives," or later "manifestations of the commitment of the church and of Christians." While this passage does not directly answer the question, when it is read against the backdrop of John Paul's methodological understanding, some conclusions, or at least inferences, become quite probable.

First, the exclusion of conferences of bishops suggests that bishops have no more magisterial authority as a body than as individuals. This is further underscored by a later statement that the Pontifical Commission *Justitia et Pax,* "which has corresponding bodies within the individual bishops' conferences," has the function of coordinating the level three activities and commitments. In this schema, apparently both the Pontifical Commission and the bishops' conferences coordinate the application of Catholic social doctrine, but they do not contribute to its development.

Second, the link of theological thinking with praxis could well reflect a certain awareness of experience as a starting point for theological thinking; however, given the operative methodology, it seems rather to imply that such thinking ought to be concerned with the application of social doctrine to social action.

And finally, the third location of engaged attention distinguishes between the church and Christians. Since the encyclical greeting includes "all men and women of good will," this is a possible reference to those Christians who are not Roman Catholic. Such an interpretation, however, would then omit reference to social action by persons from other major religious traditions. Given the two-track methodology, namely doctrine and its application, a case can be made for a distinction between the magisterium, which develops social doctrine, and Christians who apply that teaching in their historical circumstances. Such a distinction is a clear departure from *Octogesima adveniens.*

Libertatis Conscientia

In 1986 the Congregation for the Doctrine of the Faith issued *Libertatis conscientia* as the second and positive instruction dealing with theology of liberation.[35] *Libertatis conscientia* no. 72 is of particular interest to us for two reasons. First, John Paul II subsequently quotes this passage with *Octogesima adveniens* no. 4 in *Sollicitudo rei socialis;* and second, this passage serves as the single footnoted reference in a section listing "essential documents describing and defining the nature of social doctrine" from *Guidelines for Teaching the Church's Social Doctrine in Forming Priests.*[36]

In *Libertatis conscientia* no. 72, one reads

The church's social teaching is born of the encounter of the gospel message and of its demands...with the problems emanating from the life of society. This social teaching has established itself as a doctrine *(doctrinae corpus)* by using the resources of human wisdom and the sciences. It concerns the ethical aspect of this life. It takes into account the technical aspects of problems but always in order to judge them from the moral point of view.

Being essentially oriented toward action, this teaching *(doctrina)* develops in accordance with the changing circumstances of history. That is why, together with principles that are always valid, it *(doctrina)* also involves contingent judgments. Far from constituting a closed system, it *(doctrina)* remains constantly open to the new questions which continually arise; it requires the contribution of all charisma, experiences and skills.

As an "expert in humanity" the church offers by her social doctrine *(doctrina sociali)* a set of principles for reflection *("principiorum doctrinalium")* and criteria for judgment *("criteriorum iudicandi")* and also directives for action *(regulas et impulsiones ad agendum)* so that the profound changes demanded by situations of poverty and injustice may be brought about, and this in a way which serves the true good of humanity.

Footnote 107 to the text attributes the preceding expressions to *Octogesima adveniens* no. 4 and to John Paul II's address at Puebla.[37] Footnote 108 refers the expression *regulas et impulsiones ad agendum* to John XXIII's *Mater et magistra* no. 235.[38] As noted earlier, *Mater et magistra* no. 236 lists the "three stages which should normally be followed in the reduction of social principles into practice," that is, observation, judgment, and action. Several noteworthy changes have occurred in *Libertatis conscientia.*

First, the trio Observe, Judge, Act is tied to Christian action alone. This departs from *Octogesima adveniens* no. 4, wherein principles, norms, and directives along with the gospel were the resources used by the Christian community to assess the local situation for appropriate action. Since all three terms were used in *Octogesima adveniens,* there would be no need to refer to *Mater et magistra* no. 236, unless one wanted to link Observe, Judge, Act solely with the "reduction of social principles into practice," and break the link with the development of social teaching. Such an interpretation is valid only when the single sentence from *Octogesima adveniens* no. 4 concerning principles of reflection, norms for judgment, and directives for action is taken from its context.

Second, the church already has and offers the principles, criteria, and directives. Thus the Christian only has to put them into practice. This point is further strengthened by the change from *"principia cogitandi"* in *Octogesima adveniens* to *"principiorum doctrinalium"* in *Libertatis conscientia.* Note, however, that the document stops short of calling these modifications of the three stages "principles that are always valid." By contrast, in *Octogesima adveniens* the Christian community participates in working out the social teaching in history.

Third, the starting point is social doctrine, not the local situation. Fourth, the gospel and social problems gave birth to the social doctrine of the church, which then "established itself as a doctrine by using the resources of human wisdom and the sciences." Apparently once spawned by the gospel, social doctrine relies on the human sciences to become *doctrinae corpus* and to determine permanently valid principles and contingent judgments. The gospel is a progenitor of Catholic social doctrine, not an active dialogue partner with it in the local situation. This initial explanation of both the unchanging and the historical nature of social teaching will appear again.

Fifth, social doctrine advances in history via continuously arising new questions; it is not constituted in the course of history as in *Octogesima adveniens.*

Sollicitudo Rei Socialis

In *Sollicitudo rei socialis* (1987), John Paul II commemorates the twentieth anniversary of *Populorum progressio* and offers some additional insights on his reinterpretation of *Octogesima adveniens* no. 4. In the introductory paragraphs, the pope addresses the permanent and contingent dimensions of social doctrine as the second of his two reasons for writing, expressing his desire,

> following in the footsteps of my esteemed predecessors in the See of Peter, to reaffirm the continuity of the social doctrine *(doctrinae socialis)* as well as its constant renewal. In effect, continuity and renewal are a proof of the perennial value of the teaching *(doctrinae)* of the Church. This twofold dimension is typical of the teaching in the social sphere. On the one hand it is constant, for it remains identical in its fundamental inspiration, in its "principles of reflection" *(cogitationis rationibus),* in its "criteria of judgment" *(iudicii normis),* in its basic "directives for action" *(legibus principibus, quae actionem moderantur),* [6] and above all in its vital link with the Gospel of the Lord. On the other hand, it is ever new, because it is subject to the necessary opportune adaptations suggested by the unceasing flow of events which are the setting of the life of people and society.[39]

According to this paragraph, the constancy of social doctrine rests in its unspecified fundamental inspiration, in its link with the gospel, and in principles of reflection, criteria of judgment, and basic directives for action. The last point carries a footnote reference to *Libertatis conscientia* no. 72 and *Octogesima adveniens* no. 4, as if both of them confirmed this statement. In fact *Sollicitudo rei socialis* takes *Liberatatis conscientia* a step farther with its explicit identification of the principles, norms, and directives as constant elements of social doctrine. One might hope for some distinction between the three dimensions based on content, method, and specific action suggestions, if one could not hope for fidelity to the original context. If, however, all three are equally constants, specific actions become right or wrong in and of themselves, apart from circumstances, intentions, and actors. In addition to extending the position of *Libertatis conscientia* no. 72, the quotation of *Octogesima adveniens* no. 4 in order to prove that social doctrine entails perennial truths taught by the magisterium is a clear distortion of Paul VI's earlier stress on the local community, the historically constituted nature of social teaching, and the undesirability of one universal papal teaching.

Although the doctrine is constant, it can in fact be adapted, and applied to specific situations. These situations apparently do not change the doctrine itself but shape how the permanent truth might best be accepted in the local situation. This point becomes clearer in no. 8:

> In addition, the social doctrine of the church *(socialis christianorum doctrina)* has once more demonstrated its character as an application of the word of God to people's lives and the life of society as well as to the earthly realities connected with them, offering "principles of reflection," "criteria of judgment," and "directives of action" *(principia...a recta ratione postulata...orientationesque quasdem).* [20] Here, in the document of Paul VI, one finds these three elements with prevalently practical orientation, that is, directed toward moral conduct.[40]

In addition to confirming that social doctrine is to be applied to situations, this paragraph relies on the interpretation made in *Libertatis conscientia,* namely that Observe, Judge, Act is the method used to reduce social principles into action alone. No mention is made of the larger context, namely, analysis by the local community, judgment in the light of the gospel and social teaching, as well as discernment of the community's options for action, all this in consultation with the Holy Spirit and the larger ecclesial, Christian, and human communities.

The loss of this context is also apparent in the very structure of the encyclical. *Sollicitudo rei socialis* begins with an introduction and review of social doctrine (nos. 1–10). Only in Section 3 does it begin a survey of the contemporary world, that is, the signs of the times (nos. 11–26). Sections 4 and 5 return to development (nos. 27–34) and a theological reading of contemporary social problems (nos. 35–40), before section 6 (nos. 41–45) gives some practical guidelines. Although Observe, Judge, Act could provide the underlying structure of *Sollicitudo rei socialis,* a presentation of social doctrine precedes the magisterial effort at observation, judgment, and action. In addition it is the magisterium, not the Christian community, that employs this method.

The twin poles of judgment in *Octogesima adveniens* have become one: Social doctrine is the contemporary application of the gospel in the social order. Consequently if the gospel is unalterable, then social doctrine is permanent and always valid. Since social doctrine is unchanging, all that remains is the propagation and dissemination of the doctrine. *Sollicitudo rei socialls* speaks of evangelization in this vein:

> As her instrument for reaching this goal, the church uses her social doctrine *(sociali sua doctrina).* In today's difficult situation, a more exact awareness and a wider diffusion of the "set of principles for reflection, criteria for judgment and the directives for action" proposed by the church's teaching, [72] would be of great help in promoting both the correct definition of the problems being faced and the best solution to them.[41]

In summary, in *Sollicitudo rei socialis,* John Paul II stresses the continuity of social doctrine back to the gospel itself in a kind of unbroken chain. The principles of reflection, criteria of judgment, and basic directives for action no longer reflect how the Christian uses social doctrine, but have become the content of social doctrine. In addition, this doctrine is constant and not historically constituted. The constancy of social doctrine precludes a starting point in the contemporary situation.

Finally, when social doctrine is universally valid, the Christian community need only apply it to the local situation and not engage in its historically contextualized development. This interpretive shift is possible when a single sentence in *Octogesima adveniens* no. 4 is used out of its original context, where both the activity of the local church and the nature of social teaching are viewed as historically constituted.

Guidelines for Teaching the Church's Social Doctrine

Although the document *Guidelines for Teaching the Church's Social Doctrine in Forming Priests* (1988) was issued by the Congregation for Catholic Education, it is relevant to this study. Its introduction cites *Octogesima adveniens* no. 4, alluding to the church's limits in providing solutions to all problems due to the different situations in which Christians are engaged. This apparently accurate use of *Octogesima adveniens* no. 4 is, however, qualified by the following:

> On the other hand, she can and must, in the "light which comes to her from the Gospel" provide the principles and necessary guidelines for the correct organization of social life, for the dignity of the human person, and for the common good. The Magisterium, in fact, continues to intervene often in this field with a doctrine that all the faithful are called upon to know, teach, and apply.[42]

Thus, while the church is limited in providing solutions to all problems, it does have principles and guidelines from magisterial doctrine, which the faithful are to learn, teach, and apply. The qualification seems to suggest that the absence of solutions is in fact a limitation coming from the diversity and magnitude of the problems, but not from the historically constituted nature of the social doctrine itself. This differs from Paul VI's position in *Octogesima adveniens.*

The *Guidelines* then address "The Nature of Social Doctrine" (nos. 3–13). In no. 3, *Libertatis conscientia* no. 72 alone is named as the "essential document describing and defining the nature of social doctrine." The same paragraph distinguishes between "principles which are always valid" and "contingent judgments," a distinction also found in *Libertatis conscientia* no. 72.

No. 6 describes three interconnected and inseparable dimensions of social doctrine: the theoretical, the historical, and the practical. The theoretical dimension refers to the universal criteria and permanent principles formulated in organic and systematic reflection. The practical dimension includes the application of the principles in the concrete situations in which Christians find themselves. The historical dimension refers to the use of principles with a view to the real social order in magisterial documents. This dimension could be said to be conscious of historical realities. As such it differs from the theoretical, but is not yet application. This is a helpful clarification on the current magisterium's understanding of historical consciousness, but it is a far cry from historically constituted social teachings.

No. 7 presents the triad Observe, Judge, Act as the inductive-deductive methodology of social doctrine without reference to *Octogesima adveniens* no. 4, although it does mention *Mater et magistra* no. 236. A most enlightening contribution of this paragraph is the attribution of the various stages to various groups. To Observe is the function of the human and social sciences, apparently with no recourse to faith;[43] to Judge is the "function proper to the Magisterium of the Church,"[44] while "real Christians" are invited to Act by following the doctrine.[45] The gospel is mentioned in the judging phase as including a scale of values to which the church adapts. The Holy Spirit appears to be mentioned in the acting phase as a "particular assistance promised by Christ to His Church," which matures the pastoral experience and the reflection of the magisterium.[46] This mention, however, seems to link the particular assistance to the magisterium alone as a reason for the "real Christian to follow this doctrine."

Octogesima adveniens no. 4 is cited in no. 8 when the conversation turns to discernment of the "entire Christian community, and each one in particular, to 'scrutinize the signs of the times' and to interpret reality in the light of the evangelical message."[47] Either this paragraph is inconsistent with the above distinctions in phases and roles, or the discernment described belongs properly in the action phase, so that the Christian is invited to discern how to apply the conclusions reached by the judgment of the magisterium. Discernment, then, has separated from development of social teaching as a whole, and is relegated to the action phase alone. Therein the entire community is charged to discern, that is,

> to arrive, in light of permanent principles, at an objective judgment about social reality and, according to the possibilities and opportunities offered by the circumstances, to make concrete the most appropriate choices which may

eliminate injustices and favor the political, economic and cultural transformations needed in individual cases.[48]

So it has come to this. *Octogesima adveniens* no. 4 is not about constituting social teaching in the course of history with the help of the Spirit in the community and with broad consultation. Rather the Spirit is linked to the magisterium; the methodological steps are parsed out among the social sciences, the magisterium, and the faithful; and discernment has been relegated to the application of social doctrine. *Octogesima adveniens* no. 4 is not about the initiative of local communities in the continuing development of social teaching; rather, "real Christians" apply the most appropriate course of action from among those already judged by the magisterium as social doctrine.

In the only other acknowledgment of *Octogesima adveniens* no. 4, the passage is linked with the effort to make social doctrine concrete "by proposing principles for reflection and permanent values, criteria for judgment and directives for action." Observe, Judge, Act as a whole is here separated from the development of social teaching and transferred into the realm of concrete application.[49] The context is the final sentence of the section, "Formation of the Historical Heritage," directed to illustrating a central thesis, namely that, although there is a consistent and permanent corpus that constitutes social doctrine, it is not a closed system, because it responds to new problems or to old problems in new garb.[50]

Centesimus Annus

As a kind of whimper, in *Centesimus annus* (The Hundredth Year) (1991) *Octogesima adveniens* no. 4 is referred to in a footnote only once. In the context of a discussion on capitalism, the encyclical notes:

> The church has no models to present; models that are real and truly effective can only arise within the framework of different historical situations through the efforts of all those who responsibly confront concrete problems in all their social, economic, political, and cultural aspects as these interact with one another.[51]

Footnote 84 cites *Gaudium et spes* no. 36, which admits the autonomy of disciplines like economics, and *Octogesima adveniens* nos. 2–5, which make the stronger statement that the church does not have a unified message or a solution with universal validity, nor is it the mission or ambition of the church to have such a solution or message. However, the statement in *Centesimus annus* appears with no immediate reference to Catholic social doctrine or teachings.

CONCLUSIONS

In the course of the twenty years of magisterial teaching we have surveyed, a single sentence referring to principles, norms, and directives drawn from social doctrine has been separated from the whole of *Octogesima adveniens* no. 4. This is in line with the method of magisterial reinterpretation as it has been practiced for centuries. This particular reinterpretation, however, entailed a number of interrelated shifts that together amount to a distortion of the original text.

First, in considering the question, Who participates in the development of Catholic social teaching? a shift occurred from the local Christian community to the magisterium alone. Second, with regard to the starting point, a shift occurred from analysis of the local situation to permanent principles of Catholic social doctrine. Third, in considering the contribution of history, a shift occurred from history as a constitutive dimension of social teaching to an awareness of historical contingencies in the application of social teaching. Fourth, with regard to the place of the gospel, a shift occurred from the gospel as an active partner along with social teaching in dialogue with the signs of the times to the gospel as a primary, distant source of social doctrine. Fifth, the principles of reflection, norms of judgment, and directives for action drawn from social doctrine became the content of social doctrine. Thus the three stages are no longer aspects of a method used by local communities. Sixth, once the principles, norms, and directives became identified with social doctrine, the role of the local Christian community shifted from participation in the actual development of social teaching to mere application of permanently valid principles determined by the magisterium. Seventh, there is consequently a shift from Paul VI's claim that a unified message and a universal solution is neither the papal ambition nor its mission.

Finally, with regard to the relationship of church and world, a shift took place from an ecclesiology that saw the church as a pilgrim people in the world to an ecclesiology of the church as the guardian of truth that it dispenses to the world. We argue, however, that both of these ecclesiological dimensions are needed as a kind of ongoing self-corrective mechanism. The diminishment of one of them results in the impoverishment of social teaching as a whole.

This study, however, points to more than just one example of papal reinterpretation; it indicates an overall effort to reject or at least minimize historically contextualized methodologies in favor of theologies built on ahistorical truths, universally valid principles, and a suspicion of the material, historical world. This effort may be well intentioned, and it may correct some aspects of historically constituted theologies. At the same time, it implicitly minimizes, or even seems explicitly to discard, much of the scholarly achievement that has become part of the church's theological heritage in this century.

Such an approach contradicts the reality of social movements and their contribution to social thought in areas stretching from family planning to pacifism to human rights to environmental issues. Participation is essential to human dignity. This connection already has been made in Catholic social teachings in the political and economic arenas, as well as in some social arenas external to the institutional church. But participation does not characterize the church's most recent social teaching, which is thus in danger of losing its credibility. To avert this danger, the nonmagisterial contribution to the development of the church's social teaching must be actively embraced. For in truth of fact, Catholic social teachings are not shaped by the magisterium alone. This reality must be acknowledged and celebrated.

There are inadequacies inherent in the claim of a universal and permanent social doctrine. First, such an approach cannot adequately address the major issues of unity and diversity in human life today. Second, such an option is unable to make sense of change. Third, as long as ahistorical, permanent realities remain the center focus, the power of social, political, religious, and economic structures and movements to shape lives and meaning is downplayed. Finally, an ahistorical approach to Catholic social teaching practically ignores the Incarnation and with that not only history's revelatory possibilities but also a rich world of signs and symbols so central in community formation.

These inadequacies reveal that an ahistorical, unchanging framework for Catholic social teachings is fraught with limitations, whether in terms of providing meaningful principles for action on behalf of justice or in terms of presenting a method for thinking about key aspects of our era. We suggest that the credibility and integrity of Catholic social teaching requires that it retrieve the fundamental insights sketched in *Gaudium et spes* and elaborated in *Octogesima adveniens.*

Notes

1. Paul VI, *Octogesima adveniens, Acta Apostolicae Sedis* 63 (1971) 401–44.

2. Donal Dorr, *Option for the Poor: A Hundred Years of Vatican Social Teaching* (Maryknoll, N.Y.: Orbis, 1983); Mary Elsbernd, "Rights Statements: A Hermeneutical Key to Continuing Development in Magisterial Teaching," *Ephemerides Theologicae Lovanienses* 62 (1986) 308–32.

3. Marie-Dominique Chenu, *La "doctrine sociale" de l'Église comme idéologie* (Paris: Cerf 1979); Charles E. Curran, *Directions in Catholic Social Ethics* (Notre Dame: University of Notre Dame, 1985); George Grima, "Method in the Social Teaching of the Church," *Melita Theologica* 33 (1982) 11–33; and David Hollenbach, *Claims in Conflict: Retrieving and Renewing the Catholic Human Rights Tradition* (New York: Paulist, 1979).

4. Michael Schuck makes this point well: "contemporary commentators sometimes ascribe to the popes a more plebiscitary understanding of what it means to read the 'signs of the times' than is warranted by the encyclicals" (*That They Be One* [Washington: Georgetown University, 1991] 157).

5. Curran, *Directions* 33–36; Stephen B. Bevans, *Models of Contextual Theology* (Maryknoll, N.Y.: Orbis, 1992) 42–46; John Coleman, "Development of Church Social Teaching," *Origins* 11 (1981) 34–41; Ronald Modras, "Karl Rahner and John Paul II: Anthropological Implications for Economics and the Social Order," in *The Annual Publication of the College Theology Society* 31: *Religion and Economic Ethics,* ed. Joseph F. Gower (Washington: Georgetown University, 1985) 123–50, esp. 142–47; and George H. Williams, *The Mind of John Paul II: Origins of His Thought and Action* (New York: Seabury, 1981). It is probable that the magisterial writings of John Paul II, like that of the popes of the previous centuries, are in fact influenced by the historical realities of these

times. Given the reality of a God who reveals Godself in history, Incarnation, word, and sacrament, it can hardly be otherwise.

6. Bevans, *Models,* 42–46.

7. Modras, "The Thomistic Personalism of Pope John Paul II," *The Modern Schoolman* 59 (1982) 117–27. See also Karol Wojtyla, "Personalism Tomistyczny," *Znak* 13 (1961) 664–76. Modras notes that "Karol Wojtyla's philosophical career has been largely dedicated to achieving an ethics of absolute norms above the contingencies of history" ("Karl Rahner and John Paul II," 148). See also J. Bryan Hehir, "John Paul II: Continuity and Change in the Social Teaching of the Church," in *Readings in Moral Theology 5: Official Catholic Social Teaching,* ed. Charles E. Curran and Richard A. McCormick (New York: Paulist, 1986) 247–63 at 256.

8. Liberation theology, feminist theology, black theology, as well as the movements of small Christian communities and national conferences of bishops have continued to experience and articulate the place of the local Christian communities.

9. The exploration of social location as it is found in liberation, feminist, black, womanist, mujerista theologies continues to probe this strand with implications for Catholic social thought.

10. Perhaps nowhere is his pain as clear as in his 1968 Christmas radio message; see "Radio message de Noël (December 20, 1968)," in *Documents pontificaux de Paul VI. Vol. 7, 1968* (Saint-Maurice: Éditions Saint-Augustin, 1971) 793–99. See also his response to the suffering connected with the Biafran struggle, in "The Heart of Africa," *The Pope Speaks* 14 (1969) 213–46, at 221.

11. Each of these letters written by the Secretary of State conveys the apostolic blessing and thoughts of Paul VI: "Lettre de la secrétairerie d'État au Président des Semaines Sociales de France (June 30, 1968)," in *Documents pontificaux* 7.403–409, at 404; and "Lettre de la secrétairerie d' État au Président des Semaines Sociales d'Italie (September 15, 1968)," in *Documents pontificaux* 7.561–69, at 569.

12. See *The Pope Speaks* 13 (1968) 144–46.

13. Official translations of magisterial documents render *homo* by "man" in spite of the Latin term's inclusive meaning. Editorial preference and reading ease require that the editorial *sic* be omitted from subsequent quotations of magisterial documents.

14. Recall the special growth of the YCS/YCW movements in the middle decades of this century. This context sheds some light on Roger Heckel's comment in the inaugural booklet of a proposed series, *The Social Teaching of John Paul II* (Vatican City: Pontifical Commission *Justitia et Pax,* 1980) 2: "In the spirit of *Octogesima,* 4, these booklets are essentially *working* documents" (emphasis original).

15. John XXIII, *"Mater et magistra," AAS* 53 (1961) 401–64, at 456.

16. Coleman makes a similar point, namely that the question is, What have Catholic social teachings formed? To which he responds: "They have formed over the past ninety years men and women who have found in them a charter to become concerned about institutional and structural reform, to support organization for justice, to heed the papal call to respect human dignity and to go to the poor. These men and women and the Catholic movements they have spawned are the best exegesis of the documents" ("Development," 40–41).

17. My use of terms reflects the precise Latin term wherever possible, that is, *doctrine* (teaching) or teachings, although I should prefer to employ the term *social teachings,* which conveys the historically constitutive nature of magisterial teachings. Occasionally I use "Catholic social thought" as a term broader than "magisterial teachings."

18. For a further illustration, see *Populorum* nos. 2 and 3, in which Paul VI opts for the Leonine expression "the social question," when exhorting persons to shed the light of the gospel on the contemporary situation.

19. In the context of no. 43, divine law does not appear to be used in the specific Thomistic sense. Rather it is mentioned as one more instance highlighting the inseparability of religious and the social-question orientation. This paragraph also refers to faith and daily life, religious values and social enterprises, world and Christian spirit, as well as witness to Christ and human society. Divine law is paired with "laws proper to each discipline."

20. *Gaudium et spes* no. 43.

21. It is the task of another study to determine if this is in fact the beginning of lay participation in the formation of Catholic social teachings.

22. *Gaudium et spes* no. 1.

23. See Modras, "Karl Rahner and John Paul II"; Modras, "Thomistic Personalism"; John Hellman, "John Paul II and the Personalist Movement," *Cross Currents* 30 (1980–1981) 409–19; Bevans, *Models,* 42–46; John Carmody, *The Encyclical Theology of Pope John Paul II,* Warren Lecture Series in Catholic Studies (Tulsa: University of Oklahoma, 1990); George Huntston Williams, *The Mind of John Paul II* (New York: Seabury, 1991); Charles E. Curran, "The Changing Anthropological Bases in Catholic Social Thought," in Curran, *Directions,* 32–36; and Richard McBrien, "Papal, Bishops' Ships 'Passed in the Night,'" *National Catholic Reporter* 23 (October 2, 1987) 1 and 28–30. In the 1980s several French-language studies appeared specifically about the social teaching of John Paul II: P. Georges M. M. Cottier, "Profil herméneutico-épistémologique de la doctrine sociale de l'Église," *Seminarium* 29 (1989) 223–31; Ph.-I. André-Vincent, *La Doctrine sociale de Jean Paul II* (Paris: France-Empire, 1983).

24. See Modras, "Karl Rahner and John Paul II," 138.

25. "The essential meaning of this 'kingship' and 'dominion' of man over the visible world, which the creator himself gave man for his task, consists in the priority of ethics over technology, in the primacy of the person over things, and in the superiority of spirit over matter" (John Paul II, *"Redemptor Hominis,"* Origins 8 [1979] 625–44, at 635); Latin text in *AAS* 71 (1979) 257–324.

26. Cf. ibid., 636, in which transformation of economic structures depends on individual conversion.

27. Cf. ibid., 632.

28. Paul VI, *"Evangelii nuntiandi,"* AAS 68 (1976) 5–76, at 29–30, does in fact use the singular construction "social doctrine"; cf. Heckel, *Social Teaching* 23, who holds that John Paul II uses these terms and a number of others as equivalent.

29. *Origins* 8 (February 8, 1979) 529–38, at 538 (III. 7).

30. Cf. John Paul II, "Address to the Workers in Monterrey (January 31, 1979)," in *Osservatore Romano*, February 19, 1979, 7 (English ed.): "I make a forceful appeal to the public authorities, contractors and workers, to reflect on these principles and to deduce the consequent lines of action. It must also be recognized that there is no lack of examples of those who put into practice, in an exemplary way, these principles of the social doctrine of the Church."

31. John Paul II's inaugural encyclical promulgated shortly after Puebla is included among the social encyclicals, given its treatment of human dignity, human rights, and the common good.

32. Heckel does not shed light on this quotation with his comment: "By way of a direct quote, a summary reference, or further development, John Paul II often refers to *Octogesima* 42, in which Paul VI clearly illustrated the constituent features of the social teaching of the Church" (*Social Teaching,* 24). Even if John Paul II understood the constituent features of Catholic social teaching as its historical consciousness and its accompanying nature, the connection to daring creative resolves and dignity are not clear.

33. The scriptures are referred to in footnotes ninety-eight times; all other references combined equal twenty-three, including eleven references to *Gaudium et spes* nos. 33–39 ("Man's Activity throughout the World") and nine references to the *Summa theologiae*.

34. The primary nature of the magisterium is highlighted in the next paragraph, in which the social encyclicals and *Gaudium et spes* are called the "documents of the supreme magisterium of the Church."

35. *"Libertatis conscientia,"* AAS 79 (1987) 554–99; an English translation, " Instruction of Christian Freedom and Liberation," appeared in *Origins* 15 (April 17, 1986) 513–28.

36. The English edition appears in *The Pope Speaks* 34 (1989) 293–342. The Italian edition appears in *Seminarium* 29 (1989) 135–211.

37. *"Oratio habita initio Conferentiae de Puebla,"* AAS 71 (1979) 203. The references in the Latin text depart from their quoted citations.

38. *AAS* 53 (1961) 461 is the citation given. The correct reference, however, appears to be no. 236 on p. 456. The formulation in *Mater et magistra* no. 236 bears little resemblance to that in *Libertatis conscientia.*

39. *AAS* 80 (1988) 513–86, at 515.

40. The Latin terms are included in the text as quoted. Footnote 20 gives the same citations as footnote 6, although the Latin text of *Sollicitudo rei socialis* no. 8 is altered yet again.

41. *Sollicitudo rei socialis* no. 41. Footnote 72 again cites both *Libertatis conscientia* no. 72 and *Octogesima adveniens* no. 4. In spite of the quotation marks, the quoted words again deviate from both sources.

42. See *The Pope Speaks* 34 (1989) 293–340, at 295.

43. "Seeing is perception and study of real problems and their causes, the analysis of which, however, belongs to the human and social sciences" (ibid., 298).

44. "Judging is interpretation of that same reality in the light of the sources of social doctrine which determine the judgment pronounced with regard to social phenomena and their ethical implications. In this intermediate phase is found the function proper to the Magisterium of the Church which consists precisely in interpreting reality from the viewpoint of faith and offering 'what it has of its own: a global view about man and humanity'" (ibid.); a footnote at this point cites *Populorum progressio* no. 13.

45. "Acting is aimed at implementing these choices....By inviting the faithful to make concrete choices and to act according to the principles and judgments expressed in its social doctrine, the Magisterium offers the fruit of much reflection and pastoral experience matured under the particular assistance promised by Christ to His Church. It is up to the real Christian to follow this doctrine and to make it 'the foundation of his wisdom and of his experience in order to translate it concretely into forms of action, participation and commitment'" (ibid.); a footnote at this point cites *Evangelii nuntiandi* no. 38.

46. Ibid.

47. Ibid.

48. Ibid.

49. Ibid., 300 (no. 11). In addition to *Octogesima adveniens* no. 4, footnote 69 also cites *Mater et magistra* no. 454, *Oratio (Puebla)* 203 (III, no. 7), and *Libertatis conscientia* no. 72.

50. Ibid., 300 (nos. 11–12); see also 312 (nos. 27–28).

51. *"Centesimus annus,"* Origins 21 (1991) 1–24 at 17; Latin text in *AAS* 83 (1991) 793–867, at 846.

Part Four

MARRIAGE, SEXUALITY, GENDER, AND FAMILY

13. Marriage and Sexuality: Magisterial Teaching from 1918 to the Present

John Gallagher

This chapter first appeared in *Human Sexuality and Personhood* (St. Louis: Pope John Center, 1981).

THE CODE OF CANON LAW

This paper traces the teaching of the Roman Catholic magisterium from 1918 to the present. It was in the year 1918 that the modern Code of Canon Law came into force. The code contains certain theological statements about marriage. One such statement concerns the ends of marriage. Paragraph One of Canon 1013 states: "The primary end of marriage is the procreation and education of children; its secondary end is mutual help and the allaying of concupiscence."

In view of the subsequent controversy, it is well to look closely at what the code actually says. There is a widespread impression that the code says that the mutual love of spouses is only a secondary end of marriage. In fact, however, the code does not speak of the mutual love of spouses as an end of marriage in either way, as a secondary end or as a primary end.

This raises an interesting point. An end is the object of an act of will. One can, no doubt, have as one's purpose in marriage a growth in love. Love then can be said to be an end of marriage. However, it is an end in a special way. The love in question is itself an act of will responding to those further ends and goods that are the objects of love—namely, the persons who are loved and their welfare. Love is in this case an end that is a response to a more ultimate good or end. For this reason some thinkers who hold that love is central to Christian marriage may not wish to express that centrality by calling love an end of marriage.

The code does not give mere biological generation as the principal end of marriage. That end is procreation and education. Canon 1113 explains this. It states: "Parents are bound by a most serious obligation to provide to the best of their power for the religious and moral as well as for the physical and civil education of their children, and also to provide for their temporal welfare." The code sees marriage as an institution whose principal end is the total human good of the next generation.

What is the authority of the code's theological teaching about marriage? By including certain theological principles in the code, the church was not interested primarily in settling theological disputes. She was interested primarily in providing some theological background for law. For this purpose she adopted certain theological principles commonly accepted in the church at the time. Some of these principles had already been taught authoritatively by popes and councils. Some had not. The inclusion of a theological principle in the code need not mean that the principle was being taught with new authority.

CASTI CONNUBII

On December 31, 1930, Pope Pius XI published the encyclical, *Casti Connubii,* on Christian marriage. To some extent this encyclical was a response to the Lambeth Conference of 1930, at which for the first time the Church of England withdrew its official objections to artificial contraception. *Casti Connubii* does not limit itself to the problem of artificial contraception, however. It covers a wide range of topics concerning which the modern world either rejects or ignores the traditional teaching of the Catholic Church.

This encyclical seems to presuppose what one might call an organic notion of marriage. Some "reformers" would like to get rid of the institution of marriage or at least radically restructure it. Such efforts are suspect to those who have an organic notion of social institutions. A medical doctor does not begin with an abstract idea of what a rationally constructed human body should be, and then proceed to tear apart the human body and put it together along more rational lines. The human body exists and functions before any physician studies it. Analogously, marriage exists and functions before any theorist studies it. Marriage draws upon and channels certain human energies and instincts, it fulfills certain needs, and it embodies certain principles learned by trial and error, long before it is studied theoretically. In the organic view, the reformer of marriage should not try to destroy the existing institution and rebuild a substitute, according to some abstract and partial view of what is needed and what is possible. The reformer of marriage, like the physician, should be humble, learning from the existing thing and respecting requirements that flow from its nature.

Casti Connubii does not explicitly adopt this organic view, but it seems to imply it. Paragraph 6 states: "The nature of matrimony is entirely independent of the free will of man, so that if one has once contracted matrimony he is thereby subject to its divinely made laws and properties."[1] Paragraphs 49 and 50 argue that matrimony was instituted by God who is the author of nature. The argument seems to be that it was in creating the nature of things that God created marriage. Marriage is not something arbitrarily set up by God but an institution that arises because of the nature of human beings. The encyclical draws from this, that because matrimony is created by God it has laws that human beings should obey, laws that they cannot change. The point is elaborated in Paragraph 95, which contains a quotation from Pope Leo XIII.

It is a divinely appointed law that whatsoever things are constituted by God, the author of nature, these we find the most useful and salutary, the more they remain in their natural state, unimpaired and unchanged; inasmuch as God, the Creator of all things, intimately knows what is suited to the constitution and the preservation of each, and by his will and mind has so ordained all things that each may duly achieve its purpose. But if the boldness and wickedness of men change and disturb this order of things, so providentially disposed, then indeed things so wonderfully ordained will begin to be injurious, or will cease to be beneficial, either because, in the change, they have lost their power to benefit, or because God Himself is thus pleased to draw down chastisement on the pride and presumption of men.

Of special interest to our purpose is Pius's discussion of the ends of marriage. He quotes Canon 1013. "The primary end of marriage is the procreation and the education of children."[2] Elsewhere he reemphasizes the primacy of procreation. "Thus, amongst the blessings of marriage, the child holds first place."[3] The child is destined not only for a noble and dignified life in this world but also for eternal life. The sublime end of matrimony is to bring forth children who will become members of Christ and who will enjoy eternal life with God.[4]

Among the secondary ends of marriage, Pius XI includes the two mentioned by canon law, mutual aid and the quieting of concupiscence. To these he adds a third, the cultivation of mutual love.[5]

It is clear that Pius does not consider these unitive aspects (mutual love, mutual aid) to have only minor importance. Concerning the union of spouses he speaks of "the generous surrender of his own person made to another for the whole span of life."[6] Furthermore:

> By matrimony, therefore, the minds of the contracting parties are joined and knit together more intimately than are their bodies, and that not by any passing affection of sense or heart, but by a deliberate and firm act of the will.[7]

The mutual love of spouses motivates them to help each other. Pius expands the scope of this traditional category, mutual help.

> This outward expression of love in the home demands not only mutual help but must go further; must have as its primary purpose that man and wife help each other day by day in forming and perfecting themselves in the interior life, so that through their partnership in life they may advance ever more and more in virtue, and above all that they may grow in true love toward God and their neighbor.[8]

There is some reason to believe that Pius XI was not completely satisfied with calling these unitive elements merely secondary ends of matrimony. Of the love between husband and wife he says that it "pervades all the duties of married life and holds pride of place in Christian marriage."[9] Of the mutual help of spouses he says:

This mutual inward molding of husband and wife, this determined effort to perfect each other, can in a very real sense, as the Roman Catechism teaches, be said to be the chief reason and purpose of matrimony, provided matrimony be looked at not in the restricted sense as instituted for the proper conception and education of the child, but more widely as the blending of life as a whole and the mutual interchange and sharing thereof.[10]

It seems that Pius XI is insisting on two points, which in the theology of the day, were not easily expressed in one simple formula. The first point is that marriage has an essential orientation to children. The second point is that the mutual love and aid between spouses has an importance that is not adequately expressed by calling them secondary ends of marriage. However, to add a second primary end to marriage presents its own difficulties, as we shall see in discussing a later document. Pius XI resorts to the vague formula of two primacies according to two different points of view.

On sexual relations outside of marriage, the encyclical restates the church's traditional teaching as follows:

Nor must we omit to remark, in fine, that since the twofold duty entrusted to parents for the good of their children is of such high dignity and of such great importance, every lawful use of the faculty given by God for the procreation of new life is the right and the privilege of the marriage state alone, by the law of God and of nature, and must be confined absolutely within the sacred limits of that state.[11]

The order of the argument here is worth noting. Pius does not base his rejection of fornication and adultery only on an analysis of biological sexuality. His basis is the nature and end of the institution of marriage. That sex should be properly oriented toward procreation is a truth seen in the context of the orientation of marriage toward procreation.

In Paragraphs 53 to 59, Pius XI condemns artificial contraception as gravely sinful, and instructs confessors to hold to this teaching. Some writers have complained that here Pius resorts to biologistic reasoning. Biologistic reasoning in moral matters begins by discovering in a physical faculty an orientation toward some goal and then makes that orientation into a moral principle. In sexual ethics, the biologistic approach sees that the sexual organs and sexual responses are so constituted as to produce offspring, and concludes that therefore the production of offspring is the proper good of sex, and that any use of sex for any other purpose is immoral. Biologistic reasoning in ethics is open to serious objections.

Does Pius XI actually resort to a biologistic approach in condemning artificial contraception? Certain passages could suggest that he does. He states that artificial contraception is "intrinsically against nature," and that, "since, therefore, the conjugal act is destined primarily by nature for the begetting of children, those who in exercising it deliberately frustrate its natural power and purpose sin against nature and commit a deed which is shameful and intrinsically vicious."[12] In the context of the whole encyclical, however, it seems that what is "according to nature" is to be determined not by considering the physical aspect by itself but by looking at the nature and purpose of matrimony.

Paragraph 59 states that one partner in a marriage has a duty to try to convince the other not to use artificial contraceptives. However, one is not bound to refuse to have sexual intercourse with a spouse who insists on using contraceptives. The same paragraph states that spouses may have sexual intercourse when, for natural reasons either of time or defect, conception cannot occur. Intercourse at such times may be for such ends as mutual aid or the cultivation of mutual love, and one is free to pursue such secondary ends so long as they are subordinated to the primary end and so long as the intrinsic nature of the act is preserved. Pius thus rejects the rigorist opinion of some earlier theologians who allowed sexual intercourse only for the purpose of procreation and only when procreation is possible. In 1930 the researches of Ogino and of Knaus into periodic infertility had not yet led to widespread use of periodic continence as a way to prevent pregnancy. It is not clear, then, that in *Casti Connubii* Pius XI is thinking of periodic continence as a long-term strategy for avoiding pregnancy.

As the encyclical situates the meaning of sex in the context of marriage, so it briefly situates marriage in the context of society as a whole. The stability of matrimony is a fruitful source of habits of integrity and guards the well-being of the nation.[13] "The prosperity of the state and the temporal happiness of its citizens cannot remain safe and sound where the foundations on which they are established, which is the moral order, is weakened, and where the very fountainhead from which the state draws its life, namely wedlock and the family, is obstructed by the vices of its citizens."[14]

HERBERT DOMS AND THE MEANING OF MARRIAGE

The 1930s saw a lively controversy in the Catholic Church regarding the position expressed in the Code of Canon Law regarding the primary and secondary ends of marriage. In 1935 Herbert Doms, a German diocesan priest, published a book[15] that appeared in 1939 in an English translation as *The Meaning of Marriage*.[16] Doms objected that canon law seemed to say that the meaning of marriage comes only from what is called its primary end, the procreation and education of children. Doms does not deny that marriage has this end, but he insists that it has a meaning in itself apart from this end.

> The constitution of marriage, the union of two persons, does not consist in their subservience to a purpose outside themselves for which they marry. It consists in the constant vital ordination of husband and wife to each other until they become one. If this is so, there can no longer be sufficient reason, from this standpoint, for speaking of procreation as the primary purpose (in the sense in which St. Thomas used the phrase) and for dividing off the other purposes as secondary...perhaps it would be best if in the future we gave up using such terms as "primary" and "secondary" in speaking of the purpose of marriage.[17]

Doms distinguishes the meaning of marriage from the ends of marriage. The meaning of marriage and of sexual activity within marriage consists in the actual realization of the unity of the two persons. Besides this meaning there are two ends of marriage. The personal end is the mutual completion and perfection of the spouses on every level. The specific end (i.e., that which gives marriage its distinctive nature) is the child. These two ends are equally primary, and one is not subordinate to the other.

THE ROMAN ROTA, 1944

The views of Doms stirred up considerable reactions. They failed, however, to convince Rome on the central point. A decree of the Holy Office on April 1, 1944,[18] stated that the procreation and education of children is to be considered the primary end of marriage, and no other ends are to be considered as equally principal ends. Other ends are to be considered secondary and subordinate to the one primary end. In this decree, and in a "sentence" of the Holy Roman Rota earlier in the same year,[19] Doms is not named, but it is clear that his position is being rejected.

The sentence of the Rota appeals to a principle, which can be found in St. Thomas, that the end specifies a reality. Applied to activity it means that the end determines the nature of the activity. If your end is to remove a brain tumor, this requires one type of activity. If your end is to pass an examination in mathematics, this requires a different type of activity.

One activity may serve two ends at the same time. You may run home from work both as a means to keep fit and as a means to get home. Doms claimed that marriage has two ends, both equally primary, and one is not subordinate to the other. In the view of the Rota this would mean that in marriage there are two distinct aspects, the marriage as directed toward the mutual completion and perfection of the spouses, and the marriage as directed toward the child; these two aspects would be only accidentally, not essentially, united. If they had no essential relation to each other, there would be no theological reason for keeping them together. If someone wanted to have one without the other, there would be no reason not to do so. This is a consequence that the Rota would not accept.

In summary, the Rota seems to have rejected the notion that marriage has two primary ends, because this would destroy the essential relationship between the ends and leave the way open for allowing marriage with no procreative orientation. It is noteworthy that the acceptance by many Catholic theologians of two primary ends of marriage has been followed, a few years later, by the acceptance of deliberately childless marriages.

One may ask: What is wrong with deliberately childless marriages? The 1944 sentence of the Rota did not discuss this question,

because Doms and his followers had not denied that marriage has procreation and education of children as an essential end.

If the two ends of marriage are not independent, how are they
united? The Rota states that the secondary end is subordinate to the
primary end. That is, the mutual help and perfecting of spouses is
ordered to the procreation and education of children. This raises a
question. May spouses pursue these secondary ends not only insofar as
they are ordered to procreation but also for other reasons? Surely they
may; in fact, to develop one's love for one's spouse and to help one's
spouse *only* as ordered to procreation seems to offend against the very
meaning of the love of one's spouse. However, if one can pursue these
unitive ends not merely as subordinate to procreation, do they not
thereby become primary ends? Here the Rota's explanation of the relation between the unitive and the procreative aspects of marriage left
room for controversy.

POPE PIUS XII

When Pope Pius XII enters the discussion, he expresses concern
that the secondary end be shown to be very important.[20] On the other
hand he holds firmly to the notion of primary and secondary ends as
expressed in canon law. He states also that the secondary end is subordinate to the primary end. The unitive aspects are placed by the will of
nature and of the creator at the service of the offspring.[21]

In the address to the midwives Pius XII repeats the church's rejection of artificial contraception, and adds that this moral teaching is valid
for all time, a law that is natural and divine. Why is artificial contraception wrong? In some passages Pius XII seems to argue biologistically,
from the nature of the physical sexual faculty considered in itself.[22]
Elsewhere he seems to argue from the nature of marriage.[23] Further study
is needed to show whether these two approaches can be fitted together.

Pius XII dealt with a number of practical moral questions concerning sex and marriage. In the address to the midwives he discussed periodic
continence. There he first repeats the teaching of Pius XI that spouses may
engage in sexual intercourse when the wife cannot conceive. May a couple restrict the marital act to only infertile periods in order to avoid conception? Pius XII replies that married couples who engage in sexual

intercourse have a general duty to provide for the conservation of the human race. However, he says, serious reasons, often put forward on medical, eugenic, economic, and social grounds, can exempt from that obligatory service, even for a considerable period of time, even for the entire duration of the marriage.[24]

Pius XII rejected the use of artificial insemination.[25] He considers three situations: In the first the mother is not married. In this case the use of artificial insemination offends against the requirement that procreation take place within marriage. In the second situation the mother is married but the semen is from a man other than her husband. This is immoral because only the husband and wife have rights over the body of the other for purposes of generating new life. The bond of origin created by physical paternity creates a duty to protect and educate the child, but this cannot take place properly in this second type of situation. In the third type of situation the semen is from the husband of the woman. Artificial insemination is wrong even in this case because marriage and the marital act are not merely organic functions for the transmission of seed. The marital act is a personal act that expresses the mutual giving of spouses. This makes it the proper context for conception. Here, interestingly, Pius XII appeals explicitly to an aspect of the sexual act that is beyond the merely physical. Finally, according to Pius XII, artificial means may be used to facilitate conception after natural intercourse.

Pius XII rejects experiments in *in vitro* fertilization as immoral and absolutely illicit.[26] His reasons for rejecting artificial insemination using semen from the husband would rule out *in vitro* fertilization.

In an address on September 12, 1958, Pius discusses some moral issues related to genetics.[27] When genetic factors are likely to cause a couple to produce defective offspring, a prenuptial examination to discover the likelihood of such a result is licit. If the likelihood of defective offspring is great, authorities may even make such examinations obligatory. For genetic reasons one may advise a couple not to marry but one may not forbid them to marry. "Marriage is one of the fundamental human rights, the use of which may not be prevented." If the discovery of the genetic difficulty comes after marriage one may advise the couple not to have children, but one may not forbid them to have children.

Vatican II

The Second Vatican Council dealt with marriage and the family in *The Constitution on the Church in the Modern World (Gaudium et Spes)* sections 46–52. There were differences of opinion among the council fathers concerning earlier drafts of this document. One group wanted the document to follow closely the formulations of canon law and of papal documents on such crucial matters as the ends of marriage. Another group wanted to depart quite sharply from such formulations. Some wanted to open for discussion the question of artificial contraception. Pope John XXIII set up a commission to study the question. Pope Paul VI instructed the council not to pronounce on the question. He himself would pronounce on it after studying the report of the commission.

The treatment of marriage in *Gaudium et Spes* contains much from earlier papal statements, but the council gives its own particular emphasis to the material. Central to its discussion of marriage and family is what it calls "married love" or "spousal love." As a matter of human will, this love is much more than physical desire, but it includes physical expression. It is distinct from other types of friendship in that it is expressed and perfected through the physical marital act that both signifies and promotes the mutual self-giving of the spouses.[28] This spousal love wells up from the fountain of divine love and is structured on the model of Christ's love for the church. This spousal love is caught up in the divine love and can lead the spouses to God.

Spousal love leads to mutual help and service:

> Thus a man and a woman, who by the marriage covenant of conjugal love "are no longer two, but one flesh" (Matt 19, 6), render mutual help and service to each other through an intimate union of their persons and of their actions. Through this union they experience the meaning of their oneness and attain to it with growing perfection day by day. As a mutual gift of two persons, this intimate union, as well as the good of the children, imposes total fidelity on the spouses and argues for an unbreakable oneness between them.[29]

The council expresses clearly the orientation of marriage toward children:

> By their very nature, the institution of marriage itself and
> conjugal love are ordained for the procreation of children,
> and find in them their ultimate crown.[30]

Clearly the council fathers are arguing not from a narrowly bio-logical basis. It is the nature of marriage itself and of conjugal love to be oriented toward procreation.

Although it does not state whether or not artificial contraception is licit, the Constitution does discuss the problem. It stresses that parents are to procreate responsibly, taking account of their own welfare and that of their children. They are to consider the material and the spiritual condition of the times, the interests of the family group, of temporal society, and of the church. In some situations there will be a conflict between different factors. There may be strong reasons to limit the num-ber of children. At the same time sexual abstinence can create problems. It may, for example, make it difficult to maintain the faithful exercise of love and the full intimacy of spousal life. The judgment about whether to have children is to be made by the parents, but it is not to be made arbitrarily. Moral duty involves not motive only but also the observance of objective standards. These standards, in the area of sexual behavior, are those that "based on the nature of the human person and his acts, pre-serve the full sense of mutual self-giving and human procreation in the context of true love."[31] Parents are to reject abortion. They are to have an informed conscience, one conformed to the divine law and submissive to the teaching of the church, which interprets divine law.

Possibly the most controversial points about the treatment of mar-riage and the family in *Gaudium et Spes* concern what the document does not say. In at least one case an omission was a triumph for one point of view at the council. This case is the omission in the document of the old terminology of primary and secondary ends of marriage and the omission of any explanation of mutual help of spouses as merely subor-dinate to the procreation and education of children.

The conciliar text on marriage and the family left several ques-tions unanswered. The problem of artificial contraception was, of course, deliberately left unresolved. Another question concerns whether there is an intrinsic relationship between the unitive and procreative ends of marriage. If there is no such intrinsic relationship, then the way is open, as we have seen, to allow a type of marriage that is deliberately not oriented toward children.

THE PAPAL COMMISSION, 1966

In June 1966, the papal commission on birth control reported to Pope Paul VI. Four documents eventually came to light. One was the "Theological Report of the Papal Commission on Birth Control." This document, which has since become known as "the majority report," was signed by nineteen of the theologians and by a number of the other experts on the commission. It represents the view of a substantial majority of those on the commission. A second document, "Pastoral Approaches," is in agreement with the majority report. They both advocate a change in the church's official teaching in order to allow artificial contraception in some cases. A third document, the so-called minority report, was signed by four theologians on the commission who disagreed with the majority report and who advised that no change be made in the church's teaching. A fourth document is a working paper by some of the theologians who advocated change in the church's teaching. It defends their position against arguments in the third document.[32]

The position of the first document, the majority report, can be summarized in six points. First, although it would allow artificial contraception in some cases, yet it insists that sex and marriage are properly oriented toward the procreation and education of children. The union of spouses is not to be separated from the procreative finality of marriage. Conjugal love and fecundity are in no way opposed but complement each other. The community of life of spouses provides the proper framework for the procreation and education of children.

Second, the majority report approaches the problem from the point of view of the totality of the marriage. It wishes to take its moral direction not from a consideration of the sexual act or faculty by itself but from a consideration of what is good for the marriage as a whole. This allows the majority report to allow artificial contraception in certain cases while insisting on the procreative orientation of all sexual acts. In other words, the majority report does not fall into the trap of separating two independent ends for marriage and then justifying artificial contraception as a pursuit of one end while excluding the other. It insists that if artificial contraception is used, it must respect the procreative finality of marriage. How can it do so? The union of spouses, their mutual help, their love and their life together all have a procreative orientation. That is, they exist not only for their own sake but also for the sake of children. Therefore, if artificial contraception in a particular situation helps the union of the couple, it indirectly serves the procreative end of marriage. Furthermore, if artificial contraception helps parents to provide for the proper care of already existing children, it serves the procreative end of marriage.

Third, the majority report is somewhat situationist in approach. It does not see artificial contraception as intrinsically morally evil. (It does refer to a physical evil that is present in artificial contraception.) To decide what is morally good in a particular case, one must consider the different values involved and try to harmonize them as well as possible. The majority report advocates this situationist approach in the case of artificial contraception, but this need not mean that it would suggest such an approach in all areas of ethics. Its outright and apparently universal rejection of abortion suggests that it does not adopt a situationist approach to that question.

Fourth, the authors of the majority report believe that they are being faithful to tradition. They hold that the values that the church in the past protected by a universal exclusion of artificial contraception can now best be protected by allowing it in certain cases. They seem to be distinguishing two levels of moral norms. On one level are basic values, which are seen to endure from century to century. Concerning contraception, one such value, apparently, is the orientation of marriage to children. On another level are the more specific rules by which such values are applied in particular times and situations. As conditions and available information change, so the church's teaching on this second level may change.

Fifth, the majority report condemns any contraceptive mentality. It states that couples should be willing to raise a family with full acceptance of the various human and Christian responsibilities that are involved. The marriage as a whole should be procreative.

Sixth, the majority report stresses education. It expects couples to make their own judgment about what is best in their particular situation. To do so properly, they need a profound knowledge and appreciation of the values involved. There is an obvious danger of conforming not to gospel values but to popular opinion and pressure.

The minority report argues at some length against various positions in the majority report. Clearly, however, for the four authors of the minority report the questions of tradition and authority are crucial. They maintain that the question of artificial contraception cannot be solved by reason alone. They seem to believe that reasons put forward by either side cannot settle the matter. The matter is to be settled then by tradition and authority. The Catholic Church has traditionally rejected each and every act of artificial contraception as gravely wrong. The church could not have erred on so important a matter.

The minority report denies that the traditional teaching of the Catholic Church against contraception was based on a biologistic argument. It states that the traditional teaching does not appeal to some general principle that man must use all physical faculties in accord with the biological orientation of the faculty. Artificial contraception is wrong not because it goes against the biological orientation of simply any faculty, but because it goes against the orientation of the generative faculty. The generative faculty is concerned with the generation of new life, and life is not under man's dominion. By analogy, just as human life once constituted *in facto esse* is inviolate, so is the process inviolate in which the human life is *in fieri.*

HUMANAE VITAE

In August 1968, more than two years after receiving the commission reports, Pope Paul VI published the encyclical letter *On Human Life (Humanae vitae).* He begins by acknowledging that a new state of affairs has given rise to questions that necessitate reexamination of the church's traditional teaching on artificial contraception.

In his relatively brief discussion of marriage and conjugal love, Pope Paul incorporates much of the material on marriage and the family in *Gaudium et Spes.* Much of what he says conforms with the majority report. Marriage, he states, is the wise institution of the Creator to realize in mankind His design of love. "By means of the reciprocal gift of self, proper and exclusive to them, husband and wife tend toward the communion of their beings in view of mutual perfection, to collaborate with God in the generation and education of new lives."[33] Conjugal love is fully human, of the senses and of the spirit at the same time. Not only an instinct or a sentiment, it is also an act of will intended to endure and to grow so that husband and wife become one only heart and one only soul. This love is not exhausted by the communion between husband and wife but is destined to continue, raising up new lives. As Vatican II has said, the pope notes, marriage and conjugal love are by their nature ordained for the begetting and educating of children.

Paul VI proceeds then to rule out the use of artificial contraception and repeats the traditional teaching that each and every marriage act must remain open to the transmission of life. He continues,

> That teaching, often set forth by the magisterium, is founded upon the inseparable connection willed by God and unable to be broken by man on his own initiative, between the two meanings of the conjugal act: the unitive meaning and the procreative meaning. Indeed, by its intimate structure, the conjugal act, while most closely uniting husband and wife, capacitates them for the generation of new lives, according to laws inscribed in the very being of man and of woman. By safeguarding both these essential aspects, the unitive and the procreative, the conjugal act preserves in its fullness the sense of true mutual love and its ordination toward man's most high calling to parenthood. We believe that the men of our day are particularly capable of seizing the deeply reasonable and human character of this fundamental principle.[34]

The sequence of the argument seems to be as follows: Marriage and conjugal love have both a unitive and a procreative meaning, the two being essentially bound together. Marital sexual relations should preserve the full meaning of conjugal love and so should combine both unitive and procreative meanings. Artificial contraception prevents this from happening.

Why does Pope Paul's conclusion regarding artificial contraception differ from the conclusion of the majority report? On the nature of marriage and of spousal love, Paul VI seems to be in general agreement with the majority report. The difference seems to lie in two opposed ways of applying general norms to particular cases. Specifically, Pope

Paul holds that artificial contraception is intrinsically evil and can never be allowed. This rules out any appeal to the totality of a marriage for reasons to justify artificial contraception in particular cases. It rules out allowing artificial contraception as a lesser evil in certain situations.

The encyclical does not give reasons for adopting the notion of intrinsic evil or for rejecting an appeal to the total good of the marriage or for not allowing contraception as a lesser evil. These provide an important area for theological investigation, because they constitute the apparent reasons for Pope Paul's rejection of the conclusions of the commission.

Why did be hold to these views against the advice of the majority report? He states that the conclusions of the commission were not definitive but required his personal further study "…above all because certain criteria of solutions had emerged which departed from the moral teaching on marriage proposed with constant firmness by the teaching authority of the Church."[35] Therefore, although he does not dwell at length on the question of tradition and magisterial authority, this seems to be an important reason, perhaps the primary reason, for his conclusions concerning contraception.

Paul VI agrees with *Gaudium et Spes* that parents should be responsible in deciding the number of children "…either by the deliberate and generous decision to raise a numerous family, or by the decision, made for grave motives and with due respect for the moral law, to avoid for the time being, or even for an indeterminate period, a new birth."[36] When there are legitimate reasons for avoiding pregnancy, periodic abstinence may be used for that purpose. Paul VI argues that periodic abstinence is significantly different from artificial contraception. The former makes legitimate use of a natural process whereas the latter impedes the development of a natural process.

DECLARATION ON SEXUAL ETHICS

In December 1975, the Congregation for the Doctrine of the Faith published the *Declaration on Certain Questions Concerning Sexual Ethics*. Its main purpose was to warn against certain contemporary errors.

The declaration insists that there are objective moral standards that accord with the nature of human beings. These standards are known by a natural law written in the hearts of men. Revelation gives further knowledge of moral standards. Certain moral norms, including certain sexual moral norms, are immutable exigencies of human nature, not mere products of a culture which change as cultures change.

According to the declaration (and here it is following *Gaudium et Spes,* Section 51) the objective moral standards governing sexual acts are those that preserve the full sense of mutual self-giving and human procreation in the context of true love. That is, sexual norms are valid if they preserve the full sense of mutual self-giving and human procreation in the context of true love. Once again, the unitive and the procreative are bound together.

From this basis the declaration proceeds to an evaluation of various types of sexual behavior. It condemns premarital sex, because only in a stable marriage can the full sense of mutual self-giving and human procreation in the context of true love be maintained. Premarital sex cannot be properly procreative because it lacks the stable family unit in which children can be properly nurtured. Only in the stable commitment of marriage is there assurance of sincerity and fidelity, protection against whim and caprice.

The same basis is used to condemn homosexual actions. They are wrong because they do not provide for a full sense of mutual self-giving and human procreation in the context of true love. The same criteria rule out masturbation, which, the declaration teaches, is intrinsically and seriously disordered.

The declaration points out that psychology can help to show how various factors, such as adolescent immaturity, may reduce responsibility in the case of sexual sin. However, one should not go so far as to presume easily that people are not seriously responsible when they transgress in sexual matters. If responsibility is to be evaluated in particular cases, one should take account of the person's habitual behavior and his or her sincere use of the means necessary to overcome sexual sin. In other words, the declaration seems to say, if the person normally tries sincerely to do what is right, and seriously makes use of prayer and other means, then there is some reason to believe that a particular failure may not be fully responsible and so should not be considered a serious sin.

The declaration comments on the notion of fundamental option. It opposes the idea that mortal sin occurs only in a formal refusal of love of God or in a complete and deliberate closing of oneself to love of neighbor. Mortal sin can occur because of the rejection of God that is implied in choosing anything which is seriously morally disordered. Thus, a sexual sin can be a mortal sin.

Furthermore, it is possible for a mortal sin to occur in one act. On the other hand, the declaration points out, "it is true that in sins of the sexual order, in view of their kind and their causes, it more easily happens that free consent is not fully given."

The declaration goes on to point out that chastity as a virtue does not consist only in avoiding faults. It involves something positive. It is a virtue of the whole personality, regarding both interior and outward behavior. An important point, in the declaration's view, is that chastity frees the person to more fully follow Christ.

QUESTIONS

From this brief outline of official Roman Catholic teaching since 1918, several questions emerge. I will note only three questions that bear on the tasks of this workshop.

First, what is the relation between the unitive and procreative aspects of marriage? More generally, why are sex and marriage essentially directed toward procreation? Vatican II, the majority report of the papal commission, and *Humanae vitae* all agree that sex and marriage are essentially ordered toward procreation. Such agreement is not automatic today, however, among Catholic theologians. Outside of the church there is relatively little support for the church's official teaching on this point.

The second question is, Given the general orientation of sex and marriage toward procreation, why must we conclude that artificial contraception is wrong in each and every case? Why must we accept that artificial contraception is intrinsically evil? Why may we not appeal to the total good of marriage, to other values in a particular situation, to allow artificial contraception in particular cases, at least as a lesser evil? More generally, may not the demands of the situation justify exceptions to other rules of sexual ethics?

The third question is, What weight is to be given to the traditional teaching of the Roman Catholic Church in sexual and marriage ethics? Some hold that the condemnation of artificial contraception has been taught infallibly.[37] Others would limit the scope of the church's authority to teach on morals infallibly to the area of general principles and to things certainly revealed in scripture. The majority report seemed to distinguish two levels: On a level of fundamental values, the church's teaching continues unchanged. On another level, change can be accepted without being unfaithful to tradition. Is this an acceptable middle position?

Notes

1. *Casti Connubii,* Paragraph 5. Quotations from *Casti Connubii* used in this paper are taken from the translation in *The Church and the Reconstruction of the Modern World, The Social Encyclicals of Pius XI,* ed. Terence P. McLaughlin (Garden City, N.Y.: Doubleday, 1957).
2. Paragraph 17.
3. Paragraph 11.
4. See paragraphs 11–13.
5. Paragraph 59.
6. Paragraph 9.
7. Paragraph 7.
8. Paragraph 23.
9. Paragraph 23.
10. Paragraph 24.
11. Paragraph 18.
12. Paragraph 54.
13. Paragraph 37.
14. Paragraph 123.
15. *Vom Sinn Und Zweck Der Ehe* (Breslau: Osterdeutsche Verlag).
16. Published in New York by Sheed and Ward.
17. *The Meaning of Marriage,* 87–88.
18. *Acta Apostolicae Sedis* 36 (1944) 103.
19. An English translation of the relevant parts of this sentence is available in *Love and Sexuality,* ed. Odile M. Liebard (Wilmington, N.C.: McGrath, 1978) 71–83.

20. See, for example, his allocution to the Sacred Roman Rota on October 29, 1941, *Clergy Review* 22 (1942) 84–88; his address to the midwives, October 29,1951, in *Love and Sexuality*, 117.

21. See address to midwives, *Love and Sexuality,* 117, and address of May 19, 1956, ibid., 175–76.

22. See, for example, his address of Nov. 12, 1944, in *Love and Sexuality,* 92.

23. See his address to the midwives in *Love and Sexuality,* 116.

24. *Love and Sexuality,* 113.

25. Address on September 29, 1949, *Love and Sexuality,* 96–100; address to the midwives, October 29, 1951, *Love and Sexuality,* 117–18.

26. Address on May 19, 1956, *Love and Sexuality,* 177.

27. *Love and Sexuality,* 240–41.

28. *Gaudium et Spes,* Section 49.

29. *Gaudium et Spes,* Section 48. Quotations from *Gaudium et Spes* in this paper are taken from *The Documents of Vatican II,* ed. Walter M. Abbott (London-Dublin: Geoffrey Chapman, 1966).

30. Section 48. See also section 50.

31. Because these words are central to our discussion and are often quoted, it will be useful to quote the Latin of the original text. That text, having noted that the moral judgment must not depend only on a sincere intention or an evaluation of motives, continues, *"...sed objectivis criteriis, ex personae eiusdemque actuum natura desumptis, determinari debet, quae integrum sensum mutuae donationis ac humanae procreationis in contextu veri amoris observant."* It might be argued that in emphasizing that the couple must preserve the full sense of mutual self-giving and human procreation in the context of true love, this text rules out artificial contraception. However, that can hardly have been the general understanding of the text by the council fathers. Having been instructed by Pope Paul VI not to pronounce on the issue of artificial contraception, they would not be likely to try to settle the issue even in principle.

32. The first, third, and fourth documents were published in *The Tablet* 221 (1967) 449–54; 478–85; 510–13. The first and second documents are available in *Love and Sexuality,* 296–320.

33. *On Human Life* (Jamaica Plain, Boston: Daughters of St. Paul, 1968), Section 8.

34. Section 12.

35. Section 6.

36. Section 10.

37. See "Contraception and the Infallibility of the Ordinary Magisterium," J. C. Ford and G. Grisez, *Theological Studies* 39 (1978) 258–312, esp. 312.

14. Magisterial Teaching on Marriage 1880–1986: Historical Constancy or Radical Development?

Joseph A. Selling

This chapter first appeared in *Historia: Memoria futuri: Mélanges Louis Vereecke,* ed. Réal Tremblay and Dennis Billy (Rome: Accademia Alfonsiana, 1991).

Important questions have been asked and continue to be asked with respect to marriage and conjugal life. The magisterium has attempted to give some clear answers to these questions but has not always succeeded in its efforts. Often laypersons find themselves more confused than convinced; a phenomenon that was not unknown at the time of the *Humanae vitae* event. One response to this confusion has been that the faithful have been deprived of reasonable explanations on the part of priests and theologians whose role it supposedly is to interpret the judgments of the magisterium in a manner that is understandable and acceptable for all persons. It would be short-sighted to deny that in the case of the debate over the responsible regulation of fertility, there was a certain hesitation on the part of many to provide such an "acceptable" interpretation of the 1968 encyclical. Until the present time, few have suggested that perhaps one of the reasons for this hesitation might have been a similar state of confusion on the part of those priests and theologians. An explanation for this state of affairs might be that what the magisterium has taught on these subjects over the past 100 years has gone through such profound change that it is difficult to discern precisely what that teaching might be.

The above survey reflects upon only five sources since 1880, although these five have been recognized as preeminently expressive of what the magisterium has taught in this area. What we have found in these sources is a continuous development in magisterial teaching that is hard to recognize as "constant." Leo XIII's *Arcanum divinae sapientiae* was concerned primarily with legislative jurisdiction with respect to marriage and the evil of divorce. The source of common errors about marriage, he suggested, was the notion that marriage was a "natural institution," one that was not determined and defined by God himself. In correcting this error, Leo XIII put forth his concept of marriage, which he saw as complete at the time of creation, only to be raised to the dignity of a sacrament by Christ. Marriage, he wrote, had two essential properties, "unity and perpetuity." All its other characteristics belonged to the "natural order" of creation, including its orientation to the procreation and education of children and the submission of the wife to her husband as the head of the conjugal unit and the family. The "rights and duties" of marriage were attributed to conjugal and family life in general and were not equated with the performance of sexual acts. Leo XIII did not characterize procreation as a duty nor did he ascribe any meanings or purposes to "the conjugal act," even though his teaching presumes that the natural purpose of this act would be procreation alone.

The 1917 codification of canon law was concerned to describe the nature of the marital contract as accurately as possible in order to insure that marital consent would be fully and freely given. To this end, marriage is defined functionally as having a primary and a secondary end. These ends, however, apply to marriage alone and are not said to be realized through the marriage act, which itself is euphemistically characterized merely as "apt" for procreation. The contract of marriage entails rights and duties. However, these are not described in the same way that *Arcanum* had suggested but rather are restricted to the *ius in corpus*. There is not even a "right" to a specifically procreative act spelled out in the text since at the time distinguishing between fertile and infertile acts of sexual intercourse was virtually impossible.

Pius XI's *Casti connubii* represents one of the most elaborate teachings of the magisterium on marriage and conjugal life. In it we find for the first time the appropriation of Augustine's *tria bona* for explaining the meaning of marriage, although there is some ambiguity with respect to whether these *bona* should be interpreted in a hierarchical fashion. Overall, Pius XI's teaching resembles that of Leo XIII, especially in his understanding of domestic life. However, this pope was forced to deal with the question of known infertility when judging the moral permissibility of the conjugal act. In response to this question, he states that the couple could engage in sexual intercourse known to be infertile because doing so would have significance for the secondary ends of marriage, which the couple could intend in their activity. Nevertheless, Pius XI was careful to avoid the notion that these secondary ends alone could function as a sufficient justification, leaving the hierarchy of ends intact and applying them exclusively to marriage, not to the performance of the marital act as such.

In 1951, in his "Address to the Midwives," Pius XII addressed the difficult question of periodic continence and the licitness of the procreation-excluding intention. In doing so, he shifted the question away from the meaning or purpose of the marital act and onto the "duty" of a married couple to contribute to the propagation of the human race when they engage in this "right of marriage." However, he characterized this as a positive duty from which the couple could be excused because of "serious reasons" (indications). At the same time, neither the willingness of the couple to accept a child, should their efforts fail, nor the mere integrity of the sexual act were considered to be sufficient to justify this practice. No vague "openness to procreation" provided any moral justification.

The concern of Pius XII to counteract the setting forth of "personal values" in marriage as primary for the relationship caused him to withdraw from the possible opening that had been suggested by his predecessor for transferring the ends of marriage onto the purposes or meanings of the marriage act. In fact, he became explicit about the absolute subordination of these secondary ends and understood sexual intercourse in marriage to have only one purpose: "the great and unique law, *generatio et educatio prolis.*"

While Pius XII solved the problem of the relationship between the practice of periodic continence and the realization of the primary end of marriage, his teaching eventually opened new questions about the meaning of marriage itself and eventually about the possibility of inducing infertility while maintaining the integrity of the sexual act. However, before these questions entered into public debate, the Second Vatican Council took place and substantially changed the entire understanding of marriage and conjugal life.

Gaudium et spes made a significant contribution in defining marriage and conjugal life in quite different terms than the previous magisterial teaching. The conciliar teaching effectively abandoned the doctrine of the ends of marriage and opted for a scripturally inspired notion of covenant to describe the conjugal relationship. This was seen as a relationship between equal partners, having a meaning and purpose in itself, regardless of whether children were forthcoming. The procreation of children was described as a supreme gift and the ultimate crown of both marriage and conjugal love, while the task and the project of having and raising children were to be taken on with a "generous human and Christian sense of responsibility."

Within the perspective of the Pastoral Constitution, sexual acts were understood to be an expression of conjugal love and were characterized as "noble and worthy." Conjugal love itself, and not specifically the marital act, was "unitive" in the sense of involving the whole person in a lasting and exclusive relationship. Marital sexual behavior, therefore, must always be understood in terms of the whole of conjugal life. Its "meaning," or "purpose," was in service to that relationship, a covenant *(foedus),* which served as the basis for speaking of marriage as a sacrament.

When *Humanae vitae* was published in 1968, its primary concern was to pass judgment on the practice of "artificial" contraception. The resulting perspective adopted by this papal letter placed a heavy emphasis upon the structure, meaning, and purpose of sexual acts. However, in place of continuing the development that magisterial teaching had taken from 1880 to 1965, Paul VI took up the option that Pius XII had left behind and completed the transfer of the ends of marriage onto the conjugal act. In doing so, he changed the vocabulary from "ends" *(fines)* to "meanings" *(significationes).* The subsequent teaching, on the "two meanings of the conjugal act" *(Humanae vitae,* 12), may have followed the line from Pius XI to Pius XII, but it did so by developing this teaching a step farther, not by repeating a teaching that was "constant." In fact, the position of Paul VI clearly goes beyond that of Pius XII in that the "serious reasons" argument is substituted by the council's notion of "responsible parenthood." Then, Paul VI implied that the mere integrity of the act of sexual intercourse was sufficient to guarantee the moral acceptability of the couple's behavior. The new norm became "openness to procreation," going considerably beyond what Pius XII had explicitly taught.

Unfortunately, this development, even though it might somehow be connected with "previous magisterial teaching," now appeared out of place, *Gaudium et spes* having abandoned the structure that had already proven itself inadequate. It is not surprising that some received the teaching of *Humanae vitae* as a virtually "new" teaching of the magisterium. However, in the light of the history of the teaching of the magisterium on marriage and conjugal life, *Humanae vitae* can be better characterized either as a radical development of the line of teaching of Leo XIII, Pius XI, and Pius XII, or a departure from the developing teaching of Leo XIII, Pius XI, Pius XII, and the Second Vatican Council. It would demand stretching one's imaginative capabilities to understand this encyclical—and the subsequent teaching that has emerged from the magisterium—as typical of "constant teaching" in most any sense of that term.

15. Family and Catholic Social Teaching

Lisa Sowle Cahill

This chapter first appeared in *Family: A Christian Social Perspective* (Minneapolis, Minn.: Fortress, 2000).

Since the publication of John Paul II's *On the Family*[1] in 1981, the Roman Catholic Church has seen a resurgence of the domestic church metaphor. In recent usage, the family is called a "church" in order to encourage church participation by all families, to foster prayer and religious catechesis in the home,[2] and to promote family dedication to the common good.

The family's social mission is thought to derive from Christian identity. "Christian families, recognizing with faith all human beings as children of the same heavenly Father, will respond generously to the children of other families....With families and through them, the Lord Jesus continues to 'have compassion' on the multitudes."[3] But responsibility to the common good is also part of human nature and natural morality, which, like Christian morality, demand that families rise above egotistic familism. "Thus, far from being closed in on itself, the family is by nature and vocation open to other families and to society and undertakes its social role."[4]

These points will be expanded below, and criticisms will be discussed. For the present, it is sufficient to stress two aspects of Catholic teaching about domestic church. First, it addresses economic inequities and holds Christian families responsible for just distribution of material and social wealth, not limited to almsgiving but demanding structural change. All families have both a right and a duty to enhance and benefit from the common good of the whole society.

Second, and on a truly novel note compared to Christian family teaching of centuries past, the domestic church is a sphere of relative gender equity. As recently as 1930, Pope Pius XI was still calling for the subordination of women to men in a scheme that placed the family as a civil institution within an equally hierarchical model of society. Now, according to John Paul II, it is important to underline "the equal dignity and responsibility of women with men. This equality is realized in a unique manner in that reciprocal self-giving by each one to the other and by both to the children which is proper to marriage and the family."[5] Unlike contemporary proponents of male headship, John Paul II does not advocate the submission of women to men in the family.[6] (That this defense of gender equality should not be received with a wholly uncritical attitude will be demonstrated below.)

These two aspects owe much to our late modern cultural ethos, prizing individuality and individual freedom. This ethos has encouraged expanded roles for both sexes and greater social consciousness of the unacceptability of great disparities of advantage among classes and races. Hence, a socially transformative approach to family is not unique to the Catholic tradition. It is a general characteristic of modern Christian ethics. Walter Rauschenbusch, writing just as the papal social tradition was emerging around the turn of the century, likewise saw the family's emotional bonds as a school for other-concern.[7] Recent Roman Catholic symbolization of the family as domestic church, however, will provide the focus of this chapter, since it is in this tradition that the metaphor has been most extensively developed and most explicitly linked to social justice concerns.

The next chapter will consider how African American experiences of family expand the vision of domestic church. Catholic social teaching converges with and supports the insight of African American scholars that successful institutions of civil society, including the family, must be linked with larger national and federal institutions in order to represent broad public accountability for the common good. The U.S. Catholic bishops relate the domestic church metaphor to gender, race, and class in the United States in their pastoral letters on economics, on family, and on welfare reform. Their pastoral statement "Always Our Children" encourages families to accept and support their gay and lesbian children, even when they do not fully affirm their identities.[8]

In the original Catholic social encyclical, *On the Condition of Labor (Rerum Novarum),* authored in 1891 by Leo XIII, the subject of family arises in relation to work and the right of a workman to support his dependents. This encyclical is a response to industrialization, the exploitation of the working classes by capital owners, and the rise of atheistic socialism. According to Leo, capitalists may own and accumulate property but must provide workers with decent conditions and pay them a living wage adequate to support a family.

The encyclical co-opts the socialist critique of greed and exploitation, while still maintaining that "private ownership must be held sacred and inviolable."[9] It is a duty of property owners and of the state, if need be, to ensure that workers are adequately paid. Yet the essential acceptability of capitalism remains untouched. Distinctions of class and wealth are assumed by the encyclical and presented as the natural concomitants of the social roles essential to an organically functioning society. Workers are counseled to be industrious, honest, and modest so that their employers and social superiors will be "won over by a kindly feeling toward" them.[10] Marxist class struggle is definitely out.

Workers are supposed to be male.[11] "Women...are not suited to certain trades; for a woman is by nature fitted for homework, and it is that which is best adapted at once to preserve her modesty and to promote the good upbringing of children and the well-being of the family."[12] Women remain within the domestic sphere, providing traditional female services for the welfare of the family and of society. These services are not to be remunerated in any direct way; women and children are economically dependent on the male workforce. According to the 1931 encyclical of Pius XI, *Reconstructing the Social Order (Quadragesimo Anno),* "the wage paid to the workingman should be sufficient for the support of himself and of his family....It is wrong to abuse the tender years of children or the weakness of women" (71).

Christine Firer Hinze provides a trenchant critique of such assumptions and their impact on Catholic social teaching. She deplores not only the gendered assignment of social roles and the division of domestic from economically productive labor but also the lack of common social accountability for children. In the end, she argues, the notion of a family wage is viable and worth retrieving but only if domestic work is included in the definition of repaid labor. She commends John

Paul II for placing domestic labor in the category of family wage-deserving work and mentioning measures such as "grants to mothers."[13] Unfortunately, as Hinze realizes, it is still presupposed that mothers will be primary parents, responsible for family and domestic labor.

Hinze also draws attention to more fundamental questions about the economic system beneath the public-private and wage-labor framework. "The institutions and ideology of the capitalist, free market economy that have underpinned the notion of a family living wage must be subjected to more thorough critique and reconsideration."[14] For instance, the "logic of capitalism" might corrupt the domestic sphere itself and even undermine the institution of marriage. These larger questions will receive further attention at the end of this chapter, in response to recent proposals for welfare reform.

If we look at family order in earlier encyclicals on marriage, we find much the same scenario as in those on labor economics. Leo XIII, the initiator of the modern social tradition, portrays the family as the basic cell of society. In a passage that could have been written two or three centuries earlier by a Puritan divine, Leo declaims,

> This is a suitable moment for us to exhort especially heads of families to govern their households...and to be solicitous without failing for the right training of their children. The family may be regarded as the cradle of civil society, and it is in great measure within the circle of the family that the destiny of States is fostered....If in their early years [children] find within the walls of their homes the rule of an upright life and the discipline of Christian virtues, the future welfare of society will in great measure be guaranteed.[15]

In an 1880 encyclical titled *On Christian Marriage,* Leo specifically employs the Christ-church analogies of Ephesians 5 to insist on male headship, even while espousing mutual love and companionship. "The husband is the chief of the family and the head of the wife. The woman...must be subject to her husband and obey him...."[16] Children, meanwhile, are to "submit to the parents and obey them," although "the power of fathers of families" is limited by the "rightful freedom" of children to choose spouses and marry.[17]

Half a century later, Pius XI likewise proposes an "order of love," in which the "primacy of the husband" grants him authority over wife and children. As for the wife, household order requires "ready subjection" and "willing obedience."[18] She is the "heart" of the family, who acknowledges her husband as its "head." Nonetheless, the gender picture in Catholic teaching is beginning tentatively to change. Pius warns that good family order does not mean the woman should be treated as a minor or deprived of the liberty that "fully belongs" to her "in view of her dignity as a human person."[19] Unfortunately, this does not include the right to be the principal authority even in the home, to reject maternal and domestic roles, or "to conduct and administer her own affairs."[20]

The place of the family in the larger society is also slowly changing in these encyclicals. First of all, class divisions and economic disparities are less taken for granted. Second, the family becomes more than a separate cell within the social hierarchy. David Hollenbach has argued that the writings of Pius XI, for instance, imply an organic view of society, in which subsidiary parts cooperate in a solidaristic, not merely hierarchical, way. Institutions that meet essential needs and responsibilities of persons are harmonized and integrated in the well-functioning and just society.[21] Already Pius XI is demanding that large or poor families that are not self-supporting should be provided for jointly by public and private funds, for "it is incumbent on the rich to help the poor." The common good and "the very life of civil society itself" demand that the state take necessary action to relieve poor families and parents of children, whether married or unmarried.[22] While moving toward a vision of solidarity in the common good, however, this tradition tends to underplay the intransigence of human selfishness and sinful structures, and so to trust that moral persuasion can motivate social change without the need for serious conflict.

In the middle of the twentieth century, the popes adopt an increasingly international view of socioeconomic justice and become more critical of global economic trends. They begin to see the situations of families in poor nations as integrally connected with the patterns of consumption and expansion of the wealthier nations. A landmark encyclical is Paul VI's *On the Development of Peoples.* Insisting that no one has an absolute right to own and dispose of property, Paul rejects an economic ethos ruled by competition and urges that aid to developing countries is a duty of human solidarity and justice.[23] "At stake are the survival of so many innocent children and, for so many families overcome by misery, the access to conditions fit for human beings; at stake are the peace of the world and the future of civilization."[24]

JOHN PAUL II AND FAMILIES

The social teaching of John Paul II develops this trajectory. Specifically, he takes an international view of social justice, is critical of global capitalism without repudiating the market, sees families as interdependent agents within civil society, and terms the Christian family a "domestic church" dedicated to the common good and rightfully participating in the benefits social belonging bestows.

In his 1988 encyclical *On Social Concerns,* John Paul II expands on the international outlook of the Second Vatican Council and on the themes of *On the Development of Peoples.* He urges Christians to adopt "the option or love of preference for the poor."[25] A key principle of social relations in this encyclical is solidarity, to which structural sin is identified as the principal obstacle. The materialism and consumerism that often propel market relations undermine the "authentic liberation" of all peoples.[26] The pope targets problems that affect poor families, especially children, such as unemployment, homelessness, and lack of clean water, hygiene, and health care.

In a later encyclical, authored not long after the disintegration of Communist societies in Eastern Europe, the pope gives qualified support to free enterprise as an effective means of maximizing human resources to meet human needs. The injustices of market systems still come in for strong criticism, however, including their tendency to deprive some families of the means to live, while fostering a consumerist attitude toward children and family relationships, not to mention social commitments in general.[27] Human society can be built up properly only if "each person collaborates in the work of others and for their good. Man works in order to provide for the needs of his family, his community, his nation and ultimately all humanity."[28]

John Paul II has addressed family issues repeatedly during his pontificate. The most important statement remains *On the Family* (1981); subsequent pieces include the *Charter on the Rights of the*

Family (1983) and his *Letter to Families* (1994) in observance of the UN International Year of the Family. The latter pieces reveal somewhat different orientations. Whether this is more due to shifts in the papal perspective, to forces and questions that at the time had a high ecclesial or social profile, or to the character of the advisors and drafters upon whom the pope relied is difficult to say. In a sense, the perspectives are complementary and may be addressed to different, though not mutually exclusive, audiences.

The *Charter* defends family social rights as entitlements but seems most concerned about state policies that interfere in family self-determination. *On the Family* seems more concerned about engaging society in general and families in particular in serving the poor by supplying basic needs. The *Letter* spends proportionately more space than either defending the "norm" of the two-parent family and showing why contraception and divorce are incompatible with papal teaching about marital love. Perhaps the *Charter* intends to assert the basic social claims of families living under conditions of widespread deprivation, especially in the Third World, in which families lack basic material goods and in which social policies are geared to limit population. The *Letter*, on the other hand, reproaches the wealthier inhabitants of industrialized cultures for capitulation to individualistic liberal values, perceived to lead to family "breakdown."

Among these, it is *On the Family* that contains the flagship exposition of family as domestic church. It also forwards a defense of the social and familial rights of women. It does not address global economic inequities and their impact on families at any great length. The mission of the domestic church is construed in such a way, however, that the plight of society's less-fortunate members is kept in frequent view. Outlining problems facing families today, the pope mentions consumerism, deteriorating family relations, divorce, abortion, and a "contraceptive mentality." But he also calls to mind the fact that many Third World families "lack both the means necessary for survival, such as food, work, housing and medicine and the most elementary freedoms."[29]

A keynote of the document is the exhortation, "Family, become what you are."[30] Families are by nature intimate communities of love, basic cells of society,[31] and participate in, contribute to, and benefit from the common good. This means families must be guaranteed the necessary material and social preconditions of participation. It is the social responsibility of those who are able to contribute to the welfare and full participation of others to do so. Christian families make a "'preferential option' for the poor and disadvantaged."[32] Families naturally educate members in empathy and altruism, expanding care for the common good to ever larger circles of society. John Paul II is advancing not just an evangelical ideal but "an authentic family humanism."[33]

The family is defined as domestic church in light of this calling:

> The Christian family is...called to experience a new and original communion which confirms and perfects natural and human communion....The Christian family constitutes a specific revelation of ecclesial communion, and for this reason too it can and should be called 'the domestic church'....[The Christian family is] 'a school of deeper humanity.' This happens where there is care and love for the little ones, the sick, the aged; where there is mutual service every day; when there is a sharing of goods, of joys and of sorrows.[34]

Families should "devote themselves to manifold social service activities" that cannot be met adequately by "the public authorities' welfare organization."[35] They also should take the initiative in ensuring that laws and other institutions support families well. While the state should not needlessly usurp the autonomy of families, neither should families be abandoned to hostile social forces or left without effective institutional links to the assets their society can offer.

> In the conviction that the good of the family is an indispensable and essential value of the civil community, the public authorities must do everything possible to ensure that families have all those aids—economic, social, educational, political and cultural assistance—that they need in order to face all their responsibilities in a human way.[36]

As noted at the outset of this chapter, *On the Family* makes headway against traditional patriarchal headship by presenting marital love as in principle a relationship of equals. John Paul II nowhere advocates women's submission, and in fact, concludes not only that women should not be limited to domestic roles alone but that "the equal dignity and responsibility of men and women fully justifies women's access to public functions."[37] There is an important caveat, however. Women's advancement in family and society should in no way erode their "femininity" or reduce the recognition given to "the value of their maternal and family role, by comparison with all other public roles and all other professions," which ought to be "harmoniously combined" with maternal duties.

An irreducible ambivalence in the papal approach to gender owes to John Paul II's firm espousal of a complementarity model of equality. The liabilities of such models have been frequently noted. They tend to devolve in practice to less socially valued roles for women, with a smaller sphere of freedom, self-determination, and social leadership than is allotted to men.[38] For example, the pope urges men to fulfill their responsibilities as fathers in cooperation with mothers but envisions only the parental role of men as revealing divinity, to wit, "the fatherhood of God." On the other hand, discrimination against women and "machismo," or "a wrong superiority of male prerogatives which humiliates women" are ruled out.[39] At the very least, this is a long way from the views of Leo XIII and Pius XI, writing less than a century before.

More recent papal writings exhibit even stronger advocacy for women, especially in view of women's low status internationally. The pope's theory of complementarity, however, also gets reinforced. Positions on women's ecclesial, social, and sexual roles that depend on complementarity and define women's nature as maternal are continually reemphasized: Women are not allowed access to contraception, abortion, or divorce under any circumstances; they are not to be ordained priests. Hence, John Paul II's assertion of women's equality in principle is partly, but not fully, supported by the kinds of institutional practices he envisions as serving the common good at the concrete level (in marriage, family, church, and civil society in general).

Violence and discrimination against women in heavily patriarchal societies, extensive populations of which too frequently suffer under the additional burden of poverty, are rightly higher on the papal agenda than the equal rights of women in developed nations. Celebration of the dignity of the maternal role may be a useful instrument to enhance women's standing in the former situations. Expansion beyond this role, however, is key in the latter ones, and justice for women is a moral mandate in *all* societies. Yet, when addressing women, parents, and families in prosperous societies, the pope's concern about the permanency of marital commitments and responsibility for children can overshadow his commitment to women's social advancement. A deeper and more troublesome issue is whether women's advancement requires more flexibility on some of the magisterial sexual norms (especially the absolute ban on contraception) that go back to a time when women were directly and vehemently asserted to be subordinate to men, destined for domesticity alone, and ideally fulfilled as mothers.

To many North Americans, the papal eulogization of mothers sounds regressive. North American and European Catholics are well aware that the exclusion of women from the ordained priesthood, justified on the same theory of complementarity that is elsewhere used to promote women's well-being, is at odds with the education of girls and the vocational expectations of adult women that most modern societies take for granted. To some Catholics, the pope's countercultural views on women's full equality in the church represent a bulwark of tradition against cultural flux. To many others, his notion that women are by nature maternal; that, even when not literally mothers, their "special genius" consists in nurturing maternal behavior in all other relationships; and that the "special" feminine vocation to love provides a rationale for exclusion from the church's most respected leadership roles, are simply incredible. Beyond that, these views undermine the ostensible sincerity of papal statements about women's equality in family and society.[40]

Justice for women must include just relations in family *and* church. A complementarity model of justice for women, advanced under the aegis of "domestic church," can endanger women's hard-won growing equality in the family by suggesting that family relations ought to emulate the unequal status of women within church structures. Margaret Farley has aptly argued that most families in the world today, including most Western families, are still essentially patriarchal in structure and that this structure needs to be changed. She questions whether the Catholic Church can serve as a prophetic voice in this regard unless and until it "can model in its structures the coequal discipleship which was part of the original vision of Christianity."[41]

These criticisms find their target. They may explain why the domestic church metaphor has not met wide acclaim among laity in the North American church. Yet the pope's writings on women, their parental and familial roles, and the compatibility of such roles with public professional roles are best seen in larger perspective. Putting the pope's writings on women and family in a broader view will not silence fair observations of a lurking gender inequity under the defenses of women's dignity. But it can at least bring John Paul II's genuine accomplishments and the legitimate priority he tends to give to global social concerns into focus. The two factors important to an adequate perspective are the primacy of John Paul II's concern for the most oppressed women among the cultures of the world and the advance represented by the remarks of this pope about gender and family in relation to recent predecessors. A good example of his perspective, its genuine novelty, and its notable limits is his *Letter to Women,* written in preparation for the 1995 United Nations World Conference on Women in Beijing.

This letter opens by thanking women in different walks of life, most of them defined in reproductive and familial terms—mothers, wives, daughters, sisters, and "consecrated women" (virgins). On a new note, however, the pope also thanks "women who work"—not because of unfortunate economic necessities that draw them regrettably away from home but because women in the "social, economic, cultural, artistic and political" areas "make an indispensable contribution to the growth of a culture."[42] The pope laments the fact that women still suffer discrimination, that "they have often been relegated to the margins of society and even reduced to servitude," and adds that if "objective blame" belongs to the church in contributing to these situations, "for this I am truly sorry."[43] Referring to the great process of women's liberation,"[44] he upholds "real equality in every area," including "equality of spouses with regard to family rights."[45] He denounces abuses such as sexual violence against women.[46]

Again, the pope admires the "genius of women"; women's vocation is to give of themselves, since "more than men," women "see persons with their hearts."[47] There are differences "specific to being male and female." Christ has chosen men to be "icons" of himself, through the ministerial priesthood. Women should imitate Mary the mother of

Jesus. Men and women have different roles, considered of equal value, in the economy of salvation.[48]

In the *Letter to Families* composed just before the *Letter to Women,* the family is defined as the fundamental community in which persons learn how to be truly human and how to build in the world a "civilization of love." Again, the pope insists that the civilization is neither utopian nor exclusively Christian. It is part of the human ideal of family life; family love can educate for and inspire social change. But the Christian family, a domestic church, is specially graced to nourish communities in which persons are recognized and valued in themselves.[49]

Given the pope's view of women's unique role in recognizing the individuality of persons and in making a loving response to all, the special vocation of the family would then seem to rest especially with women. Women, it would seem, are more closely associated by nature than men with the upbuilding of a "civilization of love." Strikingly, in the *Letter to Families,* the fatherhood of men is interpreted precisely in relation to and by virtue of the maternal role of women. Both the civilization of love and the successful raising of children will depend on the father's "willingness…to become willingly involved as a husband and father *in the motherhood of his wife.*"[50] The family structure primarily indicated by the wording of the *Letter* is the nuclear family, since it presents the family as constituted by, and beginning in, marriage and especially in the sexual relations of the couple, in which love is expressed and a child conceived. A substantial portion of the document is devoted to abortion as a violation of the welcome to life that families should provide.[51] The principle of subsidiarity is applied to the family to support needed public assistance to parents, but even more to limit outside interference in the right of parents to bear, raise, and educate children according to church teaching and in observance of the norms the pope believes to express genuine human well-being.[52] All of this amounts to a vision of women in the home, a private, autonomous sphere of love, in which the mother is constantly prepared for the arrival of another birth, and in which she above all others exemplifies empathy and devotion.

The Holy See's 1983 *Charter on the Rights of the Family* presents a somewhat more balanced picture: States, nations, and societies are called to responsibility to offer supportive institutions so that families may flourish.[53] It is asserted without doubt that the family as an institution is based on marriage and exists, with "inalienable" rights, prior to any state. But society, particularly "the State and International Organizations, must protect the family through measures of a political, economic, social and juridical character." Poverty and the well-being of children—before or after birth, in or outside marriage, with parents or as orphans—are among the concerns of the *Charter.* The preponderance of articles, however, still addresses the rights of families over social interference in religious, marital, reproductive, and child-raising decisions. Despite significant and admirable advances, the official Roman Catholic approach to family matters is still overly concerned with reproductive issues, not sufficiently attuned to gender and race as intersecting causes of economic inequities that affect families, and too quick to assume that an audience of ecclesial and political rank-holders will endorse and effect wide-ranging changes.

Notes

1. John Paul II, *On the Family* (Apostolic Exhortation, *Familiaris Consortio*) (Washington, D.C.: U.S. Catholic Conference, 1981). Reference to this and other official Catholic documents will be made by section or paragraph number, not page. This customary means of citation enables reference across languages and editions. *On the Family* (no. 49) defines the family as a domestic church or church in miniature.

2 Family prayer and spirituality will not be addressed at length in the present work, though they are important in a Christian family perspective. A more extended treatment may be found in Florence Caffrey Bourg, *Christian Families as Domestic Churches: Insights from the Theologies of Sacramentality, Virtue, and the Consistent Ethic of Life* (Ph.D. diss., Boston College, 1998). Bourg is assistant professor of theology at the College of Mount St. Joseph in Cincinnati, Ohio.

3. *On the Family,* no. 41.

4. Ibid., no. 42.

5. Ibid., no. 22.

6. John Paul II discusses Ephesians 5 many times in his writings, using it as a model of marital love, without ever endorsing female submission or male "headship." Perhaps the most explicit treatment of this topic occurs in *On the Dignity and Vocation of Women (Mulieris Dignitatem,* 1988), *Origins* 18/17 (October 6, 1988) 261–83. The pope interprets Ephesians 5:22–23 to mean "mutual subjection out of reverence for Christ" (cf. Eph 5:21). He specifically

limits the analogy of spousal subjection to the relation between Christ and church, since, whereas in the latter, "the subjection is only on the part of the church; in the relationship between husband and wife the 'subjection' is not one-sided but mutual" (no. 24).

7. Walter Rauschenbusch, *Dare We Be Christians?* (Cleveland, Ohio: Pilgrim Press, 1993) 21–22. This work was published originally in 1914.

8. National Conference of Catholic Bishops' Committee on Marriage and Family, "Always Our Children: A Pastoral Message to Parents of Homosexual Children and Suggestions for Pastoral Ministers," *Origins* 27/17 (October 9, 1997) 285, 287–91.

9. Leo XIII, *On the Condition of Labor (Rerum Novarum),* no. 35, in William J. Gibbons, *Seven Great Encyclicals* (Paramus, N.J.: Paulist Press, 1966).

10. Ibid., no. 44.

11. See Christine Firer Hinze, "Bridge Discourse on Wage Justice: Roman Catholic and Feminist Perspectives on the Family Living Wage," in *Feminist Ethics and the Catholic Moral Tradition,* ed. Charles E. Curran, Margaret Farley, and Richard A. McCormick (Mahwah, N.J.: Paulist Press, 1996) 511–40. This essay first appeared in *The Annual of the Society of Christian Ethics,* 1991.

12. Leo XIII, *On the Condition of Labor,* no. 20.

13. John Paul II, *On Human Work (Laborem Exercens),* no. 19 (Washington, D.C.: U.S. Catholic Conference, 1981). See Hinze, "Bridge Discourse," in Curran et al., *Feminist Ethics,* 521.

14. Hinze, "Bridge Discourse," 31–32.

15. Leo XIII, *On Christian Citizenship (Sapientiae Cristianae,* 1890), no. 42, ed. Etienne Gilson, *The Church Speaks to the Modern World: The Social Teachings of Leo XIII* (New York: Doubleday, 1954).

16. Leo XIII, *On Christian Marriage (Arcanum Divinae Sapientiae),* no. 11, ed. Gilson, *Social Teachings of Leo XIII.*

17. Ibid., nos. 12 and 15.

18. Pius XI, *On Christian Marriage (Casti Connubii,* 1930), no. 26, ed. Terence P. McLaughlin, *The Church and the Reconstruction of the Modern World: The Social Encyclicals of Pius XI* (New York: Doubleday, 1957).

19. Ibid., no. 24. Although like earlier popes and theologians, both Catholic and Protestant, Pius XI still maintains that procreation is the primary purpose of sex and marriage, he makes increasingly central the mutual and equal love of spouses. The marital love that is intrinsic to "the blending of life as a whole" "can in a very real sense...be said to be the chief reason and purpose of matrimony."

20. Ibid., no. 74.

21. See David Hollenbach, *The Right to Procreate and Its Social Limitations: A Systematic Study of Value Conflict in Roman Catholic Ethics* (Ph.D. diss., Yale University, 1975) 326–27.

22. Pius XI, *On Christian Marriage*, nos. 120–22.

23. Paul VI, *On the Development of Peoples* (*Populorum Progressio*, 1967), nos. 23, 26, 44, 48 (New York and Mahwah, N.J.: Paulist Press, 1967).

24. Ibid., no. 80.

25. John Paul II, *On Social Concerns* (*Sollicitudo Rei Socialis*, 1988), no. 42, *Origins* 17/38 (3 March 1988).

26. Ibid., no. 46; see also no. 39.

27. John Paul II, *The Hundredth Year (Centesimus Annus)*, nos. 15, 39, *Origins* 21 (1991).

28. Ibid., no. 43.

29. John Paul II, *On the Family*, no. 6.

30. Ibid., no. 17.

31. Ibid., nos. 42, 46.

32. Ibid., no. 47.

33. Ibid., no. 7.

34. Ibid., no. 21. The reference given for the phrases "domestic church" and "school of deeper humanity" are two documents of the Second Vatican Council, *Lumen Gentium*, no. 11, and *Gaudium et Spes* 52, respectively. The phrase "'church in miniature' *(ecclesia domestica)*" occurs within a discussion of evangelization and in building up the kingdom of God in history (no. 49).

35. Ibid., no. 44.

36. Ibid., no. 45.

37. Ibid., no. 23.

38. See virtually all of the essays in Curran et al., eds., *Feminist Ethics and the Catholic Moral Tradition,* especially those by Barbara Andolsen, Christine Gudorf, and Anne Patrick. See also Margaret A. Farley, "The Church and the Family: An Ethical Task," *Horizons* 10/1 (1983) 50–71.

39. John Paul II, *On the Family*, no. 25.

40. The "charter document" for these views is John Paul II, *On the Dignity and Vocation of Women (Mulieris Dignitatem*, 1988), *Origins* 18/17 (October 6, 1988) 261–83. See especially nos. 28, 30, 31.

41. Farley, "Church and the Family," 67.

42. John Paul II, *Letter to Women*, no. 2, *Origins* 25/9 (27 July 1995).

43. Ibid., no. 3.

44. Ibid., no. 6.

45. Ibid., no. 4.

46. Ibid., no. 5.

47. Ibid., no. 12.

48. Ibid., no. 11.

49. *Letter to Families,* no. 15.

50. Ibid., no. 16. Italics added.

51. Ibid., no. 21 ff.

52. Ibid., nos. 8, 10, 16.

53. *Charter on the Rights of the Family* (October 22, 1983). Obtained on the Internet from Catholic Resources on the Internet: http://www.wf_f.org/ Charter. html.

16. Encountering the Other: The Modern Papacy on Women

Christine E. Gudorf

This chapter first appeared in *Social Compass* 36 (1989).

WOMEN IN PUBLIC AND PRIVATE REALMS

Papal teaching on women illustrates the clash that exists between papal social teaching on the one hand and papal teaching on the private realm of church and family on the other.[1] Since women belong to and are treated by the popes as being part of both realms, papal teaching on women has a schizophrenic quality. Papal social teaching on politics, economics, and social policy in the public realm is characterized by a social-welfare liberalism assuming equality, pluralism, democracy, social dynamism, and optimism about creating a just egalitarian order through gradual altruistic efforts within existing social structures.

Papal teaching on the private realm, on the other hand, continues to be characterized by assumptions of static institutions rooted in divine and natural law, hierarchy, and paternalism. Private-realm institutions of both church and family interact with the public realm. But in the papal perspective, the church's interaction with the world is largely limited to the gift of its teachings; the world offers little to the church other than a field for evangelization. Pope John Paul II agrees with Pope John XXIII that (social scientific) study of the world only shows the church how to present its eternal truths more effectively.[2] The family is similarly understood as "the church of the home" whose chief role is as refuge from an inhumane world.[3] The world's influence on the family is usually portrayed as detrimental and to be resisted. In short, the social relations the church teaches as appropriate for the world are not appropriate for church or family.

269

Social Teaching on Women

   The public-realm teaching on women since the early 1960s has focused on the equality of women, their right to be accorded equal education, work, pay, and political rights and to be protected from discrimination against their gender.[4] Before Vatican II, popes assumed and explicitly taught women's inequality and subordination to men, as well as condemned advocates of both women's equality and public roles for women.[5] The Second World War seems to have been the transition point: the fact that women both held jobs while men fought, and especially in Europe, worked after the war due to the death of husbands, fathers, and potential spouses, led to an acceptance of women's need to enter the public realm through employment. Pius XII recognized both this fact and the fact that women's entry into the public realm made it necessary for them to acquire rights there. But he hoped that, for the good of the family, women would not exercise all their new-found rights.[6]

   Since the time of John XXIII the popes have repeated the message that women are equal and should be granted equal rights. Whereas earlier teaching had defined the paternal role as governing, protective, and supportive (in a material sense), and the maternal role in terms of indiscriminate love, personal service, and religious and moral instruction,[7] the Council and succeeding popes make fewer gender distinctions between the educative role of parents.[8]

   Most contemporary commentary, secular as well as ecclesiastical, on papal teaching on women concentrates on the recent social teaching on women's equality and the need to end discrimination against women. One reason for this is that the language of liberal rights is found in the more authoritative, and more accessible, papal documents, such as social-teaching encyclicals. This liberal message is also more familiar and understandable to secular writers. Nevertheless, the great bulk of papal treatment of women contains a very different message and is found in less well-known sermons and addresses, especially in more devotional speeches on Mary and the saints, and in addresses to local groups.

   Another interesting note is that the theme of women's equality is not elaborated to the same extent as are the devotional private-realm messages. The popes do not describe or condemn specific discriminative practices against women. More than half of all U.S. women workers have quit their jobs or been fired because of sexual harassment,[9] which is certainly not an exclusively U.S. phenomenon; but on this issue, the popes are silent. Violence against women, whether by rape or battery, is similarly a massive problem all over the world, affecting up to one out of every four families in the United States;[10] and yet the popes are silent. Unlike many other areas of papal teaching, there are no personal stories or remarks from the popes about public roles for women, no models advocated for emulation. When examples of Mary and the saints are presented as models, the aspects of their lives that are highlighted are never responsible leadership or public careers, but rather their role as background supporters who help share the world through prayer and child-rearing. For example, John Paul II wrote of Mary as "the woman who is honored as Queen of Apostles without herself being inserted into the hierarchical constitution of the church. Yet this woman made all hierarchy possible because she gave to the world the Shepherd and Bishop of our souls."[11] The teaching on traditional roles for women seems much more deeply rooted in the personal life and spirituality of John Paul II (and that of his predecessors) than is the egalitarian message, however strongly he intellectually supports equality of the sexes.

Private-Realm Teaching on Women

Because of the shift to affirming the equality of women, papal teaching on the private realm required changes not always gracefully achieved. John XXIII insisted on both the equality of women and the authority of husbands in the family: "Within the family, the father stands in God's place. He must lead and guide the rest by his authority and the example of his good life."[12] He later explained,

> It is true that living conditions tend to bring about almost complete equality of the sexes. Nevertheless, while their justly proclaimed equality of rights must extend to all the claims of personal and human dignity, it does not in any way imply equality of functions.
>
> The Creator endowed woman with natural attributes, tendencies and instincts, which are strictly hers, or which she possesses to a different degree from man; this means woman was also assigned certain tasks.

> To overlook this difference in the respective functions
> of men and women or the fact that they necessarily comple-
> ment one another, would be tantamount to opposing nature:
> the result would be to debase woman and to remove the true
> foundation of her dignity.[13]

John never fully describes how the different and complementary functions of men and women are unequal, but he does go on to refer to an argument often made by his predecessors: To claim full equality for women would be to jeopardize all rights for women. His predecessors claimed for the church the achievement of having elevated the dignity and status of women chiefly through elevating marriage—the intimate but hierarchically ordered link between men and women.[14] The implication is that women accept unequal status in marriage in return for some benefits and protection, or that women can press for equality that so offends men that men will deny any status and protection to women. The nature of men will not allow women full equality. John's assumption that hierarchy is natural, that all social units require a head because authority cannot be shared but only wielded by some over others,[15] is undoubtedly linked to this pessimistic view of men's nature.

Since the time of John XXIII, we rarely find women urged to submit to the headship of their husbands, although this was common before the Second World War.[16] Nor is women's nature described in the same traditional terms. Pope Benedict XV bewailed that one of the worst effects of the First World War was the removal of fathers and husbands from the home, which allowed immorality to flourish there.[17] Pius XI condemned communism for advocating the removal of women from the "tutorship of man," and female athletics for threatening women's virtue.[18] Post-Vatican II popes have not elaborated this female need for moral control and protection. Even more striking is that since formal acceptance of women's equality was given, there have been no papal descriptions of women's nature as making them less capable of reason. The claim of women's irrationality and consequent inability to discriminate was the source of the central inconsistency in pre-Vatican II papal teaching on women. For the early twentieth-century popes had adopted pedestalized understandings of woman as the superior religious and moral force *at the same time* as they insisted that woman's nature made her incapable of competent choice. Papal acceptance of women as innately religious and moral was clearly determined more by women's greater acquiescence to church authority in an age when the church as an institution was under siege, than by church teaching on male and female nature.

Equality and Pedestalization

Despite the shift toward equality for women in Church social teaching, papal teaching on the nature and role of women still demonstrates a romantic pedestalization of women. The predominant theme is motherhood. This is as true of John Paul II today as it was of Pius XII in the 1940s and 1950s. Women are understood to have been created to be mothers,[19] either physically as wives, or spiritually as with women religious. One arresting aspect of John Paul's thought is that motherhood is not an element of what it is to be a woman but rather that motherhood defines womanhood.[20] Like his predecessors, John Paul prefers the teaching of 1 Timothy 2:15, that women are saved through motherhood, to Jesus' teaching that women will be saved and venerated not for their maternity but for their participation in the larger project of the Kingdom of God (Luke 11:27–28, Mark 3:31–35).

John Paul II represents the "biology is destiny" school of thought with regard to women and shares with others in that school the failure to understand the male sex in similar biological terms. In fact, despite the inadequacy of John Paul's teaching on women (and that of his predecessors) the greater problem is its treatment of men. In an attempt to persuade women to acquiesce to traditional divisions of power that favor men, the popes have lifted women's pedestal so high as to deny in many ways the basic humanity and Christian potential of men.

Like his predecessors, John Paul often speaks of a mother's role in the family as "irreplaceable,"[21] and deals with motherhood by referring to the example of Mary, "who conceived spiritually before she conceived physically."[22] Conception and birth are miraculous moments for John Paul II. He sees them as central to the feminine mystique:

> What is happening in the stable, in the cave hewn from rock,
> is something very intimate, something that goes on
> "between" mother and child. No one from outside has

access to it. Even Joseph, the carpenter from Nazareth, is but a silent witness.[23]

> ...we should stand by the expectant mother; [that] we should devote special care to mothers and to the great event that is peculiarly theirs: the conception and birth of a human being. This event is the foundation on which the education of a human being builds. Education depends upon trust in her who has given life.
>
> Motherhood is a woman's vocation. It is a vocation for all times; it is a vocation today. The words of a song popular among young people in Poland comes to my mind at this moment: "The mother who understands everything and in her heart embraces each of us." The song goes on to say that the world has a special "hunger and thirst" for this motherhood which is woman's "physical" and "spiritual" vocation, as it is Mary's.[24]

While childbirth can perhaps be described as an experience touching woman alone, John Paul's placing of conception in the same category raises serious questions about his understanding of sexual intercourse. Furthermore, his description of mothers alone as "detecting the cry of the infant" or understanding children and loving each of them, excludes men from relational intimacy in the family. John Paul II's understanding of the role of men in families often seems to revolve around material support. Men's role is, like Joseph's, to remain loyal to one's wife and to the children to whom she is linked by a mysterious love, even though men are excluded from that mysterious love. "Do not abandon her!" he writes to husbands about their wives.[25] After all, "such was the mystery in which Mary was included, but Joseph was unaware of this mystery."[26]

No wonder that men abandon women and children in large numbers if they share John Paul's understanding of men as being excluded from the central relationship in families. In an age when economic necessity and less economic discrimination against women combine to pressure many women to take on part of men's traditional role as breadwinner, what is left for men to value in their familial role?

Two decades ago John XXIII addressed the issue of working wives and mothers. In an address to working women, he said,

Everyone knows that outside work, as you might naturally expect, makes a person tired and may even dull the personality; sometimes it is humiliating and mortifying besides. When a man comes back to his home after being away for long hours and sometimes after having completely spent his energies, is he going to find in it a refuge and a source for restoring his energies and the reward that will make up for the dry, mechanical nature of the things that have surrounded him?

Here again there is a great task waiting for women; let them promise themselves that they will not let their contacts with the harsh realities of outside work dry up the richness of their inner life, the resources of their sensitivity, of their open and delicate spirit; that they will not forget those spiritual values that are the only defense of their nobility; last of all, that they will not fail to go to the fonts of prayer and sacramental life for the strength to maintain themselves on a level with their matchless mission.

They are called to an effort perhaps greater than that of men; if you take into consideration women's natural frailty in some respects and the fact that more is being asked of them. At all times and in all circumstances they are the ones who have to be wise enough to find the resources to face their duties as wives and mothers calmly and with their eyes wide open; to make their homes warm and peaceful after the tiring labors of daily work, and not to shrink from the responsibility of raising children.[27]

Evidently John believed that jobs do not damage and deplete women to the same extent that they do men. Most of the world agrees; government studies in the United States show that married working women put in working weeks averaging seventy-two to seventy-six hours, compared with their husbands' average working week of forty-two hours.[28] When women return from work, they begin their second job at home, with an average of less than two hours a week of assistance from their husbands. How can this be reconciled with the papal proclamations of women's equality?

Recent popes, including John Paul II in particular, insist that in seeking to free women from discrimination societies must prevent employment from detracting from women's irreplaceable role in the family.[29] Although the policies to achieve this end are yet unclear, John Paul's suggestions seem to revolve around pressure to keep married women from jobs by providing economic incentives for them to stay home.[30] There is no attempt to redistribute the work of the home between the spouses, even in the present before such schemes could be implemented. Furthermore, the implementation of such schemes is far beyond the capability of most nations of the world. In the Third World it is not uncommon for half the men to lack stable employment. Many scrape by in the informal sector with help from wives who work as ambulatory vendors or servants and then return home to take up their second job. In such nations, incomes for housewives are utopian dreams. Women have often been described by sociologists as carrying the double burden of paid employment and housework/childcare. In the passage quoted earlier, John adds another burden for women: that of responsibility for the emotional and spiritual well-being of the family, for making the home into an intimate refuge. Both Paul VI and John Paul II seem to assume that this psychological burden is naturally and exclusively women's.[31] This burden is perhaps more debilitating for women than extra hours of work.

It is inescapable that papal assertions of sexual equality are best understood to refer to equal dignity in the eyes of God. But equal dignity should connote some equality in vocation. If men's only responsibility is to support the family materially, how is his vocation the equal of the wife's, much less the working wife's? Can men be regarded as other than deficient humans when they seem to carry few relational responsibilities? How can they be Christians? Where are men's opportunities for personal service, for sensitivity, for love in any intimate sense? If men's roles in the family do not teach them to be sensitive to the needs of others, to the demands of justice within the home, how can they possibly love well? How will their sons have models for learning to love well as men?

Furthermore, if men lack the compassion and nurturance of women and if these gifts of women are required to keep the home as a refuge for men and children to counteract the harshness of the public sphere, then there can be no conversion of the public sphere. The call to evangelize

the world becomes impossible when the only people considered capable
of creating true human community are restricted to domestic refuges.

Gender Complementarity

Papal assumptions of gender complementarity[32] are problematic in
themselves, even without the added complexity of historical shifts in
gender roles. The problem is that traditional assertions of gender complementarity have the effect of positing both men and women as being
incomplete outside marriage. More recent treatment of complementarity
tends to explain gender complementarity in terms of human sociality.[33]

It is necessary to affirm that we are inherently social, that we
become human through social relations, and that we grow through expo-
sure to different kinds of people. It is also necessary to oppose the typi-
cally modern assumption of autonomous selves for whom social
relations are voluntary and not intrinsic. We do need to relate to both
men and women in order to develop our own gender identity successfully and to enrich our ability to relate to different people. But gender
complementarity in papal teaching reaches much farther than this; it
assumes that traits and roles are essentially sex-based, so that a man will
be more different from all women than from any man. Because of this,
our most intimate human relationship, the marital relationship, is
assumed to be the place in which we come face to face with our complement and thus are made whole through the challenge to communicate
with and bond to this opposite.

But the popes seem to forget their teaching on complementarity of
the sexes when they discuss celibacy. Not only are celibates who lack the
intimate marital bond with an opposite not characterized in terms of a
lack of wholeness and completeness, but they are not encouraged to
develop close nonsexual relationships with their sexual opposites in
order to compensate for the lack of sexual intimacy that more normally
forces growth in wholeness.[34] In fact, the segregation of seminarians from
women continues to be a major concern of the popes, in opposition to
recent trends in the United States and other countries.[35] Despite data cir-
culating among bishops regarding low levels of emotional development
and interpersonal relationships, and high levels of alcoholism, depression, and sexual activity among Catholic priests,[36] we do not find John

Paul II supporting relationships with women as being valuable in the priestly formation process. It has become clear that in a society in which intimacy is more or less restricted by convention to sexual, especially marital, relationships, those forbidden marriage will be relationally deprived. Such analysis usually leads to the conclusion that celibates and all of us would benefit from sanctioning greater emotional intimacy in nonsexual relationships such as friendships with both sexes, rather than limiting necessary intimacy to relationships not accessible to all.

But papal thought is not open to this direction for two reasons: fear of sexuality, especially of women, and fear for the stability of marriage. Friendships between the sexes are regarded as dangerous threats to celibacy both for priests and single laity because of the presumed power of the sex drive. Given the patriarchal structure of the church and the training of the clergy, the threat to celibacy represented by the sex drive is interpreted as a threat from women and becomes intertwined with historic conceptions of women as polluting. Even within marriage, intimacy is understood to be easily corrupted by sexual desire, which John Paul II cannot distinguish from lust. He is thoroughly classical in this regard. Both Augustine and Thomas Aquinas agreed that sexual desire is both sinful and difficult to avoid within marriage; only the great good of procreation made this constant temptation to sin tolerable within marriage.[37]

The second reason for resisting a call for a diffusion of intimate nonsexual relationships within society is rooted in papal fear for the stability of marriage. As we have seen, recent popes present women as being natural nurturers and intimates, compassionate sharers who create webs of relationships around them. The popes, especially John Paul II, see women as domesticating men by offering them the intimacy only available within the refuges created by women. Men are not viewed as naturally bound to family as women are. Instead, women bind men to family through men's need for intimacy—for unconditional acceptance, for sexual gratification, for nurture—which traps him into the role of husband and father, tames his natural drive toward unrooted competition and achievement, and binds him to the home. His tie is to woman and only through her to children. His role within this family, which both gratifies him and traps him, is material support, a role in which he must be able to take pride if his benefits from the arrangement are to outweigh his sacrifice. Even if the popes believed that intimacy were possible outside the family, they might well suppress it in order to protect the family institution.

Such an understanding of gender roles agrees with much of the data of contemporary sociologists. Women's dependence on men through marriage is largely material; the primary result of divorce for women in the United States is poverty for themselves and their children.[38] Children are regarded as being much more closely bound to mothers than to fathers; the vast majority of children are awarded by mutual agreement to the mother in cases of divorce although this is slightly less common in the recent past.[39] Men's psychological need for women seems to be much greater than women's need for men. In the United States married men suffer less anxiety, depression, and emotionally related health problems than single or divorced men; divorced and widowed men remarry more often and much sooner than divorced or widowed women.[40] Married women, on the other hand, tend to higher degrees of depression, anxiety, and mental illness than both husbands and single women. Men have greater problems adjusting to divorce and death of a spouse than do women.[41]

Papal concern for the stability of family and reluctance to support any equality that might free women of double workloads and men for growth in relationality, is undoubtedly influenced by traditional theology of marriage.

Saint Augustine, for example, proposed the primary purposes of marriage to be first, producing offspring, and second, a cure for lust and formation of a marital bond (ordered to partnership in the rearing of children).[42] The papal view is distinctly clerical—that is, it is based on children's experience of marriage as revolving around them and their needs, rather than on spouse's experience of marriage. Since the 1960s' debate on contraception there have been vocal assertions by laity of an understanding of marriage contrary to that of St. Augustine and the clergy. Key to these lay perceptions is an understanding of intimacy neither as a byproduct of procreation nor as a commodity offered by wives to trap husbands into material support, but a mutual creation that exists for its own sake. An important aspect of this marital intimacy is sexual intercourse, central neither for the sake of procreation nor as an outlet for human lust. Collette Potvin, the wife in one of the three couples appointed to the Pontifical Commission on Population, the Family and

Birth during Vatican II represented many of the laity when she responded
to a cleric on the Commission who had just asked whether the sex act was
necessary for married couples. As reported by Robert Kaiser,

> She described herself as "simply a wife, married 17 years,
> with five children." She had had three miscarriages and a
> hysterectomy; perhaps from that point of view she had a
> clearer point of view than the scientists and the theologians.
> She looked up at the group, hesitated a moment, then dared
> a needed preamble: "To understand woman, you need to
> stop looking at her as a deficient male, an occasion of sin, or
> an incarnation of the demon of sex, but rather as Genesis
> presents her: a companion to man. Where I come from, we
> marry primarily to live with a man of our choice. Children
> are a normal consequence of our love and not the goal. The
> physiological integrity of the conjugal act is less important
> than the repercussions of that love on the couple and on
> their family. And that conjugal act is the principal way we
> have of showing our love for each other."
>   …Because no one had dared speak so plainly, she
> would. Directly and with no false modesty, she explained
> what lovemaking meant to her and Laurent (her husband).
> "Marvellous moments," she said, "when each of us accepts
> the other, forgives the other, and can give the best of our-
> selves to the other." The morning after such a communion,
> she said, she felt more serene, more patient with her chil-
> dren, more loving to everyone. Nothing contributed more to
> her family equilibrium. She described the spiritual sense of
> well being that accompanied what she called "the conjugal
> orgasm": "a sense of joy, a feeling of accord on every
> level"—and all of it accompanied by "a rainbow of wonder-
> ful tingling sensations."[43]

For many lay people, the papal teaching on marriage fails to
understand the great power and gift that resides in marriage as a sacrament. It trivializes marriage by assigning to it a physical goal beyond the
relationship itself. Papal teaching on marital sex can be compared with
teaching Christians to have faith in order to be saved from hellfire,

rather than because faith is a fulfilling way of life, a joyous communion with God and neighbor. The sacramental sign in marriage is sexual orgasm, and the nature of sacramental signs is that they create what they celebrate: in marriage, mutual love.[44] Intercourse is more than an expression of love, certainly more than an outlet for lust or a reward offered men for their fidelity to family. And like the Eucharist, another sacramental sign, it should be encouraged as a part of the life of faith.

If the popes could understand that this intimate relationship between equals is central, and the birth of children only an expression, although an important one, of marital love, then perhaps John Paul might not see fathers as so peripheral to family. His fixation on the biological link between mother and child is not necessary when the experience of the couple themselves is that this child is a mutual creation of their love and a challenge to that love to grow and expand to include this child. If John Paul could recognize the existence of strong mutual sexual love between men and women, then perhaps he would realize that men are capable of intimacy and nurture, and that women need not carry the burden of providing intimate, nurturing refuges for society but can share the task of humanizing the world with men.

Notes

1. See Christine E. Gudorf, "Renewal or Repatriarchalization? Responses of the Roman Catholic Church to the Feminization of Religion," *Horizons,* Fall 1983.

2. John XXIII, *Mater et Magistra, Acta Apostolicae Sedis (AAS)* 53 (1961) pp. 456–7, 236–9; *Pacem in terris, AAS* 55 (1963) 301, 160. John Paul II took this position in "Libertatis Nuntius," August 6, 1984. He told the Peruvian bishops that he not only approved this document written by Ratzinger but wrote opening sections of it. *The Pope Speaks (TPS)* 29, 289–310.

3. "Este hora," address in Mexico, January 28, 1979, in *TPS* 24, 66; *Familiaris Consortio,* No. 51, *TPS,* 27, 3, 214.

4. *Gaudium et Spes,* Nos. 52, 60, *AAS* 58 (1966) 1073–4, 1080–1; *Pacem in terris,* No. 15, *AAS* 55 (1963) 261; *Octogesima Adveniens,* No. 16, *AAS* 63 (1971) 413; *Justitia in Mundo,* Pt. III, *AAS* 63 (1971) 933–41; *Familiaris Consortio,* Nos. 22, 23, *AAS* 74 (1982) 106–9.

5. Pius XI, "Lux veritatis," December 25, 1931, *AAS* 23 (1931) 516; *Divini Redemptoris, AAS* 29 (1937) 71; *Casti Connubii, AAS* 22 (1930) 549–50; Pius XII, address to Catholic Action, April 24, 1943, *AAS* 35 (1943) 34; also see Chapter 5 in Christine E. Gudorf, *Catholic Social Teaching on Liberation Themes* (Lanham, Md.: University Press of America, 1980).

6. Address to Italian women, *AAS* 37 (1945) 291–2.

7. *Gaudium et Spes,* Nos. 50, 52, 103, *AAS* 58 (1966) 1070–2, 1073–4, September 24 address to U.S. bishops, "It is a Real Joy," *TPS* 28, 360–5; "Sono lieto," March 9, 1985, *TPS* 30, 358; "Considerando che," October 22, 1983, *TPS* 29, 78–85.

8. An excellent example is Pius XII's treatment of women in "Le vingt cinquième," *Osservatore Romano,* July 28, 1955, or his October 21, 1945, address, *AAS* 37 (1945) 292.

9. The documentary "The Workplace Hustle" describes two studies conducted during the 1980s, one by the U.S. Department of Labor, the other by the U.S. Department of Health and Human Services.

10. Between 25 and 50 percent of women in the United States have experienced at least one attempted or completed rape; between 15 and 21 percent of women who have been married in the United States have been battered. See Diana Russell, *Rape in Marriage* (New York: Macmillan, 1983) 64, 57, 89.

11. "Mary, Sign of Hope for All Generations," October 7, 1979, *TPS* 7, 345.

12. *Ad Petri Cathedram, AAS* 51 (1959) 509–10.

13. "Convenuti a Roma," *AAS* 53 (1961) 611; translation, *TPS* 7, 345.

14. Leo XIII, *Arcanum, Acta Sanctae Sedis* 12, 390; Pius XI, *Casti Connubii, AAS* 22 (1930) 567–8, Pius XII, "Dilette figlie," *TPS* 3, 367; September 10, 1941, address, *Atti e discorsi* 4, 111–12.

15. *Pacem in terris, AAS* 55 (1963) 270.

16. Leo XIII, *Quod Apostolici Muneris,* December 28, 1878, *ASS* 11, 373–4; Pius XII, *Casti Connubii, AAS* 22 (1930) 549–50; Pius XII, September 10, 1941, to newlyweds, *Atti e discorsi* 3, 224–5; "Der Katolische Deutsche," July 17, 1952, *AAS* 44 (1952) 718–19.

17. *Divini Redemptoris, AAS* 29 (1937) 71.

18. "A Lei, Vicario Nostro," *AAS* 20 (1928) 136–7.

19. "E'giunto al termine," January 10, 1979, *TPS* 24, 82; *Laborem exercens*, No. 19, *AAS* 73 (1981) 626–9; *Familiaris Consortio*, No. 25, *AAS* 74 (1982) 107–9; "I am Pleased," June 7, 1984, *TPS* 29, 250.

20. John Paul II, "Motherhood, which is women's 'physical' and 'spiritual' vocation, as it is Mary's," in "E'giunto al termine," *TPS* 24, 182.

21. *Laborem exercens,* No. 19, *AAS* 73 (1982) 107–9.

22. "Mary, Hope of All Generations," October 7, 1979, *TPS* 24, 366–70.

23. "Chi troviamo," December 25, 1978, *TPS* 24, 166.

24. "All' indirizzo," December 22, 1979, *TPS* 24, 181–2.

25. "Family Stability and Respect for Life," March 19, 1981, *TPS* 26, 174–9.

26. Ibid.

27. "Ci e gradito," *Osservatore Romano,* December 8, 1960, *TPS* 7, 172–3.

28. Heidi I. Hartman, "The Family as the Locus of Gender, Class and Political Study: The Example of Housework," *SGINS* 6 (Spring 1981) 379–80; Wanda Minge Klevana, "Does Labor Time Decrease with Industrialization? A Survey of Time Allocation Studies," *Current Anthropology* 21 (June 1980) 283–5.

29. "E'giunto al termine," *TPS* 24, 182; *Laborem exercens,* No. 19, *AAS* 73 (1981) 625–9; *Familiaris Consortio, AAS* 74 (1982) 107–9.

30. "Considerando che" (Charter of Rights of the Family), October 22, 1983, article 10, *TPS* 29, 78–85; "I am Pleased," June 7, 1984, *TPS* 29, 250.

31. "A tutti," December 8, 1974, *Osservatore Romano,* December 10, 1974; "Soyez les bienvenues," April 18, 1975, *Osservatore Romano,* April 19, 1975.

32. Pius XII, address to Italian women, October 21, 1945, *AAS* 37 (1945) 291–2; "Convenuti a Roma," *AAS* 53 (1961) 611; *Gaudium et Spes, AAS* 58 (1966) 1074; "Apres plus," *TPS* 21, 165; "Soyez les bienvenues," April 18, 1975, *TPS* 20, 37; "Parati semper," March 31, 1985, *TPS* 30, 210.

33. Vincent Genovesi, S.J., *In Pursuit of Love: Catholic Morality and Human Sexuality* (Wilmington, Del.: Michael Glazier, 1987), for his description and discussion of Ruth T. Barnhouse, "Homosexuality," *Anglican Theological Review* 58 (1976) 107–24, 129–30, and her *Homosexuality: A Symbolic Confusion* (New York: Seabury, 1977) 172–4. See also Edward A. Malloy, *Homosexuality and the Christian Way of Life* (Lanham, Md.: University Press of America, 1981) 88.

34. John Paul II does not address the need for any personal relationships in priestly training other than priest-priest, except with prayer relationships; whereas a relationship with Mary is advocated strongly. Traditionally, the feminine symbols of Mary and the "Mother" church replace all live women. See John Paul II, "Augustinum Hipponensem," August 28, 1986, *TPS* 31, 363, and also "Este hora," January 28, 1979, *TPS* 24, 49–67.

35. For example, John Paul argues against making the priest more like the laity in "Ecce nunc," March 16, 1986, *TPS* 31, 163.

36. See *The National Catholic Reporter* coverage of clerical AIDS, homosexuality, pedophilia, and active heterosexuality over the past two years, especially Bill Kenkelen, "Priests' AIDS Deaths," December 12, 1986; Jason

Berry, "Homosexuality, Pedophilia: 'no direct linkage,'" March 6, 1987, and the extensive two-part study of priestly sexuality/lifestyle by Jason Berry in the February 27 and March 6, 1987, issues.

37. Augustine, *On Marriage and Concupiscence,* Book 1, Chapter 17, No. 15; St. Thomas Aquinas, *Summa theologiae* 1, 98, 2.

38. "Twenty Facts on Women Workers," U.S. Department of Labor, Office of the Secretary, Women's Bureau, 1982.

39. Gwendolyn L. Lewis, "Changes in Women's Role Participation," in *Women and Sex Roles,* ed. Irene Frieze (New York: Norton, 1978).

40. Jessie Bernard, *The Future of Marriage* (New York: World, 1972).

41. Ibid.

42. Augustine, *On Marriage and Concupiscence,* Book 1, Chapter 19, No. 7.

43. Robert Blair Kaiser, *The Politics of Sex and Religion: A Case History in the Development of Doctrine* (Kansas City: Leaven, 1985) 141–2.

44. Charles A. Gallagher et al., *Embodied in Love: Sacramental Spirituality and Sexual Intimacy* (New York: Crossroad, 1986).

Part Five

MORE THEORETICAL EXPLANATIONS OF CHANGE IN OFFICIAL CATHOLIC MORAL TEACHINGS

17. Development in Moral Doctrine

John T. Noonan, Jr.

This chapter first appeared in *Theological Studies* 54 (1993).

That the moral teachings of the Catholic Church have changed over time will, I suppose, be denied by almost no one today. To refresh memories and confirm the point, I will describe four large examples of such change in the areas of usury, marriage, slavery, and religious freedom, and then analyze how Catholic theology has dealt with them.

USURY

The first is the teaching of the church on usury. Once upon a time, certainly from at least 1150 to 1550, seeking, receiving, or hoping for anything beyond one's principal—in other words, looking for profit—on a loan constituted the mortal sin of usury. The doctrine was enunciated by popes, expressed by three ecumenical councils, proclaimed by bishops, and taught unanimously by theologians. The doctrine was not some obscure, hole-in-the-corner affection, but stood astride the European credit markets, at least as much as the parallel Islamic ban of usury governs Moslem countries today. There were lawful ways of profiting from the extension of credit, but these ways had been carefully constructed to respect the basic prohibition; it was a debated question at what point they crossed the line and were themselves sinfully usurious. The great central moral fact was that usury, understood as profit on a loan, was forbidden as contrary to the natural law, as contrary to the law of the church, and as contrary to the law of the gospel.[1]

All that, we know, has changed. The change can be exaggerated. Even at the height of the prohibition of usury not every form of credit transaction was classified as a loan from which no profit might be sought. The idea of legitimate interest was also not absent. Formally it can be argued that the old usury rule, narrowly construed, still stands: namely, that no profit on a loan may be taken without a just title to that profit. But in terms of emphasis, perspective, and practice, the old usury rule has disappeared; the just title to profit is assumed to exist. The centrality of "Lend freely, hoping nothing thereby," construed as a command, has disappeared. We take interest as profit on our banking accounts. We expect our banks to profit from their lending business. Our entire financial world is built on profitable charges for credit. The idea that it is against nature for money to breed money or that it is contrary to church law to deposit in a savings institution with the hope of a profit or that hoping for profit at all from a loan breaks a command of Christ—all these ideas, once unanimously inculcated with the utmost seriousness by the teaching authority of the church, are now so obsolete that one invites incredulity by reciting them.

MARRIAGE

Usury was a moral doctrine dependent on economic conditions that could change. Let us now consider, as something related to fundamental unchanging human nature, moral doctrine on adultery, bigamy, and marriage. Monogamy without divorce is the law of the gospel, established by words attributed to Jesus himself and related by him to the primordial order established by God (Matt 19:2–9). Within the New Testament, however, a perceptible change occurs. If, of two married unbelievers, one converts and the other does not but deserts the convert, St. Paul teaches that the convert is free: "Neither a brother nor a sister is a slave in these matters" (1 Cor 7:10–16). The implication, teased out in patristic times, is that the convert can commit what otherwise would be adultery and bigamy and enter a second marriage in the Lord.[2]

Until the sixteenth century, this so-called Pauline privilege remained the solitary exception to Christian monogamy. Then, on behalf of African slaves torn from their African spouses and shipped to South America, the privilege was radically extended. The slave who wanted to convert could not know whether his absent spouse would abandon him or not. No matter, Gregory XIII ruled in 1585, it was important that such converts be free to remarry "lest they not persist in their faith." On their behalf, the pope dissolved their old marriages and declared them free to enter a second marriage that would otherwise have been adulterous and bigamous.[3]

The next step in this direction was taken under the impetus of the great canonist Cardinal Pietro Gasparri in the 1920s. In a case from Helena, Montana, Gerard G. Marsh, unbaptized, had married Frances R. Groom, an Anglican. They divorced; Groom remarried. Two years later Marsh sought to marry a Catholic, Lulu La Hood; Pius XI dissolved Marsh's marriage to Groom "in favor of the faith" of Miss La Hood. Apparently exercising jurisdiction over the marriage of two non-Catholics (Groom and Marsh), the pope authorized Marsh to marry a Catholic under circumstances that but for the papal action would (morally, not civilly) have constituted bigamy for Marsh and adultery for La Hood.[4] Prior to 1924 the teaching of the church, expressly grounded both on the commandment of the Lord and on the natural law, was that marriage was indissoluble except in the special case of conversion of an unbeliever. The teaching was unanimously expressed by papal encyclicals and by the body of bishops in their universal ordinary teaching. Then, in 1924, by the exercise of papal authority, the meaning of the commandment against adultery was altered; what was bigamy was revised; and a substantial gloss was written on the Lord's words, "What God has joined together let no man put asunder."

SLAVERY

Let us now examine two examples taken from an area more fundamental than justice in lending, more fundamental than rectitude in sexual relations—examples that bear on the basic conditions of moral autonomy. I mean moral doctrine on human liberty. And first, moral doctrine on a human being's right to be free from ownership by another human being.

Once upon a time, certainly as late as 1860, the church taught that it was no sin for a Catholic to own another human being; to command the labor of that other human being without paying compensation; to determine where he or she lived and how much he or she was fed and clothed; to restrict his or her education; to pledge him or her for a loan, forfeit him or her for a default, sell him or her for cash; to do the same to his or her offspring; and to discipline him or her by physical punishments if he or she were rude or boisterous or slack in service. I refer, of course, to some of the features of chattel slavery as it existed in the United States, as it was upheld by American law, and as it was applied by Catholic laymen, bishops, and religious orders with the approval of ecclesiastical authority. No qualm of conscience troubled that leading Catholic jurist, Chief Justice Roger Taney, as he wrote Dred Scott, or disturbed the slaveholding Maryland Province of the Society of Jesus.[5] That loving one's neighbor as one's self was observed only in a Pickwickian way by holding one's neighbor in bondage was not a commonplace of Catholic moral thought.

It was Catholic moral doctrine that slaves should be treated humanely, and that it was good to give slaves freedom. With some qualifications it was Catholic moral doctrine that slaves should be allowed to marry.[6] But Catholic moral doctrine considered the institution of slavery acceptable. St. Paul had accepted it, returning Onesimus to his master (Phlm 11–19) and instructing the Christian slaves of Corinth to obey their masters (1 Cor 7:21).

The premier moralist of the West, St. Augustine, said succinctly that Christ "did not make men free from being slaves." The greatest of reforming popes, Gregory I, accepted a young boy as a slave and gave him as a gift to another bishop; his famous decision to send missionaries to England is said to have arisen from his musings as he browsed in a slave market in Rome.[7]

The greatest of Catholic jurisprudents, Henri de Bracton, thought slavery was contrary to natural law, but accepted it as an institution of the law of nations; he merely copied the great Catholic lawgiver, Justinian. St. Antoninus of Florence followed St. Thomas in acquiescing in the civil law permitting slave status to follow birth to a slave woman. Paul III praised the benevolent effects of slavery on agriculture while approving the traffic in slaves in Rome. The eminent Jesuit moralist Cardinal Juan De Lugo was in harmony with the moralists' tradition when he found slavery "beyond the intention of nature," but "introduced to prevent greater evils." Near the end of the seventeenth century, the master French theologian, Bishop Bossuet, declared that to condemn slavery would be "to condemn the Holy Spirit, who by the mouth of St. Paul orders slaves to remain in their state."[8]

In 1839 Gregory XVI condemned the slave trade, but not so explicitly that the condemnation covered occasional sales by owners of surplus stock.[9] In the first treatise on moral theology written for Americans, Bishop Francis Kenrick in 1841 declared it no sin against nature to own slaves treated in a humane way and added that, even if Africans had been brought to America unjustly, long lapse of time had cured any defect in title on the part of those who had inherited them.[10] Up until actual abolition occurred, the church was mute on the institution. Or, rather, the church endorsed the institution as compatible with Christianity; indeed as Bossuet observed, expressly approved in Christian scripture.

Again, all that has changed. In the face of the repeated teachings of modern popes, beginning with Leo XIII, on the rights of labor, uncompensated slave labor is seen as a moral outrage. In the light of the teachings of the modern popes and the Second Vatican Council on the dignity of the human person, it is morally unthinkable that one person be allowed to buy, sell, hypothecate, or lease another or dispose of that person's children.[11] And all the usual and inevitable corollaries of chattel slavery (the denial of education, the denial of vocational opportunity, the destruction of the family) have been so long and so vigorously denounced by bishops and moral theologians that today there is a rampart of authority condemning the conditions without which such slavery could not exist. Slavery has disappeared from most of the world. The Catholic Church stands as one of the great modern teachers excoriating it as evil.

RELIGIOUS FREEDOM

Finally, I turn to moral doctrine on the freedom that should attend religious belief. Once upon a time, no later than the time of St. Augustine, it was considered virtuous for bishops to invoke imperial force to compel heretics to return to the church. Augustine's position was expressly grounded in the gospels.[12] At a later point in time (the rule is well-established in St. Thomas Aquinas), it is doctrine that a relapsed heretic will be judged by the ecclesiastical authorities and remanded to the secular authorities for execution. Forgers are put to death for debasing the currency. Why should not those disloyal to the faith be killed for falsifying it? God may pardon them; the church and the state should not.[13]

For a period of more than 1,200 years, during much of which the Catholic Church was dominant in Europe, popes, bishops, and theologians regularly and unanimously denied the religious liberty of heretics. No theologian taught that faith may be freely repudiated without physical consequences; no pope extended the mantle of charitable tolerance to those who departed from orthodox belief. On the contrary, it was universally taught that the duty of a good ruler was to extirpate not only heresy but also heretics.[14] The vast institutional apparatus of the church was put at the service of detecting heretics, who, if they persevered in their heresy or relapsed into it, would be executed at the stake. Hand and glove, church and state collaborated in the terror by which the heretics were purged.

Nor did doctrine change markedly as the Protestant Reformation led to the acceptance not of religious liberty but of religious toleration in parts of Europe. Tolerance is permission of what is frankly described as an evil, but a lesser evil. Eventually, as religious peace became the norm in eighteenth- and nineteenth-century Europe, the hypothesis was advanced and accepted that in such circumstances it was for the common good to refrain from religious persecution.[15] The thesis required that in ideal circumstances the state be the physical guarantor of orthodoxy.

All that changed quite recently—only 30 years ago. Then the Second Vatican Council taught that freedom to believe was a sacred human right; that this freedom was founded on the requirements of the human person; that this freedom was at the same time conveyed by Christian revelation; and that the kind of respect that must be shown for human freedom of belief had been taught from the beginning by Jesus and his Apostles, who sought not to coerce any human will but to persuade it. No distinction was now drawn between the religious freedom of infidels (in theory always respected) and the religious freedom of heretics, once trampled on in theory and practice. Now each human being was seen as the possessor of a precious right to believe and to practice in accordance with belief. Religious liberty was established. The state's interference with conscience was denounced.[16]

The minority in opposition strenuously maintained that the teaching of the magisterium was being abandoned; they cited express texts and hitherto unchallenged papal statements. Archbishop Marcel Lefebvre, a leader of the minority, debating the document at the council, said sarcastically that what was proposed was "a new law," which had been condemned many times by the church. What was being taught did not come from the tradition of the church, but from "Hobbes, Locke and Rousseau," followed by rejected Catholic liberals such as Lamennais. Pius IX had rejected it. Leo XIII had "solemnly condemned it" as contrary "to Sacred Scripture and Tradition."[17] A commentator after the fact calmly observed that the council had "reversed the teaching of the ordinary papal magisterium."[18] The doctrine regnant from 350 to 1964 was, in a cryptic phrase, reclassified as conduct occurring through "the vicissitudes of history."[19]

ANALYSIS

Enough has been said, I trust, to suggest the nature of the problem. Wide shifts in the teaching of moral duties, once presented as part of Christian doctrine by the magisterium, have occurred. In each case one can see the displacement of a principle or principles that had been taken as dispositive—in the case of usury, that a loan confers no right to profit; in the case of marriage, that all marriages are indissoluble; in the case of slavery, that war gives a right to enslave and that ownership of a slave gives title to the slave's offspring; in the case of religious liberty, that error has no rights and that fidelity to the Christian faith may be physically enforced. These principles were replaced by principles already part of Christian teaching: in the case of usury, that the person of the lender, not the loan, should be the focus of evaluation; in the case of marriage, that preservation of faith is more important than preservation of a human relationship; in the case of slavery, that in Christ there is "neither free nor slave" (Gal 3:28); and in the case of religious liberty, that faith must be free. In the course of this displacement of one set of principles, what was forbidden became lawful (the cases of usury and marriage); what was permissible became unlawful (the case of slavery); and what was required became forbidden (the persecution of heretics).

It is true that the moral doctrine of the Catholic Church can be seen as *sui generis;* it belongs to no type and so yields no laws. Change depends on two free agencies: human will and the Holy Spirit. No a priori rules can bind or predict their course.[20] Nonetheless, when a palpable change has taken place (and surely usury, slavery, religious liberty, and divorce are cases in point) it should be possible to look back and determine what the conditions of change were; to observe the extent of the change that was possible; and to construct a provisional theory as to the limits to change. At least, in Newman's words, one might propose "an hypothesis to account for a difficulty."[21]

While a large literature exists on the development of doctrine, examination reveals that this literature is focused on changes in theological propositions as to the Trinity, the nature of Christ, the Petrine office, or Marian dogma. I have found no well-known writer on development who has addressed the kinds of change I have described; no great theologians have immersed themselves deeply in these mutations of morals. One exception, as will be noted, is Bernard Häring, but he does not theorize at length. But perhaps we can profit by analogy if we look at what theologians have had to say about changes in propositions of faith.[22]

One approach, of which Bishop Bossuet and Orestes Brownson are representative, has been to deny that any real change has ever occurred; there has only been an improvement in expression. For Bossuet and Brownson the invariance of Catholic teaching was a mark of the true church, to be triumphantly contrasted with "the variations" found among Protestants. A second approach, of which Spanish seventeenth-century theology affords an example, took the position that it is possible for the church to work out the logical implications of scripture and so reach, and declare as true, propositions not contained in scripture; real advances occur.[23]

A third, and highly influential, theory was put forward in 1843 by John Henry Newman. Writing still as an Anglican, yet as one about to become a Catholic, Newman produced a work that is part detective story (What is the true church?) and part apologia (All the apparent defects of the true church are defensible). His mind, teeming with images, offered a variety of ways of understanding how the church's doctrine of today was not literally the same as the church's doctrine of yesterday, but yet the church was still faithful to her Founder. Doctrine, he declared, developed. In the later *Apologia pro vita sua,* development became one of the "principles" of Catholic Christianity.[24] What was meant by development was illustrated in the *Essay on Development* by analogy: by analogy to the beliefs of a child as these beliefs matured in the mind of the child become adult; by analogy with the thought of a poet, whose verse contained more than was explicit in his mind as he composed; by analogy with any organic life as it grows from bud to flower; and by analogy to the course of an idea embraced by a society, an idea whose detailed consequences can be grasped only as the idea is lived out in the society. By all these comparisons Newman confessed that changes had occurred in the doctrine of the church, but he maintained that the changes had been rooted in the original revelation and were a perfection, not a distortion, of it. True development, he wrote, "corroborates, not corrects, the body of the thought from which it proceeds."[25]

The modernists took the idea of development and ran away with it. Doctrine became the projection of human needs, changing in response to those needs. Control of doctrine by the objective content of revelation disappeared.[26] The church rejected modernism and retained Newman's conclusion that there was genuine growth in doctrine from unchanged foundations. Vatican II put it tersely: "Insight grows both into the words and the realities that have been handed on."[27] Change, that was in fact doctrinal progress, was celebrated. The central reality, in relation to which insight grew, was Jesus Christ, himself "both the mediator and the plenitude of the whole revelation."[28]

How would any of these approaches work if applied to moral doctrine? To deny that real change had occurred, as Bossuet and Brownson did, would be an apologetic tactic incapable of execution and unworthy of belief. To say, as did the seventeenth-century Spanish, that the unfolding had been by logical implication would be equally incredible. The acceptance of slavery did not imply freedom; the endorsement of religious persecution did not entail respect for religious freedom. The method might indeed be used if the most basic principles, such as "Love your neighbor as yourself," were the starting point. But would logic alone suffice?

Newman's complex set of analogies is different. At one level of doctrine, of course, one cannot maintain that the church's present championing of freedom, personal and religious, "corroborates" an earlier stage in which the church defended chattel slavery and religious persecution. At another level, Newman's notion of an idea maturing can be criticized by taking his analogy with organic life literally; he can then be caricatured as supposing that spiritual growth is similar to vegetative growth.[29] But Newman's rich range of arguments and metaphors cannot be so neatly written off. In a passage dealing with the nature of development in general that I read as decisive, he declares:

> The development then of an idea is not like investigation worked out on paper, in which each successive advance is a pure evolution from a foregoing, but it is carried on through and by means of communities of men and their leaders and guides; and it employs their minds as its instruments and depends upon them while it uses them....It is the warfare of ideas under their varying aspects striving for the mastery....[30]

This passage acknowledges an objectivity in the idea or ideas at issue; at the same time it fully recognizes that development occurs by conflict, in which the leading idea will effect the "throwing off" of earlier views now found to be incompatible with the leading idea more fully realized.[31] Principles, broadly understood, underlie and control specific changes.[32] Newman's approach is adaptable to the development of moral doctrine.

The modernist position that human needs will shape doctrine carries the cost of eliminating any objective content; it is, as Pius X put it, "the synthesis of all the heresies."[33]

Finally, there is the position of Vatican II: there can be and is a growth in insight into a reality that is Jesus Christ. It comes from "the contemplation of believers, the experience of spiritual realities, and the preaching of the church."[34] As Bernard Häring has amplified the words of *Dei verbum:* "Christ does not become greater through ongoing history, but our knowledge of the plan of salvation which is revealed in the world in Christ does become more complete and close to life in our hearts through the working of the Spirit in the history of the church and above all in the saints."[35]

To hold that moral doctrine changes with increased insight into Christ is an attractive proposition. It entails one obvious danger. When one sees more deeply into Christ, is one looking into a mirror merely reflecting one's own deepest feeling? The answer must be that the church has the mission of determining what is only the projection of subjective feelings and what is an authentic response to Christ as revealed.

If insight into Christ is taken from the realm of faith to that of morals and applied to our four examples, it will be found to afford at least a partial explanation of what has happened. On the great question of religious liberty, a stronger appreciation of Christ's own methods has led to repudiation of all violence in the enforcement of belief. On the great question of human slavery, a better grasp of the fellowship effected by Christ has made the holding of any person in bondage intolerable.

In the other cases one factor facilitating change was a deeper, less literal, reading of the words of Christ. When "Lend freely, hoping nothing thereby" had been understood as a peremptory command, it came to be understood as an exemplary exhortation.[36] When "What God has joined together, let no man put asunder" had been read as absolute, the possibility of exception has been eventually envisaged and expanded. In these cases, too, one could say that the reality of Christ was better reached by the abandonment of the letter.

Yet it would be preposterous to imagine that all these profound changes occurred simply by the acquiring of deeper insights into Christ. Human beings do not reach moral conclusions in a vacuum apart from the whole web of language, custom, and social structure surrounding them. A society composed entirely of free human beings was unknown in the Mediterranean world of the first centuries; a society in which the state did not support religion was equally unknown. Only as social structures changed did moral mutation become possible, even if the change in social structures, as it might reasonably be argued, was owed at least in part to the perception that structures fostering liberty were more congruent with deeper insight into Christ.[37]

Those structures could not have shifted without experience. The central European experience leading first to religious tolerance and then to religious liberty was the experience of the evil of religious persecution. The experience was long and bloody and sufficient to demonstrate how demoralizing the enforcement of religion by force was. Equally, I would argue, it was the centuries-old experience of slavery that led to the conclusion that slavery was destructive both for the slaves and for the masters.[38]

Experience as such, taken as "raw experience," the mere participation in this or that phenomenon, is, however, not the key. Raw experience carries with it no evaluation. But experience, suffered or perceived in the light of human nature and of the gospel, can be judged good or bad. It was the experience of unfreedom, in the gospel's light, that made the contrary shine clear.[39]

The negative experience of religious persecution was reinforced by the American experience of religious freedom, for America launched the great experiment of a nation committed to the nonestablishment of any national religion and the free exercise of religion. The American experiment had blemishes, such as the persecution of the Mormons and of the Jehovah's Witnesses, and the denial of constitutional freedom to conscientious objectors to unjust war. But the American ideal and its relative success were clear and were taught to Europe by Tocqueville, Lamennais, and Lacordaire. In the end, the theologians built on the American experience, guided in no small part by an American theologian, John Courtney Murray. Finally, sealing all by fire, was the experience of religious unfreedom under the terrible dictatorships of the twentieth century. Without those experiences, negative and positive, and without the elaboration of the ideal by Tocqueville and Murray, the changes made by Vatican II could not have occurred.[40]

The advance on slavery also depended on articulation by individuals who were ahead of the theologians and the church. In Catholic France, Montesquieu challenged the morality of slavery, writing with fine irony of blacks: "It is impossible that we should suppose those people to be men, because if we should suppose them to be men, we would begin to believe that we ourselves are not Christians."[41] It was eighteenth-century Quakers and Baptists and Methodists and nineteenth-century Congregationalists who led the fight against slavery in the English-speaking world, and it was the French Revolution that led to its abolition in the French Empire. The gospel, as interpreted by Protestants and as mediated by Rousseau and the revolutionaries of 1789, achieved much.[42] Only after the cultures of Europe and America changed through the abolitionists' agency, and only after the laws of every civilized land eliminated the practice, did Catholic moral doctrine decisively repudiate slavery as immoral. Only in 1890 did Pope Leo XIII attack the institution itself, noting that slavery was incompatible "with the brotherhood that unites all men."[43] At the end of the argument and articulation and legal upheaval that had gone on for two centuries, the requirement of Christ was clear.

In contrast, the change regarding divorce and remarriage, adultery and bigamy, appears to have been almost entirely an internal process. But was it? St. Paul's original modification of monogamy responded to conditions he encountered affecting conversion. His rule worked well enough until the extreme conditions of African slavery in South America suggested the need for radical expansion. And that change was not improved upon until, in modern religiously mixed societies, it became common for unbaptized persons and Catholics to fall in love and want to be married. Then a new expansion was made. Canonistic ingenuity and exaltation of papal power played a dominant part. The canonists responded to changed external conditions as they discovered the true meaning of Christ's command.

The change with regard to usury, basically effected in the course of the sixteenth century although formally acknowledged only in the nineteenth, came from the convergence of several factors. Europe moved from an agricultural to a commercial economy. Moral theologians began to give weight to the experience of otherwise decent Christians who were bankers and who claimed banking was compatible with Christianity. The morality of certain types of credit transactions (the so-called triple contract and the personal annuity and the foreign exchange contract) were all reexamined and reevaluated in the light of credit transactions already accepted as legitimate. Perhaps above all, the perspective of moral analysis shifted from focus on the loan in itself to focus on the lender and the investment opportunity the lender lost by lending. All these factors—commercial developments, attention to experience, new analyses, and shift in perspective—produced a moral doctrine on usury that was substantially different from that taught throughout the Middle Ages and substantially similar in practice to what is accepted today. All these factors, plus reevaluation of the words of Christ, created the new moral doctrine.[44]

CONCLUSION

When morals are at issue, the process of change requires a complex constellation of elements. Every society, including the church, lives by rules that keep its vital balance. Change one, and the balance is jeopardized. Hence there is a conservative tendency to keep the rules as they are, there is fear when they are given up, and sometimes, nostalgia for the loss.

Change is also resisted for other reasons: There is a praiseworthy desire to maintain intellectual consistency. There is a longing in the human mind for repose, for fixed points of reference, for absolute certainty. There is alarm about the future: What else can change? There is the theological conviction that as God is unchanging, divine demands must also be unchanging. How could one have gone to hell yesterday for what today one would be held virtuous in doing? How could one have done virtuously yesterday what one would be damned for doing today? How could one once have been bound to a high and demanding standard that later is said to be unnecessary? How could one once have been permitted to engage in conduct that is later condemned as uncharitable? A mutation in morals bewilders. Hence there is a presumption of rightness attending the present rules, and authority is rightly vigilant to preserve them. Not every proposed mutation is good; the majority, it could be guessed, might be harmful.

But a new balance can be struck. The consistency sought should not be verbal nor literal; nor can conformity to every past rule be required. The consistency to be sought is consistency with Christ. The human desire for mental repose is not to be satisfied in this life. One cannot predict future changes; one can only follow present light and in that light be morally certain that some moral obligations will never alter. The great commandments of love of God and of neighbor, the great principles of justice and charity continue to govern all development. God is unchanging, but the demands of the New Testament are different from those of the Old, and while no other revelation supplements the New Testament, it is evident from the case of slavery alone that it has taken time to ascertain what the demands of the New Testament really are. All will be judged by the demands of the day in which they live. It is not within human competence to say with certainty who was or will be saved; all will be judged as they have conscientiously acted. In new conditions, with new insight, an old rule need not be preserved in order to honor a past discipline.

Another response to change is to ignore it, to deny explicitly or implicitly that it has occurred, to be aware of the mutations described here and find them without significance—just so many well-established and well-known historical facts. Denial of that sort also betrays fear of change, fear that change is simply chance. Mutations are muted. But why should believers in Christ have such a fear? The Spirit guides the church. The acts of development have a significance beyond themselves. "The idea of development was the most important single idea Newman contributed to the thought of the Christian Church."[45] The idea of development had this importance because it contained an explanation of the passage from the past and a Delphic prophecy of the future.

In the church there can always be fresh appeal to Christ, there is always the possibility of probing new depths of insight. To grow is to change, and the gospel parable of the mustard seed promises growth (Matt 13:31–32). The kingdom of heaven, we are told, is like a householder who from his storeroom brings forth things old and new (Matt 13:52). Our world has grown by mutation; should not our morals, especially when the direction and the goal are provided by the Lord? "[H]ere below to live is to change. And to be perfect is to have changed often."[46] Must we not, then, frankly admit that change is something that plays a role in Catholic moral teaching? Must not the traditional motto *semper idem* be modified, however unsettling that might be, in the direction of *plus ça change, plus c'est la même chose?* Yes, if the principle of change is the person of Christ.

Notes

1. On the whole topic, see John T. Noonan, Jr., "Authority on Usury and on Contraception," *Tijdschrift voor Theologie* 6 (1966) 26–50, republished in *Cross Currents* 16 (1966) 55–79 and *The Wiseman Review* (Summer 1966) 201–29. The standard definition of usury was given by Gratian, *Decretum, Corpus iuris canonici,* ed. E. Friedberg (Leipzig, 1879–1881) 2.14.3.1. The Second Council of the Lateran condemned usury (G. D. Mansi, *Sacrorum conciliorum nova et amplissima collectio* [Paris, 1901–1920] 21.529–30); the Third Council of the Lateran declared usury to be condemned "by the pages of both Testaments" (Mansi 22.231). The Council of Vienne declared that anyone "pertinaciously affirming that to practice usury is no sin should be punished as a heretic" (Clement, *Constitutiones* 5.5, *Corpus iuris canonici,* ed. E. Friedberg).

2. See John T. Noonan, Jr., *Power to Dissolve* (Cambridge: Harvard University, 1972) 343.

3. Ibid. 356, citing Gregory XIII, *Populis et nationibus*, reprinted as Document VII in the appendix to *Codex iuris canonici* (Rome: Vatican, 1917).

4. *Power to Dissolve,* 370–71.

5. According to Ambrose Marechal, Archbishop of Baltimore, the province in 1826 owned as personal property "about 500 African men" (Marechal to Cardinal Della Sornaglia, January 15, 1826, in Thomas Hughes, S.J., *History of the Society of Jesus in North America: Documents* [New York: Longmans, Green, 1908] 1.1.544). Anthony Kohlmann, S.J., commenting on this assertion, put the number of slaves at half this figure; he added that their value was less than Marechal supposed because "those over 45 cannot be alienated," the clear inference being that those under 45 could be sold (ibid. 545).

6. Gratian, *Decretum* 2.29.2.8 upheld the validity of slave marriages but required the consent of the slaves' owners. In the United States, Bishop Francis Kenrick thought that "the majority" of slave agreements did not have "the force of marriage" since "the intention of contracting a perpetual bond is lacking to them" (Francis P. Kenrick, *Theologia moralis* [Philadelphia, 1843] 3.333).

7. Augustine, *On Psalm 125* no. 7 (J. P. Migne, *Patrologiae cursus completus. Series latina* [hereafter *PL*] (Paris, 1844–1891) 37.1653; Gregory, *Epist.* 7.30 (*PL* 77.887 [accepts slave]). For the story of the slave market, see Bede, *Historia ecclesiastica gentis anglorum,* ed. George H. Moberley (Oxford: Clarendon, 1869) 2.1; cf. Anon., *The Earliest Life of Gregory the Great,* ed. and trans. Bertram Colgrave (Cambridge: Cambridge University, 1968) 91.

8. Henri de Bracton, *De legibus et consuetudinibus Angliae,* ed. S. E. Thorne (Cambridge: Harvard University, 1970–77) 2.30, following *Justinian, Digesta* 50.17.32; Antoninus, *Summa Sacrae theologiae* (Venice, 1581–82) 3.3.6; Paul III, *Motu proprio,* November 9, 1548, trans. in John F. Maxwell, *Slavery and the Catholic Church* (Chichester: Rose, 1975) 75; Lugo, *De iustitia et iure* 6.2, *Disputationes scholasticae et morales* (Paris, 1899) vol. 8; Jacques B. Bossuet, *Avertissement sur les lettres du Ministre Jurieu,* in Bossuet, *Oeuvres complètes* (Lyons, 1877) 3.542.

9. Gregory XVI, *In supremo apostolatus, Acta,* ed. Antonio Maria Bernasconi (Rome: Vatican, 1901) 2.388. Bishop John England was at pains to explain to Secretary of State John Forsyth that none of the bishops at the Provincial Council of Baltimore thought that Gregory XVI's condemnation affected the American institution of slavery: see John England, *Works,* ed. Ignatius A. Reynolds (Baltimore: J. Murphy, 1849) 3.115–119. The Holy Office in 1866 ruled that the buying and selling of slaves was not contrary to natural law (Holy Office to the Vicar Apostolic of the Galle tribe in Ethiopia, June 20, 1866, *Collectanea S.C. de Propaganda Fide* [Rome, 1907] I n. 1293).

10. Kenrick, *Theologia moralis,* vol. 2, tract 5.2.6.

11. E.g., Vatican II, *Gaudium et Spes* no. 67, in *Decreta, Declarationes,* ed. secretaria generali concilii oecumenici Vaticani II (Rome: Typis polyglottis Vaticanis, 1966) 790 (*Constitutiones* 790).

12. Augustine to Boniface, *Epistula* 185, *PL* 33.803.

13. Thomas Aquinas, *Summa theologiae,* ed. Pietro Caramello (Turin: Marietti, 1952) 2–2, q. 11, a. 3 (death penalty; comparison of forgery); q. 11, a.4 ad 1 (church "cannot imitate" God in reading hearts and so does not keep relapsed heretics "from peril of death" imposed by the state).

14. Lucius III, *Ad abolendam (Decretales Gregorii IX,* 5.7.9).

15. John A. Ryan and Francis J. Boland, *Catholic Principles of Politics* (New York: Macmillan, 1940) 317–21. The same teaching appears in John A. Ryan and Moorhouse F. X. Millar, S.J., *The State and the Church* (New York: Macmillan, 1924) 35–39.

16. Vatican II, *Dignitatis humanae personae* no. 2, Second Vatican Council, *Constitutiones* 55.

17. Lefebvre, Intervention, Sept. 20, 1965 (*Acta Synodalia Sancti Concilii Oecumenici Vaticani II* [Rome, 1976] 4.1, 409).

18. J. Robert Dionne, *The Papacy and the Church* (New York: Philosophical Library, 1987) 193.

19. *Dignitatis humane personae,* 11.

20. See Karl Rahner, S.J., *Theological Investigations* I, trans. C. Ernst (Baltimore: Helicon, 1961) 41.

21. John Henry Newman, *An Essay on the Development of Christian Doctrine,* ed. Charles Frederick Harrold (New York: Longmans, Green, 1949) 28.

22. Consider as representative of recent work, Jan Hendrik Walgrave's *Unfolding Revelation: The Nature of Doctrinal Development* (London: Hutchinson, 1972). It has no discussion of moral doctrine. Jaroslav Pelikan's massive work, *The Christian Tradition: A History of the Development of Doctrine* (Chicago: University of Chicago, 1971–1989) does not deal with any of the four changes used as examples here; in other words, the development of moral doctrine is no part of his comprehensive treatment of "the development of doctrine." A recent sensitive account of the history of moral theology offers no theory of development; see John A. Gallagher, *Time Past, Time Future: A Historical Study of Catholic Moral Theology* (New York: Paulist, 1990). But John Mahoney, *The Making of Moral Theology* (New York: Oxford/Clarendon, 1987) 320 observes that "the Church has a great difficulty…in handling the subject of change as such." Mahoney goes on to note that change is "an unavoidable element of human existence" and to suggest that change in moral doctrine is sometimes the right response to changed conditions (326–27).

23. See Owen Chadwick, *From Bossuet to Newman: The Idea of Doctrinal Development* (Cambridge: Cambridge University, 1957) 20 (Bossuet); 171 (Brownson); 25–44 (Spanish).

24. Newman, *Apologia pro vita sua,* ed. Charles Frederick Harrold (New York: Longmans, Green, 1947) 79.

25. Newman, *Essay on Development* 2.5.6, p.186. Newman wrote as an Anglican but did not amend the quoted passages when he revised the *Essay* as a Catholic. On the analogies, see Chadwick 151, 155. Aidan Nichols sees Newman's fundamental metaphor as that of a seal cutting a design of wax (*From Newman to Congar: The Idea of Doctrinal Development from the Victorians to the Second Vatican Council* [Edinburgh: T. & T. Clark, 1990] 44).

26. See John T. Noonan, Jr., "The Philosophical Postulates of Alfred Loisy" (M.A. thesis, Catholic University of America, 1948).

27. Vatican II, *Dei verbum* 8, Second Vatican Council, *Constitutiones* 430.

28. Ibid. 8, 424.

29. Compare the criticism of Newman's metaphor by Ambroise Gardeil, *Le Donné révélé et la théologie* (Paris: J. Gabalda, 1910) 156, noting the difference between "la vie d'un végétal et la vie d'un esprit."

30. Newman, *Essay on Development* 1.1.6, p. 74.

31. Ibid.

32. Ibid. 2.5.2, p. 167.

33. Pius X, *Pascendi dominici gregis,* September 8, 1907 (*Acta sanctae sedis* 40.632; Eng. trans. in *All Things in Christ,* ed. Vincent A. Yzermans [Westminster, Md.: Newman, 1954] 117).

34. Vatican II, *Dei verbum* no. 8, Second Vatican Council, *Constitutiones* 430.

35. Bernard Häring, *My Witness for the Church,* trans. Leonard Swidler (New York: Paulist, 1992) 122.

36. Urban III treated the words of Christ on lending as mandatory (Urban III, *Consuluit, Decretalia Gregorii IX* 5.19.10, *Corpus iuris canonici,* ed. E. Friedberg). Domingo de Soto is the first major scholastic theologian to challenge this interpretation (*De iustitia et iure libri decem* [Lyons, 1569] 6.1.1).

37. Cf. Louis Vereecke, *Storia della teologia morale moderna* (Rome: Lateran, 1979) 1.4–5 (moral theology is where the unchanged gospel encounters changing cultures).

38. See Thomas Jefferson, *Notes on the State of Virginia,* ed. William Peden (Chapel Hill: North Carolina, 1955) Query 18.

39. See Roger Williams, *The BLOUDY TENENT, of Persecution, for Cause of Conscience, discussed, in A Conference between TRUTH and PEACE* (1644), reprinted and ed. Samuel L. Caldwell, *The Complete Writings of Roger Williams* (New York: Russell & Russell, 1963) 3.3–4.

40. See Alexis de Tocqueville, *Democracy in America,* trans. Henry Reeve, rev. Francis Bowen (New York: Alfred A. Knopf, 1945) 308–9; John

Courtney Murray, "Governmental Repression of Heresy," *Proceedings of the Catholic Theological Society of America* 3 (Washington: Catholic Theological Society, 1948) 161.

41. Charles de Secondat, Baron de Montesquieu, *L'Esprit des lois,* in his *Oeuvres complètes* (Paris, 1843) 5.309.

42. See David Brian Davis, *The Problem of Slavery in Western Culture* (Ithaca: Cornell University, 1966) 291, 333, 401.

43. Leo XIII, *Catholicae ecclesiae*, November 20, 1890 (*Acta sanctae sedis* 23.257).

44. See John T. Noonan, Jr., *The Scholastic Analysis of Usury* (Cambridge: Harvard University, 1956) 199–201.

45. Owen Chadwick, *Newman* (Oxford: Oxford University, 1983) 47.

46. Newman, *Essay on Development* 1.1.7, p. 38.

18. Catholic Medical Ethics: A Tradition Which Progresses

Raphael Gallagher

This chapter first appeared in James F. Keenan et al., eds., *Catholic Ethicists on HIV/AIDS, Prevention* (New York: Continuum, 2000).

Cardinal Newman advanced a hypothesis to account for the difficulty that the evident development of doctrine posed. Ethical issues pose a different though analogous quandary for the theologian. On the one hand there is the myriad of new questions, strikingly so in the biomedical area; on the other hand there is the unmistakable evidence that moral theology has changed its use and formulation of some principles and rules in response to new questions. If moral theological rules are not permanent, but change, how can they help us respond to new problems? Understanding how the tradition of moral theology has developed could be useful toward an adequate response to a crisis such as AIDS.

Instead of talking about the relationship between existing moral theological rules and AIDS, I will look at another issue: How was the principle of totality used in justifying organ transplants? Of course, to the contemporary reader, the need to justify organ transplants may seem unnecessary. However, at one point in history we needed that justification because it seemed wrong to take the organ that God gave one person and give it to another.

When moral theologians invoked the principle of totality to justify these donations, they were interpreting the principle in a wholly different way. Still, their predecessors had over the centuries also applied the principle of totality in a variety of ways. The principle developed, then, through the moral tradition.[1] But we cannot simply assert that development occurs: The why and how of this development are worth examining to discern what lessons we may learn in the application of other principles to other cases.

WHY A MORAL TRADITION DEVELOPS

The manuals taught that self-mutilation was wrong according to the principle of nonmaleficence. Furthermore, this view was considered to be immutable, since the manuals held that the action was intrinsically evil.[2] The individual's body was defined as a self-contained physical totality of which God alone was sovereign. Initial efforts to widen the application of totality to include the needs of society were rejected precisely on these grounds: One cannot redefine the physical nature of an action.

Theoretical discussion and practical medical advances were to question this presumption. On the level of theory, it was pointed out that there is a difference between charity as an internal end of the agent *(finis operantis)* and the bond of charity as the good of virtue *(bonum virtutis)* that became a legitimate qualifying circumstance. On the practical level, the breakthrough in the possibility of kidney transplants made it possible to envisage that a good done for another was not necessarily the direct result of an evil done to oneself: Medicine made it safe to live a full life on one kidney.

What we see here is the transformative development of a principle (totality) through the recovery of a virtue (charity) into a reformulation of the principle that we can now, perhaps, call totality as solidarity. That this is a case of development, and not abandonment, is evidenced by the retaining of the term *totality,* though obviously with a new meaning. The hesitancy about the possibility of transplants was overcome by the recovery of a more genuinely Christian view of the person in society: An individual is never an end in oneself, and we have an obligation to return something to society in lieu of all we have received from it.

It was the moral prophets of a previous generation who unfroze the presumed immutable principle of bodily totality through a recovery of a more comprehensive vision of charity and social solidarity. The basic insight that enabled the development to occur was an anthropological one: We looked at the person as a more integrated social-spiritual-moral reality. The body was no longer seen as a private physical entity:

It was seen to have a social significance, something that scientific advances helped to make clear.

Acquiring a fuller anthropological vision of the meaning of the body facilitated another development. A questioning of the appropriateness of the particular principles and their application began to occur. The older formulation of the principle of totality is given a presumptive priority: There is a prima facie duty not to harm oneself or to use a person as a means in any situation. But once we enter into what Aristotle called the particulars of a case, we begin to see that we cannot properly understand an action without a consideration of the various contingencies and variabilities.

A moment of interpretive uncertainty occurs: Is the case we are studying really covered by the principle of totality? This interpretive uncertainty forces us to hesitate: This can be the result of either ambiguity (is this really an act of self-mutilation?) or conflict (the duty of self-preservation versus the duty of helping another person in greater need). What happens is that a more correct specification of the action in question enables us to ask whether the prima facie presumption in favor of a particular principle holds up in view of the doubts raised by new cases and new evidence. In the issue of transplants it clearly did not: Development occurs in that an older formulation of a principle is found to be not applicable in a particular case. This change in the application of the principle of totality is an aspect of the underlying anthropological shift that I noted. Once totality is understood in terms of the spiritual-moral person, rather than in those of the merely physical body, it is obvious that the application of the principle will change.

These reasons for development are all aspects of the fact that moral theology includes the art of practical deliberation. There is, consequently, an ongoing need to interpret and decipher what is occurring in changing circumstances.[3] It is rarely immediately obvious what virtue requires: integrity and character. Centrally important as they are for the moral life, they do not yield automatic solutions to specific problems. The moral theologian must incorporate the skill of practical hesitancy into a theological method: Hesitancy implies doubt; doubt implies uncertainty; and uncertainty implies the possibility of development. This possibility of development is, for some, bewildering because it seems to imply that right and wrong changes depending on the decade we live in. The theoretic explanation of the reason for moral development offered here is more nuanced: What develops is the insight into the anthropological value that is presumed in the principle. Quite simply, when the theory of a particular principle is tested in practice, it can become clear that the formal application of the principle would, in fact, undercut the presumed anthropological value.

In the development of the principle of totality what happened was that the anthropological meaning of the principle was expanded. The principle was not abandoned, tempting as that option must have seemed to some. With the expanded anthropological horizon, something new became clear: The principle of totality could be seen to be of benefit to the donor as well as to the recipient. The benefit to the recipient was always clear, but it is only when we work with a wider anthropology that we can see that the donor is also a beneficiary. Totality is, thus, not abandoned; it develops a new meaning on the basis of an anthropological insight.

A useful analogy is St. Thomas's discussion of theft: The principle "do not steal" is not applicable in certain circumstances in which the protections that normally surround property no longer apply because certain normally presumed conditions are lacking. Once we accept the need for practical deliberation as an aspect of moral theology, it seems logically imperative to posit the possibility of development, particularly when we consider that what we are deliberating about is the anthropological meaning of the human.

I believe the above reasons for moral development can be seen as operative in the period between the end of World War II and the opening of Vatican II. Organ transplants were generally forbidden at the beginning of this period, given that they were judged to be a direct mutilation of one's physical body. A first move in the direction of development happened when it was suggested that mutilation was not covered by the principle of double effect (thus removing the problem of "direct" mutilation) but, rather, by the principle of totality. This is not a view held by all, but I suggest it is a tenable position on the basis that the principle of totality is an aspect of anthropology while the principle of double effect is an aspect of the practical application of a principle. Largely due to a pioneering thesis by B. Cunningham, it was increasingly accepted that the totality referred to was not simply one's own physical body but the mystical body of Christ.[4] As the possible justification for transplants was thus established, medical progress began to convince moralists that the appropriate principle to invoke was, indeed, totality but no longer understood in a restrictive physical sense. It was not that something was "wrong" in 1945 and "right" in 1962, *tout court.*

In the light of the arguments advanced above, the reasons for development are coherent rather than random in that there is a gradual discovery of an anthropological insight. A principle develops in the light of and in response to the questions that are put to it by new cases. The principle of totality is an excellent example: The new cases raised the basic anthropological question of what it means to be human. Development occurs, therefore, through a process of differentiation and distinction, and this, of a fundamental kind. The insight that the body is a social organism rather than a self-referring physical entity was the catalyst for developing the principle of totality. A new anthropological horizon of meaning became possible.

HOW A MORAL TRADITION DEVELOPS

Understanding why a tradition develops leads to a second question for the theologian: How is this development expressed and articulated?

The use of distinctions with a view to greater clarity suggests itself as the first step in how moral theology has developed its principles and rules.[5] Take the older and, for the manuals, standard definition of mutilation: the destruction of some part or the suppression of some function of the body. The ambiguity of this definition was exposed once theologians saw that the definition did not distinguish between sterilizing and nonsterilizing mutilations, a critical distinction for the manual tradition. Further, the view that mutilation was intrinsically evil was undermined by the observation that in some cases mutilation was both justifiable and licit.

It is possible for a tradition to find a coherent way of development by using distinctions in order to understand the total picture. True, moral theology has too often used distinctions to obfuscate and confuse. This need not necessarily be so. A carefully made distinction helps to maintain a dialectic between what we understand a principle to be and what our experience of reality is telling us. From this dialectic emerges a greater clarity, precisely because of the proper distinction, and from the emergent clarity it is possible to develop one's theory.

Using distinctions in a discerning way not only develops the tradition in terms of accurate formulation. There is the further benefit of indicating which principle one should use in which case. Mutilation, once covered by moral theologians under the rubric of the double-effect theory, was later treated under the principle of totality, in its various formulations. Transplants opened the possibility of competing principles: the good of one's own body versus the good of humanity in a more general sense. Unless one accepted the positive value of distinguishing, precisely in order to clarify and unify, moral theology would have remained frozen, unable to distinguish between a physicalist understanding of totality and one that was more anthropologically inclusive of the spiritual and social dimensions of the human.

Given the importance of magisterial statements in the tradition of moral theology, it is not surprising that the interpretation of such texts gives a further clue as to how tradition develops. Earlier in this century, most moralists seemed to agree that the principle of (physical) totality was the only principle applicable in instances of bodily mutilation. In defense of this position it became standard to quote a classic text of Pius XI in *Casti Connubii,* which upheld that the good of a part was always subordinate to the good of the whole.[6] Once theologians began to examine the historical context of the philosophical attitudes that the pope was attacking, it became clearer that such a restrictive interpretation of the magisterial text was not necessarily consonant with the papal intention. This indicated that, in using magisterial statements, a theologian should not merely repeat the verbal text but, crucially, should seek the intention of the text within the context in which it was written. Textual criticism, in this sense, was a determining factor in a development to which we have already alluded: the move away from a physicalist understanding of totality to seeing it as totality interpreted through charity-solidarity.[7] It was this development of the principle that allowed for the resolution of the problem of transplants.

How a tradition develops has, in the above three modes, been illustrated in what might seem like marginal details: distinctions, clarifications, and textual criticism. Underlying these is one central issue: Once the basic anthropological reference-schema is changed, there is an inevitability in how principles and rules develop.[8] I will use a series of assertions, followed by a qualification, to illustrate this. The body is a value but not the highest value; God is sovereign of life, but humans have a responsibility of stewardship; totality is an important principle, but wholeness is a better indicator of the human vocation. These three positions indicate important anthropological shifts that have occurred within moral theology. The first part of the anthropological assertion is never denied; however, the qualifying clause in each case has implications for moral principles. Mutilation, to take a precise example, would be judged in a different way depending on whether one followed the first part of the above assertions or whether one accepted the qualifying clause. The acceptance of the qualifications is of profound anthropological consequence. It is my belief that it is at this point we can best see how the tradition has developed in recent decades.

In an anthropological horizon of physical bodily integrity, obligations to the self, and a biocentric view of life, transplants are defined in a restrictive way, as in the moral manuals. In an anthropological horizon of social harmony, responsibilities toward the good of society, and a transcendental view of the human destiny, transplants are judged quite differently. The anthropological horizon changes: A transplant can be a gift that transforms our self-understanding and transforms a role-construction of society into a mutually supportive community. Transplants can become, in this changed definition of anthropological responsibility, a meritorious Christian gesture.

Looking over the developments within moral theology and its use of principles with regard to mutilation and transplants, I think a four-stage pattern is discernible. At first the moral tradition is presumed to be immutable, and there is nothing to do but apply the unchangeable principle and rule. In a second moment, more obvious in the early part of this century, it is the physicalist interpretation of natural law that is the stabilizing reference point. By mid-century, these first two stages are subsumed into a voluntarist (and, at times, literalist) interpretation of magisterial texts. In a fourth moment, the central reference point becomes the spiritual-social consideration of the human person in relation to others and with God.

No doubt, this general schema may appear too neat and simple. I use it not to defend the schema in detail but to indicate how a change within the dominant horizon of anthropological reference is a decisive catalyst in moral development. It is important to note how the change in anthropological emphasis refers back to the earlier arguments. Moral theology, using practical discernment, often has to move into new or strange territory. This is relatively straightforward when there is a simple development of case studies within a stable paradigm. It becomes more problematic when the major reference points are changed, as in the anthropological shift just noted. Development then becomes more a questioning of presumed positions than a positive addition of new formulations; these come later.[9]

Within the issues under consideration here, one can note a questioning of underlying ideas (the definition of the body, the meaning of human nature, and the like) that tries to ensure that any moral principles used correspond to the best possible formulation of the relevant facts and eschew any false use of ideologies. How development occurs is, thus, not just through positive additions and clarifications; the negative elimination of outdated ideas has also been a crucial factor, even if the full fruits of this stage of development are yet to be reaped. The fact, for instance, that there may not be consensus on a definition of "the person adequately considered" does not mean that we have to revert to older biological formulas. An anthropological benchmark has been struck, and it too will be filled out in time by the use of distinctions and clarifications.

I have noted a number of ways how a moral tradition develops: greater clarity though more precise distinctions; a more accurate choice of the appropriate principle; the use of proper norms for textual interpretation; changes within the horizon of interpretive reference; and a *via negativa* elimination of ideas that obfuscate proper moral classification.[10] In each of these ways, one can note a slighter or greater development of the tradition. We now turn to the more important consideration: Can the why and how of development indicate any signposts or parameters for further development?

SIGNPOSTS FOR THE FUTURE

A basic premise of this chapter is that moral theology is formed within a tradition. The arguments presented above suggest that it is a tradition that can develop in a coherent way. By coherence I do not wish to imply that every step is at once logically clear; this need not necessarily be so. The coherence is connected with the direction of moral development. This always seeks a more accurate understanding of the anthropological basis of any principle. Given this sense of coherence, I believe we can establish three processes that may apply to future development, and from these we can formulate three further likely inferences as to how that development is likely to take shape.

It is evident, firstly, that development has occurred in overlapping stages: The point at which one formulation of a principle ends and another begins is never exactly definable. The principle of totality was, for instance, variously defined in terms of physicalist, ecclesiastically positivist, and personalist categories. I am referring here to the statement of the principle as a normative theory rather than entering the separate question of metaethical verification. Though the stages overlap, there is no doubt that, by the end of the process, the first stage of the formulation of the principle had been superseded. Future development is likely to follow this same stage-by-stage pattern of redimensioning the formulation of principles.

Secondly, the evidence shows that the development of a principle includes residual elements of the previous definition (or formulation) of the principle. With regard to transplants, the principle of nonmaleficence ("do no harm") was, with time, seen to be less important than the principle of beneficence ("do good to others"). But the consensus around the principle of beneficence did not cancel crucial residual elements of the principle of nonmaleficence: For instance, mentally incompetent persons would be ruled out as donor-candidates because of an inability to give free consent. This process will apply to future development: The present formulation of a principle can be said to have a prima facie claim if compelling reasons or conflicting cases force us to reconsider the formulation.

In this reconsideration, the evidence shows that moral theology attempts to preserve, at least in a shadow form, values that are considered enduring. The benefit to the donor, which is one of the gains of the developed principle of totality as solidarity, does not cancel the enduring benefit to the recipient, which clearly remains a constant factor.

The third process that seems incontrovertible in the light of the evidence studied is that the development of moral principles involves a process of theological reception. Development is slow, and occasionally contorted. One could argue that the justification of transplants is "self-evident." Why was moral theology so tardy in responding? My analysis would suggest that the careful distinctions and clarification of cases were not refusals to be realistic. The issues at stake are most serious, involving the definition of life, relationships in society, and the future direction of humanity. The way moral theology tends to develop does not block progress but allows time and space for the reception of new insights to be tested in a variety of appropriate ways. This infuriates many people, of course, but I judge that this painstaking process of reception is the more normal route of theological development.[11]

From the above I believe we can draw three likely inferences for future developments: First, it is more likely that moral principles will function as a hermeneutic of interpretation rather than as a probabilist theory of reflex principles. This will happen not just because of the (happy) demise of the casuistry of the manuals, but more importantly, because of interpretive uncertainties with regard to new evidence and the necessity of deciphering the practical meaning of obligation in unforeseen circumstances. Principles will remain, but their interpretive function will be different.

Linked to this is a second inference. Moral theology is concerned with all that really matters in life, and what matters most is the need for personal survival in a crisis of suffering. Principles will function, therefore, as a mode of deciphering what is ultimately important for the person in this dilemma of pain and distress. It was more usual for principles to function in the broadest sense, as a method of meaning-making in the face of life's inevitable moral dilemmas. I am impressed by the evidence, particularly from studies in medical anthropology, that the urgent current quest is not the search for meaning (some forms of suffering seem utterly meaningless) but the need for personal survival.[12] If this is true, it would imply that principles serve this latter need rather than the former search.

The third inference is a placing of the first two in the context of faith, and more specifically, of theodicy. The heart of moral theology is neither the principle nor its function, new or old. Moral theology's first question is how, in this experience, God is revealed to us. Too often the theodicy question was absent from moral theology.[13] This happened because of presumptions about the centrality of sin and a certainty that principles clearly reflected God's will. If our primary sensitivity is to the suffering person(s) we encounter then, I believe, the experience of God will be formulated differently. That this would have consequences for the formulation and application of principles and rules seems obvious.

I have focused on the questions of how and why a moral principle develops. I believe a certain pattern has emerged. Principles seem to function as a way of pausing before perplexity and diversity; they are a sort of plateau on which the moral theologian works out residual hesitations about the implications of any development for the anthropological meaning of the human. The tradition develops because principles, however important, are seen to be at the service of the fuller truth that always lies ahead. Precisely because it is a tradition and not an abstract theory, moral theology can develop to meet new challenges along the lines indicated above.[14] If my central analysis is correct—namely, that the principle of totality developed because of an insight into anthropology—the application to the crisis of AIDS seems almost too banal to mention. It is humanity that has AIDS and not simply an isolated person. Any moral principle that tries to deal with whatever aspect of AIDS simply by referring to the past applications of the principle will fail the test for development which my analysis indicates. It was the anthropological question of what life means (a physical entity or a social organism) that was determinative in the development of the principle of totality. AIDS is forcing us to ask the question: How can human life survive now? That it can and will, I have no doubt. But those of us who use moral principles in dealing with AIDS must pause and hesitate, precisely because of the human dimension of AIDS. The epidemic raises the question of the *humanum* on every level: the behavioral choices that people make, the political options implicit in medical programs, the religious inferences in attributing blame. If it was a new anthropological insight that enabled the principle of totality to develop into its current understanding, we may be surprised at how placing the AIDS crisis in its wider anthropological context may enable a development of some principles that, at first sight, seem immutable. What is at stake is the quality of human survival. That should make any theologian pause for thought in the use of principles and in the discernment of their possible development.

Notes

1. A wider historical perspective can be found in Thomas R. Kopfensteiner, *Paradigms and Hermeneutics: The Essential Tension between Person and Nature in the Principle of Totality*, *dissertatio ad doctoratum* (Rome: Gregorian University, 1988).

2. A standard presentation is available in Henry Davis, *Moral and Pastoral Theology* (London: Sheed and Ward, 1949), 2:141–99.

3. The issues are well presented by Richard Miller, *Casuistry and Modern Ethics* (Chicago: University of Chicago Press, 1996), 17–27, 168–72.

4. B. Cunningham, *The Morality of Organic Transplantation* (Washington, D.C.: Catholic University of America Press, 1944).

5. This paragraph owes much to the insightful article of John Mahoney, "The Challenge of Moral Distinctions," *Theological Studies* 53 (1992): 663–82.

6. Encyclical Letter *Casti Connubii, AAS* 22 (1930), at 565.

7. A notable early contribution on this point was that of Gerald Kelly, "The Morality of Mutilation: Toward a Revision of the Treatise," *Theological Studies* 17 (1956): 322–44.

8. These arguments are treated at greater length by Antonio Autiero, "Quale obbligo c'è di donare un organo?" in *La Questione dei Trapianti: tra Etica, Diritto, Economia*, ed. S. Fagiuoli (Milan, 1997), 139–49.

9. Though not sharing all his conclusions, I am indebted to the contribution of John T. Noonan, "Development in Moral Doctrine," *The Context of Casuistry*, ed. James Keenan and Thomas Shannon (Washington, D.C.: Georgetown University Press, 1995), 188–204.

10. As background material to these arguments I suggest a rereading of some articles that have become standard reference points: G. Kelly, "Pope Pius XII and the Principle of Totality," *Theological Studies* 16 (1955): 373–96; M. Nolan, "The Positive Doctrine of Pius XII on the Principle of Totality," *Augustinianum* 3 (1963): 28–44, and 4 (1964): 537–59; Augustine Regan, "The Basic Morality of Organic Transplants between Living Humans," *Studia Moralia* 3 (1965): 320–61 and "Man's Administration of his Bodily Life and Members: The Principle of Totality and Organic Transplants between Living Donors," *Studia Moralia* 5 (1967): 179–200.

11. That patient and closely argued debate leads to a good quality of development is implicit in the study of David Kelly, *The Emergence of Roman Catholic Medical Ethics in North America* (New York: Mellen Press, 1979).

12. For an introduction to the issues, a useful article is A. Kleinman, "'Everything That Really Matters': Social Suffering, Subjectivity, and the Re-Making of Human Experience in a Disordering World," *Harvard Theological Review* 90 (1997): 315–25.

13. Strong arguments for its inclusion can be found in J. B. Metz, "God and the Evil of the World," *Concilium* 5 (1997): 3–8.

14. Allen Verhey and Stephen E. Lammers, ed., *Theological Voices in Medical Ethics* (Grand Rapids, Mich.: William B. Eerdmans, 1993) is a useful overview of how traditions develop in medical ethics.

19. Progress in the Moral Tradition

Marciano Vidal

This chapter first appeared in James F. Keenan et al., eds., *Catholic Ethicists on HIV/AIDS Prevention* (New York: Continuum, 2000).

In the following pages, I attempt to analyze the meaning of tradition in the field of moral theology. More precisely, I am concerned with developing the criteria that govern progress within the Christian moral tradition. This question bears great epistemological import, since together with scripture and the magisterium, tradition constitutes one of the proper theological "loci."[1]

"Human reason needs to be added to these three strictly theological places." According to what John Paul II has recently reminded us once again in his encyclical *Fides et Ratio,*[2] human reason is the necessary mediation to live and express the meaning of faith. This articulation between the specifically theological places and human reason was happily formulated by Vatican II when it said that the moral problems of our times need to be analyzed "in the light of the gospel and human experience."[3] In this way, human mediation is not reduced to "reason," but rather assumes the full meaning of "human experience." Moreover, the theological places obtain unity when they are understood as the "gospel." Even more, the copula "and" stresses the relation between the gospel and human experience. This expression leads us to see the connection as neither an incoherent juxtaposition nor as a confusion nor as a sterile copulative.

I have recalled this basic structure of moral-theological epistemology in order to place tradition within this framework and to emphasize the importance that tradition has in constituting a coherent ethical-theological discourse. One needs to say, however, that this question, generally acknowledged by everyone as of great importance, has been hardly studied.[4]

I have two goals. First, I mean to offer a description of the state of the question, confirmed in magisterial statements. Second, I give a number of systematic perspectives over two aspects of progress in moral tradition: the forms of development in the Christian moral tradition and some advances achieved during the last few decades in the field of Catholic ethics.

Lacking enough specific theological reflection on the development of tradition in the field of Christian ethics, we need to turn to the texts of the magisterium if we want to know the state of the question, naturally, still in an embryonic or basic stage. I limit my references to three documents of church teachings: the Constitution *Dei Verbum* from Vatican Council II (1965), and John Paul II's encyclicals *Veritatis Splendor* (1993) and *Centesimus Annus* (1991).

DEI VERBUM (DV)

To my knowledge, there is no study analyzing the references that *DV* made to the question of progress in tradition and Christian ethics. I consider, however, that turning to this document is of great interest and importance if we want to put the question about the possibility and form of moral development within the tradition of the church correctly. I point to those perspectives that I consider most decisive and pertinent.

The Meaning of Tradition

Undoubtedly, the most decisive orientation of *DV* consisted in referring to divine revelation in personalist[5] categories of communication.[6] These categories do not originate from the "truth" of God but from God's "wisdom and goodness."[7] These categories seem to invite humans into the trinitarian dynamism and so "to become sharers in the divine nature."[8] Making use of the same expression adopted by the Council of Trent, Vatican II calls divine revelation "gospel."[9] Such a category denotes a rich scriptural flavor and allows for ecumenical convergence.

Broadly understood here as divine revelation, the gospel is "source of all saving truth and moral discipline." Vatican II borrowed this formulation from Trent.[10] Thus, Christian ethics is implicated by faith in general terms. This implication with different nuances often appears underlined in recent documents of the magisterium.[11]

Vatican II's concern with tradition was, before anything else, to deepen and express its relationship with scripture anew.[12] It also offered valuable perspectives to understand its nature and its functionality.[13]

The council text does not use the word *tradition* consistently.[14] One can distinguish between apostolic or constitutive tradition (the sacred tradition) and postapostolic or church tradition (continuing tradition). The apostolic tradition, which includes the sacred scriptures, "comprises everything that serves to make the people of God live their lives in *holiness and to increase their faith*."[15] I emphasize these words to highlight the moral content of the apostolic tradition.[16] As opposed to the scriptures, this moral content of the tradition lacks a particular organ of verification.[17] It is the entire life of the church that manifests the "moral content of the apostolic tradition." "In this way the church, in her doctrine, life and worship, perpetuates and transmits to every generation all that she herself is, all that she believes."[18]

The riches of the apostolic tradition "are poured out in the practice and life of the church, in her belief and her prayer." That tradition becomes a living presence through the conversation of the church, spouse of the Trinity. The text attributes to the Holy Spirit the fact that "the living voice of the gospel rings out in the church."[19] Constituted as such, the tradition appears to convey a richer theological meaning (trinitarian, ecclesiastical, and eschatological) than the cold and miserly one given by the neoscholastic epistemology: "place of probation."[20] Although the council did not teach in detail and with precision what is the subject of the tradition,[21] it clearly stated that the entire church, infallibly and in communion, lives and fleshes out the "living voice of the gospel."[22] The "great tradition" is constituted, then, through the life of the entire church; the smaller "traditions" obtain their meaning by referring themselves to this greater tradition.[23]

The Dynamic Character of Tradition

In this theological context, Vatican II introduces the dynamic character of tradition. Vatican II explicitly refers to Vatican I at this point and labors within the framework provided by the previous council. Vatican II makes the next general statement: "The tradition that comes from the apostles makes progress in the church, with the help of the Holy Spirit." We would want to know the concrete meanings of this important statement. The council seems to limit "growth" to the "insight into the realities and words that are being passed on." Such comprehensive growth takes place through the next passages: "through the contemplation (of the words and the institutions transmitted) and the study by believers who ponder these things in their hearts (see Luke 2:1–51). It comes from the intimate sense of spiritual realities which they experience. And it comes from the preaching of those who have received, along with their right to succession in the episcopate, the sure charism of truth."[24]

Although Vatican II did not dwell on it, there is no doubt that the council stressed the dynamic character of the forms and passages of progress within the church tradition: "The church is always advancing toward the plenitude of divine truth, until eventually the words of God are fulfilled in her"; "the Holy Spirit…leads believers to the full truth."[25] Such a dynamic understanding of the church tradition cannot be underestimated.[26] On the contrary, the role of creativity in tradition needs to be continuously studied, along the lines chosen by Avery Dulles or in some similar way.[27] The spirit and the letter of the Constitution *Dei Verbum* direct us toward a dynamic understanding of tradition—that is, to a living tradition.

VERITATIS SPLENDOR (VS)

John Paul II's encyclical *VS* (1993) is the recent document of the church that most powerfully shows both the normative character that tradition has in the field of ethics and its dynamic and, therefore, progressive structure. The document, however, does not provide an elaborate development of its statements.[28]

Normative Character of Tradition in Ethics

VS 27 shows in an explicit way the normative character that tradition bears in the field of ethics. This paragraph presupposes the teaching of Vatican II on the ecclesiastical sphere within which divine revelation is transmitted: "In this way the church, in her doctrine, life and worship, perpetuates and transmits to every generation all that she herself is, all that she believes."[29] Apart from this general statement, it underlines two aspects:

First, 27 emphasizes the continuity of the "ecclesiastical tradition" in relation to the "apostolic tradition." "Promoting and preserving the faith and the moral life is the task entrusted by Jesus to the apostles (see Matt 28:19–20), a task which continues in the ministry of their successors." Secondly, it insists on the signs of the ecclesiastical tradition as witnessed by the teaching of the fathers, the lives of the saints, the church's liturgy, and the teaching of the magisterium.

Adopting an expression already used by the *Catechism of the Catholic Church* (no. 83), it locates this doctrine as belonging to the "great tradition." *VS* 27 applies this very doctrine to the field of ethics: "By this same tradition Christians receive 'the living voice of the gospel,' as the faithful expression of God's wisdom and will. Within tradition, the authentic interpretation of the Lord's law develops with the help of the Holy Spirit. The same Holy Spirit present at the origin of the revelation of Jesus' commandments and teachings guarantees that they will be reverently preserved, faithfully expounded and correctly applied in different times and places."

Therefore, the encyclical *VS* comes to underline a statement usually assumed in the ethical-theological etymology: the normative character of tradition. Church ethics is "a moral teaching based upon Sacred Scripture and the living tradition of the church."[30]

"Dynamic" Interpretation of Tradition

VS does not understand tradition as a static number of truths handed down from one generation into the next. On the contrary, it means tradition as a dynamic or "living" reality. The latter adjective usually accompanies the substantive tradition. The expression "living tradition" arose in the context of nineteenth-century Catholic romanticism, more precisely in the theology of Johann Adam Möhler, and then passed into the Roman school of theology, influencing Yves Congar's reflection on tradition and traditions in particular.[31] Currently, it is a formulation that is regularly repeated in magisterial documents.[32]

Apart from the expression "living tradition," *VS* uses other verbal phrases denoting dynamism and emphasizing the dynamic character of the tradition. In no. 27 the following details appear: "This tradition, which comes from the apostles, progresses in the church"; "Within tradition, the authentic interpretation of the Lord's law develops, with the help of the Holy Spirit."

At the same time, we need not forget that the living, or dynamic, character of the ecclesiastical tradition does not point to an increase of divine revelation, since revelation was closed at the end of the apostolic age.[33]

"Doctrinal Development" within the Tradition

VS goes one step farther. It not only receives and develops the teaching of *DV* on the dynamic character of tradition, but from such a general comprehension, it deduces an important concrete application for epistemology and for the discourse of moral theology. For the first time in a church document, the principle of "doctrinal development" applied to the truths of faith is carried up to the field of ethics. Such a clear formulation of this application will not be found even in previous academic expositions of moral theology.

VS 28 formulates the principle, places it in its context, and explains how it operates. The formulation of the principle is clear: The church "has achieved a *doctrinal development* analogous to that which has taken place in the realm of the truths of faith." This principle retrieves its meaning from the context of faithfulness to the received word of God: "The church has faithfully preserved what the word of God teaches, not only about truths which should be believed but also about moral action." Here the principle is applied to three references: (1) The subject of doctrinal development is the "church assisted by the Holy Spirit." (2) The search for "all the truth (see John 16:13)," which becomes the final goal, rules over this dynamism. (3) According to the guideline given by *Gaudium et Spes,* 22, and so often quoted by John Paul II, the way to realize the evolving process is "to illuminate the mystery of the human" by scrutinizing "the mystery of the Word made flesh."

As will be noted, *VS*'s exposition on the principle of doctrinal development in the field of Christian ethics is remarkably original and doctrinally rich. Nevertheless, some decisive questions remain open to further analysis. I refer to two of them: The first one concerns the explanation of doctrinal development in a general sense, "within the limits of the truths of faith." The second one deals with the meaning of the adjective "analogous" (*similis* in the Latin original) when applied to development within the moral field: What is the distinctive characteristic of moral development when compared with development in the field of the truths of faith? *VS* does not answer these questions, leaving them open for theological reflection.

In this regard, the special contribution of *VS* is its reference in paragraph 4 to the doctrinal development of the papal magisterium: "At all times, but particularly in the last two centuries, the popes, whether individually or together with the college of bishops, have developed and proposed a moral teaching regarding the many different spheres of human life." It notes the positive function of doctrinal development for different areas of human life: "With the guarantee of assistance from the Spirit of truth, they [the popes] have contributed to a better understanding of moral demands in the areas of human sexuality, the family, and social, economic and political life." It formulates a general principle, referring to previous pronouncements by Pius XII and John XXIII: "In the tradition of the church and in the history of humanity, their teaching represents a constant deepening of knowledge with regard to morality."

The last sentence clearly shows the newness of *VS*'s contribution to the "development of doctrine" in the moral field: "In the tradition of the church" and in relation to "the history of humanity," "a constant deepening" takes place with regard to all that implies "moral knowledge." It is up to the theological reflection to explain, harmonize, and to make more concrete this doctrine.

CENTESIMUS ANNUS (CA)

One may detect some creative air in the arrangement of *CA*. In no. 3, I spot the most explicit references, that I know of, by the magisterium to "look to the future" and to read the tradition of the church with a prospective and creative hermeneutics. The pope writes: "I invite you to look to the future," when we glimpse the third millennium of the Christian era, so filled with uncertainties, but also with promises that together appeal to our imagination and creativity, and reawaken our responsibility.

It is in this context of invitation to the creative and responsible imagination that the pope asks for the unveiling of the "treasure of the church's tradition," which he says is "always living and always vital." He exposes the sense of tradition by turning to the gospel image of the "scribe who has been trained for the Kingdom of Heaven," whom the Lord compares to "a householder who brings out of his treasure what is new and what is old" (Matt 13:52). The pope does not hesitate to apply this image to the tradition of the church: this "treasure is the great out-pouring of the church's tradition, which contains 'what is old'— received and passed on from the very beginning—and which enables us to interpret the 'new things' in the midst of which the life of the church and the world unfolds." The discovered new things are "incorporated into tradition" and, thus, "they become old," "enriching both tradition and the life of faith."

I want to finish my description of the state of things with this excerpt because, in my opinion, it provides us with the spirit in which we should analyze the unsettled questions on moral progress in tradition. In the life of the church, particularly in periods like ours, "so filled with (serious) uncertainties but also (hopeful) with promises," we need to understand the tradition from a creative fidelity approach, like the scribe "who knows to communicate the new and the old."

SYSTEMATIC PERSPECTIVES: PLANNING

In light of the magisterium, I will try to offer two sets of system-atic perspectives about moral progress in the Christian tradition. I mean, more specifically, the ways or forms through which this progress may happen and the spheres in which, as a matter of fact, moral advance has taken place.

John T. Noonan, Jr., has analyzed development in Catholic moral doctrine focusing on four topics: usury, marriage (dissolution of the bond), slavery, and religious freedom. Only the last one, and to some extent the second, refer to recent situations. In order to explain evolution in moral doctrine, Noonan basically makes use of the criteria proposed by John Newman for the development of dogmatic questions.[34] He summarizes these criteria: the deeper knowledge of Christ and the meaning of human experience.[35]

For my part, I take into account Noonan's reflections, but I direct my own thoughts along complementary ways. I address recent changes, not failing to acknowledge, however, the importance of analyzing other changes that happened in the history of moral theology. Moreover, I consider those changes insofar as they bear positive progress in moral theology. Finally, I attempt to systematize those factors (or ways or forms) conditioning the advance of Catholic moral tradition.

ADVANCES IN CATHOLIC MORAL THEOLOGY

I do not intend to show all the changes and advances achieved in moral theology, which are impossible to state in this essay. I will limit my considerations to some topological examples, framed most recently by the church. Yet I present the formulation of these changes from the documents of the ecclesiastical magisterium. Thus, we will be assured that we are dealing with moral progress in the Christian tradition.

Advances in Social Ethics

It is obvious that in this field of moral theology, many advances have been achieved. I point to the most outstanding ones in the last decades:

- Agreeing with Noonan, I note first the awareness and strengthening of the *rights to religious freedom and freedom of conscience,* a "revolutionary" advance of Vatican II.[36]
- The *moral reappraisal of war:* We have shifted from the "just war" theory to "undertake a completely fresh reappraisal of war,"[37] to finally the point of saying no to war.[38]
- The formulation of *solidarity* as a "new virtue"[39] and a "new principle"[40] of social life.[41]
- The acceptance of the ethical-juridical category *human rights:* After the reticence specific to the eighteenth, nineteenth, and the first half of

the twentieth centuries, the encyclical *Pacem in terris* marked the change by stating that "the explicit acknowledgment of human rights" constitutes "the fundamental principle of work for man's welfare"[42] and "an authentic and solid foundation" of democracy.[43]

- The magisterium has introduced such nuances into the right to *private property* that one can talk about a "substantive variation" in its understanding today.[44]
- The *preferential option for the poor*[45] has been affirmed as a moral principle that "far from being a sign of particularism or sectarianism, manifests the universality of the church's being and mission,"[46] bearing noteworthy repercussions for understanding and formulating the "social responsibilities" of the Christian.[47]

Advances in Personal Ethics

Those advances that have taken place in the understanding of the person, the value of human life, and of corporal and sexual dimensions pertain to this section. These changes bear considerable influence when focusing on moral problems pertaining to bioethics and sexual ethics. I note some of them:

- In many commentators' opinion there is a progress in the *comprehension* of the person in *Gaudium et Spes,* and particularly in its reference to the "nature of the human person" (no. 51), where a "wholistic" comprehension of each human being is offered to us.
- The value of human life has gained depth, above all in John Paul II's magisterium,[48] so that one can talk about an authentic "progress" in Catholic moral theory on this value; especially in the morality of abortion, euthanasia, capital punishment, and so forth.[49]
- The understanding of the *corporal dimension* of the human condition has moved beyond the staggering biologist (or physicalist) consideration to a distinctive personalist comprehension.[50]
- *Human sexuality* is placed today within the framework of an integral vision of the person.[51]

Advances in Fundamental Ethics

Catholic moral theory has also achieved many advances in this field. I note only three:

- Chapter 5 of *Lumen Gentium* states that the *universal call to holiness* implies an extensive development in our understanding of Christian ethics.[52] This is no longer a "morality of sins" but the pursuit of the "exalted vocation of the faithful in Christ."[53]
- The limits of the morality "of acts" have been overcome by accepting the complementary category of *fundamental choice,* which "ultimately defines the moral condition of a person,"[54] although it should not be separated from the "concrete choices."[55]
- The sin of *structure*[56] or structural sin is an advance in the formulations of objective and subjective culpabilities.[57]

If we realize that these thirteen topics belong to the Vatican II era, it can be stated that in the short period of the last thirty to forty years a spectacular progress has happened in Catholic moral theory, whose implications and consequences have not been fully developed.

Factors of Moral Progress

In a schematic fashion, I point now to the factors working toward moral progress in Christian tradition. These factors are, at the same time, the ways through which the developing dynamism happens; they may be considered also as the forms adopted by moral development.

Noonan's advice is valuable: Progress in moral theory does not depend on a singular factor but rather comes from a "complex constellation of elements."[58] Thus, the following factors should not be understood separately but as building a meaningful whole:

- The most profound understanding of the mystery of Christ and its meaning to explain and orient the mystery of the human person is, without doubt, the principal and omnipresent factor in all moral advances in the Christian tradition.[59] Vatican II formulated the principle governing progress in the understanding and orientation of the human condition: "It is only in the mystery of the Word made flesh that the mystery of humanity truly becomes clear."[60] Christian ethics is nothing but a "patterned" anthropology whose original reference is Christ; this is the reason why all progress in Christian moral theory implies a more profound knowledge of the incarnate Word.

- The urgency to answer the questions posed by *historical reality* in a Christian manner constitutes the other major factor that, indissolubly bound to the ever-deeper knowledge of the mystery of Christ, prompts moral progress in the Christian tradition. Vatican II proposed a new hermeneutical category: "the signs of the times," that the church has to "read" and "interpret" in the light of the gospel.[61] All "historical newness" carries as well a "challenge" to the Christian conscience. The answer to that challenge has to be born from a "re-creation" of the data of the tradition to combine "the old things" and "the new things," according to the suggestive interpretation that John Paul II made of Matthew 13:52.[62]

- The rich and diverse *human experience,* the gift of God the creator, opens new ways to the truth that are fully revealed in Christ and inherited *(depositum)* by the church. "The church is not unaware of how much it has profited from the history and development of mankind. It profits from the experience of past ages, from the progress of the sciences, and from the riches hidden in various cultures, through which greater light is thrown on the nature of man and new avenues to truth are opened up."[63] This "vital exchange between the church and different cultures"[64] has an especially meaningful function in the field of ethics.

- The *scientific-technical advances* discover new possibilities in human realities. They present new ethical questions postulating answers that are also new within the Christian tradition. Christians have "to incorporate the findings of new sciences and teachings and the understanding of the most recent discoveries with Christian morality and thought."[65] This integration requires putting into practice a "creative fidelity," for which tradition is not an obstacle but a sphere of security and guarantee.

Moral theory, letting itself be questioned by all the factors that we have just seen, needs to advance. This is what John Paul II has noted in Catholic ethical reflection carried out in accordance with the spirit of Vatican II. "The work of many theologians who found support in the council's encouragement" has allowed that Christian truths be today "offered in a form better suited to the sensitivities and questions of our contemporaries."[66] This new presentation does not go against tradition, since "there is a difference between the deposit of the truths of faith and the manner in which they are expressed, keeping the same meaning and the same judgment."[67]

The goal of those advances in moral theory that happen in the Christian tradition is that "thus the knowledge of God will be made better known *(penitus percipi);* the preaching of the gospel will be rendered more intelligible to man's mind *(melius intelligi),* and will appear more relevant *(aptius proponi)* to his situation."[68] Therefore, while "listening to and distinguishing the many voices of our times and to interpret them in the light of the divine word,"[69] theologians know that they remain creatively faithful to Christian tradition.

Notes

1. *Dei Verbum,* 10.
2. *Fides et Ratio,* 36–48.
3. *Gaudium et Spes,* 46.
4. For two studies on the subject, see Brian Johnstone who analyzes the subject in general terms in "Faithful Action: The Catholic Moral Tradition and *Veritatis Splendor,*" *Studia Moralia* 31 (1993) 283–305. A more concrete study of the changes in usury, marriage, slavery, and religious freedom is in John T. Noonan, Jr.'s, "Development in Moral Doctrine," *Theological Studies* 54 (1993) 662–77.
5. René Latourelle, "La Révélation et sa transmission selon la Constitution *Dei Verbum,*" *Gregorianum* 47 (1966) 5–40.
6. *Dei Verbum,* 2: "By this revelation, then, the invisible God...from the fullness of his love, *addresses* men as his friends, and moves among them, in order to invite and receive them into his own *company*" (stress added).
7. Ibid., "It pleased God, in his *goodness and wisdom,* to reveal himself" (stress added).
8. Ibid., "His will was that men should have access to the Father, through *Christ...*in the *Holy Spirit,* and thus become sharers in the divine nature" (stress added).
9. Ibid., 7
10. Trent, *Tamquam fontem omnis et salutaris veritatis et morum disciplinae* (Denzinger, 1501); Vatican II: *Dei Verbum,* 7.
11. *Gaudium et Spes,* 33; *Veritatis Splendor,* 4, 27, 28, 29, 30.

12. Ibid., 9. On the postconciliar reception of this doctrine, see the study by Achim Buckenmaier, *"Schrift und Tradition" seit dem Vatikan II. Vorgeschichte und Rezeption* (Paderborn: Bonifatius, 1996).

13. Two recent works interpret the teaching of Vatican II on tradition and place it in an historical context: Angel Maria Navarro Lecanda, *"Evangelii traditio." Tradición como Evangelización a la luz de Dei Verbum* I–II (Vitoria-Gasteiz: Eset, 1997), 2 vol.; Jean Georges Boeglin, *La question de la Tradition dans la théologie catholique contemporaine* (Paris: Editions du Cerf, 1998).

14. See César Izquierdo, "La Tradición en Teología Fundamental," *Scripta Theologica* 29 (1997) 397, note 16.

15. *Dei Verbum,* 8.

16. Josef Rupert Geiselmann's opinion is well known. For him everything pertaining to faith is contained at the same time in the scriptures and tradition, whereas the latter contains its own elements pertaining to disciplinary and moral orders, and is not contained in the scriptures [*Sagrada Escritura y Tradición, Historia y alcance de una controversia* (Barcelona: Herder, 1968) 381–82; also "Tradición," *Conceptos Fundamentales de Teología* (Madrid: San Pablo, 1979), second ed., vol. II, 818.] As is well known, the council did not want to solve this theological question.

17. The apostolic tradition "lacks its own organ of transmission and, therefore, it is transmitted via church tradition that includes the magisterium of the bishops, the teaching of the Fathers and theologians, and, to some extent, the sense of the faithful" (Bartomeu Maria Xiberta, *La tradición y su Problemática actual* [Barcelona: Herder, 1964] 32).

18. *Dei Verbum,* 8.

19. Ibid., "Thus, God who spoke in the past, continues *to converse* with the spouse of his beloved Son."

20. On the theology of tradition, see M. Semeraro, "Temi eclesiologici nel capitolo secondo della *'Dei Verbum'*"; Nicola Ciola, ed., *La "Dei Verbum" trent'anni dopo* (Rome: Libreria editrice della Pontificia Università Lateranense, 1995) 123–45.

21. Angel Maria Navarro, *"Evangelii traditio,"* vol. II, 913–17, mentions this silence among the lacunae of *Dei Verbum.*

22. *Dei Verbum,* 10.

23. *Catechism of the Catholic Church,* no. 83. Yves Congar's study in *La Tradition et les traditions,* 2 vol. (Paris: Fayard, 1960), echoes in this distinction between great tradition and traditions.

24. *Dei Verbum,* 8.

25. Ibid.

26. See the open interpretation of this statement by Vicente Gómez Mier, "Sobre tradición y tradiciones de investigación," *La Ciudad de Dios* 209 (1996) 231–70, as opposed to Latourelle's minimalist stand in his article cited above.

27. Avery Dulles, "Tradition and Creativity in Theology," *First Things* 27 (November 1992) 20–27.

28. See Brian V. Johnstone, "Faithful Action," "The theme of Tradition or 'living tradition' has a central place in the encyclical" (283). "However, it does not provide an analysis of what tradition is, or how tradition functions" (284).

29. *Dei Verbum,* 8.

30. *Veritatis Splendor,* 5; it cites *Dei Verbum,* 10.

31. See M. Semetaro, "Temi eclesiologici," 123–45.

32. *Veritatis Splendor,* n. 5 ("Living Tradition of the Church"), n. 27 ("Living Tradition"); *Familiaris consortio,* n. 29 ("living tradition of the ecclesiastical community"); *Centesimus annus,* n. 3 ("the church's tradition…being ever living and vital"); *Donum veritatis,* n. 6 ("Living Tradition of the Church").

33. *Dei Verbum,* 4.

34. See Noonan, "Development," 670–72. Noonan (677) assumes Owen Chadwick's opinion in *Newman* (Oxford: Oxford University Press, 1983) 47, for whom "the idea of development was the most important single idea Newman contributed to the thought of the Christian Church."

35. Noonan, "Development," 672–75.

36. *Dignitatis Humanae,* 2.

37. *Gaudium et Spes,* 80.

38. *Centesimus Annus,* 52.

39. *Sollicitudo Rei Socialis,* 39.

40. *Centesimus Annus,* 10.

41. See its development in Marciano Vidal, *Para comprender la Solidaridad: virtu y principio ético* (Estella: Verbo Divino, 1996).

42. *Redemptor Hominis,* 17.

43. *Centesimus Annus,* 47.

44. *Populorum Progressio,* 23; *Laborem Exercens,* 14; *Sollicitudo Rei Socialis,* 42, *Centesimus Annus,* 30.

45. See Marciano Vidal, "La preferencia por el pobre, criterio de moral," *Studia Moralia* 20 (1982) 277–304.

46. Congregation for the Doctrine of Faith, *Christian Freedom and Liberation* (1986), no. 68.

47. *Centesimus Annus,* 42.

48. Particularly by means of *Evangelium Vitae* (1995).

49. See Marciano Vidal, *El evangelio de la vida humana* (Madrid: San Pablo, 1996).

334 / *Marciano Vidal*

50. *Veritatis splendor,* 50; *Donum vitae,* introduction, 3.

51. Congregation for the Doctrine of Faith, *Human Person* (1975), no. 1; Congregation for Catholic Education, *Educational Orientations on Human Love* (1983), nn. 4–6; Pontifical Council for the Family, *Human Sexuality: Truth and Meaning* (1995), nn. 8–15.

52. See Marciano Vidal, *Moral y Espiritualidad* (Madrid: PS, 1997).

53. *Optatam Totius,* 16.

54. *Persona Humana,* 10.

55. *Veritatis Splendor,* 65–70.

56. *Sollicitudo Rei Socialis,* 36.

57. See M. Vidal, "Structural Sin: A New Category in Moral Theology," in Raphael Gallagher and Brendan McConvery, eds., *History and Conscience: Studies in Honor of Sean O'Riordan, C.Ss.R.* (Dublin: Gill and MacMillan, 1989) 181–98.

58. *Noonan,* "Development," 676.

59. *Veritatis Splendor,* 28. Cf. Noonan, "Development," 672–73.

60. *Gaudium et Spes,* 22.

61. Ibid., 4.

62. *Centesimus Annus,* 3.

63. *Gaudium et Spes,* 44.

64. Ibid., 44.

65. Ibid., 62.

66. *Veritatis Splendor,* 29.

67. *Gaudium et Spes,* 62. Quoted in *Veritatis Splendor,* 29.

68. Ibid., 62.

69. Ibid., 44.

List of Contributors

E. Christian Brugger is Assistant Professor of Ethics at Loyola University, New Orleans.

Lisa Sowle Cahill is the J. Donald Monan Professor of Theology at Boston College.

Charles E. Curran is the Elizabeth Scurlock University Professor of Human Values at Southern Methodist University.

The late Émile-Joseph De Smedt was the Bishop of Bruges, Belgium, and a leading figure at the Second Vatican Council.

Avery Dulles, a Cardinal of the Roman Catholic Church, is the Lawrence J. McGinley Professor of Religion and Society at Fordham University.

Mary Elsbernd is Associate Professor of Pastoral Studies and Social Ethics at Loyola University, Chicago.

John Gallagher taught moral theology for many years and was Superior General of the Congregation of St. Basil.

Raphael Gallagher is Visiting Professor of Moral Theology at the Accademia Alfonsiana in Rome.

Patrick Granfield is Professor of Theology at the Catholic University of America.

Christine E. Gudorf is Professor of Christian Ethics at Florida International University.

Diana L. Hayes is Associate Professor of Theology at Georgetown University.

J. Bryan Hehir is the President of Catholic Charities USA.

The late John Francis Maxwell was an English diocesan priest and author of *Slavery and the Catholic Church.*

The late John Courtney Murray was a U.S. Jesuit priest who wrote extensively on church-state issues.

John T. Noonan, Jr., is a judge of the U. S. Court of Appeals for the Ninth Circuit and Robins Professor Emeritus at the University of California at Berkeley.

Joseph A. Selling is Professor of Moral Theology at the Catholic University of Leuven, Belgium.

Marciano Vidal is Professor of Moral Theology at the Universidad Pontificia Comillas in Madrid.